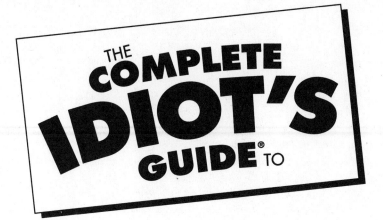

THE
COMPLETE IDIOT'S GUIDE® TO

Learning Italian

Third Edition

by Gabrielle Ann Euvino

ALPHA

A member of Penguin Group (USA) Inc.

ALPHA BOOKS

Published by the Penguin Group

Penguin Group (USA) Inc., 375 Hudson Street, New York, New York 10014, USA

Penguin Group (Canada), 90 Eglinton Avenue East, Suite 700, Toronto, Ontario M4P 2Y3, Canada (a division of Pearson Penguin Canada Inc.)

Penguin Books Ltd., 80 Strand, London WC2R 0RL, England

Penguin Ireland, 25 St. Stephen's Green, Dublin 2, Ireland (a division of Penguin Books Ltd.)

Penguin Group (Australia), 250 Camberwell Road, Camberwell, Victoria 3124, Australia (a division of Pearson Australia Group Pty. Ltd.)

Penguin Books India Pvt. Ltd., 11 Community Centre, Panchsheel Park, New Delhi—110 017, India

Penguin Group (NZ), 67 Apollo Drive, Rosedale, North Shore, Auckland 1311, New Zealand (a division of Pearson New Zealand Ltd.)

Penguin Books (South Africa) (Pty.) Ltd., 24 Sturdee Avenue, Rosebank, Johannesburg 2196, South Africa

Penguin Books Ltd., Registered Offices: 80 Strand, London WC2R 0RL, England

International Standard Book Number: 978-1-59257-276-2
Library of Congress Catalog Card Number: 2004106751

12   11   10   12   11   10

Interpretation of the printing code: The rightmost number of the first series of numbers is the year of the book's printing; the rightmost number of the second series of numbers is the number of the book's printing. For example, a printing code of 04-1 shows that the first printing occurred in 2004.

Printed in the United States of America

Note: This publication contains the opinions and ideas of its author. It is intended to provide helpful and informative material on the subject matter covered. It is sold with the understanding that the author and publisher are not engaged in rendering professional services in the book. If the reader requires personal assistance or advice, a competent professional should be consulted.

The author and publisher specifically disclaim any responsibility for any liability, loss, or risk, personal or otherwise, which is incurred as a consequence, directly or indirectly, of the use and application of any of the contents of this book.

Most Alpha books are available at special quantity discounts for bulk purchases for sales promotions, pre-miums, fund-raising, or educational use. Special books, or book excerpts, can also be created to fit specific needs.

For details, write: Special Markets, Alpha Books, 375 Hudson Street, New York, NY 10014.

Publisher: *Marie Butler-Knight*
Product Manager: *Phil Kitchel*
Senior Managing Editor: *Jennifer Chisholm*
Acquisitions Editor: *Paul Dinas*
Development Editor: *Michael Koch*
Production Editor: *Megan Douglass*

Copy Editor: *Keith Cline*
Illustrator: *Richard King*
Cover/Book Designer: *Trina Wurst*
Indexer: *Angie Bess*
Layout/Proofreading: *Angela Calvert*

Contents at a Glance

Contents

Foreword

If you're looking for a book that will teach, inspire, illuminate, and educate in a user-friendly manner that's downright fun, the *Complete Idiot's Guide to Learning Italian, Third Edition*, is the text for you.

For almost 40 years I have been a language teacher, and since 1981 I have been director of the Language Immersion Institute (LII) at the State University of New York at New Paltz. Ms. Euvino, a graduate from SUNY New Paltz, comes from the new generation of language teachers who instruct using immersion. Her mentor, the late Dr. Gianni Azzi, was a good friend of mine, and one of the most dynamic teachers I've ever known.

Anyone who takes one of Ms. Euvino's classes will invariably be affected by her "infectious enthusiasm" and "love of the Italian language" that make her classes so successful. That's why I'd have to say that the next best thing to taking one of Gabrielle's courses is to read this book.

We teach the basics to people who need to learn Italian quickly and don't necessarily have a strong background in grammar. Ms. Euvino's book is perfect for the traveler getting ready for a *viaggio* to Italy. Newlyweds will find all the language they need to make it from the airport to their hotel suite and then a little more. Wine connoisseurs and epicureans will light up when they discover the ample food-related vocabulary that fills the book like delicate *antipasti*. Sports enthusiasts, hikers, people on the go, literary types, sedentary, young or old, Italian or not, you'll be amazed by how much you can learn in such a short amount of time.

Ms. Euvino's book immerses you in the language, culture, and food of Italy while explaining the grammar in clear, concise terms that makes learning Italian easy. Her practical, down-to-earth style takes you to the streets of Italy, walks you through Rome's alleys, guides you to the canals of Venice, waltzes you to the sound of Puccini, and accompanies you to the doctor (if need be). Finally, but no less important, you will hear Ms. Euvino's voice as she continually praises the reader for their determination and *intelligenza*. After all, you deserve to be commended for trying to learn a new language.

In today's rapidly shrinking world, communication skills are vital. Drawing from her vast teaching experience, Ms. Euvino has created a book that makes studying Italian a rewarding and inspiring experience.

Dr. Henry Urbanski
Distinguished Service Professor of Russian
Founder and Director, Language Immersion Institute
State University of New York at New Paltz

Introduction

Any idiot can speak Italian, and lots of them do. The word *idiot* comes from the Greek root *idios* and means *of a particular person, private, own.* In Latin, an *idiota* simply refers to a private person. You see this root in the words *idiom* and *idiosyncrasy.*

Beware of the idiots! Lame and suffering from a speech impediment, Claudius (10 B.C.–54 A.D.) is remembered as a scholar and a competent administrator during the time he reigned. Against all odds, this "idiot" rose up to become Roman Emperor, making a fool of everyone.

The fact is, you're not an idiot, or you wouldn't be reading this book, now in its third edition—I have listened to my readers and students and have updated *The Complete Idiot's Guide to Learning Italian* with a number of additional features that include an expanded pronunciation guide, the latest technological, cultural, business, and sports terms, and more tables to facilitate learning.

How to Use This Book to Learn Italian

This book has been organized to maximize your understanding of key Italian concepts and terms. By following the lessons, you will be able to construct a solid foundation for future studies. Keep in mind that the vocabulary lists provided in each chapter are just that: word lists. You can refer to Chapter 21 to find computer terms, Chapter 10 for travel terms, Chapter 14 for food terms, or Chapter 17 for music and art. My point is this: You don't need to learn all of the verb lessons to begin developing a vocabulary that is relevant to *your* interests.

This book also offers readers the most important aspects of grammar and verbs supported by practical, contemporary *vocabolario* related to a number of real-life situations. If you feel like you could use a little extra help in the grammar department, read the book from the beginning—you'll find the answers to many of your questions in language that is clear and to the point. If you are already familiar with the basic grammatical terms and lessons offered, by all means, do not linger on that which you already know—skip ahead! Regardless of your level, learning Italian requires *pazienza* (patience) and *ripetizione, ripetizione, ripetizione* (repetition). And to help you with your practice, I've included numerous exercises so you can test what you've learned in each chapter. You can find the answers to these exercises in Appendix A.

In general, keep an eye on the appendixes—they contain helpful verb tables and other linguistic and grammatical aids.

What Else You Can Do to Improve Your Italian

It's one thing to study grammar and verbs; it's another to speak a foreign language, especially if you are trying to learn it from abroad, wherever you are. For this reason, the more you are able to integrate Italian into your daily life, the better your chances of success. If you love to cook, find a recipe book that has been translated into Italian and try to follow the directions. Buy an Italian *calendario* and you'll learn the days of the week and months in no time. If you're plugged into the World Wide Web, why not subscribe to an Italian-language bulletin? Visit a music library and listen to *Rigoletto* sung by five different artists. Start a collection of children's books. Read the Italian fashion magazines. Gather the menus of your favorite Italian *ristoranti*. Many museums, such as the Metropolitan Museum of New York, offer guided tours on tape in a number of languages, including Italian. If you're a film buff, rent Italian movies. Whatever you do, make it fun, and you'll find that you can't get enough.

How This Book Is Organized

This book is organized into four parts, followed by a series of appendixes that supplement your learning experience.

Part 1, "*Essenziali:* The Basics," lays the foundation of your Italian-language learning experience, bringing you in-depth definitions and explanations of key grammatical forms, verbs, and parts of speech. In this overview, you'll become familiar with the great Italian poets Dante, Boccaccio, and Petrarca and their influence on the Italian language. You'll study *parole simili* (cognates)—what I like to call linguistic cousins—and begin to see the relationship between the English and Italian languages. You'll learn how to spell your name in Italian, and how to properly pronounce words like *gnocchi* (*nyoh-kee*) and *famiglia* (*fah-meel-yah*) without making a fool of yourself. You'll learn how to talk about *i giorni della settimana* (the days of the week), *i mesi* (months), and *i numeri* (numbers). Finally, welcome to the vast world of nouns and articles. Learn how to determine the gender of a noun just by following a few basic guidelines; you'll find adjectives to be just as simple.

Part 2, "Building Blocks: Creating a Strong Base," has been reworked and consolidated to help you focus your energies where they will be most effective. Verbs are the spine of language and shape and form our world. Part 2 heavily focuses on developing verb skills and familiarizing you with the rules of conjugation for both regular and irregular verbs. In the meantime, you'll also learn how to talk about time and weather, ask questions, and make suggestions. I've also included essential vocabulary terms related to travel and sightseeing.

Part 3, "*La Dolce Vita,*" is filled with the fun stuff that made you want to study Italian in the first place. You'll be given ample opportunity to eat, sing, shop, and party your way to fluency. Learn about the things you love most: food, shopping, Italian holidays, the arts, music, film, and much more. Plus, you'll take your verb skills into the past with the *passato prossimo* and the *imperfetto*. Sports fans welcome: Discover more about the *tifosi*, *il calcio*, and other sports-related trivia. Art lovers will also find a generous section devoted to the Italian arts, music, and film.

Part 4, "*Minutiae,*" focuses on the details. Study the reflexive verbs while you talk about your body. Learn how to write a letter, make a phone call, navigate through the *ufficio postale*, and make plans for the *futuro*. You'll learn how to ask about getting your glasses fixed, finding a good tailor, and other vocabulary you need when things go wrong. Learn about the conditional, often used in collaboration with the subjunctive mood as in, *You would probably move to Italy if the circumstances were right*. Finally, in an updated technology and business section, you'll be given all the practical lingo you'll ever need to achieve your goals. To round off your study of Italian, I've included a basic lesson on the *passato remoto*, a highly irregular form of the past.

The final part of the book contains the appendixes.

Appendix A, "Answer Key," gives you the answers to the exercises offered throughout the book.

Appendix B, "Verb Tables," summarizes more verb tenses than you probably care to memorize.

Appendix C, "Idiomatic Expressions," reviews many commonly used Italian idiomatic expressions and gives you a chance to apply your Italian skills.

Appendix D, "Italian *Grammatica* at a Glance," offers you concise tables outlining the essentials of Italian grammar.

Appendix E, "Italian *Sinonimi*" offers readers a scaled-down version of an Italian thesaurus.

Appendix F, "Further Resources," offers an expanded resource section devoted to enhancing your study of Italian.

Appendix G, "Word List," supports your Italian studies and offers hundreds of helpful vocabulary words and exclamations used by the Italians. This word list should not substitute for a good Italian/English dictionary.

Bite-Size Extras

As an extra perk, featured throughout this book are interesting sidebars and margin notes that highlight relevant aspects of the Italian language and culture.

Buon'Idea

These boxes provide useful suggestions, study techniques and helpful resources.

La Bella Lingua

These are notes on dialect, idioms, and helpful vocabulary, which may or may not pertain directly to the lesson.

What's What

These boxes reveal idiot-proof definitions of terms.

Attenzione

These boxes highlight elements of the Italian language that merit special attention.

As a Regola

These boxes highlight or expand on aspects of Italian grammar.

Acknowledgments

When it comes to gratitude, the list just keeps growing! First, and foremost, a huge thanks to the entire team that put this book together. Special thanks go to Paul Dinas for his patience and professionalism, Megan Douglass for her excellent production abilities, Keith Cline (who copyedited this from Greece), and development editor Michael Koch for the great movie titles.

Then, my students. I love the expression, *When the pupil is ready, the teacher will appear* because you are all my teachers, and I continually learn and expand my awareness as a result of the synergy we create together. *A good teacher learns from a student's mistakes.* My job is to facilitate; that's all. You do the work. It is an honor to join you in the search for knowledge.

And finally, to the friends and family in my life for their love, counsel, gentility, and generosity. You feed my soul, nurture my spirit, and bring good things to eat. (Feed me, and I'm yours!) *Mille grazie.*

Special Thanks to the Technical Reviewer

The Complete Idiot's Guide to Learning Italian, Third Edition, was reviewed by a team of experts who double-checked the accuracy of what you'll learn here, to help us ensure that this book gives you everything you need to know about the Italian language. *Mille grazie* are extended to Stefano Spandoni for his continued expertise on this subject and a big hug to Oriana Moltisanti, who began with me as a professional but whom I now call *sorella.* Thank you so much.

Trademarks

All terms mentioned in this book that are known to be or are suspected of being trademarks or service marks have been appropriately capitalized. Alpha Books and Penguin Group (USA) Inc. cannot attest to the accuracy of this information. Use of a term in this book should not be regarded as affecting the validity of any trademark or service mark.

Part 1

Essenziali: The Basics

Pronto? Ready? Every house needs a foundation, and this part gives you the fundamentals of the Italian language. Whether it takes you five *mesi* (months) or five *anni* (years), remember that it's the *viaggio* that counts.

In this part, I'll give you a mini lesson on the history of Italian along with a quick grammar review to help prime your brain for the upcoming lessons. I'll have you rolling your *R*s with an easy-to-read pronunciation guide. Then I'll show you cognates (similar-sounding words) and how you can use them to tie the Italian language to English. Of course, you'll also learn everything you ever wanted to know about sex ... I mean, gender, and how to create plurals with the switch of a vowel. You'll also learn about adjectives and adverbs. Finally, I've thrown in a few basic greetings and salutations to get your mouth warmed up. *Buon viaggio!*

Why You Should Study
la Bella Lingua

In This Chapter

◆ The many virtues of the Italian language

◆ Where you can use Italian

◆ Developing a learning strategy

◆ There's no reason to be afraid!

It's recognizable immediately: the gentle cadence of words as melodic as *musica*, the sexy rolling of *R*'s, the soothing, sensual lilt of voices that move you as does an *opera*, *una poesia*, or a beautiful work of *arte*. It's *la bella lingua* of Italian, and there's nothing quite like it.

You've picked up this book because you want to learn Italian. Lucky for you, there are now many resources available to the student in libraries, bookstores, and on the Internet, not to mention classes, study groups, pen-pal exchanges, and chat rooms.

Steering Your Linguistic Ship

Determining your needs and setting goals should be a priority. If you don't establish a horizon point by which to steer your linguistic ship, at best you'll end up floating around in circles; at worst you'll end up on the rocks and finally, abandon your *viaggio*.

The Top Ten Most Common Reasons to Study *Italiano*

Do you really need a reason to study Italian? How about ten?

1. You're planning a trip to Italy and don't want to seem like a complete *idiota*.

2. You want to be able to watch Fellini films without having to read the subtitles.

3. You've always wanted to have an *accento*.

4. You want to understand what your *suoceri* (in-laws) are saying about you while they smile and wipe the tomato sauce off their chins.

5. You love Italian food and want to be able to know what you're ordering. You loved the *trippa* until you found out what it was.

6. You heard studying a second language helps postpone Alzheimer's. If you're going to babble, why not let it be in *italiano?*

7. You met a gorgeous attendant on the Alitalia flight you took to *Roma* last year. You want to be able to *determinare* if this is the real thing, or just a *fantasia*.

8. Your *nonni* spoke Italian and you want to reclaim a part of your *passato*.

9. You've tried studying other languages and nothing stuck. You're hoping Italian is easier. (It's all in the approach, trust me.)

10. You're interested in living in Italy and need to learn Italian as soon as *possibile*.

Integration Is the *Soluzione*

If you believe you don't have the time to learn Italian, think *ancora* (again). Most of us believe that if we can't devote X amount of time to something, why bother? We're overly ambitious, creating standards for ourselves that are, by and large, beyond our reach. By creating opportunities for you to integrate Italian into your daily life, you'll discover that you do have the time, if you make it. Five *minuti* stolen here and there, waiting in line at the *ufficio postale*, at the *banca*, or when stuck in *traffico*, can add up to more than you imagine.

Here are a few more ways to integrate Italian into your daily schedule:

♦ Listen to tapes while you're driving or doing chores, even if you're only remotely paying *attenzione*. Subliminally, you are still learning.

♦ Use your computer to access the vast accumulation of Italian language-related materials on the World Wide Web. Switch your home page to an Italian-related site. Refer to Appendix G for more resources.

♦ Play *Scarabeo*, the Italian version of Scrabble.

♦ Sponsor a weekly Italian potluck with others interested in developing their language skills. You'll love the leftovers … I know I do!

♦ Look for Italian primers and books that offer the English *traduzione* alongside the original Italian. This saves you the effort of looking up every *parola* you don't understand and gives you a general *idea* of what is being communicated.

♦ Trust the *processo*. It takes time to learn anything new; give yourself a pat on the back and try to have *pazienza*. Similar to developing the skills you now take for granted (walking, talking, swimming, riding a bicycle, driving, and so on), there will be a *periodo* in which you'll probably experience a great deal of *confusione*.

Buon'Idea

Use Post-Its to label the things that surround you. You'll soon acquire a practical *vocabolario* that you can begin using immediately. To get you started, try these helpful terms, each given with the appropriate article:

il tavolo	the table
la sedia	the chair
la porta	the door
la finestra	the window

You've already made a great start by picking up this *libro* (and I am genuinely pleased to have the honor of assisting you!).

Immerse Yourself—Literally!

Context is key: Absorb the significance of a *parola* by looking at the words surrounding it. When you learn how to decode the Italian language, you'll begin to see patterns emerge; from there, it's just a matter of time before the words begin pouring out of you!

Speaking of the power of words, inspiration often comes from the unexpected. Go to your bookstore and leaf through several books in the Italian language section. See what interests you. Children's books are another fun way of building *vocabolario*. If you're in Italy, or know someone who is, there's nothing like the local *libreria* (bookstore)—pick up a few.

Italian publications, especially magazines, are usually quite entertaining, full of glossy, color ads and interesting facts. The elegant world of *la moda* (fashion), *il viaggio* (travel), and *la cucina* (food) are three popular topics. Pick up a copy and figure out the contents by studying the titles. *L'Espresso, Oggi, Panorama,* and *Vogue Italia* are but a few. Italian newspapers include *La Repubblica, Il Corriere della Sera, Libero, Il Giornale,* and *La Stampa.* Also, the next time a friend takes a trip to Italy, ask him or her to bring back the in-flight magazine if it has both Italian and English. Alitalia produces a wonderful publication that has the Italian and the English side by side. You'll be surprised at how much you can pick up.

Here are some more tips on how to make the most of your spare time to improve your Italian:

♦ **Become a class act.** Call your local *università* and investigate whether it has an Italian department. Find out if it has a mailing list for events, and make a point of meeting other *Italophiles.* Ask if there is a language lab you can use; if so, there is usually a sizeable library to accompany its use.

♦ **Hang out with Monica Bellucci.** Every week, I force my students to sit down in front of their television sets to watch Italian movies. I'm telling you, just like I tell them, that this is not an assignment to be ignored. Needless to say, you want the subtitled versions (stay away from anything dubbed—a character is his voice). DVD players now allow viewers to watch the film with subtitles in a number of languages. Even if the film you are watching is not Italian, you can utilize this feature to your linguistic *vantaggio.*

I'll never forget the excitement in a student's voice when she told me she had finally understood the Italian when she watched a rerun of the movie *A Fish Called Wanda,* with Jamie Lee Curtis and Kevin Kline. You might remember the part when Kline starts muttering in Italian. The next time you watch the movie, see if you can determine just what, *esattamente,* Kline's character is saying.

♦ **Get the right tools.** Invest in a good bilingual *dizionario,* preferably one published in *Italia* that offers various features, such as stress accentuation (many dictionaries will indicate irregularly stressed syllables) and parts of speech. Bigger is not necessarily better—choose a *dizionario* that isn't too cumbersome so you'll be more likely to bring it with you. Don't skimp on price here—a good dictionary is something you'll keep for a long time.

Buon'Idea

You can pick up a box of flash cards at any bookstore, or you can make your own. That unused box of business cards from your old job, or unused pages from your last address book are *perfetto.* Punch holes in them and put 10 or 20 on a key ring so you can put them in your pocket or bag for "study quickies."

- **Tune in!** Find out what station has Italian news. RAI, the Public Italian television and radio network, airs programs every day. Even though it will sound as though they are speaking a million miles a *minuto*, exposing your ears to the *lingua* will evolve into understanding it.

- **Read the fine print.** Keep the owner's manual to any appliances, electronics, or cameras that include multilingual instructions. This is a great way to learn technical terms—and, once more, you don't need to pick up a dictionary; the English translation is probably already there.

- **Find birds of a feather.** Study the *lingua* with a friend. There's nothing like having a partner to keep you motivated and on your toes. Practice together, and maybe invest in a private tutor to meet with you every couple of weeks. The *costo* is usually reasonable considering the kind of *attenzione* you will receive, and it will be good incentive to keep up with your studies.

While you're at it, make some Italian friends—there's nothing like a good *conversazione* to hone your skills.

- **Play it again, Salvatore.** Make tapes of yourself speaking Italian, and then play these tapes to a native Italian speaker (your new friends, the waiter in the local *ristorante*, your *nonna*, or anyone who will listen). Ask them to evaluate your linguistic strengths and weaknesses.

Buon'Idea

Meetup.com is a free service that organizes local gatherings about anything, anywhere. Create your own local Italian study group using this valuable resource. Check them out online at www. meetup.com.

The Italians are among the most warm, hospitable, easy-going, open-minded people you will ever meet. Your attempt to speak Italian, even in the most basic of ways, will elicit nothing less than enthusiasm and delight. Say *buon giorno* (good day) every time you walk into an establishment, and watch the response. They are listening to what you are trying to express, not what mistakes you might have made.

The constant traffic up and down the peninsula over the *millenni* had the effect of creating a plethora of different dialects, some of which are quite different from the Italian you're studying here. As a result, the Italians have developed a flexible and adaptable attitude when it comes to communication. All of those hand gestures probably developed in part because of the Italian character, but ultimately,

Buon'Idea

Create a potluck once a week to celebrate the things you love most about Italy. Use food to enhance your vocabulary skills and eat your way to fluency!

the art of gesticulation developed out of necessity. Put yourself in their *scarpe* and remember the last time someone speaking English as a second language impressed you with her command of the language, the whole time murmuring, "I don't speak so good." "Are you kidding?" you wanted to ask. "You speak very well!"

Stick with me and I promise, you'll learn Italian. Now, as a fun exercise, go back through this chapter and count how many new Italian words you learned just for showing up here—and without even trying! *Bravo!*

The Least You Need to Know

- There's no time like the present to learn *la bella lingua* of Italian.

- Italian is an accessible language that anyone can learn.

- You can communicate even if your pronunciation and grammar are less than *perfetto.* Remember that *la lingua* is simply a means to communicate your thoughts to another *persona.* If you can learn to speak one language, you can learn to speak another.

- You have nothing to fear but fear itself. Whether it takes you three months or three years, one step in front of the other is the way you will achieve your goals. Find your pace. Stick with it.

- Find ways to integrate Italian into your everyday activities.

- Create a study group by finding others to celebrate with you!

Immersione Italiana

In This Chapter

- ◆ A history of the Italian language
- ◆ What's a dialect?
- ◆ What are idioms, anyway?
- ◆ Using your bilingual dictionary
- ◆ Why grammar is the key to *la bella lingua*

This chapter offers you a brief history of Italian and compares it with English. It also provides a summary of different parts of *grammatica* and attempts to take away some of the intimidation factor that often accompanies learning a new *lingua*.

Just Kicking Around

The Italians have been around for a long time, and as you know, Italian derives from Latin, the language used by the Romans. Incidentally, the province in which Rome (called *Roma* by Italians) resides is called *Lazio* (Lathium in English) because it was originally inhabited by the *Latini*.

Then came the invaders. They came from the *nord* and from the *sud*, dropping words like seeds, which in turn germinated into new words, and from there Latin's influence continued to spread, geographically and through time. However, the varied terrain and mountain ranges (the Alps and the Appenini) throughout the peninsula created pockets of *umanità*, many of which were quite isolated. Fluctuations occurred, dialects developed. Sicilians had their own language, likewise the Sards, the Neapolitans, and so on.

These were the languages brought over by the *immigranti*, my grandparents included, and often it was surprisingly difficult for two Italians, each from different provinces, to understand one another. Of course, they managed. The often exaggerated hand gestures and signs still used by the Italians today developed out of need. How else to fill in the blanks when two people from two different regions with two different languages were trying to communicate? And thus developed a genuine *tolleranza*, not to mention *pazienza*, implicit in the Italian national character.

La Bella Lingua

Latin originally developed in central Italy in the area known as Latium. Within the Italian peninsula lived the Estrucans (giving Tuscany its name), Faliscans, Oscans, Umbrians, and a slew of other tribes. The Italic languages of the tribes all contributed to the eventual development of the language we now recognize as Italian. It is not clear when Italian became a distinct language from Latin, because no Italian text has been recorded before the tenth century; however, we do know that by the fourth century, St. Jerome had translated the Bible from Latin into the language spoken by the common people.

Latin Lovers

The history of the Italian language spans centuries and begins with classical Latin, the literary language of ancient *Roma* and the language used principally by the upper classes, the educated, and later the clergy—hence the term Romance languages (from which French, Spanish, Portuguese, and Rumanian are also derived). These languages were all offshoots, or dialects. Italian is the Romance language closest to Latin.

As I mentioned, languages are like seeds that drift from one area into another, germinating wherever there is ripe soil. Latin made its way into English during the seventh century as England was converting to Christianity, and later during a revival in classical scholarship stemming from the Renaissance (*Rinascimento*, literally meaning *rebirth*). During the sixteenth and seventeenth centuries, hundreds of Latin words were incorporated into English, resulting in much of today's legal and medical *terminologia*.

As a result, many small words in modern English have their origins in Latin, a hop from Italian. Chapter 4 presents a more thorough listing of those similar words, or *cognates*. Keep in mind that English is a much broader language than Italian in terms of the sheer number of words it possesses.

You will see that in Italian it is sometimes much easier to express certain *diminutives* and *superlatives* than in English. For example, English has the pair cat/kitten. The word *kitten* is quite different from the word *cat*. In Italian, it's much easier to express a small cat: By adding the ending *-ino* to the word *gatto*, we create the word *gattino*. You're already familiar with the word *zucchini*, which comes from the Italian word *zucca* (pumpkin/squash).

A commonly used superlative in English is *-est*, which is attached to adjectives to describe the smallest, biggest, or best. In Italian, this would be expressed with the ending *-issimo*, as in the adjective *bellissimo* (very beautiful, gorgeous).

In spite of the fact that Italian has fewer words than English, Italians have no difficulty expressing themselves, as you will find out for yourself.

> **What's What**
>
> A **diminutive** is a suffix, or ending, that denotes small-ness, youth, or familiarity, such as *caro* (dear) and *carino* (cute), *ragazzo* (boy) and *ragazzino* (small boy). A **superlative** expresses the extreme, or highest degree of something, such as *bello* (beautiful) and *bellissimo* (gorgeous).

Il Dialetto: Dialect

A dialect is a variation of a language, usually particular to a region and often quite different from the standard spoken vernacular. Due to its shape and long history of outside influences, Italy has hundreds of different dialects, many of which are still used today. Some dialects are virtually identical to Italian, but with particular colloquialisms and idiomatic expressions understood only by those familiar with the dialect.

Other dialects are like different languages. For example, up north in Lombardia, you'll hear a specifically German accent and a softening of the *R*'s, a result of the district's rule by Austria at one time. In the Piedmonte region, you can hear the French influence. Down south near Napoli, you can hear Spanish and French, whereas in Calabria, certain expressions are quite clearly Greek (*kalimera* means *good day* in modern Greek and is also used in Calabria to say "hello") or Albanian in nature. The islands of *Sardegna* and *Sicilia* also have their own languages.

Many Italian *immigranti* brought their dialects to the Americas, including the United States, where they were further influenced by factors such as culture, English, and other dialects. This partly explains why the Italian spoken by many immigrants often differs greatly from the Italian presented in this book—and why you may still have difficulty communicating with your grandmother after having mastered the basics. Many variations or dialects of Italian are spoken around the world today, in such places as Switzerland and many parts of South America such as Venezuela, Argentina, and Brazil, and as far away as Australia.

La Bella Lingua

The poet **Dante Alighieri** (1265–1321) is to the Italian language what Shakespeare is to English. It was his poetry that legitimized the Italian language as we know it today, because all his predecessors wrote exclusively in Latin. His most famous work, *La Divina Commedia,* is an epic poem depicting an imaginary journey through hell, purgatory, and paradise. That work was actually influenced by another of the world's greatest poets, the Latin poet **Virgilio** (Publius Vergilius Maro, 70–19 B.C.E.), who served as Dante's guide both literally, as a writer (he was, after all, the author of the great epic adventure story the *Aeneid*), and figuratively, in the story itself.

Tuscan Italian

In modern Italy, the standard language taught in schools and spoken on television is Tuscan Italian, primarily because this was the regional dialect used by the great medieval writers Dante, Petrarca, and Boccaccio, all of whom used what was then only a spoken language. Modern Italian is often quite different from the Italian used during the Middle Ages, but, as when you compare modern English to Old English, there are also striking similarities.

Look at this excerpt from Dante's *Inferno:*

> Nel mezzo del cammin di nostra vita
> mi ritrovai per una selva oscura,
> che la diritta via era smarrita.

Note the translation:

> In the middle of our life's journey
> I found myself in a dark wood,
> out of which the straight way was lost.

The Italian has a wonderful rhyme quality—the word *vita* working with the word *smarrita.* Although the translation to English loses some of the flow and meaning of the poem, you can still get a sense of what is being communicated; and you certainly can gain an understanding of the musicality of the language. It's like looking at a photograph of a bright, sunny day where you can see the *colori* but you can't feel the warmth of the sun, experience the expanse of blue sky, or hear the *vento* rustle the leaves in the trees.

Idiomatically Speaking

Idioms are important for a complete and correct understanding of a language. They are the spice that makes language interesting. If verbs and grammar are the brain of a language, then idioms are the *personalità*. They express the various idiosyncrasies of the speaker's *tradizioni*, customs, values, and social mores.

La Bella Lingua

The works of **Francesco Petrarca** (1304–1374) differed from those of Dante. As an early humanist, Petrarca's ideas focused more on love and other earthly concerns, making him very popular during the Renaissance. His major works, *I Trionfi* and *Il Canzoniere*, were both written in the vernacular, or in everyday (as opposed to formal) speech.

Giovanni Boccaccio (1313–1375) has been rated one of the greatest literary figures of Italy. A contemporary of Petrarca, he is most known for *Il Decamerone*. Written around the time of the Black Death of 1348, *Il Decamerone* is a collection of 100 novellas, many comic, some bawdy, a few tragic—and all captivating and engaging.

Happy as a Lark

Idiomatic expressions are speech forms that cannot be understood through literal translation; they must be learned and memorized along with their meaning. Many idiomatic expressions find their roots in the truth. For example, common sense dictates that you really shouldn't put all your eggs in one basket.

Often, but not necessarily, there is an allusion to something else, as with the expression *happy as a lark*. If you were a foreigner studying English, would you understand how happy that actually was?

It's the same with Italian. Most idioms cannot be translated without losing some of their meaning, although occasionally, the same idiom can exist in two or more languages. In Italian, you can ask *Posso dare una mano?* (Can I give you a hand?) However, in Italian you would not be able to say that it's raining cats and dogs without raising an eyebrow. Do you get the picture?

So What's Your *Storia?*

Etymology is a fancy term used to describe the study of words, but you don't need to be a linguist to appreciate the *origine* of a word. By using your powers of deduction, it's often *possibile* to figure out a word's *significato* simply by looking at its root. Take the word *pomodoro*, which means tomato in Italian. Coming from the Latin words *pomum* (apple or fruit) and *oro* (signifying gold), the word derives from the Latin *aurum* (connected to the word *aurora*, meaning dawn or redness). Thus, the word *pomodoro* breaks down to literally mean *golden apple*.

The English words *Vermont* and *verdant* both share a common root: *vert* (coming from Latin *viridis* and meaning green). In Italian, the word for the season spring is *primavera*, meaning *first green*. The words *carnivore, carnal, charnel,* and *carnival* all derive from the Latin stem *carn*, meaning *flesh*. Are you a verbose person? Think *verb*, or in Latin, *verbum*, meaning *word*.

> **La Bella Lingua**
>
> Expand your horizons! Many Italian streets are named after historical and religious figures, such as *Corso Vittorio Emanuele II* and *Via Savonarola.* Use the street signs as opportunities to gain insight about Italy and its rich culture.

There's no need to rush out and take a course in *Latino.* Rather than memorizing a list of words, try creating associations with words you already know. Sometimes it's as *semplice* as adding a vowel here and there, or tacking on an Italian ending. Your cognitive *abilità* to make sense will do the rest. After you have an understanding of how the endings change from English to Italian, you'll be able to switch from one *lingua* to the other in no time at all.

Your Dictionary Is Your Best Friend

Having a good bilingual *dizionario* is essential to learning a new language, whatever your purpose may be. Use your dictionary as an adventurer would use a map. Keep it handy, somewhere where you do most of your studying so that you don't have far to reach every time a new word pops up. You'll be amazed at how often you'll use it if you're not climbing a ladder to get to the top shelf of your bookcase whenever a need arises. Most good English/Italian dictionaries indicate what kind of word it is. You should understand the significance of the abbreviations used in the definitions. The following table lists a few of them.

> **La Bella Lingua**
>
> If an explanation given in this book still leaves you confused, refer to that same topic in a different grammar book. Sometimes it takes two different explanations to fully grasp a new concept.

Dictionary Abbreviations

English Abbreviation	Italian Abbreviation	Meaning
adj.	agg.	Adjective
adv.	avv.	Adverb

English Abbreviation	Italian Abbreviation	Meaning
n.	f.	Singular feminine noun
n.	m.	Singular masculine noun
prep.	prep.	Preposition
pron.	pron.	Pronoun
v.i.	v.i.	Intransitive verb
v.t.	v.t.	Transitive verb
—	v.rifl.	Reflexive verb
fam.	fam.	Familiar/colloquial

Also take advantage of any tables, charts, or specialized vocabulary offered in your dictionary. There is often a handy summary of the language tucked away somewhere in the front or back pages. Read the small print.

Grammar Stammer

What is it about grammar that makes full-grown adults quiver at the knees and become tongue-tied? I see it all the time and assume it has something to do with conditioning. For a lot of people, aside from the need to get a good grade, grammar held little *importanza* in the big scheme of things.

If you can read a map, follow a recipe, surf the net, and do all of the things you do, you can learn grammar. For now, let's review parts of speech.

Persona, Place, or *Pasta:* Nouns

A noun (called either a *nome* or *sostantivo* in Italian) can be a person, place, thing, or idea. *Pasta, pizza,* and *pane* are all nouns.

In Italian, all nouns have a gender: They are either masculine (m.) or feminine (f.) and either singular (sg.) or plural (pl.).

Descriptively Speaking: Adjectives

An adjective (called *aggettivo*) describes a noun. An adjective can be *grande, piccolo, bello, brutto, rosso, bianco,* and all the colors of the rainbow. Unlike English, Italian adjectives agree in number and gender (sex) with the nouns they modify. For example, if the noun is singular and masculine, as in *il vino* (the wine), then the adjective must also be singular and masculine, as in *il vino rosso* (the red wine).

In Italian, the adjective is almost always placed after the noun it modifies, as in *la casa bianca* (the house white), but exceptions exist, as in *il bravo ragazzo* (the good boy). You'll get a much clearer idea of how adjectives work in a little while.

Adverbs describe verbs, adjectives, and other adverbs. They move us quickly and happily toward our goal of learning Italian. Most adverbs in English end in *-ly*. In Italian, many adverbs end in *-mente*, such as *rapidamente* and *allegramente*.

Who's He?

Pronouns substitute for nouns and refer to a person, place, thing, or idea. For example: *Robert* took a trip to Italy, and *it* (the trip) cost *him* (Robert) quite a penny. Pronouns save us from having to constantly repeat ourselves.

Italian pronouns, like nouns, reflect gender and number. There is no neuter *it* in Italian. There are several kinds of pronouns, of which the most important to remember are subject pronouns (*he, she,* and so on), direct object pronouns, and indirect object pronouns (*it*).

> **What's What**
>
> An **object pronoun** replaces the object in a sentence. In English, this is equivalent to *it*. In Italian, all object pronouns must reflect gender and plurality.

Objectively Speaking

There are two kinds of objects: direct and indirect. The direct object of a sentence is the recipient of a verb's action. The indirect object of a sentence tells to whom or for whom the action was done.

Have I Got a Preposition for You

Le preposizioni (prepositions) are words that help indicate a relationship to other words in a sentence. When you travel *through* a town, get *on* a bus, wait *for* a friend, or study the lessons *in* this book, you are using prepositions. Other prepositions include words like *above, along, beyond, before, in, on, at, to, for,* and many others. Prepositions are best learned in connection with the expressions in which they are used. For example, you may think *about* someone, but you can also think *of* going on vacation.

I Verbi Are Where the Action Is

Verbs indicate action. An infinitive verb is a verb that has not been conjugated, as in *to be, to eat,* or *to travel.* A conjugated verb is simply a form of the verb that agrees with the subject. You conjugate verbs in English all the time when you say I am, you are, and he is. Verb conjugations are discussed in greater depth throughout the book.

Intransitive verbs can stand alone, without a direct object, as *sing* does in the sentence "I sing." You can sing a song or just sing.

Transitive verbs can be followed by a direct object or require a reflexive pronoun, as in we kissed *one another*, or Robert is going *to the party*. You see, Robert can't just *go*—he must go somewhere.

Attenzione!

In Italian, the subject pronoun *io* (I) is not capitalized unless it begins a sentence.

The Italian polite form of *you*, the subject pronoun *Lei*, is always capitalized to distinguish it from *lei*, meaning *she*.

Who's the Subject?

In order to speak Italian, you're going to have to understand *i verbi*. Verbs are the action words in a sentence. The subject of the verb is the thing or person doing the action. It's not difficult to figure out.

Determining the Subject

Sentence	Subject
I want to visit Venice.	I
You want to learn Italian.	You
The bus is leaving at 4:30.	The bus *or* it
Eat, drink, and be merry!	You
Robert and I are brother and sister.	Robert and I *or* we
You are all very intelligent.	You (plural)
The Italians love life.	The Italians *or* they

Italian Subject Pronouns

Person	Singular	Plural
First	*io* (I)	*noi* (we)
Second	*tu* (you, informal)	*voi* (you)
Third	*lui/lei/Lei* (he/she/You)	*loro* (they)

Name That Subject

Just to make sure you're on track, determine the subject of the verb in the following sentences; then ascertain the appropriate subject pronoun for each sentence. (You can find the answers in Appendix A.)

1. The stars twinkled brightly.

2. Jessica knows how to have fun.

3. Leslie travels a lot.

4. My mother was a painter.

5. Louis was an engineer.

6. The food is delicious.

7. Italian is easy to learn.

8. Anna flies a plane.

It All Depends on How You Look At It

You don't have to be a rocket scientist to use a bilingual dictionary, but a little inside knowledge of grammar doesn't hurt. It's important to remember how versatile words can be, and you do that by looking at the entire sentence. This is essential to extrapolating the meaning of the text or even a word that you don't recognize. Look at the word *inside*. Watch how the meaning changes in the following sentences:

The *inside* walls of the church are covered with art. (adjective)

It is very dark *inside* the tunnel. (preposition)

The *inside* of the Coliseum was once quite beautiful. (noun)

Change *inside* to the plural, and its meaning changes:

She laughed until her *insides* hurt. (colloquial, noun)

The following is what a listing in a good Italian/English dictionary might look like:

inside (in'said) 1. *avv.* dentro, in casa, entro; 2. *agg.* interno, interiore; 3. *prep.* in, dentro; 4. *n.* interno, parte interna (*fam.*), stomaco; informazioni riservate.

Practice Makes *Perfetto*

Using the Italian definitions just given, figure out the part of speech for *inside* in each of the following sentences, and complete the translated sentences in Italian. (You can find the answers in Appendix A.)

1. We live inside the walls of the city.

Abitiamo _____ le mura della città.

2. The woman's insides hurt.

   Alla donna fa male lo _____.

3. We will arrive home inside of an hour.

   Arriviamo a casa _____ *un'ora.*

4. He has inside information on the *Palio.*

   Lui ha _____ *sul Palio.*

5. The inside of the church is dark.

   L' _____ *della chiesa è scuro.*

> ### La Bella Lingua
>
> Keep an eye out for English movies that have an Italian theme. You can improve your Italian without having to read a thing. Some titles include *Avanti, Big Night, Down by Law, The Godfather, Good Morning Babylon, Indiscretion of an American Housewife, Moonstruck, Queen of Hearts, Stealing Beauty,* and *Summertime.*

What's the Object? Who's the Subject?

Okay, imagine that you're back in the seventh grade again. The sun is shining outside the school windows, and the teacher is droning on about objects and subjects. As she's speaking, you're on the verge of falling asleep. The room is too hot, you're bored, and you're thinking, "I'm never going to need this to do anything!"

Of course, in retrospect, you know better. But you still aren't quite sure what an object is, unless it's something unidentified and coming from parts unknown.

Use a sentence from your first-grade book to look at what an object is:

Jack throws Jane a ball.

First things first. Take a *minuto* to find the *verbo* in this sentence. Remember, verbs are where the action is.

Did you figure out it was the verb *to throw? Bravi!* You're on your way. Next question: Who threw the ball? Answer: Jack did, that's who—and he is your subject.

The million-*euro* question now is, what did Jack throw? Answer: The ball! That's the direct object. A direct object is the recipient of the verb's action.

In sentences with two nouns following the verb, the first is generally the indirect object, the word that tells to whom or for whom the action was done (Jane).

Let's continue with Jack and Jane. Jane, never one to say no to a challenge, decides to keep the ball rolling. Analyze the next sentence for its subject and object pronouns:

She throws it back to him.

Did you figure out that *she* is the subject pronoun (substituting for Jane) and *it* (substituting for ball) is the object pronoun? So you see, there's nothing to worry about. You know everything you need to get this ball rolling and learn the language you've always dreamed of knowing.

Drawing from *Esperienza*

Have you ever studied another *lingua?* Perhaps you took *spagnolo* when you were in high school. At the urging of your parents, you might have studied *latino,* and after three semesters of it, all you can remember are the words *veni, vedi, vici* (came, saw, conquered). Whatever the last language was that you studied, whether it was *francese, russo, ebreo* (Hebrew), or *cinese,* it will be the first *lingua* to come out of your mouth when you try mustering up some Italian. It's *naturale*—your brain retains everything, although some of the *informazione* ends up stored away until you decide to dust off the cobwebs and reopen the files.

Your pronunciation may initially reflect those first language classes, but you'll soon be rounding your *R*'s and wooing your partner Italian-style in no time flat. If you have studied another Romance language, you'll already be familiar with the basic *struttura* of Italian. Let's take a look at some of those basic *regole* (rules):

> ### La Bella Lingua
>
> If you can't think of the Italian word, use the word you remember from the last *lingua* you studied. If your *frase* comes out one third *italiano,* one third *francese,* and one third *inglese,* it's still better than nothing.

- All Romance languages possess masculine and feminine nouns.

- The definite article (the) agrees in gender and number with the noun it modifies.

- All adjectives must agree in both gender and plurality with the nouns they modify. *Per esempio,* if a noun is feminine singular, its adjective must also be feminine singular, as in *la lingua italiana.*

- As a general rule, most adjectives come after the noun, as with *il vino buono* and *la casa bianca.*

- All Romance languages possess a polite as well as a familiar form of *you.* The polite form, *Lei,* is capitalized to distinguish it from *lei,* meaning *she,* and should be used with strangers, authority figures, and elders. The familiar form, *tu,* is used with friends and children.

Read It, Write It, Say It

Writing things down helps you to retain the things you have read or heard. Your body will remember in ways your mind will not. Studying aloud will get your mouth into the habit of helping you to *ricordare*. If you read the words, write them down, and read aloud, you'll be speaking in no time.

The Least You Need to Know

- ◆ Italian comes from Latin and is connected to a history steeped in *tradizione*.

- ◆ You have no reason to be intimidated by grammar. Understanding the different parts of speech takes away the mystery of learning a second language.

- ◆ A bilingual *dizionario* is essential to language learning and can help you identify different parts of speech and understand common Italian expressions.

- ◆ Dante, Boccaccio, and Petrarca are three of Italy's greatest writers.

Chapter 3

ng Your *Bocca* Around
BCs and 123s

ter

an pronunciation

Italian *alfabeto*

tress or not to stress

l your *nome* in *italiano*

s of the week and months

neri (numbers)

a new language is like having a box filled with puzzle pieces that
en fit together. At first, it's all just a jumble of sounds and letters
, but soon your *confusione* is replaced with *comprensione* as a clear
erges. This chapter gives you the nuts and bolts of Italian, and
nt to what the average Italian four-year-old knows. (*Don't worry,*
ime.)

Italian Pronunciation

Initially, it seems as though anyone speaking Italian is singing. There is a *continuità* and *fluidità* that reminds you of a beautifully sustained note.

With few exceptions, Italian pronunciation is very easy to learn. Almost all Italian words end in a *vocale* (as in vocal and meaning *vowel*) and are often pronounced as if joined together. As a phonetic language, in Italian, what you see is what you say—at least most of the time. After you learn how to read the music, you'll be able to play along with anyone.

The key is to understand the basic differences between the English and Italian rules of pronunciation. For example, in Italian, the word *cinema* is written exactly the same as in English; however, in Italian it is pronounced *chee-neh-mah.* The same *ci* is used in the greeting *ciao.*

CAUTION

Attenzione!

When pronouncing Italian words, keep your tongue and mouth alert. Emphasize double consonants without overstressing letters or syllables; otherwise you'll end up sounding like someone trying a little too hard.

You'll find that certain Italian sounds may initially present a challenge to the English speaker, most notably the rolled *R* and the letter combination *gli* (pronounced *ylee,* like million). Nevertheless, after some time even these sounds will come easily to the attentive listener.

Italian requires clean diction with clearly pronounced vowels. Double consonants in words such as *anno* (year), *birra* (beer), and *gatto* (cat) should be emphasized. Avoid sounding overly nasal or guttural.

You will see less of the pronunciation spelled out for you in later chapters. Flip back to this chapter if you are not sure how a word should be pronounced. Unless otherwise indicated, equal stress should be given to two-syllable words such as *cento* (*chen-toh*).

Your ABCs

The Italian language uses the Latin alphabet. Unlike English, however, the Italian alphabet contains only 21 letters, borrowing the letters *j, k, w, x,* and *y* for words of foreign origin.

As you read, you'll discover that the spelling of Italian words follows a logical pattern.

A Is for *Ancona*

When spelling out words, rather than using proper names like you do in English (*T* as in Tom), Italians often use the names of Italian cities. For example, *A come Ancona, I come Imola, T come Torino* (*A* as in *Ancona*, *I* as in *Imola*, *T* as in *Torino*), and so on. A practical way of remembering the *alfabeta* is to learn how to spell your name in Italian. The Italian equivalent is given beside the letter. The stressed syllable is in bold. Examples of foreign letters are given with commonly used nouns.

Letter	Italian Name of Letter	Pronunciation	Example	Pronunciation
A	a	*a*	Ancona	*ahn-**koh**-nah*
B	bi	*bee*	Bologna	*boh-**loh**-nyah*
C	ci	*chee*	Cagliari	***kahl**-yah-ree*
D	di	*dee*	Domodossola	*doh-moh-**doh**-soh-lah*
E	e	*eh*	Empoli	***em**-poh-lee*
F	effe	*ehf-fay*	Firenze	*fee-**ren**-zay*
G	gi	*jee*	Genova	***jeh**-noh-vah*
H	acca	*ahk-kah*	hotel	*oh-tel*
I	i	*ee*	Imola	***ee**-moh-lah*
J*	i lunga	*ee loon-gah*	jolly	*jah-lee*
K*	cappa	*kahp-pah*	kaiser	*ky-zer*
L	elle	*ehl-lay*	Livorno	*lee-**vor**-noh*
M	emme	*ehm-may*	Milano	*mee-**lah**-noh*
N	enne	*ehn-nay*	Napoli	***nah**-poh-lee*
O	o	*oh*	Otranto	*oh-**tran**-toh*
P	pi	*pee*	Palermo	*pah-**ler**-moh*
Q	cu	*koo*	quaderno (notebook)	*kwah-**der**-noh*
R	erre	*ehr-ray*	Roma	*roh-mah*
S	esse	*ehs-say*	Sassari	***sah**-sah-ree*
T	ti	*tee*	Torino	*toh-**ree**-noh*
U	u	*oo*	Udine	***oo**-dee-neh*
V	vu	*voo*	Venezia	*veh-**neh**-zee-ah*
W*	doppia vu	*doh-pee-yah voo*	Washington	***wash**-eeng-ton*
X*	ics	*eeks*	raggi-x	*rah-jee eek-say*

continues

continued

Letter	Italian Name of Letter	Pronunciation	Example	Pronunciation
Y*	ipsilon	*eep-see-lohn*	York	*york*
Z	zeta	*zeh-tah*	Zara	*zah-rah*

*These letters have been borrowed from other languages.

Getting the Accent

In this case, we're not talking about what Sophia Loren and Roberto Benigni have when speaking English. Italian uses the grave accent (`), pronounced *grav*, on words where the stress falls on the final syllable: *caffè, città, università*.

You may also see the acute accent (´) used (especially in older text and phrasebooks), particularly with the words *benché* (although) and *perché* (because/why). Don't be surprised to find conflicting examples.

The written accent is also used to distinguish several Italian words from others that have the same spelling but a different meaning.

è	is	*e*	and
sì	yes	*si*	oneself
dà	gives	*da*	from
sè	himself	*se*	if
là	there	*la*	the
lì	there	*li*	the
né	nor	*ne*	some

CAUTION

Attenzione!

Some Italian letter combinations are seldom found in English. These sounds include the *gl* combination in words such as *figlio* (son; pronounced *fee-lyoh*); the word *gli* (the; pronounced *ylee*, like the *ll* in the English word *million*); and the *gn* combination, seen in words such as *gnocchi* (potato dumplings; pronounced *nyoh-kee*), and *bagno* (bathroom; pronounced *bah-nyoh*, like the *ny* sound in *canyon* or the *ni* sound in *onion*).

The following examples illustrate how an apostrophe is often used to indicate the dropping of a final vowel.

l'animale instead of *lo animale* (the animal)

d'Italia instead of *di Italia* (of Italy)

dov'è instead of *dove è* (where is)

Don't Get Stressed Out

As a rule, most Italian words are stressed on the next-to-last syllable, such as *signorina* (*see-nyoh-**ree**-nah*), and *minestrone* (*mee-neh-**stroh**-neh*).

Exceptions exist, making rules rather difficult to follow. Some words are stressed on the third-to-last syllable, such as *automobile* (*ow-toh-**moh**-bee-leh*) and *dialogo* (*dee-**ah**-loh-goh*).

Other words—mostly verb forms—are stressed on the fourth-to-last syllable, such as *studiano* (***stoo**-dee-ah-noh*) and *telefonano* (*teh-**leh**-foh-nah-noh*).

Finally, stress should be placed on the last syllable when you see an accent mark at the end of a word, such as *città* (*chee-**tah***), *università* (*oo-nee-ver-see-**ta***), and *virtù* (*veer-**too***).

I've indicated in the early chapters where to put the stress in words of three syllables or more, and in words of two syllables with an accented (and thus stressed) syllable. In the future, consult a good dictionary when you are unclear about which syllable should be emphasized. Generally, you will see either an accent placed above or a dot placed below the stressed vowel.

As a *Regola*

For the purposes of clarity, the pronunciation used in this text is designed to be read phonetically.

Always remember to enunciate vowels clearly and not to slur your words. Say what you see.

Double *RR*s should be held and emphasized when trilled.

Double consonants should always be emphasized—but never as separate sounds. They should be joined and slide into one another, as in the word *pizza* (*pee-tsah*).

I Giorni: Days

When pronouncing days of the week, the accent tells you to emphasize the last syllable. Italians have adopted the English way of expressing the end of the week by using the English word *weekend*, but you will also hear *il fine settimana*.

Days of the Week

English	L'Italiano	Pronunciation
Monday	lunedì	*loo-neh-**dee***
Tuesday	martedì	*mar-teh-**dee***
Wednesday	mercoledì	*mer-koh-leh-**dee***
Thursday	giovedì	*joh-veh-**dee***
Friday	venerdì	*ven-er-**dee***
Saturday	sabato	***sah**-bah-toh*
Sunday	domenica	*doh-**meh**-nee-kah*
The weekend	il fine settimana	*eel fee-neh seh-tee-**mah**-nah*

I Mesi: Months

The original *calendario* used by the Romans was based on a 10-month year. The months *luglio* (July) and *agosto* (August) were added in *onore* of Julius Caesar and Augustus. If you're planning your next *viaggio* or want to talk about *l'astrologia*, knowing the month is *importante*. Like the days of the week, the months are not capitalized in Italian.

La Bella Lingua

The word *calendar* originally comes from the Latin word *calends*, signifying the day of the new moon. During the Middle Ages, the *calender* was what money lenders called their account books, being that the monthly interest was due on the *calends*. The original "old style" Roman calendar, instituted by Julius Caesar in 46 B.C.E., was used until 1583 when Pope Gregory XIII made official the "new style" calendar—also referred to as the Gregorian calendar.

I Mesi (The Months)

Month	*Mese*	Pronunciation
January	gennaio	*jeh-**nah**-yoh*
February	febbraio	*feb-**rah**-yoh*
March	marzo	*mar-tsoh*
April	aprile	*ah-**pree**-leh*
May	maggio	*mah-joh*
June	giugno	*joo-nyoh*
July	luglio	*loo-lyoh*
August	agosto	*ah-**goh**-stoh*
September	settembre	*seh-**tem**-breh*
October	ottobre	*oh-**toh**-breh*
November	novembre	*noh-**vem**-breh*
December	dicembre	*dee-**chem**-breh*

La Bella Lingua

The days of the week correspond to these planets.

lunedì: la luna (the Moon)

martedì: Marte (Mars)

mercoledì: Mercurio (Mercury)

giovedì: Giove (Jupiter)

venerdì: Venere (Venus)

sabato: Saturno (Saturn)

domenica: (Sunday; refers to God's day)

Rolling Your *R*s

There are a few sounds in Italian that are not found in English, the most obvious being the rolled *R*. Some people can roll their *R*'s forever, but if you are not one of them, here's a mini-guide on rolling your *R:* Place the tip of your tongue so that it's touching the roof of your

La Bella Lingua

In linguistic parlance, the term *rhotacism* is defined, among other things, as the incorrect use or overuse of *R*'s in pronunciation.

mouth just behind your front teeth. Now curl the tip of your tongue and exhale. You should get the beginning trill of a rolled *R*. After you get it, be subtle—a little trill will do.

The Long and the Short of It: *Vocali*

The Italian word for vowel (*vocale*) is almost the same as the English word *vocal*, a good reminder that Italian vowels should always be pronounced clearly. If you can master the vowels, you're already halfway to the point of sounding Italian. The following table shows how the vowels are pronounced. Read aloud to practice.

Pronouncing Vowels Properly

Vowel	Sound	Example	Pronunciation
a	*ah*	artista	*ar-**tee**-stah*
e	*eh*	elefante	*eh-leh-**fahn**-teh*
i	*ee*	isola	***ee**-zoh-lah*
o	*oh*	opera	***oh**-peh-rah*
u	*oo*	uno	*oo-noh*

The Hard and Soft of It: *Consonanti*

The following table contains a list of *consonanti* (consonants) and includes letters recognized in foreign languages. When you get the hang of it, Italian is so easy to pronounce that it would be just as simple to read the words without the pronunciation guide. Most Italian consonants are pronounced like the English ones. It's the different letter combinations that take a little study. Roll on.

Pronouncing Consonants Properly

Letter	Sound	Example	Pronunciation	Meaning
b	*bee*	bambino	*bahm-**bee**-noh*	child *m.*
c + a, o, u	hard *c* (as in cat)	candela	*kahn-**deh**-lah*	candle
c + e, i	*ch* (as in chest)	centro	*chen-troh*	center/downtown
ch	hard *c* (as in cat)	Chianti	*kee-**ahn**-tee*	Chianti (a red wine)

Letter	Sound	Example	Pronunciation	Meaning
d	*dee*	due	*doo-eh*	two
f	*eff*	frase	*frah-zeh*	phrase
g + a, o, u	hard *g* (as in go)	gatto	*gah-toh*	cat
g + e, i	*j* (as in gem)	gentile	*jen-**tee**-leh*	kind
gli	*ylee* (as in million)	figlio	*fee-lyoh*	son
gn	*nya* (as in onion)	gnocchi	*nyoh-kee*	potato dumplings
h	silent	hotel	*oh-tel*	hotel
j*	*juh* (hard *j*)	jazz	*jaz*	jazz
k*	*kuh* (hard *k*)	koala	*koh-**ah**-lah*	koala
l	*ell*	lingua	*leen-gwah*	language
m	*em*	madre	*mah-dreh*	mother
n	*en*	nido	*nee-doh*	nest
p	*pee*	padre	*pah-dreh*	father
q	*kew*	quanto	*kwahn-toh*	how much
r	*er* (slightly rolled)	Roberto	*roh-**ber**-toh*	Robert
rr	*err* (really rolled)	birra	*bee-rah*	beer
s (at beginning of word)	*ess* (as in see)	serpente	*ser-**pen**-teh*	snake
s	*s* (as in rose)	casa	*kah-zah*	house
sc + a, o	*sk*	scala	*skah-lah*	stair
sc + e, i	*sh*	scena	*sheh-nah*	scene
t	*tee*	tavola	***tah**-voh-lah*	table
v	*v*	vino	*vee-noh*	wine
w*	*wuh*	Washington	***wash**-eeng-ton*	Washington
x*	*eeks*	raggi-x	*rah-jee eeks*	x-ray
y*	*yuh*	yoga	*yoh-gah*	yoga
z	*z*	zebra	*zeh-brah*	zebra
zz	*ts*	pazzo	*pah-tsoh*	crazy

These letters are used in words of foreign origin.

La Bella Lingua

The best way to remember how a particular letter combination should be pronounced is to simply recall a word that you already know. *Ad esempio,* the word *ciao* is pronounced with the soft *c,* as in *chow.* Other words with the *c + i* combination include *cinema* (cinema), *bacio* (kiss), and *amici* (friends).

The word Chianti is pronounced with a hard *c,* as in kee-**ahn**-tee. When you come across other words (such as chi [who] and perchè [why]) with this *combinazione,* you'll know just how they're pronounced.

Practice Those Vowels

Now try to pronounce these words, focusing just on the vowels.

A

Say *ah,* as in *father:*

madre	fila	canto	casa	strada	mela
mah-dreh	fee-lah	kahn-toh	kah-zah	strah-dah	meh-lah
(mother)	(line)	(song)	(home)	(street)	(apple)

E

Say *eh,* as in *make* or *let:*

padre	sera	festa	bene	età	pensione
pah-dreh	*seh-rah*	*fes-tah*	*beh-neh*	*eh-**tah***	*pen-see-**oh**-neh*
(father)	(evening)	(party)	(well)	(age)	(motel, pension)

I

Say *ee,* as in *feet:*

idiota	piccolo	pulire	in	idea	turista
*ee-dee-**oh**-tah*	***pee**-koh-loh*	*poo-**lee**-reh*	*een*	*ee-**deh**-ah*	*too-**ree**-stah*
(idiot)	(small)	(to clean)	(in)	(idea)	(tourist)

O

Say *oh,* as in *note* or *for:*

donna	bello	cosa	albero	gatto	uomo
doh-nah	*beh-loh*	*koh-zah*	***ahl**-beh-roh*	*gah-toh*	*woh-moh*
(woman)	(beautiful)	(thing)	(tree)	(cat)	(man)

U

Say *oo*, as in *crude:*

luna	una	cubo	lupo	tuo
loo-nah	*oo-nah*	*koo-boh*	*loo-poh*	*too-oh*
(moon)(a)	(cube)	(wolf)	(your)	(yours)

Give Me the Combo

Italian pronunciation follows a pretty consistent, easy-to-remember format. The rules change depending on what *vocale* is connected to what *consonante*.

The following examples illustrate many letter combinations you'll find in Italian. To ask someone how to say something in Italian, you can use this expression: *Come si dice …?* (How do you say …?)

Buon'Idea

Use what you know to remember the rules of Italian pronunciation. *Ciao,* as you know, is pronounced *chow.* It's safe to assume that any other words with the *ci* combination follow this rule. Examples include *Cina* (China), *cinema* (cinema), and *cipolla* (onion).

C Is for Casa

Look at all that you can do with the letter *c.*

Letter Combination	*Sound*	*Pronunciation Guide*	
c + a, o, u	*k*	Say *c*, as in *camp*	
casa	amico	caro	bocca
kah-zah	*ah-**mee**-koh*	*kah-roh*	*boh-kah*
(house)	(friend)	(expensive/dear)	(mouth)
colore	conto	cultura	giacca
*koh-**loh**-reh*	*kohn-toh*	*kool-**too**-rah*	*jah-kah*
(color)	(bill/check)	(culture)	(jacket)
Letter Combination	*Sound*	*Pronunciation Guide*	
c + h	*k*	Say *c*, as in *camp*	
chiamare	occhio	perché	Machiavelli
*kee-ah-**mah**-reh*	*oh-kee-yoh*	*per-keh*	*mah-kee-ah-**veh**-lee*
(to call)	(eye)	(why)	(Machiavelli)

chiaro	chiuso	macchina	ricchi
*kee-**ah**-roh*	*kee-**yoo**-zoh*	***mah**-kee-nah*	*ree-kee*
(clear/light)	(closed)	(car)	(rich, *m.p.*)

Letter Combination	Sound	Pronunciation Guide	
c + e, i	*ch*	Say *ch*, as in *cherry*	

accento	cena	città	ceramica
*ah-**chen**-toh*	*che-nah*	*chee-**tah***	*cheh-**rah**-mee-kah*
(accent)	(dinner)	(city)	(ceramic)
ciao	bacio	Francia	cioccolata
chow	*bah-choh*	*frahn-chah*	*choh-koh-**lah**-tah*
(hi/bye)	(kiss)	(France)	(chocolate)

G Is for Gamba

Practice getting your *g* sounds right.

Letter Combination	Sound	Pronunciation Guide	
g + a, o, u	*g*	Say *g*, as in *great*	

gamba	lago	gufo	prego
gahm-bah	*lah-goh*	*goo-foh*	*preh-goh*
(leg)	(lake)	(owl)	(you're welcome)
gambero	mago	strega	gusto
***gahm**-beh-roh*	*mah-goh*	*streh-gah*	*goo-stoh*
(shrimp)	(wizard)	(witch)	(taste)

The letter combination *gh* is also pronounced like the *g* in *go*, as in *funghi* (mushrooms).

Letter Combination	Sound	Pronunciation Guide	
g + e, i	*j*	Say *g*, as in *gem*	

gelato	giovane	giacca	viaggio
*jeh-**lah**-toh*	***joh**-vah-neh*	*jah-kah*	*vee-**ah**-joh*
(ice cream)	(young)	(jacket)	(voyage)
formaggio	gente	giorno	maggio
*for-**mah**-joh*	*jen-teh*	*jor-noh*	*mah-joh*
(cheese)	(people)	(day)	(May)

Letter Combination	Sound	Pronunciation Guide	
g + n	*ny*	Say *onion*	
lavagna	signore	legno	gnocchi
*lah-**vah**-nyah*	*see-**nyoh**-reh*	*leh-nyoh*	*nyoh-kee*
(blackboard)	(sir, Mr.)	(wood)	(potato dumplings)
ragno	compagna	signora	guadagno
rah-nyoh	*kohm-**pah**-nyah*	*see-**nyoh**-rah*	*gwah-**dah**-nyoh*
(spider)	(countryside)	(Mrs., Ms.)	(earnings)

S Is for *Scandalo*

The letter *s* is quite slippery.

Letter Combination	Sound	Pronunciation Guide	
sc + a, h, o, u	*sk*	Say *sk*, as in *skin*	
sconto	scusa	scandalo	pesca
skohn-toh	*skoo-zah*	***skahn**-dah-loh*	*pes-kah*
(discount)	(excuse)	(scandal)	(peach)
scuola	schifo	fiasco	schizzo
skwoh-lah	*skee-foh*	*fee-**ah**-skoh*	*skee-tsoh*
(school)	(disgust)	(fiasco)	(sketch, squirt)

Letter Combination	Sound	Pronunciation Guide	
sc + e, i	*sh*	Say *sh*, as in *sheet*	
sci	pesce	scena	lasciare
shee	*peh-sheh*	*sheh-nah*	*lah-**shah**-reh*
(skiing)	(fish)	(scene)	(to leave something)
sciroppo	sciocco	sciopero	scelto
*shee-**roh**-poh*	*shee-**oh**-koh*	***shoh**-peh-roh*	*shel-toh*
(syrup)	(fool)	(strike)	(choice)

Did you notice any similarity between the words you just read and their English counterparts? You know more than you think! It's *importante* to see how much Italian and English share. Remember that a lot of English derives from Latin. It helps to make associations with familiar words. Each time you do this, you are creating a bridge from one shore to another. For example, the word *luna* (moon) comes from

Attenzione!

Say "Ah!" The real key to success is to make sure you are pronouncing your vowels correctly: *a* (*ah*), *e* (*eh*), *i* (*ee*), *o* (*oh*), and *u* (*oo*). Practice your vowels the next time you sing "Old McDonald had a farm"!

Latin, as we see in the English word *lunatic.* It was once believed that lunacy came from the full moon. All sorts of associations can be made to *illuminate* (*illuminare*) these connections.

Diphthongs

No, a diphthong is not a teeny-weeny bikini. The term *diphthong* (*dittongo* in Italian) refers to any pair of vowels that begins with one vowel sound and ends with a different vowel sound within the same syllable. The term literally means *two voices* (*di* = two; *thong* = tongue/voice) and originally comes from Greek.

Italian utilizes many diphthongs such as *olio* (pronounced *ohl-yoh*), *quanto* (*kwahn-toh*), and *pausa* (*pow-sah*). Keep in mind that not all pairs of vowels form diphthongs.

Double Consonants

Any time you see a double consonant in a word, such as *birra* (beer) or *anno* (year), it is important to emphasize that consonant, or you may be misunderstood. Take a look at a few words whose meanings change when there is a double consonant. As you will see, in some cases you *definitely* want to emphasize those double consonants:

What's What

In Italian, two vowels do not necessarily produce a diphthong. The word *zia* (*zee-ah*) maintains two distinct, separate sounds and consequently does not produce a diphthong. On the other hand, the word *Italia* (*ee-tahl-yah*) does produce a diphthong. Keep in mind that diphthongs are always pronounced as one sound.

ano (*ah-noh;* anus)	*anno* (*ahn-noh;* year)
casa (*kah-zah;* house)	*cassa* (*kahs-sah;* cash register)
pena (*peh-nah;* pity)	*penna* (*pehn-nah;* pen)
pene (*peh-neh;* penis)	*penne* (*pen-neh;* pens)
sete (*seh-teh;* thirsty)	*sette* (*set-teh;* seven)
sono (*so-noh;* I am)	*sonno* (*sohn-noh;* sleepy)

Double consonants will not be highlighted in the pronunciation. It's up to you to emphasize them. Practice pronouncing the following words, remembering to slide the syllables together:

mamma	sorella	cappello	atto	pazzo	bocca	Anna
mah-mah	*soh-**reh**-lah*	*kah-**peh**-loh*	*ah-toh*	*pah-tsoh*	*boh-kah*	*ah-nah*
(mom)	(sister)	(hat)	(act)	(crazy)	(mouth)	(Ann)

As a *Regola*
Unless beginning a word, a single *s* is pronounced like *z*, as in the name *Gaza*, or *s*, as in *busy* and the Italian word *casa* (house).
A double *ss* is pronounced like the *s* in the English word *tassel* and the Italian word *passo* (pass).
A single *z* is pronounced like the *z* in the word *zebra*.
A double *zz* is pronounced like the *ts* in the English word *cats* and the Italian word *piazza* (plaza).

Bambino, I Got Your Numero

In Italy, as in many other European countries, the currency adopted is the euro (EUR). This can be pretty handy because you can use euros in other European countries like France and Germany. Its value changes, so please check the actual exchange rate before traveling. Be ready to manage a lot of coins, because there are no bills under 5 euros. Remember also that sometimes people talk absolute money referring to the old currency, lira, whose value was about 2,000 liras for 1 euro. If you want to make a date, tell the time, or find out prices, you need to know your cardinal numbers (1, 2, 3, …).

Fortunately, you don't need to use Roman numerals to do your math. Numbers that express amounts, known as cardinal numbers, are called *numeri cardinali* in Italian.

Numeri Cardinali

Number	Italian	Pronunciation
0	zero	*zeh-roh*
1	uno	*oo-noh*
2	due	*doo-weh*
3	tre	*treh*
4	quattro	*kwah-troh*
5	cinque	*cheen-kweh*
6	sei	*say*
7	sette	*seh-teh*
8	otto	*oh-toh*
9	nove	*noh-veh*
10	dieci	*dee-**yay**-chee*

continues

Numeri Cardinali (continued)

Number	Italian	Pronunciation
11	undici	**oon**-dee-chee
12	dodici	**doh**-dee-chee
13	tredici	**treh**-dee-chee
14	quattordici	kwah-**tor**-dee-chee
15	quindici	**kween**-dee-chee
16	sedici	**say**-dee-chee
17	diciassette	dee-chah-**seh**-teh
18	diciotto	dee-**choh**-toh
19	diciannove	dee-chah-**noh**-veh
20	venti	ven-tee
21	ventuno	ven-**too**-noh
22	ventidue	ven-tee-**doo**-weh
23	ventitrè	ven-tee-**treh**
24	ventiquattro	ven-tee-**kwah**-troh
25	venticinque	ven-tee-**cheen**-kweh
26	ventisei	ven-tee-**say**
27	ventisette	ven-tee-**seh**-teh
28	ventotto	ven-**toh**-toh
29	ventinove	ven-tee-**noh**-veh
30	trenta	tren-tah
40	quaranta	kwah-**rahn**-tah
50	cinquanta	cheen-**kwahn**-tah
60	sessanta	seh-**sahn**-tah
70	settanta	seh-**tahn**-tah
80	ottanta	oh-**tahn**-tah
90	novanta	noh-**vahn**-tah
100	cento	chen-toh
101	centuno	chen-**too**-noh
200	duecento	doo-ay-**chen**-toh
300	trecento	treh-**chen**-toh
400	quattrocento	kwah-troh-**chen**-toh
500	cinquecento	cheen-kway-**chen**-toh

Number	Italian	Pronunciation
1.000	mille	*meel-lay*
1.001	milleuno	*meel-lay-**oo**-noh*
1.200	milleduecento	*mee-lay-doo-eh-**chen**-toh*
2.000	duemila	*doo-eh-**mee**-lah*
3.000	tremila	*treh-**mee**-lah*
10.000	diecimila	*dee-ay-chee-**mee**-lah*
20.000	ventimila	*ven-tee-**mee**-lah*
100.000	centomila	*chen-toh-**mee**-lah*
200.000	duecentomila	*doo-eh-chen-toh-**mee**-lah*
1.000.000	un milione	*oon mee-**lyoh**-neh*
1.000.000.000	un miliardo	*oon mee-**lyar**-doh*

Number Crunching

You'll need your *numeri* to tell time in Chapter 9. For now, keep in mind these brief notes on writing numbers in Italian:

♦ Italian uses a period to indicate units of thousands.

English	Italian
2,000	2.000

♦ In Italian, you must use commas in decimal numbers. It is read as *e* (and):

English	Italian
1.25	1,25

Get Help!

The best way to learn how to speak another language is to spend time listening to it. If you don't have live entertainment, some suggestions include these:

♦ **Audiocassettes.** Visit your local *biblioteca* (library) or *libreria* (bookstore) to see what they have on hand. Audiocassettes are excellent for developing listening skills. You may want to see if your local *università* has a language lab you can use.

♦ **Language CD-ROMs for the computer.** If you're computer savvy, invest in an Italian/English *dizionario* or educational translation program appropriate for your computer and purposes. Some even have programs that will pronounce the words for you.

♦ **Internet.** There are many wonderful sites now offering audio samples. For some suggestions, refer to Appendix G.

♦ *Musica.* Listen to an Italian radio station; you can listen to almost all of them on the Internet using programs like Windows Media Player. In addition, you may want to invest in some *musica* you've never heard before. Aside from *opera*, you'll find Italian hip-hop, rock and roll, rap (yes, rap even in Italian), and traditional folk songs, often with lyrics. Listen to the different dialects.

Buon'Idea

Expand your *lessico.* Play the Italian name game with friends interested in learning Italian. Using the letters of a famous Italian name, see how many Italian words you can come up with. Keep your Italian dictionary close by.

For example: Leonardo Di Caprio

leone (lion)	*capra* (goat)
lepre (hare)	*rana* (frog)
principe (prince)	*cena* (dinner)
onore (honor)	*delirio* (delirium)

Pazienza and *Pratica* Pay Off

Anyone who has ever studied—or even heard someone studying—a new musical instrument knows that the first time you pick up a violin, you're not going to sound like a *virtuoso.* Fortunately, learning Italian is much easier than playing a *violino.*

The Least You Need to Know

♦ Let your tongue do the talking. Tickle a single *R*, but rrrrrrroll your double *RR*s. Rev them like an engine, purr like a cat, or growl like a bear.

♦ Don't slur—enunciate vowels, yet keep your Italian from sounding forced and unnatural.

♦ Fluidity is key. Slide syllables together!

♦ Look for interesting Italian websites and language cassettes to support your language studies.

Chapter 4

You Have *Amici:* Cognates

In This Chapter

- ◆ Bridging the gap between languages by using cognates

- ◆ You know a lot more Italian than you think

- ◆ Breaking it down: the nouns, verbs, and adjectives you already know

- ◆ Why you should beware of false friends (in the Italian language, that is!)

What if you were told that you were already halfway to speaking Italian? Remember that English, although a Germanic language, contains many words of Latin origin. The list of Italian words you already know is longer than you can imagine. Some are virtually the same, whereas most are easily identified by their similarity to English. *Telefono, attenzione, università, automobile, studente*—the list goes on and on.

Cognates: A Bridge Between Languages

Cognates serve as the stepping-stones between the banks of different languages. Any words that are similar to and look the same as other words in a foreign language are called *cognates*, or, in Italian, *parole simili* (literally, similar words). By learning how to dissect a word, searching for clues that will help reveal the mystery of its meaning, you will discover how much you already know.

> ### What's What
>
> Cognates are words in different languages that derive from the same root and are similar in both spelling and meaning, such as with the words *familiar* and *familiare*, *possible* and *possibile*, and so on. **False cognates** can be misleading; in Italian, the word *parenti* means *relatives*, not *parents*, as one might think. *Ape* refers to *bees* and *cane* is a *dog*.

Did I Hear *Biscotto?*

I love to teach beginner Italian just to be able to see the reactions on students' faces when they put *due e due* (two and two) together. We call it the "ah-hah!" moment and we devote the beginning of every *lezione* to sharing our most recent revelations. Allow me to demonstrate. Study the following words, isolating the common denominator that connects them all.

- ◆ Biscotto
- ◆ Manicotti
- ◆ Ricotta
- ◆ Panna cotta
- ◆ Terra cotta

I've always thought someone should use a *biscotto* as a weapon in a mystery novel; they're hard enough to put an eye out! And what makes those delicious little biscuits so hard? If you've ever made them, you know that they are cooked (*cotto*) once, cooled, and cooked again. The *bi-* refers to two, as you can infer from the words *bicicletta* (bicycle), *binario* (binary; track), and *bifocale* (bifocal).

Next, using your taste buds as memory enhancers, look at the word *ricotta* (recooked). This soft cow's milk cheese is stuffed into *manicotti*, hand-cooked pasta sleeves (ah-hah!). The word for hands is *mani*; other related Italian cognates include *manuale* (manual), *manoscritto* (manuscript), and *manico* (handle).

Now, check out the word *terra cotta*. We have established that *cotta* means *cooked*. Can you deduce the significance of the word *terra?*

If you intuited *earth* you were right! *Congratulazioni!* What other words can you think of related to *terra?*

As a *Regola*

English has only one definite article: *the.* Italian has several definite articles, all of which indicate gender (masculine or feminine) and number (singular or plural). When you look at the following list of cognates, you'll notice that all Italian nouns are marked by a definite article. Although the gender of nouns is easily identifiable in Italian, it is best to learn the noun with its appropriate definite article. It might seem confusing at first. For now, keep in mind the following:

- ◆ *Il* is for masculine singular nouns.
- ◆ *Lo* is for masculine singular nouns beginning with s + consonant, or z.
- ◆ *L'* is for any singular noun that begins with a vowel.
- ◆ *La* is for feminine singular nouns.

Trucchi of the Trade

Many English words can be made into Italian simply by changing the endings. Look what happens with the following examples.

English to Italian Endings	English to Italian Examples
-ty → *-tà*	identity → *identità*
-ble → *-ibile*	possible → *possibile*
-tion → *-zione*	action → *azione*
-ous → *-oso*	famous → *famoso*
-ent → *-ente*	president → *presidente*
-ence → *-enza*	essence → *essenza*
-ism → *-ismo*	socialism → *socialismo*

If It Looks Like a Duck ...

The Italian language has only a few perfect cognates—such as the words *banana,* *opera, panorama, pizza, via,* and *zebra.* Although the endings and pronunciations may be slightly *differente,* near cognates are essentially the same.

Let's start with cognates of place and time. Study the places and the times and dates in the following two tables to get *un'idea* of how many *parole simili* exist between

Italian and English. Nine out of ten times, your initial gut response will be correct—trust it!

Buon'Idea

Collect menus from your favorite Italian *ristorante* and study the *ingredienti* for each *piatto*. Often, what sounds exotic is simply a description of the food. Angel-hair pasta, called *capellini*, literally means *thin hairs*. The ear-shaped pasta called *orecchiette* refers to *little ears*. *Calzone* comes from the word *calza*, due to its resemblance to a cheese-filled *sock*.

Where in the *Mondo:* Places

Where to begin? Wherever you are. Look at the cognates in the following table. Each noun is given with the appropriate definite article to get you started understanding the concept of gender.

La Bella Lingua

Why memorize a hundred words when you can study a handful of endings? The *possibilità* are endless!

Although exceptions exist, it's amazing how many English words can be easily converted into Italian by substituting a little letter:

English		Italiano	Examples
al	→	o	practical → pratico
c	→	z	force → forza
k, ck	→	c, cc	sack → sacco
ph	→	f	telephone → telefono
th	→	t	theater → teatro
x	→	s, ss	external → esterno
xt	→	st	extreme → estremo
y	→	i	style → stile

Places

Italiano	English	Italiano	English
l'aeroporto	the airport	l'appartamento	the apartment
l'agenzia	the agency	la banca	the bank
il bar	the bar	l'oceano	the ocean
il caffè	the café	l'ospedale	the hospital
il castello	the castle	il paradiso	the paradise
la cattedrale	the cathedral	la piazza	the plaza
il centro	center/downtown	il ristorante	the restaurant
il cinema	the cinema	lo stadio	the stadium
il circo	the circus	la stazione	the station
la città	the city	lo studio	the studio/office
la corsa	the course/track	il supermercato	the supermarket
la discoteca	the discothèque	il teatro	the theater
la farmacia	the pharmacy	la terrazza	the terrace
il giardino	the garden	l'ufficio	the office
il mercato	the market	l'ufficio postale	the post office
la montagna	the mountain	il villaggio	the village
il museo	the museum		

It's About Time

You don't know what time it is? Sure you do—the following table lists some cognates related to time.

Time and Dates

Italiano	English	Italiano	English
l'anniversario	the anniversary	il minuto	the minute
annuale	annual	la notte	the night
biennale	biannual	l'ora	the hour
la data	the date	il secondo	the second
la festa	the holiday (as in "festive")	il tempo	the time (also, weather)
il millennio	the millennium		

How *Intelligente* You Are!

Convert the following words into Italian by changing the endings accordingly. (You can find the answers in Appendix A.)

1. position   _____posizione_____

2. incredible   _____

3. nation   _____

4. presence   _____

5. identity   _____

6. pessimism   _____

7. prudent   _____

8. continent   _____

9. religious   _____

10. difference   _____

As a *Regola*

The letter *e* is actually a word, meaning *and*. The accented letter *è* is also a word, meaning *is*.

Adjectives: How *Grande!*

Thinking about everything you've learned so far in this chapter on cognates, cover the English translation in the following table with a piece of paper, and try to guess the meanings of these adjective cognates.

Cognate Adjectives

Italiano	English	Italiano	English
alto	tall	moderno	modern
ambizioso	ambitious	naturale	natural
biondo	blond	necessario	necessary
bruno	brunette	nervoso	nervous
calmo	calm	normale	normal
cortese	courteous	numeroso	numerous
curioso	curious	onesto	honest
delizioso	delicious	organizzato	organized
differente	different	popolare	popular
divorziato	divorced	possibile	possible
eccellente	excellent	povero	poor
elegante	elegant	pratico	practical
energico	energetic	rapido	rapid
falso	false	ricco	rich
famoso	famous	romantico	romantic
forte	strong (as in fortitude)	saggio	wise (as in sage)

Italiano	English	Italiano	English
fortunato	fortunate	serio	serious
frequente	frequent	sicuro	secure, sure
geloso	jealous	sincero	sincere
generoso	generous	splendido	splendid
gentile	kind, gentle	sposato	married (think spouse)
grande	big, grand	strano	strange
ignorante	ignorant	stupendo	stupendous
importante	important	stupido	stupid
impossibile	impossible	terribile	terrible
incredibile	incredible	tropicale	tropical
intelligente	intelligent	ultimo	last, ultimate
interessante	interesting	violento	violent
lungo	long	virtuoso	virtuous
magnifico	magnificent		

Sostantivi Nouns

While I'm listing cognates, I thought I'd save you the trouble and throw in some nouns as a bonus. Remember: a noun is a person, place, or thing. I've listed the following Italian nouns according to their gender. Your job is to simply write down what they mean in English.

Masculine Nouns

Study the different articles used in front of these masculine nouns. Do you see a pattern beginning to emerge? (You can find the answers in Appendix A.)

Masculine Cognates

Italian Masculine Nouns	English Translation	Italian Masculine Nouns	English Translation
l'aeroplano	_____	il motore	_____
l'anniversario	_____	il museo	_____
l'arco	_____	il naso	_____

continues

Masculine Cognates (continued)

Italian Masculine Nouns	English Translation	Italian Masculine Nouns	English Translation
l'attore	_____	l'odore	_____
l'autobus	_____	il paradiso	_____
il caffè	_____	il presidente	_____
il colore	_____	il profumo	_____
il comunismo	_____	il programma	_____
il continente	_____	il rispetto	_____
il cotone	_____	il salario	_____
il direttore	_____	il servizio	_____
il dizionario	_____	il socialismo	_____
il dottore	_____	lo spirito	_____
l'elefante	_____	lo studente	_____
il fatto	_____	il tassì	_____
il gruppo	_____	il tè	_____
l'idiota	_____	il telefono	_____
il limone	_____	il treno	_____
il meccanico	_____		

Feminine Nouns

Try the same thing with these feminine nouns in the following table. (You can find the answers in Appendix A.)

Feminine Nouns

Italian Feminine Nouns	English Translation	Italian Feminine Nouns	English Translation
l'arte	_____	l'identità	_____
la bicicletta	_____	l'inflazione	_____
la carota	_____	l'insalata	_____
la chitarra	_____	la lampada	_____

Italian Feminine Nouns	English Translation	Italian Feminine Nouns	English Translation
la classe	_____	la lettera	_____
la condizione	_____	la lista	_____
la conversazione	_____	la medicina	_____
la cultura	_____	la musica	_____
la curiosità	_____	la nazione	_____
la depressione	_____	la persona	_____
la dieta	_____	la possibilità	_____
la differenza	_____	la probabilità	_____
la discussione	_____	la professione	_____
l'emozione	_____	la regione	_____
l'esperienza	_____	la religione	_____
l'espressione	_____	la rosa	_____
la festa	_____	la scultura	_____
la figura	_____	la temperatura	_____
la fontana	_____	la turista	_____
la forma	_____	l'università	_____
la fortuna	_____	la violenza	_____
l'idea	_____		

Now you're using that *cervello* (brain) of yours! Go ahead, tell the world you're studying Italian. My, aren't you proud?

English Words Used in *Italiano*

Many English nouns have been incorporated into Italian. In Italian, these words are given a gender and, with a few exceptions, are pronounced similarly. Each word is shown with the appropriate Italian definite article.

l'antenna	il cinema	l'hotel	lo shock
l'area	il cocktail	il jazz	lo shopping
l'autobus	il computer	i jeans	lo snob
il bar	l'idea	la radio	lo sport

il blues	il film	il rock and roll	il weekend
il camping	l'hamburger	lo shampoo	lo zoo

See if you can come up with additional examples.

Trojan Horses—False Friends

A **false cognate** is a word in Italian that sounds like an English word but means something different. Fortunately, in Italian there aren't many false cognates, or *falsi amici*. Your *dizionario* will also provide useful information regarding false friends. Look for examples such as this one:

> **mansione** *f.* office, function, capacity; *(compito)* task, job. ATTENZIONE: **mansione** ≠ mansion.

How do you know when you're correctly using a cognate? Test your new skills out and see how far you can go. Most of the time, your first guess is right. Trust your *instinti* (instincts), but don't kick yourself in the *stinco* (shin) if it takes a little while. The following table shows you a few false cognates that are good to know.

False Friends

Italian Word	Meaning	Italian Word	Meaning
ape	bee (≠ ape)	lunatico	moody (≠ lunatic)
argomento	issue (≠ argument)	magazzino	department store (≠ magazine)
camera	room (≠ camera)	marrone	brown (≠ maroon)
come	how (≠ come)	morbido	soft (≠ morbid)
con	with (≠ convict)	pesante	heavy (≠ peasant)
commozione	emotion (≠ commotion)	rumore	noise (≠ rumor)
fabbrica	factory (≠ fabric)	sano	healthy (≠ sane)
fattoria	farm (≠ factory)	sensibile	sensitive (≠ sensible)
firma	signature (≠ firm)	stampa	press (≠ stamp)
grosso	large (≠ gross)	testa	head (≠ test)
libreria	bookstore (≠ library)		

How Much Do You Understand Already?

Read the following sentences and try to determine their meaning. Check your pronunciation guide (especially with those *c*'s and *g*'s) to make sure you sound like a native. (You can find the answers in Appendix A.)

1. La città è bella.
2. Il ristorante è terribile.
3. La giacca è grande.

4. Il museo è interessante.
5. Il servizio è buono.
6. La montagna è alta.

Your Turn

Now write and say the following sentences in Italian. Look back at your cognate list to make sure you are using the appropriate article. The equivalent of *is* in Italian is *è*. (You can find the answers in Appendix A.)

1. The doctor is elegant.
2. The president is famous.
3. The bank is rich.

4. The violence is terrible.
5. The discussion is important.
6. The idiot is stupid.

As a *Regola*

In Italian, adjectives must agree in number and gender with the nouns they modify or describe. In general, masculine nouns use adjectives ending in *-o*, and feminine nouns use adjectives ending in *-a*. Everything has to agree, as in *la lingua italiana* or *il dizionario italiano*.

Verbi

Remember that verbs are the action words in a sentence. Italian verbs seem tricky because they have so many forms, or tenses, such as the present, past, future, conditional, and so on. Many Italian verbs, especially irregular ones, change significantly after they are conjugated. Therefore, when you look up a verb in a dictionary, it is important to be able to identify its *infinitive form*.

What's What

The **infinitive** of a verb is simply a verb in its unconjugated form, as in *to eat, to study,* or *to travel*. With few exceptions, there are three kinds of verb endings (also known as verb families) in Italian: *-are, -ere,* and *-ire*.

This isn't *difficile* after you understand the basic rules of verbs. Think of it as a mystery and you must get to the *root* of the *problema*. In linguistic terms, the root of a verb tells you everything. I'll show you what I mean.

Study the following words and identify their roots (which should be easy since I've highlighted them for you). Try to guess their significance.

      studiare   to _____

      assistere   to _____

      dormire   to _____

Maybe the meaning won't always be so obvious, but you should still be able to identify the roots of most verbs.

Try to *determinare* the meaning of the following verb cognates. (You'll learn more about verbs in Part 2.) (You can find the answers in Appendix A.)

Put It All Together

It's time for you to test yourself and see where you stand. How much have you learned so far? Test the *acqua* with the following exercises.

Traduzione, Per Favore

You shouldn't have too much of a *problema* deciphering the meaning of these cognate-rich sentences. (You can find the answers in Appendix A.)

1. L'Italia fa parte del continente europeo.

2. Lo studente studia la matematica e la storia.

3. L'attore è molto famoso nel cinema.

4. Il meccanico ripara l'automobile.

5. Il cuoco prepara un'insalata e un antipasto.

6. Il dottore conversa con il paziente.

7. La famiglia desidera un appartamento moderno e grande.

8. La turista giapponese visita il museo e la cattedrale.

9. Il presidente presenta il programma.

10. Roberto preferisce la musica classica.

What's Your Take?

Imagine that you have just arrived in Italy, and you want to express your opinions to a fellow traveler. Use what you have learned in this chapter and try to express the following. (You can find the answers in Appendix A.)

1. The chocolate is delicious.

2. The restaurant is excellent.

3. The city is splendid and magnificent.

4. The perfume is elegant.

5. The conversation is interesting.

6. The doctor is sincere.

7. The student is intelligent.

8. The museum is important.

9. The cathedral is high.

10. The train is fast.

As a *Regola*

Italian adjectives ending in -e are used for both masculine and feminine singular nouns:

un libro importante (an important book)

una lezione importante (an important lesson)

Are You Well Read?

The following literary titles here all contain cognates. Give their English equivalents. (You can find the answers in Appendix A.)

Barzini: *Gli Italiani*

Dante: *La Divina Commedia*

Eco: *Il Nome della Rosa*

Machiavelli: *Il Principe*

Morante: *La Storia*

Pirandello: *6 Personaggi in Cerca d'Autore*

The Least You Need to Know

◆ Italian and English share many common roots.

◆ Come up with other words that can express your meaning, and you may find a cognate more often than you think. For example, *guardare* is *to look at.* Think of a guard standing at his post looking over the landscape.

◆ Beware of false friends. You may think you are saying one thing when you actually are saying another.

◆ Learn how to dissect a word to decipher its meaning.

Person, Place, or *Cosa:* Nouns and Articles

In This Chapter

- ◆ Common greetings, salutations, and exclamations
- ◆ Determining gender
- ◆ Nouns
- ◆ Definite and indefinite articles
- ◆ Producing plurals

The only way to learn a foreign language is to fumble and mumble your way through it. This chapter offers you the greetings and exclamations you can begin to use immediately. You'll learn how to address strangers and how to gab with your *amici*. I've also thrown in a few basic *frasi* related to communication that will help you begin speaking immediately.

You'll also be introduced to nouns and noun markers, and I'll explain the birds and bees of gender and show you how to make plurals.

Come Sta?

You should be looking for ways to practice your new salutations whenever there's an opportunity. Maybe it's when you speak to the elegant *signora* who greets you every Friday night at your local Italian *ristorante*. Perhaps it's with your *nonna*, if you can get her to speak in Italian. But if you have no friends or family to practice with, then it'll have to be the television screen as you watch Fellini's *Amarcord* for the fifth time.

Ciao

To start, it helps to know the basics. These are the first things (after the swear words) anyone learns in a foreign language.

Straniero in a Strange Land

You almost always want to begin a *conversazione* with a stranger in the polite form of address. It gives you a chance to warm up to someone and then switch into the *tu* after a relationship has been established. The following table offers you some helpful greetings and salutations you can use with anyone. As you read aloud, try to sound *naturale.* To help you with the pronunciation, the stress has been indicated in words of three syllables and more. If it has not been indicated, each syllable should be pronounced equally. Emphasize those doubled consonants when you see them.

Formal and Generic Salutations and Expressions

Italiano	Pronunciation	English
Buon giorno	*bwon jor-noh*	Good morning/Good day/Good afternoon/Hello (use until early afternoon)
Buona sera	*bwoh-nah seh-rah*	Good evening (begin using after 3 P.M.)
Buona notte	*bwoh-nah noh-teh*	Good night/Good-bye
Signore	*see-**nyoh**-reh*	Mr./Sir
Signora	*see-**nyoh**-rah*	Mrs./Ms.
Signorina	*see-nyoh-**ree**-nah*	Miss
Come sta?	*koh-meh stah*	How are you?
Sto bene, e Lei?	*stoh beh-neh, eh leh*	I am well, and you?
Molto bene	*mol-toh beh-neh*	Very well
Non c'è male	*nohn cheh mah-leh*	Not bad
Abbastanza bene	*ah-bah-**stahn**-zah beh-neh*	Pretty well

Italiano	Pronunciation	English
Come si chiama?	*koh-meh see kee-**ah**-mah*	What is your name?
Mi chiamo	*mee kee-**ah**-moh*	My name is (literally, "I call myself") ....
Piacere.	*pee-ah-**cheh**-reh*	It's a pleasure.
ArrivederLa.	*ah-ree-veh-**der**-lah*	Until next time

What's What

Arrivederci means *to re-see one another;* the word is commonly used to say "good-bye" to friends or colleagues. ***ArrivederLa*** is used under more formal circumstances. ***Ci vediamo*** is also used often to express "see you later." ***Ciao*** is similar to saying "hi" and "bye." The term ***salve*** is used in a similar fashion.

The Most Important *Frasi* in Any Language

The following table summarizes the most important *frasi* you should learn in any *lingua*. Here they are in Italian.

Pleasantries

English	Italiano	Pronunciation
Greetings	Salve	*sal-veh*
Yes	Sì	*see*
No	No	*no*
Please	Per favore	*per fah-**voh**-reh*
	Per piacere	*per pee-ah-**cheh**-reh*
Thank you	Grazie	***grah**-tsee-yeh*
Excuse me	Mi scusi	*mee skoo-zee*
You're welcome	Prego	*pray-goh*
I'm sorry	Mi dispiace	*mee dees-pee-**ah**-cheh*
Help!	Aiuto!	*ah-**yoo**-toh*
Where is ...?	Dov'è ...?	*doh-**veh***
How much?	Quanto?	*kwahn-toh*

> ### La Bella Lingua
>
> All the ways to say "thank you":
>
> | | |
> |---|---|
> | Grazie | Thank you |
> | Mille grazie | Thanks a million |
> | Tante grazie | Thanks so much |
>
> ... and to say "you're welcome":
>
> | | |
> |---|---|
> | Prego | You're welcome |
> | Niente | It's nothing |

Informal Greetings and Salutations

Some useful informal greetings and phrases you can use in more casual, friendly situations are given in the following table. Mix and match.

Informal Salutations

Italiano	Pronunciation	English
Ciao!	*chow*	Hi!/Bye-bye!
Saluti!	*sah-**loo**-tee*	Greetings!
Salve!	*sahl-veh*	Hello!
Come stai?	*koh-meh stah-ee*	How are you?
Come va?	*koh-meh vah*	How's it going?
Va bene.	*vah beh-neh*	Things are good.
Va benissimo.	*vah beh-**nee**-see-moh*	Things are great.
Non c'è male.	*nohn cheh mah-leh*	Not bad.
Okay	*oh-kay*	Okay
Così così	*koh-**zee** koh-**zee***	So-so
Arrivederci.	*ah-ree-veh-**der**-chee*	See you later.
A più tardi	*ah pyoo tar-dee*	Until later
A domani.	*ah doh-**mah**-nee*	See you tomorrow.
A presto.	*ah pres-toh*	See you soon.

Comunicazioni

You'll want to explain that you're studying Italian. The following expressions will tell you how to tell them what you're doing.

Communications

Italiano	Pronunciation	English
Capisco.	*kah-**pee**-skoh*	I understand.
Non capisco.	*non kah-**pee**-skoh*	I don't understand.
Non parlo italiano.	*non par-loh ee-tah-lee-**ah**-noh*	I don't speak Italian.
Studio italiano.	***stoo**-dee-oh ee-tah-lee-**ah**-noh*	I am studying Italian.
Parla inglese?	*par-lah een-**gleh**-zeh*	Do you speak English?
Capisce?	*kah-**pee**-sheh*	Do you understand?
Che cosa significa?	*keh koh-zah seeg-**nee**-fee-kah*	What does it mean?
Che?	*keh*	What?
Come?	*koh-meh*	How?
Dov'è ...?	*doh-veh*	Where is ...?
Lo ripeta per favore.	*loh ree-**peh**-tah per fah-**voh**-reh*	Please repeat that.
Non lo so.	*non loh soh*	I don't know.
Parli lentamente per piacere.	*par-lee len-tah-**men**-teh per pee-ah-**cheh**-reh*	Please speak slowly.

Expressing Your Honest *Opinione*

You can sound like a veritable Italian with just a few exclamations. Start with *Che bello!*

Exclamations

Expression	Pronunciation	Meaning
Che bello!	*keh beh-loh*	How beautiful!
Che brutto!	*keh broo-toh*	How ugly!
Che chiasso!	*keh kee-**ah**-soh*	What a ruckus!
Che disastro!	*keh dee-**sas**-troh*	What a disaster!

continues

Exclamations   (continued)

Expression	Pronunciation	Meaning
Eccellente!	*eh-cheh-**len**-teh*	Excellent!
Fantastico!	*fan-**tas**-tee-koh*	Fantastic!
Favoloso!	*fah-voh-**loh**-zoh*	Fabulous!
Magnifico!	*mag-**nee**-fee-koh*	Magnificent!
Meraviglioso!	*meh-rah-vee-**lyoh**-zoh*	Marvelous!
Orribile!	*oh-**ree**-bee-leh*	Horrible!
Ridicolo!	*ree-**dee**-koh-loh*	Ridiculous!
Stupendo!	*stoo-**pen**-doh*	Stupendous!
Terribile!	*teh-**ree**-bee-leh*	Terrible!

Nouns

Once upon a time, the masculine energy of *il sole* (the sun) ruled the earth during the day, and the feminine energy of *la luna* (the moon) ruled the night. When politically correct English speakers came across the land, they called this sexism and made everything neuter. Not so in Italian. In this chapter, you might not learn everything you wanted to know about sex, but you *will* learn about *sostantivi* (nouns) and gender.

Determining Gender: He vs. She

Unlike English, where women are women and men are men, and everything else is a nongender, in Italian, every single noun (person, place, thing, or idea) is designated as masculine or feminine. The sun, the stars, and the moon all have a specific gender. How is this determination made? Sometimes it's obvious, sometimes there are clues, and sometimes it's just downright tricky. A *dizionario* comes in handy during these times of confusion, and if you imagine yourself as a mystic unveiling the mysteries of the *mondo*, determining gender can be an *avventura* you never imagined.

Masculine or Feminine

All Italian nouns are either *maschile* or *femminile*. Whether you're talking about *il gatto* (the cat), *il cane* (the dog), or *la macchina* (the car), all nouns are one gender or the other.

The reason *why* a particular noun is masculine or feminine is not always obvious. Determining a noun's gender, however, is quite easy in Italian. The clue is in the endings. Whether a noun is masculine or feminine, the endings are almost always *consistente*.

Remember this basic rule of thumb: Nouns ending in *-o* (*libro, ragazzo, gatto*) are generally masculine, whereas nouns ending in *-a* (*casa, scuola, pizza*) are feminine.

Occasionally, you will come across a word that does not conform to this rule (*animale, cane, computer*), making memorization necessary; but even then, the article preceding the noun will often indicate its gender. Words of foreign origin tend to be masculine.

> ### As a *Regola*
>
> If a word ends in -a, it is generally feminine. If a word ends in -o, it is masculine. Some words end in -e and require memorization. The article always reflects gender.

Everyone Must Agree

The gender of a noun affects its relationship with other words in a *frase*, including adjectives (a word that describes a noun). If you learn the definite articles along with the nouns, it is easier for you to form sentences correctly later.

The key word here is *agreement.* Everyone and everything has to get along. Nouns and adjectives must always agree. For example, if we want to say "the small cat" (*il gatto piccolo*), the adjective small (*piccolo*) must agree in gender with the word *cat* (*il gatto*). We'll get to adjectives later; just keep in mind that they follow the same rules.

An Article Is Not What You Read in a *Giornale*

Before you get into Italian nouns, there's one little challenge you must face: the noun marker that precedes the noun. The term *noun marker* refers to an article or adjective that tells us whether a noun is masculine (m.) or feminine (f.), singular (s.) or plural (p.). The noun markers shown in the following table are singular, definite articles expressing *the* and indefinite articles expressing *a, an,* or *one.*

Singular Noun Markers

English	Masculine	Feminine
the	il, lo, l'	la, l'
a, an, one	un, uno	una, un'

What's What

Definite articles are the singular masculine (*il, lo, l'*) and feminine (*la, l'*) articles that precede Italian nouns and correspond with *the* in English. Unlike the English *the*, these articles show the gender of a noun. The plural masculine (*i, gli*) and plural feminine (*le*) articles reflect gender and plurality.

A **noun marker** can be any of a variety of articles, such as *il, lo, l', la, i, gli, le* (the equivalent of *the* in English) and *uno, una, un'* (the equivalent of *a* in English).

You use the definite article in front of a day to describe something you always do:

*Andiamo in chiesa **la** domenica.* (We go to church on Sundays.)

*Faccio yoga **il** mercoledì.* (I do yoga on Wednesdays.)

The Definite Article

What?! Five different singular definite articles? You're probably thinking this is a little too much grammar for you. Rest assured; it's not as confusing as you think. Here's how these definite articles work in the singular:

- *Il* is used in front of singular, masculine nouns beginning with a consonant (other than *z* or *s* + a consonant), such as *il ragazzo* (the boy), *il sole* (the sun), and *il vino* (the wine).

- *Lo* is used in front of all singular, masculine nouns that begin with a *z* or an *s* followed by a consonant, such as *lo zio* (the uncle), *lo studio* (the study), and *lo sci* (the ski/skiing).

- *L'* is used in front of all singular nouns, both masculine and feminine, that begin with a vowel, such as *l'uomo* (the man), *l'opera* (the opera), and *l'atleta* (the female athlete).

- *La* is used in front of all other singular, feminine nouns, such as *la ragazza* (the girl, the girlfriend), *la musica* (the music), and *la luna* (the moon).

An Indefinite Article

Indefinite articles (*a/an*) are simple to use. Remember that they are used only before *singular* nouns.

Masculine:

- *Un* is used before singular masculine nouns beginning with either a consonant or a vowel, such as *un palazzo* (a building), *un signore* (a gentleman), and *un*

> *animale* (an animal). This does not include those nouns beginning with a *z* or an *s* followed by a consonant.

♦ *Uno* is used just like the definite article *lo* before singular masculine nouns beginning with a *z* or an *s* followed by a consonant, such as *uno zio* (an uncle) and *uno stadio* (a stadium).

Feminine:

♦ *Una* is used before any feminine noun beginning with a consonant, such as *una farfalla* (a butterfly), *una storia* (a story), and *una strada* (a street).

♦ *Un'* is the equivalent of *an* in English and is used before all feminine nouns beginning with a vowel, such as *un'italiana* (an Italian woman), *un'amica* (a friend), and *un'opera* (an opera).

Singular Nouns

Some nouns in Italian are easy to mark because they obviously refer to masculine or feminine people. Pay special attention to their endings.

Gender-Obvious Nouns

Masculine Noun	Feminine Noun	Pronunciation	English
il padre		*eel pah-dreh*	the father
	la madre	*lah mah-dreh*	the mother
il marito		*eel mah-**ree**-toh*	the husband
	la moglie	*lah mol-yeh*	the wife
il nonno		*eel noh-noh*	the grandfather
	la nonna	*lah noh-nah*	the grandmother
il fratello		*eel frah-**teh**-loh*	the brother
	la sorella	*lah soh-**reh**-lah*	the sister
il cugino		*eel koo-**jee**-noh*	the cousin *m.*
	la cugina	*lah koo-**jee**-nah*	the cousin *f.*
il ragazzo		*eel rah-**gah**-tsoh*	the boy
	la ragazza	*lah rah-**gah**-tsah*	the girl
lo zio		*loh zee-oh*	the uncle
	la zia	*lah zee-ah*	the aunt

continues

Gender-Obvious Nouns (continued)

Masculine Noun	Feminine Noun	Pronunciation	English
l'uomo		*lwoh-moh*	the man
	la donna	*lah doh-nah*	the woman
l'amico		*lah-mee-koh*	the friend *m.*
	l'amica	*lah-mee-kah*	the friend *f.*

Pretty soon you'll be watching Fellini films and won't have to read *i sottotitoli* (subtitles) anymore. Let's add a few more words to your *vocabolario*.

La Bella Lingua

The word *ragazzo* can mean boy or boyfriend. The word *ragazza* can mean girl or girlfriend.

CAUTION

Attenzione!

All nouns, with the exception of one's immediate family members, require an article in front of them.

Hermaphrodites

A few nouns, such as *artista*, *dentista*, and *musicista* can be either masculine or feminine. All you have to do is change the identifier—without altering the spelling—to refer to either gender. The gender of nouns beginning with a vowel, such as *artista*, are difficult to determine (except in context), because the noun marker *l'* is always used. Study the following sentences to see how this works:

Il dentista mangia la cioccolata.

La dentista mangia la frutta.

L'artista è molto brava.

The following table shows several examples of either-gender nouns.

Either-Gender Nouns

Italiano	English	Italiano	English
l'artista	the artist	l'erede	the heir
l'atleta	the athlete	il/la giovane	the youth
il/la cantante	the singer	il/la nomade	the nomad
il/la dentista	the dentist	il/la parente	the relative
il/la dirigente	the director/executive	il/la turista	the tourist

Irregular Masculine Nouns

Some nouns ending in *-e* or *-i* may be masculine or feminine and therefore require you to memorize their gender. See the following table for common masculine nouns ending in *-e*. One trick is to remember that nouns such as *valore* (value) that end in *-ore* are masculine.

Masculine Nouns Ending in -e

Masculine	English	Masculine	English
il cane	the dog	l'onore	the honor
il colore	the color	il pesce	the fish
il dolore	the pain	il serpente	the snake
il mare	the ocean	il sole	the sun
il nome	the name/noun	il valore	the value

Irregular Feminine Nouns

Although many of the following nouns are considered irregular, it is still possible to see the patterns. Nouns such as *stazione* (station) that end in *-zione* are feminine. Most singular nouns ending in *-i* are also generally feminine.

As a *Regola*
Italian words ending in *-azione* are often the equivalent of English words ending in *-tion*, such as *occupazione* (occupation). These words are always feminine. Most words of foreign origin ending in a consonant are masculine, such as *l'autobus, il bar, il computer, il film,* and *lo sport.*

Feminine Nouns Ending in -e

Feminine	English	Feminine	English
l'automobile	the car	l'oasi	the oasis
la crisi	the crisis	la pulce	the flea
la lepre	the hare	la stazione	the station
la nave	the ship	la tesi	the thesis
la notte	the night	la traduzione	the translation

Rules Are Made to Be Broken

Just to drive you *pazzo*, there are a few exceptions to these rules. Remember that rules are man-made, designed by linguists to make sense of an otherwise chaotic *universo*. All languages, including Italian, are dynamic. They evolve, expand, and contract over time, in accordance with trends, other cultural influences, and values.

Disconcerting Genders

Sometimes the ending of a word completely changes that word's significance. The only way to remember these oddities is to memorize them. In any event, fear not: Even if you get the gender wrong, 99 percent of the time the person to whom you are speaking will understand what you're saying. The following table provides a list of words whose meanings change according to the ending.

Disconcerting Genders

Masculine	Feminine	Masculine	Feminine
il ballo (dance)	*la balla* (bundle, bale)	*il muro* (interior wall)	*le mura* (city walls)
il collo (neck)	*la colla* (glue)	*il partito* (political party)	*la partita* (sports match)
il colpo (blow)	*la colpa* (fault, guilt)	*il porto* (port)	*la porta* (door)
il costo (cost)	*la costa* (coast)	*il posto* (place)	*la posta* (mail)
il filo (thread)	*la fila* (line)	*il punto* (detail, dot)	*la punta* (tip)
il foglio (sheet of paper)	*la foglia* (leaf)	*lo scopo* (aim, end)	*la scopa* (broom)
il legno (wood)	*la legna* (firewood)	*il torto* (mistake)	*la torta* (cake)
il manico (handle)	*la manica* (sleeve)	*il velo* (veil)	*la vela* (sail, sailing)
il mento (chin)	*la menta* (mint)		

More Misbehaving Males

Quite a few Italian nouns that end in *-a* are masculine, many of which derive from Greek. Look at the following table for a few of these misbehaving masculine nouns. Note the prevalence of cognates ending in *-ma*, such as *emblema* (emblem), *poema* (poem), and *problema* (problem).

Masculine Nouns That End in -*a*

Noun	Pronunciation	English
il cinema	*eel **chee**-neh-mah*	the cinema
il clima	*eel klee-mah*	the climate
il cruciverba	*eel kroo-chee-**ver**-bah*	the crossword (puzzle)
il dramma	*eel drah-mah*	the drama
l'emblema	*lem-**bleh**-mah*	the emblem
il papa	*eel pah-pah*	the pope
il pianeta	*eel pee-ah-**neh**-tah*	the planet
il poema	*eel poh-**eh**-mah*	the poem
il problema	*eel proh-**bleh**-mah*	the problem
il programma	*eel proh-**grah**-mah*	the program

Those Rebellious Females

Feminine nouns can be troublemakers, too. The following table mentions some of them.

Feminine Nouns That End in -*o*

Noun	Pronunciation	English
la foto (short for *fotografia*)	*lah foh-toh*	the photo
la mano	*lah mah-noh*	the hand
la moto (short for *motocicletta*)	*lah moh-toh*	the motorcycle
la radio	*lah **rah**-dee-yoh*	the radio

Sex Changers

Certain words can be made feminine by changing the ending to *-a*, *-essa*, or *-ice*, depending on the gender of the person performing the action. You'll learn more about professions in Chapter 9.

Noun Endings

Masculine	Feminine	English
l'attore	l'attrice	actor/actress
l'avvocato	l'avvocatessa	lawyer
il cameriere	la cameriera	waiter/waitress
il direttore	la direttrice	director
il dottore	la dottoressa	doctor
il maestro	la maestra	teacher
il padrone	la padrona	boss
il pittore	la pittrice	painter
il poeta	la poetessa	poet
il professore	la professoressa	professor
lo studente	la studentessa	student

In modern usage, the feminine endings of professionals such as actors, doctors, professors, and lawyers are used with less frequency than they used to be. It is appropriate, for example, to refer to a male or female lawyer as *l'avvocato*.

The Apple Doesn't Fall Far

Fruit is almost always referred to in the feminine as *la frutta*, but a piece of fruit is referred to as *un frutto*. When a specific fruit is made masculine, it becomes the fruit tree.

> *l'arancia* (the orange) ➜ *l'arancio* (the orange tree)
>
> *la ciliegia* (the cherry) ➜ *il ciliegio* (the cherry tree)
>
> *la mela* (the apple) ➜ *il melo* (the apple tree)
>
> *la pera* (the pear) ➜ *il pero* (the pear tree)

Practice Makes *Perfetto*

Determine the gender by placing the appropriate definite article in front of the following nouns. You might have to consult a dictionary for a couple of them. Don't forget to look at the endings! (You can find the answers in Appendix A.)

1. ___ *casa* (house)
2. ___ *cane* (dog)
3. ___ *albero* (tree)
4. ___ *piatto* (plate)
5. ___ *lezione* (lesson)
6. ___ *estate* (summer)
7. ___ *chiesa* (church)
8. ___ *straniero* (foreigner)
9. ___ *cattedrale* (cathedral)
10. ___ *pianeta* (planet)

Compound Nouns

Simply defined, compound nouns are comprised of two or more nouns. The majority of compound nouns are masculine, although exceptions exist. Of course, you must develop enough of an Italian vocabulary to recognize the different words independent of one another; however, after you begin to see how words interact within the greater picture, you'll find yourself feeling much more confident the next time you guess at a new word's meaning.

Masculine Compound Nouns

In addition to the following masculine compound nouns, try to figure out the significance of this compound noun: *nontiscordardimé.* Cover the English with a piece of paper and see how well you do.

l'asciugamano	towel (literally, dry the hand)
il bucaneve	snowdrop
il cruciverba	crossword
il girasole	sunflower (literally, turn sun)
il guardaroba	wardrobe
il pescespada	swordfish
il portacenere	ashtray (literally, carry ash)
lo scolapasta	colander

Feminine Compound Nouns

Fortunately, there are fewer feminine compound nouns to remember. The following list shows a few of them. Again, cover the English with a piece of paper and see how well you can guess their meaning.

l'acquaforte	etching (literally, strong water)
la banconota	banknote
la belladonna	deadly nightshade

la cartapecora	parchment (literally, sheep paper)
la ferrovia	railway (literally, iron way)
la madreperla	mother of pearl
la terraferma	mainland

More Is Better: Making Plurals

In English, it's relatively easy to talk about more than one thing; usually, you just add an *-s* to the word, although there are many plurals that confuse people learning English as a second language. How many "childs" do you have, or rather, children? Fortunately, forming plural nouns in Italian is as easy as floating in a gondola. Yes, you do have to memorize the endings, and again, the ending must always reflect gender. But you don't have to memorize a hundred different words just to say more than one. The following table illustrates how the ending should change in the plural.

Attenzione!

In certain cases, the plurals of certain nouns and adjectives follow different rules:

1. Singular feminine nouns and adjectives ending in *-ca* or *-ga* form the plural by changing the endings to *-che* or *-ghe*.

   ami**ca** ➔ ami**che**

   bian**ca** ➔ bian**che**

2. Singular feminine nouns ending in *-cia* and *-gia* form the plural with …
   cie/gie (if a vowel precedes the singular ending).

   cami**cia** ➔ cami**cie**

   vali**gia** ➔ vali**gie**

   ce/ge (if a consonant precedes the singular ending).

   aran**cia** ➔ aran**ce**

   piog**gia** ➔ piog**ge**

3. Singular masculine nouns and adjectives ending in *-co* and *-go* generally form the plural by replacing the singular endings with *-chi* and *-ghi*.

   pac**co** ➔ pac**chi**

   bian**co** ➔ bian**chi**

   la**go** ➔ la**ghi**

   lar**go** ➔ lar**ghi**

Plural Endings

Singular		Plural	Singular		Plural
-o	→	*-i*	ragazzo	→	ragazzi
-a	→	*-e*	donna	→	donne
-ca	→	*-che*	amica	→	amiche
-e	→	*-i*	cane	→	cani

Do We Agree? Plural Noun Markers

When an Italian noun refers to more than one thing, you must change the noun marker.

The following table outlines the definite articles and demonstrates how singular noun markers change in the plural. Remember that funny rule about the definite article *lo*, which is used only in front of words beginning with *s* (or *z*) + a consonant. The same applies to *gli* (pronounced *ylee* as in the word *million*).

The Definite Article (The)

Gender	Singular	Plural	When It's Used	Examples
Masculine	lo	→ gli	In front of all masculine nouns beginning with a z or s + consonant	lo zio → gli zii lo studente → gli studenti
	l'	→ gli	In front of all masculine nouns beginning with a vowel	l'amico → gli amici
	Il	→ i	In front of all other masculine nouns	il nonno → i nonni
Feminine	l'	→ le	In front of all feminine nouns beginning with a vowel	l'amica → le amiche
	la	→ le	In front of all other feminine nouns	la sorella → le sorelle

As a *Regola*

Family names do not change endings in the plural. Use the article to indicate plurality. For example, if you were talking about the Leonardo family, you would say *i Leonardo* (the Leonardos).

Nouns ending in a consonant (such as many words of foreign origin) or accented on the last vowel do not change form in the plural. Only the article changes. For example:

l'autobus	→	gli autobus
il caffè	→	i caffè
la città	→	le città
l'università	→	le università

The Rules

The following summarizes everything you could ever want to know about making plurals:

◆ *Gli* is used in front of all plural, masculine nouns beginning with a *z* or an *s* followed by a consonant, and plural, masculine nouns beginning with a vowel, such as *gli studenti* (the students), *gli zii* (the uncles), *gli animali* (the animals), and *gli amici* (the friends).

◆ *I* is used in front of all plural, masculine nouns beginning with all other consonants, such as *i ragazzi* (the boys) and *i vini* (the wines).

◆ *Le* is used in front of all plural, feminine nouns, such as *le ragazze* (the girls), *le donne* (the women), and *le automobili* (the cars).

Plural Spelling

Look at what happens to the nouns in the following table when made plural.

Singular and Plural Nouns

Singular Noun	English	Plural Noun	English
la monaca	the nun	le monache	the nuns
l'amica	the friend *f.*	le amiche	the friends *f.*
l'amico	the friend *m.*	gli amici	the friends *m.*
il nemico	the enemy *m.*	i nemici	the enemies *m.*

Singular Noun	English	Plural Noun	English
l'ago	the needle	gli aghi	the needles
il luogo	the place	i luoghi	the places

You already know one plural—*spaghetti!* Because you could never eat one *spaghetto*—which isn't a real word—you must always use it in the plural. Let's try a sentence: *In Italia, mangiano gli spaghetti al pomodoro.*

La Pratica

Try making the following nouns plural using the rules you just learned. I've done the first one for you. (The answers are in Appendix A.)

1. *il libro* (the book)   →   _i libri_   (the books)

2. *il gatto* (the cat)   →   _____   (the cats)

3. *la ragazza* (the girl)   →   _____   (the girls)

4. *la stazione* (the station) →   _____   (the stations)

5. *l'amico* (the friend, *m.*) →   _____   (the friends)

6. *l'amica* (the friend, *f.*) →   _____   (the friends)

Irregular Plural Nouns

Some masculine nouns become feminine when pluralized. As you can see, many parts of the body are included. (Consult Chapter 18 for additional body parts.)

Irregular Plural Nouns

Singular	Plural
il braccio (the arm)	*le braccia* (the arms)
il dito (the finger)	*le dita* (the fingers)
il ginocchio (the knee)	*le ginocchia* (the knees)
il labbro (the lip)	*le labbra* (the lips)
la mano (the hand)	*le mani* (the hands)
il miglio (the mile)	*le miglia* (the miles)
il paio (the pair)	*le paia* (the pairs)
l'uovo (the egg)	*le uova* (the eggs)

Always Plural

Some nouns are only used in the plural. For instance, when you look for your glasses, it is assumed that you are referring to the ones you see with.

Always Plural Nouns

Italiano	English
le forbici	scissors
le pinzette	tweezers
le redini	reins
i pantaloni	pants
le mutande	underwear
gli occhiali	eyeglasses

Practice Those Plurals

You've just arrived in Rome, and you need to pick up a few odds and ends. You're in a *negozio* (store) and want to buy more than one of the following items. Start by saying *Cerco …* (I am looking for …) and the plural of the item. Don't forget to use the appropriate article. (You can find the answers in Appendix A.)

Example: *il regalo* (gift)
Answer: *Cerco i regali.* (I am looking for the gifts.)

1. *la cartolina* (postcard)
2. *la rivista* (magazine)
3. *la collana* (necklace)
4. *il profumo* (perfume)
5. *la cravatta* (tie)
6. *la penna* (pen)

What Have You Learned About Gender?

You've always wanted to be in a movie. You remember watching all those spaghetti westerns where tall men wore big hats and the women always looked pretty, even with dirt smudged across their cheeks. You're in Rome visiting the famous movie studio *Cinecittà* where those films were made, and you see a listing for auditions. Determine whether the part requires a male or female role. (You can find the answers in Appendix A.)

Attrice matura (40–50 anni), cercasi con la capacità di parlare l'inglese e il francese per interpretare il ruolo di una contessa. Aspetto distinto. Inviare curriculum con foto a Via Garibaldi 36, Roma.

Attore forte, atletico, giovane, cercasi con i capelli chiari per interpretare il ruolo di Cesare. Presentarsi il 25 giugno ore 9:00 alla palestra Superforte, secondo piano.

Uomini e donne veramente sexy, cercasi per apparire nudi in una scena sulla spiaggia: Varie età. Esperienza non necessaria. Telefonare al 06/040357.

The Least You Need to Know

- It's best to use the polite salutations and expressions with strangers. You can let your hair down in more casual situations.

- Certain endings are almost always masculine (-*o*, -*i*, consonants) or feminine (-*a*, -*e*).

- Some nouns can be changed from masculine to feminine by adding an appropriate ending.

- Always look at the article to determine the gender and plurality of a noun.

- Plural nouns end in either -*i* or -*e*.

Chapter 6

Che Bella Famiglia: Adjectives and Adverbs

In This Chapter

- ◆ Introducing your *famiglia*
- ◆ Describing things: adjectives
- ◆ Expressing possession using *di*
- ◆ Using possessive adjectives
- ◆ Forming and using adverbs

You've covered the nouns and their noun markers, and are ready to add some *colore.* In this chapter, you'll learn all about adjectives, adverbs, and how to express possession.

One of the *Famiglia*

In Italy, one of the first things people want to know about is your *famiglia.* Do you have *fratelli* or *sorelle?* Are you *d'origine italiana* or one of the many who have fallen in love with the *cultura,* the beautiful landscapes, and the *arte?* The following table explains who's who in *la famiglia.*

Family Members

Female	Pronunciation	Meaning	Male	Pronunciation	Meaning
madre	*mah-dreh*	mother	padre	*pah-dreh*	father
moglie	*moh-lyeh*	wife	marito	*mah-**ree**-toh*	husband
nonna	*noh-nah*	grandmother	nonno	*noh-noh*	grandfather
figlia	*fee-lyah*	daughter	figlio	*fee-lyoh*	son
bambina	*bahm-**bee**-nah*	infant	bambino	*bahm-**bee**-noh*	infant
sorella	*soh-**reh**-lah*	sister	fratello	*frah-**teh**-loh*	brother
cugina	*koo-jee-nah*	cousin	cugino	*koo-jee-noh*	cousin
zia	*zee-ah*	aunt	zio	*zee-oh*	uncle
nipote	*nee-**poh**-teh*	granddaughter	nipote	*nee-poh-teh*	grandson
nipote	*nee-**poh**-teh*	niece	nipote	*nee-poh-teh*	nephew
suocera	***swoh**-cheh-rah*	mother-in-law	suocero	***swoh**-cheh-roh*	father-in-law
nuora	*nwoh-rah*	daughter-in-law	genero	***jen**-eh-roh*	son-in-law
cognata	*koh-**nyah**-tah*	sister-in-law	cognato	*koh-**nyah**-toh*	brother-in-law
matrigna	*mah-**tree**-nyah*	stepmother	padrigno	*pah-**dree**-nyoh*	stepfather
sorellastra	*soh-reh-**lah**-strah*	stepsister	fratellastro	*frah-teh-**lah**-stroh*	stepbrother
madrina	*mah-**dree**-nah*	godmother	padrino	*pah-**dree**-noh*	godfather
ragazza	*rah-**gah**-tsah*	girlfriend	ragazzo	*rah-**gah**-tsoh*	boyfriend
fidanzata	*fee-dahn-**zah**-tah*	fiancáe	fidanzato	*fee-dahn-**zah**-toh*	fiancá
vedova	***veh**-doh-vah*	widow	vedovo	***veh**-doh-voh*	widower

---

As a *Regola*

When discussing the collective *children*, Italian reverts to the masculine plural: *i figli.* The same goes for friends: *gli amici.* One's *genitori* (parents) can be simply referred to as *miei* (coming from the possessive adjective *my*, as in *my parents*). The word *nipote* is used to describe niece or nephew and granddaughter or grandson and shares the same root as *nepotismo* (nepotism).

Are You Possessed?

You will always be somebody's somebody: your mother's child, your brother's sister, your dog's owner, your wife's husband. In English, we use *'s* or *s'* to show possession. In Italian, there are two ways of showing possession.

You show possession by using *di*, as follows:

> *Silvia è la figlia di Peppe.*
> Silvia is the daughter of Peppe.

You can also show possession by using a possessive adjective, as in the following familiar *espressioni:*

> *Dio mio!*   My God!
> *Mamma mia!*   Mother of mine!

Using *Di* to Show Possession

The simplest way to express possession is to use *di*, meaning *of.* Look at the following example to see how this works.

> *Questa è la casa di Mario.*
> This is Mario's house. (This is the house of Mario.)

Forming Contractions with *Di*

Notice how the endings of the contractions correspond to the articles, and pay attention to how *di* changes when forming a contraction. Contractions are explained in more detail in Chapter 10. All of the following examples correspond in translation to *of the.*

> **As a *Regola***
>
> The terms *il signore, la signora,* and *la signorina* are often used in place of *the man, the woman,* and *the young woman.*

Contractions with *Di*

Singular	Plural
di + il = del	di + i = dei
di + lo = dello	di + gli = degli
di + l' = dell'	di + le = delle
di + la = della	

Frasi using contractions with *di* include …

> *Ecco [sono] le chiavi **della** macchina.*
> Here [are] the car keys. (Here are the keys of the car.)

> *Quello è il figlio **del** presidente.*
> That is the president's son. (That is the son of the president.)

If you can't remember your possessive adjectives yet, try simply using *di* followed by the name of the possessor to indicate the subject:

> *Il libro di Rosetta.*
> The book of Rosetta.

> *La macchina di Antonio.*
> The car of Antonio.

Possessive Adjectives

Italian possessive adjectives correspond in English to the possessive pronouns and convey the idea of my, your, his, her, and so on.

CAUTION

Attenzione!

Compare the English possessives to their Italian counterparts in these examples. Contrary to English usage, Italian forms do not distinguish between his and her; pay special attention to how *suo* and *sua* are used.

*Gino ama **sua** madre e **suo** padre.*
Gino loves **his** mother and **his** father.

*Beatrice ama **sua** madre e **suo** padre.*
Beatrice loves **her** mother and **her** father.

The following table summarizes the use of possessive adjectives. Remember that the Italian possessive adjective is almost always preceded by the definite article.

Possessive Adjectives

| | Singular | | Plural | |
Possessive	Masculine	Feminine	Masculine	Feminine
my	il mio	la mia	i miei	le mie
your	il tuo	la tua	i tuoi	le tue
his/her (its)	il suo	la sua	i suoi	le sue
Your*	il Suo	la Sua	i Suoi	le Sue
our	il nostro	la nostra	i nostri	le nostre
your	il vostro	la vostra	i vostri	le vostre
their	il loro	la loro	i loro	le loro

*Polite

A Sense of Belonging

Determine the appropriate possessive adjective using the previous list for the following nouns. (The answers are in Appendix A.)

Example: her house
Answer: *la sua casa*

1. his house _____

4. his books _____

2. my school _____

5. your (familiar) friend Mario _____

3. her books _____

As a *Regola*
When speaking of immediate family members, there is no article required before the possessive adjective: *Mio fratello abita a Roma.* (My brother lives in Rome.)

Making Introductions Using Demonstratives

If you are in mixed company, it's always considered polite to introduce your new friends and family to one another.

You can express the demonstrative pronouns *this* and *these*, shown in the following table, if you want to say, "*This* is my sister and *these* are my parents."

The Demonstratives This and These

Gender	This	These
Masculine	*questo libro* (this book)	*questi libri* (these books)
	*quest'anno** (this year)	*questi anni* (these years)
Feminine	*questa penna* (this pen)	*queste penne* (these pens)
	*quest'idea** (this idea)	*queste idee* (these ideas)

All singular nouns beginning with a vowel take quest'.

Questo Is My Brother ...

When referring to singular nouns denoting family members (*madre, padre, sorella, fratello* ..., and not *mamma, babbo* ...), there's no need to put an article in front of the person being possessed. If you are introducing your *fratello* (brother), then you must still use the masculine singular demonstrative pronoun *questo*, as follows:

Questo *è* **mio** *fratello.*   This is my brother.

If it's your mother you are introducing, you must use a feminine singular demonstrative pronoun, as follows:

Questa *è* **mia** *madre.*   This is my mother.

In most other cases, you must include the article before the noun. Even if a friend may feel just like family, she should be introduced using the article. For example:

Questa *è* **la mia** *amica Anna.*   This is my friend Anna.

As a *Regola*
As a reminder, in both nouns and adjectives, the singular ending *-e* turns to *-i* in the plural: *il signore intelligente* ➔ *i signori intelligenti.*

Who Is Who

You'll need to know how to use the following expressions to make introductions. As you move forward in your studies, you may want to come back to this chapter to see how much *progresso* you've made.

Helpful Introductory Expressions

Italiano	English
Vorrei presentare	I'd like to present ....
Conosce ...?	Do you know ...?
È un piacere conoscerti.*	It's a pleasure to meet you. (informal)
È un piacere conoscerLa.*	It's a pleasure to meet you. (polite)
Il piacere è mio.	The pleasure is mine.
Questo è mio fratello.	This is my brother.
Questa è mia sorella.	This is my sister.
Questi sono i miei amici.	These are my friends. (mixed gender)
Queste sono le mie amiche.	These are my (girl)friends.

Both of these constructions use the direct object pronoun. You'll learn more about these in Chapter 15.

Alto, Bruno, e Bello

What a bland world it would be without descriptive adjectives. Everything would be all *azione* and no *illustrazione*. If *i verbi* are the skeleton of a language and nouns are the flesh, adjectives are the details of color and nuances of light. They're *bianco* and *rosso* (as in *vino*), or *bello* or *brutto, grande* or *piccolo*, and all of what's in between.

Modifying Adjectives

Similar to Spanish and French, Italian adjectives must reflect both the gender (masculine or feminine) and number (singular or plural) of the nouns and pronouns they describe. Fortunately, the endings used for adjectives are similar to noun endings. Similar to a *concerto*, everything has to work together. Keep in mind the following:

♦ If describing a masculine noun, simply leave the adjective as is. (Adjectives default to the masculine—it goes way back before women's lib.)

   *Tuo fratello è un **ragazzo simpatico**.*
   Your brother is a nice boy.

♦ In most cases, when you change an adjective to the feminine, the ending will be *-a*.

   *Tua sorella è una **ragazza simpatica**.*
   Your sister is a nice girl.

♦ Many adjectives that end in *-e*, such as *intelligente, giovane, grande, verde, triste*, and *cortese*, are used to describe both masculine and feminine nouns. The plural endings of these adjectives follow the same rules as nouns ending in *-e*.

> ### La Bella Lingua
>
> To indicate that you're in a good or bad mood, use the expressions *Sono di buon umore* (I am in a good mood) and *Sono di cattivo umore* (I am in a bad mood).

Modifying Those Adjective Endings

You've already seen how many Italian adjectives are cognates to English in Chapter 4. Look at the endings in the following table, and compare them to the noun endings you learned in Chapter 5.

Adjective Endings

Endings	Examples
o → i	famoso → famosi
a → e	curiosa → curiose
ca → che	magnifica → magnifiche
e → i	intelligente → intelligenti

Character Analysis

Using the adjectives you just learned, try describing the people around you. (The answers are in Appendix A.)

Example: *Il mio fidanzato è generoso, intelligente, sincero, e ricco.*
Answer: My fiancé is generous, intelligent, sincere, and rich.

1. Your significant other (or your fantasy) _____

2. Your mother _____

3. Your brother, sister, or cousin _____

4. Your cat, dog, or other domestic companion _____

5. Your best friend _____

6. Your boss _____

Take the *Brutto* with the *Bello*

You want to describe your wonderful wife or husband, your children, your new boyfriend or girlfriend, your ex, your best friend, or your cat. Are they kind or cruel, good or bad, generous or stingy? The list of adjectives and their antonyms in the following table will add to your array of options.

Emotions and Characteristics

English	Italiano	Pronunciation	English	Italiano	Pronunciation
ambitious	ambizioso	*ahm-bee-zee-oh-zoh*	lazy	pigro	*pee-groh*
beautiful	bello	*beh-loh*	ugly	brutto	*broo-toh*
blond	biondo	*bee-ohn-doh*	brunette	bruno	*broo-noh*

English	Italiano	Pronunciation	English	Italiano	Pronunciation
calm	calmo	*kahl-moh*	nervous	nervoso	*ner-voh-zoh*
clever/sly	furbo	*foor-boh*	slow/dull	lento	*len-toh*
courageous	coraggioso	*koh-rah-joh-zoh*	cowardly	codardo	*koh-dahr-doh*
courteous	cortese	*kor-teh-zeh*	discourteous	scortese	*skor-teh-zeh*
cute/pretty	carino	*kah-ree-noh*	unattractive	bruttino	*broo-tee-noh*
fat	grasso	*grah-soh*	skinny	magro	*mah-groh*
funny	buffo	*boo-foh*	boring	noioso	*noy-oh-zoh*
generous	generoso	*jeh-ner-oh-zoh*	stingy	tirchio	*teer-kee-yoh*
good	bravo	*brah-voh*	evil	cattivo	*kah-tee-voh*
happy	allegro	*ah-leh-groh*	sad	triste	*tree-steh*
healthy	sano	*sah-noh*	sick	malato	*mah-lah-toh*
honest	onesto	*oh-nes-toh*	dishonest	disonesto	*dee-soh-nes-toh*
intelligent	intelligente	*een-tel-ee-jen-teh*	stupid	stupido	*stoo-pee-doh*
kind/polite	gentile	*jen-tee-leh*	impolite	scortese	*skor-teh-zeh*
loyal	fedele	*feh-deh-leh*	unfaithful	infedele	*een-fed-eh-leh*
lucky	fortunato	*for-too-nah-toh*	unlucky	sfortunato	*sfor-too-nah-toh*
married	sposato	*spoh-zah-toh*	divorced	divorziato	*dee-vor-zee-ah-toh*
nice	simpatico	*seem-pah-tee-koh*	mean	antipatico	*ahn-tee-pah-tee-koh*
organized	organizzato	*or-gah-nee-zah-toh*	unorganized	disorganizzato	*dee-zor-gah-nee-zah-toh*
perfect	perfetto	*per-feh-toh*	imperfect	imperfetto	*eem-per-feh-toh*
proud	fiero	*fee-yeh-roh*	ashamed	vergognoso	*ver-goh-nyoh-zoh*
romantic	romantico	*roh-mahn-tee-koh*	practical	pratico	*prah-tee-koh*
sensitive	sensibile	*sen-see-bee-leh*	insensitive	insensibile	*een-sen-see-bee-leh*
sincere	sincero	*seen-cheh-roh*	insincere	bugiardo	*boo-jar-doh*
strong	forte	*for-teh*	weak	debole	*deh-boh-leh*
tall	alto	*ahl-toh*	short	basso	*bah-soh*
young	giovane	*jyoh-vah-neh*	old	vecchio	*veh-kee-yoh*
wise	saggio	*sah-joh*	uncultured	incolto	*een-kol-toh*

Antonimi (Antonyms)

Learning things in batches helps your brain retain more information. Use the following list of adjectives and their opposites to help you expand your horizons.

Adjectives and Their Antonyms

English	Italiano	Pronunciation	English	Italiano	Pronunciation
big	grande	*gran-deh*	small	piccolo	***pee**-koh-loh*
clean	pulito	*poo-**lee**-toh*	dirty	sporco	*spor-koh*
complete	completo	*kom-**pleh**-toh*	incomplete	incompleto	*een-kohm-**pleh**-toh*
dear	caro	*kah-roh*	inexpensive	economico	*eh-koh-**noh**- mee-koh*
first	primo	*pree-moh*	last	ultimo	***ool**-tee-moh*
full	pieno	*pee-**yeh**-noh*	empty	vuoto	*vwoh-toh*
good	buono	*bwoh-noh*	bad	male	*mah-leh*
hard	duro	*doo-roh*	soft	morbido	***mor**-bee-doh*
heavy	pesante	*peh-**zahn**-tay*	light	leggero	*leh-**jeh**-roh*
hot	caldo	*kahl-doh*	cold	freddo	*fray-doh*
long	lungo	*loon-goh*	short	basso	*bah-soh*
new	nuovo	*nwoh-voh*	used	usato	*oo-**zah**-toh*
next	prossimo	***proh**-see-moh*	last	ultimo	***ool**-tee-moh*
normal	normale	*nor-**mah**-leh*	strange	strano	*strah-noh*
open	aperto	*ah-**per**-toh*	closed	chiuso	*kee-**yoo**-soh*
perfect	perfetto	*per-**feh**-toh*	imperfect	imperfetto	*eem-per-**feh**-toh*
pleasing	piacevole	*pee-ah-**chay**-voh-leh*	displeasing	spiacevole	*spee-ah-**chay**-voh-leh*
real	vero	*veh-roh*	fake	finto	*feen-toh*
safe/sure	sicuro	*see-**koo**-roh*	dangerous	pericoloso	*peh-ree-koh-**loh**-zoh*
strong	forte	*for-teh*	weak	debole	***deh**-boh-leh*
true	vero	*veh-roh*	false	falso	*fahl-zoh*

I Colori

Colors are adjectives and must agree with the nouns they are describing, whether masculine or feminine, singular or plural. Check out the rainbow in the following table.

Colori

Color	Colore	Pronunciation
beige	beige	*behj*
black	nero	*neh-roh*

Color	Colore	Pronunciation
blue	blu	*bloo*
brown	marrone	*mah-**roh**-neh*
gold	oro	*or-oh*
gray	grigio	*gree-joh*
green	verde	*ver-deh*
orange	arancione	*ah-ran-**choh**-neh*
pink	rosa	*roh-zah*
purple	viola	*vee-**oh**-lah*
red	rosso	*roh-soh*
silver	argento	*ar-**jen**-toh*
white	bianco	*bee-**ahn**-koh*
yellow	giallo	*jahl-loh*

La Bella Lingua

To describe any color as light, simply add the adjective *chiaro* to the color to form a compound adjective, as in *rosso chiaro* (light red).

To describe any color as dark, add the word *scuro*, as in *rosa scuro* (dark pink). (*Rosa* is masculine unless you are talking about *la rosa*, the flower.)

One Yellow Banana, Please

Fill in the blank with the adjective modified by the subject and then translate the sentences. (You can find the answers in Appendix A.)

> Example: La banana è _____. (yellow)
> Answer: La banana è gialla.

1. La casa _____ (white) è _____ (clean).

2. Il Colosseo è molto _____ (old).

3. Le montagne in Svizzera sono _____ (high).

4. Il negozio è _____ (closed) la domenica.

5. Quest'albergo è _____ (inexpensive).

6. La lingua_____ (Italian) è _____ (easy).

It's a Colorful *Mondo*

I colori are easy to learn in Italian—even easier if you connect them to things you know, such as *white as snow.* The Italian language is riddled with fun *espressioni* having to do with *i colori.* Here are some of them with both the literal translation and the figurative one.

mettere nero su bianco
to put black to white
(to put down in writing)

rosso come un peperone
red as a pepper

vedere rosa
to see pink (to see through
rose-colored glasses)

essere nero
to be black
(to be in a bad mood)

vedere nero
to see black (to be angry
or pessimistic)

un numero verde
a green number
(a toll-free number)

Bello and *Quello*

The adjectives *bello* (beautiful, handsome, nice, good, fine) and *quello* (that/those) follow the same rules, as you can see in the following table. Both have forms similar to those of the definite article.

Bello and *Quello*

Gender	Singular	Plural	When It Is Used
Masculine	bello/quello	begli/quegli	Before *s* + consonant or *z*
	bell'/quell'	begli/quegli	Before vowels
	bel/quel	bei/quei	Before consonants
Feminine	bella/quella	belle/quelle	Before all consonants
	bell'/quell'	belle/quelle	Before vowels

Generally speaking, *bello* and *quello* come before the noun, like in English. *Bello* is used to describe anything wonderful: a good meal, a sunset, a beautiful person. If you want to sound like an Italian, use this *espressione* the next time you are moved by something you find extraordinary: *Che bello!* (How beautiful!).

*Che **bei** bambini!*
What beautiful children!

> *Quelle **belle** donne sono anche simpatiche.*
> Those beautiful women are also nice.

When the adjective *bello* follows the verb *essere*, it retains its full form. (However, it must still reflect the gender and number of the noun it describes.)

> *Quell'albergo è **bello.***
> That hotel is beautiful.

> *Quella ragazza è **bella.***
> That girl is beautiful.

Make the Connection

Fill in the appropriate forms of the definite article and its corresponding forms of *quello*, and translate. (You can find the answers in Appendix A.)

Definite Article	Translation	Quello	Translation
1. _il_ libro	_the book_	_quel_ libro	_that book_
2. _____ libri	_____	_____ libri	_____
3. _____ penna	_____	_____ penna	_____
4. _____ penne	_____	_____ penne	_____
5. _____ articolo	_____	_____ articolo	_____
6. _____ articoli	_____	_____ articoli	_____
7. _____ studente	_____	_____ studente	_____
8. _____ studenti	_____	_____ studenti	_____

Buono Is Good

Similar to the rules followed by the indefinite articles, the adjective *buono* (good) changes form in the singular when preceding a noun. (However, when following the verb *essere* or the noun it modifies, it uses the regular forms *buono* and *buona* in the singular.) The plural form of this adjective is regular. Consult the following table for the different forms.

Buono

Gender	Singular	Plural	When It Is Used
Masculine	il *buono* studente	i *buoni* studenti	Before masculine nouns beginning with *s* + consonant or *z*
	il *buon* libro il *buon* amico	i *buoni* libri i *buoni* amici	Before all other masculine nouns (both consonants and vowels)
Feminine	la *buona* ragazza	le *buone* ragazze	Before feminine nouns beginning with a consonant
	la *buon'*amica	le *buone* amiche	Before feminine nouns beginning with a vowel

How Are You? Adverbs

How are you? I hope that you're *well* and that everything is *fine*. Adverbs describe verbs or adjectives and indicate *how* you do something, such as, "She plays the piano *beautifully*," or "You are *sincerely* the *most* beautiful person I've ever met." In addition to irregular adverbs, which are covered next and need to be memorized, you can also create an adverb from an adjective.

Forming Adverbs from Adjectives

Many English adverbs end in *-ly*. In Italian, you can form several adverbs by adding *-mente* to the end of the feminine form of the adjective:

seria ➔ *seria***mente**	serious ➔ serious**ly**
profonda ➔ *profonda***mente**	profound ➔ profound**ly**
chiara ➔ *chiara***mente**	clear ➔ clear**ly**

Adjectives ending in *-le* or *-re* drop the final *-e* before adding *-mente:*

facile (easy) ➔ **facil**mente (easily)

gentile (kind) ➔ **gentil**mente (kindly)

> ### La Bella Lingua
>
> Every time you use the word *non* in a sentence, you are using an adverb. I'll bet you *never* (also an adverb) knew that the words *no* and *sì* (yes) are both adverbs. Other commonly used irregular adverbs include these:
>
> | | | | |
> |---|---|---|---|
> | better | *meglio* | never | *mai* |
> | by no means | *nemmeno* | not even | *neanche* |
> | certainly | *certamente* | really | *davvero* |
> | exactly | *appunto* | well | *bene* |
> | maybe | *forse* | | |

Take Your Place

A couple of points about the placement of adverbs will help you easily incorporate them into your growing *vocabolario*.

◆ Adverbs are generally placed after the verb:

*Puoi imparare **facilmente** l'italiano.*
You can **easily** learn Italian.

*Siete **gentilmente** pregati di lasciare un messaggio.*
You are **kindly** asked to leave a message.

*Ti parlo **seriamente.***
I'm speaking to you **seriously.**

◆ Some adverbs may come *before* the verb or adjective:

***Probabilmente** vado domani.*
I'm **probably** going tomorrow.

*Firenze è **sempre** bella.*
Florence is **always** beautiful.

> ### As a *Regola*
>
> Use these two little words to communicate more or less:
>
> | | |
> |---|---|
> | *più* | more |
> | *meno* | less |

Molti Adverbs

When talking about *quantità*, you might want less or more, depending on your mood. The following table gives you some of these.

Irregular Adverbs of Quantity

English	Italiano	English	Italiano
enough	abbastanza	quite a lot of	parecchio
hardly, scarcely	appena	rather, somewhat	piuttosto
less	meno	too	troppo
not very	poco	very, much, a lot	molto
not any more, no more	non più		

Adverbs of Time

Many adverbs relating to time—like those of place—aren't formed from an adjective. The following table offers you a selection of these timely words.

Adverbs of Time

English	Italiano	English	Italiano
after	dopo, poi	slowly	piano, lentamente
again	ancora	soon	subito
always	sempre	still	ancora
before	prima	then	allora, poi
early	presto	today	oggi
immediately	subito	tomorrow	domani
never	mai	usually	di solito
now	adesso, ora	in a hurry	in fretta
often	spesso	when	quando
quickly	presto	yesterday	ieri

As a *Regola*

It's possible to use the preposition *con* and a noun in lieu of an adverb:

Guidate con attenzione.
Drive attentively. (Drive with attention.)

Parla con sincerità.
He speaks sincerely. (He speaks with sincerity.)

Adverbs of Place

It's good to know your place. The adverbs in the following table will help.

Adverbs of Place

English	Italiano	English	Italiano
above	sopra	in back of	dietro
anywhere	dovunque	in front of	davanti
behind	indietro	inside	dentro
beneath	sotto	near	vicino
down	giù	on	sopra
down there	laggiù	on top of	su
elsewhere	altrove	outside	fuori
everywhere	dappertutto	there	ci, là, lì
far	lontano	up	su
here	qui, qua		

The More Things Change

Make the following adjectives into adverbs. Many of these adjectives will require that you make them feminine before converting them to adverbs. You can also use the formula *con* (with) + the noun, such as *con attenzione* (with attention). (The answers are in Appendix A.)

Example: *breve* (brief)
Answer: *brevemente* (briefly)

1. *dolce* (sweet) _____

2. *sincero* (sincere) _____

3. *intelligente* (intelligent) _____

4. *necessario* (necessary) _____

5. *veloce* (fast/quick) _____

6. *regolare* (regular) _____

7. *difficile* (difficult) _____

8. *probabile* (probable) _____

9. *solo* (only) _____

10. *gentile* (kind) _____

The Least You Need to Know

♦ To show possession in Italian, use the possessive adjectives or the preposition *di*.

♦ The adjective *buono* follows a pattern similar to the indefinite article.

♦ Italian adjectives must agree in gender and number with the nouns they modify.

♦ Adverbs are formed by adding *-mente* to many feminine adjectives. Many adverbs of time and place are irregular and must be memorized.

Part 2

Building Blocks: Creating a Strong Base

In this part, you're going to learn your *verbi*. You'll study subjects and conjugations, learn the differences between regular and irregular verbs, and study the many idiomatic expressions that derive from these verbs. You'll also learn how to discuss weather and time and study important travel terms. Finally, you'll learn how to use question words, ask for directions, understand the response (an important *considerazione!*), and a whole lot more. This part is loaded with useful information that can't be absorbed in one sitting; you'll probably want to have a little bite, savor the flavor, and let your mind digest the material before going too far ahead. Take your time and really absorb the *lezioni*.

Avventura Italiana: Regular Verbs

In This Chapter

- ◆ Subject pronouns
- ◆ Verb families and conjugation
- ◆ Common regular Italian verbs
- ◆ Taking conjugation a step further: asking questions
- ◆ Forming negative statements

You're going to hear me talk a lot about *i verbi*. Verbs are where the action is, so study them closely. *I verbi* are the skeleton of la *lingua*. Without *i verbi*, nothing would exist, get done, or happen. Verbs are what move us, shape us, and allow us to convey messages. If you're new to second language learning, then prepare yourself for your greatest, and most important, linguistic challenge: understanding verbs.

Remember that an infinitive verb is a verb in its unconjugated form, as in *cucinare* (to cook), *mangiare* (to eat), *dormire* (to sleep), and *viaggiare* (to travel).

Before you can begin to use verbs, you need to know your subject pronouns.

Your Loyal Subject

Determining the subject of a verb is essential to conjugation. As a reminder: To determine the subject, you need to ask the simple question, "What or who is doing the action?" The subject may be a person (Roberto), a thing (such as the car), or a pronoun replacing the noun (he, she, it, them, and so on).

What's What _____

You may see the Italian pronouns *egli* (he) and *ella* (she) serving in place of the subject pronouns *lui* and *lei*. You may also hear—depending on gender and number—the pronouns *esso, essi, essa,* and *esse* used in reference to people, animals, and inanimate objects.

Subject Pronouns

Study the subject pronouns in the following table.

Italian Subject Pronouns

Singular	Plural
io (I)	*noi* (we)
tu (you, informal)	*voi* (you)
lui/lei/Lei (he/she/You)	*loro* (they)

*The pronoun Lei *(with a capital* L*) signifies* You *(polite or formal); the pronoun* lei *signifies* she. *Both, however, are third person.*

When to Use Italian Subject Pronouns

Subject pronouns are useful for …

◆ **Clarity.** To differentiate who the subject is in cases when verb forms are the same and when there is more than one subject. For example:

Lui parla l'italiano ma lei parla il francese.
He speaks Italian but **she** speaks French.

◆ **Emphasis.** To clearly underline the fact that the subject will be performing the action. For example:

Tu viaggi in Italia; io sto qui.
You travel to Italy; **I'm** staying here.

◆ **Politeness.** To show respect and maintain a formality with another person. For example:

Lei è molto gentile.
You are very kind.

La Bella Lingua

The following *frasi* might as well be the first expressions you learn; you'll need them.

Non parlo l'italiano molto bene.	I don't speak Italian very well.
Parlate lentamente, per favore.	Speak slowly, please.
Parlate l'inglese?	Do you speak English?

Tu, Lei, Voi, and *Loro:* All You

Have you ever addressed a group of people and not known quite how to acknowledge all of them? In the southern United States, you'd say, "Y'all." In the North, you might say, "All of you." Italian solves this problem by having a separate, plural form of *you,* aptly called the second person plural. It also has an informal *you* (second person singular) used specifically with friends and family members and a separate form of *you* used in formal situations, which we call the *polite* form (third person singular). You've already seen these pronouns in an earlier table. Take a look at them again in the following table, just to make sure you understand.

Forms of You

English	Italian	When to Use	Person
you (informal)	*tu*	Informal, used with family, friends, and children	Second singular
You (polite)	*Lei*	Polite, used to show respect to strangers, authority figures, and elders; always capitalized	Third singular

continues

Forms of You (continued)

English	Italian	When to Use	Person
you (plural)	*voi*	Plural, used when addressing more than one person	Second plural
You (plural polite)	*Voi**	Plural, polite; used in extreme cases (as when addressing the pope)	Second plural

*This form, although plural, would be used to address the pope as the polite form of voi. *It probably stems from the notion that when speaking to the pope, one is also addressing God. Although Pope John Paul II often uses the first person singular form when giving his own personal opinion, he may also use the plural* noi *(we) form of the verb, as in* pensiamo *(we think), which is the traditional form used by popes.*

Hey You!

What Italian subject pronouns would you use when speaking to the following people? (You can find the answers in Appendix A.)

1. Your best friend
2. Mr. and Mrs. Carini
3. Giorgio and Filippo
4. Your in-laws
5. Your mother
6. Your baby brother
7. Your boss

Infinitively *Importante*

It is important to be able to recognize verb infinitives in order to look them up in your *dizionario* because verb conjugations are generally not included. The infinitive form of a verb is simply the unconjugated verb, as in *to love* (amare), *to dance* (ballare), and *to dream* (sognare), or *loving, dancing,* and *dreaming.* An infinitive, however, doesn't tell us who is doing the action. This is where conjugation comes in. Every time you speak, you conjugate verbs to reflect the subject of the verb. Included in this chapter are many regular verbs you might want to use as your Italian language skills progress. The list is long—rather than trying to learn all the verbs at once, use this chapter as a reference section you can come back to as *necessario.*

All in the *Famiglia*

Most of the time, Italian verbs follow certain rules. We call these regular verbs. (We'll discuss irregular verbs in Chapter 8.)

All verbs in Italian belong to one of three families, easily identified by their endings. The rules are the same for each family, so after you've learned the pattern for one verb, you know how to conjugate all the verbs in that family.

Also called the first conjugation, the *-are* family is the largest and most regular. The *-ere* family—known as the second conjugation—has its own set of rules. The *-ire* family has two methods of conjugation and is referred to as the third conjugation. These verb families include infinitive verbs such as *parlare* (to speak), *rispondere* (to respond), *partire* (to depart), and *capire* (to understand).

The Anatomy of a *Verbo*

Understanding the anatomy of a verb will help you conjugate. Keep in mind that every infinitive verb has a root that can be distinguished from its *infinitive ending. Ad esempio:*

> *parlare* (to speak)
>
> *parl-*　　　*-are*
>
> (root)(infinitive ending)

Most infinitive verbs end in *-are*, *-ere*, or *-ire*, making it very easy to distinguish infinitive verbs from other parts of speech.

To conjugate any regular verb in the present tense, keep the root, drop the infinitive ending, and replace it with the appropriate conjugation. Following this formula, you should be able to conjugate any regular verb (whether you understand its meaning or not).

La Bella Lingua

In English, the present tense can be expressed in three different ways:

The simple present: I study.

The present progressive: I am studying.

The emphatic present: I do study.

The Italian present tense expresses all three of these meanings with one word: *Studio.* (Although you can also say: *Sto studiando.)*

The Anatomy of a Verb

Conjugation	Infinitive Verb	Stem	Infinitive Ending
First	*parlare* (to speak)	*parl-*	*-are*
Second	*rispondere* (to respond)	*rispond-*	*-ere*
Third	*partire* (to depart)	*part-*	*-ire*
Third	*capire* (to understand)	*cap-*	*-ire*

The Present-Tense Conjugations

For a general overview, the following table outlines the correct endings for all three verb families, as represented by the verbs *parlare* (to speak), *rispondere* (respond), *partire* (to depart), and *capire* (to understand). (Note the two different conjugations for *-ire* verbs.)

Regular Verb Endings

Subject Pronoun	Parl<u>are</u>	Rispond<u>ere</u>	Part<u>ire</u>	Cap<u>ire</u>
io	parl**o**	rispond**o**	part**o**	cap**isco**
tu	parl**i**	rispond**i**	part**i**	cap**isci**
lui/lei/Lei	parl**a**	rispond**e**	part**e**	cap**isce**
noi	parl**iamo**	rispond**iamo**	part**iamo**	cap**iamo**
voi	parl**ate**	rispond**ete**	part**ite**	cap**ite**
loro	parl**ano**	rispond**ono**	part**ono**	cap**iscono**

What's What

The **stem** or **root** of a word or verb is the base from which other words are formed. In regular verbs, the stem remains the same when conjugated. In **irregular verbs,** the stem may change form after it has been conjugated. This is called a *stem-changing verb,* as with the verb *bere* (to drink), whose stem changes to *bev-* when conjugated.

The *-are* Family

The largest family in the batch, the *-are* verbs, are also the most regular. These are the most user-friendly verbs in the batch because they follow consistent rules.

P Is for *Parlare*

Take a look at the verb *parlare* (to speak) and see how it conjugates. (Refer to the verb tables below to see the pronunciation spelled out for you). Substitute the infinitive -*are* with the endings you just saw.

Parlare (To Speak)

Italiano	English	Italiano	English
io parl**o**	I speak	noi parl**iamo**	we speak
tu parl**i**	you speak	voi parl**ate**	you speak
lui/lei/Lei parl**a**	he/she speaks; You speak	loro parl**ano**	they speak

---

As a *Regola*

As you know, pronouncing Italian is easy; the challenge is knowing where to place the stress. When pronouncing all forms of the verbs, note that—except for *noi* and *voi*—stress should be placed on the stem of the verb, *not* the ending. Although there are exceptions, this is particularly helpful to recall when you're pronouncing the third person plural (*loro*) conjugations:

mangiano	*mahn-jah-noh*	they eat
parlano	*par-lah-noh*	they speak
vedono	*veh-doh-noh*	they see

Remember that double consonants should be emphasized but not separated, and all syllables should slide together in a flow of melodic *musica!*

Regular -*are* Verbs

The following table is a fairly comprehensive list of the -*are* verbs. Don't be intimidated by the sheer number of verbs there are—think of them as *colori* for your palette. The more you know, the better you will express yourself. For now, carefully study the verbs listed. Later, cover the translations with a piece of paper and see if you can ascertain their meaning by associating them with English words you already know. Look for cognates.

Regular *-are* Verbs

Verb	Pronunciation	Meaning
abbronzare	*ah-brohn-**zah**-reh*	to tan
abitare	*ah-bee-**tah**-reh*	to live
abusare	*ah-boo-**zah**-reh*	to abuse
accompagnare	*ah-kohm-pah-**nyah**-reh*	to accompany
adorare	*ah-doh-**rah**-reh*	to adore
affermare	*ah-fer-**mah**-reh*	to affirm
affittare	*ah-fee-**tah**-reh*	to rent
aiutare	*ah-yoo-**tah**-reh*	to help
alzare	*ahl-**tsah**-reh*	to raise/lift up
amare	*ah-**mah**-reh*	to love
ammirare	*ah-mee-**rah**-reh*	to admire
anticipare	*ahn-tee-chee-**pah**-reh*	to anticipate
arrestare	*ah-reh-**stah**-reh*	to stop/arrest
arrivare	*ah-ree-**vah**-reh*	to arrive
aspettare	*ah-speh-**tah**-reh*	to wait/expect
avvisare	*ah-vee-**sah**-reh*	to inform/advise
ballare	*bah-**lah**-reh*	to dance
bloccare	*bloh-**kah**-reh*	to block
bussare	*boo-**sah**-reh*	to knock
buttare	*boo-**tah**-reh*	to throw
calcolare	*kal-koh-**lah**-reh*	to calculate
camminare	*kah-mee-**nah**-reh*	to walk
cancellare	*kahn-cheh-**lah**-reh*	to cancel
cantare	*kahn-**tah**-reh*	to sing
causare	*kow-**zah**-reh*	to cause
celebrare	*cheh-leb-**rah**-reh*	to celebrate
cenare	*cheh-**nah**-reh*	to dine
chiamare	*kee-ah-**mah**-reh*	to call
comprare	*kohm-**prah**-reh*	to buy
consumare	*kohn-soo-**mah**-reh*	to consume
contare	*kohn-**tah**-reh*	to count
controllare	*kohn-troh-**lah**-reh*	to control/to check
conversare	*kohn-ver-**sah**-reh*	to converse

Verb	Pronunciation	Meaning
costare	*koh-**stah**-reh*	to cost
cucinare	*koo-chee-**nah**-reh*	to cook
deliberare	*deh-lee-beh-**rah**-reh*	to deliberate/to resolve
depositare	*deh-poh-zee-**tah**-reh*	to deposit
desiderare	*deh-zee-deh-**rah**-reh*	to desire
determinare	*deh-ter-mee-**nah**-reh*	to determine
detestare	*deh-teh-**stah**-reh*	to detest
dimostrare	*dee-moh-**strah**-reh*	to demonstrate
disegnare	*dee-zen-**yah**-reh*	to draw/design
disgustare	*dee-sgoo-**stah**-reh*	to disgust
disperare	*dee-speh-**rah**-reh*	to despair
diventare	*dee-ven-**tah**-reh*	to become
domandare	*doh-mahn-**dah**-reh*	to question
donare	*doh-**nah**-reh*	to donate/give
elevare	*eh-leh-**vah**-reh*	to elevate
eliminare	*eh-lee-mee-**nah**-reh*	to eliminate
entrare	*ehn-**trah**-reh*	to enter
esaminare	*eh-zah-mee-**nah**-reh*	to examine
evitare	*eh-vee-**tah**-reh*	to avoid
firmare	*feer-**mah**-reh*	to sign
formare	*for-**mah**-reh*	to form/create
fumare	*foo-**mah**-reh*	to smoke
funzionare	*foon-zee-oh-**nah**-reh*	to function
gettare	*jeh-**tah**-reh*	to throw
gridare	*gree-**dah**-reh*	to yell/scream
guardare	*gwar-**dah**-reh*	to look at something
guidare	*gwee-**dah**-reh*	to drive
immaginare	*ee-mah-jee-**nah**-reh*	to imagine
imparare	*eem-pah-**rah**-reh*	to learn
informare	*een-for-**mah**-reh*	to inform
invitare	*een-vee-**tah**-reh*	to invite
lavare	*lah-**vah**-reh*	to wash
lavorare	*lah-voh-**rah**-reh*	to work

continues

Regular *-are* Verbs (continued)

Verb	Pronunciation	Meaning
liberare	*lee-beh-**rah**-reh*	to liberate/to set free
limitare	*lee-mee-**tah**-reh*	to limit
lottare	*loh-**tah**-reh*	to struggle, to fight
mandare	*mahn-**dah**-reh*	to send
meritare	*meh-ree-**tah**-reh*	to deserve
misurare	*mee-zoo-**rah**-reh*	to measure
modificare	*moh-dee-fee-**kah**-reh*	to modify
nuotare	*nwoh-**tah**-reh*	to swim
occupare	*oh-koo-**pah**-reh*	to occupy
odiare	*oh-dee-**ah**-reh*	to hate
operare	*oh-peh-**rah**-reh*	to operate
ordinare	*or-dee-**nah**-reh*	to order
organizzare	*or-gah-nee-**zah**-reh*	to organize
osservare	*oh-ser-**vah**-reh*	to observe
parlare	*par-**lah**-reh*	to speak
partecipare	*par-teh-chee-**pah**-reh*	to participate
passare	*pah-**sah**-reh*	to pass
pensare	*pen-**sah**-reh*	to think
perdonare	*per-doh-**nah**-reh*	to forgive, to pardon
pesare	*peh-**zah**-reh*	to weigh
pettinare	*peh-tee-**nah**-reh*	to comb
portare	*por-**tah**-reh*	to bring, to carry, to wear
pranzare	*prahn-**zah**-reh*	to eat lunch, to dine
pregare	*preh-**gah**-reh*	to pray, to request
prenotare	*preh-noh-**tah**-reh*	to reserve
preparare	*preh-pah-**rah**-reh*	to prepare
presentare	*preh-zen-**tah**-reh*	to present
prestare	*preh-**stah**-reh*	to lend
provare	*proh-**vah**-reh*	to try
raccomandare	*rah-koh-mahn-**dah**-reh*	to recommend, to register
raccontare	*rah-kohn-**tah**-reh*	to tell, to recount
rappresentare	*rah-preh-zehn-**tah**-reh*	to represent
respirare	*reh-spee-**rah**-reh*	to breathe

Verb	Pronunciation	Meaning
rifiutare	*ree-fyoo-**tah**-reh*	to refuse, to reject
rilassare	*ree-lah-**sah**-reh*	to relax
riparare	*ree-pah-**rah**-reh*	to repair, to fix
riservare	*ree-zer-**vah**-reh*	to reserve, to put aside
rispettare	*ree-speh-**tah**-reh*	to respect
ritornare	*ree-tor-**nah**-reh*	to return
saltare	*sahl-**tah**-reh*	to jump
salvare	*sahl-**vah**-reh*	to save
scusare	*skoo-**zah**-reh*	to excuse
soddisfare	*soh-dee-**sfah**-reh*	to satisfy
sognare	*sohn-**yah**-reh*	to dream
sposare	*spoh-**zah**-reh*	to marry
suonare	*swoh-**nah**-reh*	to play an instrument, to sound
telefonare	*teh-leh-foh-**nah**-reh*	to telephone
terminare	*ter-mee-**nah**-reh*	to terminate
trovare	*troh-**vah**-reh*	to find
usare	*oo-**zah**-reh*	to use
vietare	*vee-eh-**tah**-reh*	to forbid/prohibit
visitare	*vee-zee-**tah**-reh*	to visit
volare	*voh-**lah**-reh*	to fly
votare	*voh-**tah**-reh*	to vote

As a *Regola*

For many verbs ending in *-iare*, such as *baciare* (to kiss), you must drop the additional *-i* if it occurs during conjugation. This serves to avoid a doubling of the vowel *-i* in the *tu* and *noi* forms.

Tu baci.   You kiss.   *Noi baciamo.*   We kiss.

Other affected verbs include these:

mangiare   (to eat)   *tagliare*   (to cut)

studiare   (to study)   *viaggiare*   (to travel)

An exception to this rule is the verb *odiare* (to hate), which retains the double *-ii.*

Exceptions

Here are a few exceptions to keep in mind:

- ◆ Most verbs ending in *-iare*, such as *cominciare* (to begin) and *studiare* (to study), drop the extra *-i* when conjugating to the *tu* and *noi* forms of the endings.

Subject	Cominciare	Studiare
io	comincio	studio
tu	cominci	studi
lui/lei/Lei	comincia	studia
noi	cominciamo	studiamo
voi	cominciate	studiate
loro	cominciano	studiano

Other verbs falling under this category include:

abbracciare (to hug)	*lasciare* (to leave something)
assaggiare (to taste)	*mangiare* (to eat)
baciare (to kiss)	*tagliare* (to cut)
cambiare (to change)	*viaggiare* (to travel)
cominciare (to begin)	

- ◆ Many verbs ending in *-care* and *-gare* add an *-h* to the stem in front of the vowels *i* and *e* to maintain the hard *c* and *g* sounds. Look at the verbs *cercare* (to search for) and *spiegare* (to explain) to see how this works.

Subject	Cercare	Spiegare
io	cerco	spiego
tu	cerchi	spieghi
lui/lei/Lei	cerca	spiega
noi	cerchiamo	spieghiamo
voi	cercate	spiegate
loro	cercano	spiegano

Other verbs falling under this category include the following:

comunicare (to communicate)	*notificare* (to notify)
giocare (to play)	*pagare* (to pay)
indicare (to indicate)	*toccare* (to touch)
navigare (to navigate)	*verificare* (to verify)

Practice Makes *Perfetto*

Use the correct form of the verb in the following sentences. If the subject is not identified in the sentence, it is given in parentheses. Don't forget to determine what your subject is and whether the verb should be conjugated in its singular or plural form. (You can find the answers in Appendix A.)

1. Paolo _____ (lavorare) in ufficio.

2. Luca ed io _____ (aspettare) il treno.

3. _____ (abitare) in una casa splendida. (tu)

4. _____ (parlare) la lingua italiana. (io)

5. _____ (passare) la notte in una bella pensione. (voi)

6. Antonella e Dina _____ (preparare) la cena.

The *-ere* Verbs

In most cases, *-ere* verbs are conjugated similarly to the *-are* verbs. Drop the infinitive ending from your root and add the endings from the "Regular *-ere* Verbs" table.

S Is for *Scrivere*

Notice how easy it is to write in Italian with the verb *scrivere* (to write). Start with *scriv-* and add the endings.

Scrivere (To Write)

Italiano	English
io scriv**o**	I write
tu scriv**i**	you write
lui/lei/Lei scriv**e**	he/she writes; You write
noi scriv**iamo**	we write
voi scriv**ete**	you write
loro scriv**ono**	they write

Regular -*ere* Verbs

As you can see from the list in the following table, there are fewer regular verbs in the -*ere* family. Study the verbs in the table.

Regular -*ere* Verbs

Verb	Pronunciation	Meaning
accendere	*ah-**chen**-deh-reh*	to light/turn on
affliggere	*ah-flee-**jeh**-reh*	to afflict
aggiungere	*ah-**joon**-jeh-reh*	to add
alludere	*ah-**loo**-deh-reh*	to allude/refer
ammettere	*ah-**meh**-teh-reh*	to admit/let in
apprendere	*ah-**pren**-deh-reh*	to learn
assistere	*ah-**see**-steh-reh*	to assist
assumere	*ah-**soo**-meh-reh*	to hire
attendere	*ah-**ten**-deh-reh*	to attend/to wait for
cadere	*kah-**deh**-reh*	to fall
chiedere	*kee-**yeh**-deh-reh*	to ask
chiudere	*kee-**yoo**-deh-reh*	to close
commettere	*koh-**meh**-teh-reh*	to commit/join
commuovere	*kohm-**woh**-veh-reh*	to move/touch/affect
comprendere	*kohm-**pren**-deh-reh*	to understand
concedere	*kohn-**cheh**-deh-reh*	to concede/grant/award
concludere	*kohn-**kloo**-deh-reh*	to conclude
confondere	*kohn-**fon**-deh-reh*	to confuse
conoscere	*koh-**noh**-sheh-reh*	to know someone
consistere	*kohn-**see**-steh-reh*	to consist
convincere	*kohn-**veen**-cheh-reh*	to convince
correggere	*koh-**reh**-jeh-reh*	to correct
correre	***koh**-reh-reh*	to run
corrispondere	*koh-ree-**spohn**-deh-reh*	to correspond
credere	***kreh**-deh-reh*	to believe
crescere	***kreh**-sheh-reh*	to grow
decidere	*deh-**chee**-deh-reh*	to decide

Verb	Pronunciation	Meaning
descrivere	*deh-**skree**-veh-reh*	to describe
difendere	*dee-**fen**-deh-reh*	to defend
dipendere	*dee-**pen**-deh-reh*	to depend
dipingere	*dee-**peen**-jeh-reh*	to paint
discutere	*dee-**skoo**-teh-reh*	to discuss
dissolvere	*dee-**sohl**-veh-reh*	to dissolve
distinguere	*dee-**steen**-gweh-reh*	to distinguish
distruggere	*dee-**stroo**-jeh-reh*	to destroy
dividere	*dee-**vee**-deh-reh*	to divide
emergere	*eh-**mer**-jeh-reh*	to emerge
esistere	*eh-**zee**-steh-reh*	to exist
esprimere	*es-**pree**-meh-reh*	to express
fingere	***feen**-geh-reh*	to pretend
godere	*goh-**deh**-reh*	to enjoy
includere	*een-**kloo**-deh-reh*	to include
insistere	*een-**see**-steh-reh*	to insist
intendere	*een-**ten**-deh-reh*	to intend
interrompere	*een-teh-**rom**-peh-reh*	to interrupt
invadere	*een-**vah**-deh-reh*	to invade
leggere	***leh**-jeh-reh*	to read
mettere	***meh**-teh-reh*	to put/place/set
muovere	***mwoh**-veh-reh*	to move
nascondere	*nah-**skon**-deh-reh*	to hide
offendere	*oh-**fen**-deh-reh*	to offend
perdere	***per**-deh-reh*	to lose
permettere	*per-**meh**-teh-reh*	to permit
piangere	*pee-**yahn**-jeh-reh*	to cry
prendere	***pren**-deh-reh*	to take
proteggere	*proh-**teh**-jeh-reh*	to protect
rendere	***ren**-deh-reh*	to render/give back
resistere	*reh-**zee**-steh-reh*	to resist
ricevere	*ree-**cheh**-veh-reh*	to receive
ridere	***ree**-deh-reh*	to laugh

continues

Regular -*ere* Verbs   (continued)

Verb	Pronunciation	Meaning
riflettere	*ree-**fleh**-teh-reh*	to reflect
ripetere	*ree-**peh**-teh-reh*	to repeat
risolvere	*ree-**zol**-veh-reh*	to resolve
rispondere	*ree-**spon**-deh-reh*	to respond
rompere	***rom**-peh-reh*	to break
scendere	***shen**-deh-reh*	to descend
scrivere	***skree**-veh-reh*	to write
sorridere	*soh-**ree**-deh-reh*	to smile
sospendere	*soh-**spen**-deh-reh*	to suspend
spendere	***spen**-deh-reh*	to spend
succedere	*soo-**cheh**-deh-reh*	to happen/occur
uccidere	*oo-**chee**-deh-reh*	to kill
vedere	*veh-**deh**-reh*	to see
vendere	***ven**-deh-reh*	to sell
vincere	***veen**-cheh-reh*	to win
vivere	***vee**-veh-reh*	to live

Practice Makes *Perfetto* II

Your plate is full and your eyes are bloodshot from the feast of verbs. Refer to the previous table and provide the correct verb form that best completes the sentences. (You can find the answers in Appendix A.)

prendere	accendere	risolvere
vedere	spendere	scrivere

1. (Loro) _____ molti soldi.

2. (Io) _____ una lettera.

3. (Tu) _____ la luce.

4. (Noi) _____ il film, *La Dolce Vita*.

5. (Lei) _____ il problema.

6. (Voi) _____ il treno.

La Bella Lingua

Some verbs are only used in the third person, such as *piovere* (to rain), *nevicare* (to snow).

The *-ire* Family

There are two groups of *-ire* verbs. The first group follows conjugation rules that are similar to those for the *-ere* verbs. As a matter of fact, they are the same except for the second person plural (*voi*), as shown in the following table.

D Is for *Dormire*

It's true, verb conjugations can put you to sleep. As an example of the first group, study the verb *dormire* (to sleep).

Dormire (To Sleep)

Italiano	English	Italiano	English
io dorm**o**	I sleep	noi dorm**iamo**	we sleep
tu dorm**i**	you sleep	voi dorm**ite**	you sleep
lui/lei/Lei dorm**e**	he/she sleeps; You sleep	loro dorm**ono**	they sleep

The *-ire* Verbs (Group I)

A handful of verbs fall under this *categoria*. The following table shows you some of them.

Group I: Regular *-ire* Verbs

Verb	Pronunciation	Meaning
aprire	ah-**pree**-reh	to open
bollire	*boh-**lee**-reh*	to boil
convertire	*kohn-ver-**tee**-reh*	to convert
coprire	*koh-**pree**-reh*	to cover
dormire	*dor-**mee**-reh*	to sleep
fuggire	*foo-**jee**-reh*	to escape
mentire	*men-**tee**-reh*	to lie
offrire	*oh-**free**-reh*	to offer
partire	*par-**tee**-reh*	to depart
seguire	*seh-**gwee**-reh*	to follow
servire	*ser-**vee**-reh*	to serve

More -*ire* Verbs (Group II)

The second group of -*ire* verbs is still considered regular but must be conjugated differently from other -*ire* verbs. After you learn the endings, you'll have no problem conjugating them.

C Is for *Capire*

A commonly used verb from this family is the verb *capire* (to understand). Look at how this verb conjugates. If you can remember this verb, the others follow quite easily:

Capire (To Understand)

Italiano	English	Italiano	English
io cap**isco**	I understand	noi cap**iamo**	we understand
tu cap**isci**	you understand	voi cap**ite**	you understand
lui/lei/Lei cap**isce**	he/she understands; You understand	loro cap**iscono**	they understand

The -*ire* Verbs (Group II)

The second group of -*ire* verbs includes interesting verbs such as *capire* (to understand), *impazzire* (to go crazy), and *tradire* (to betray)—all the verbs you'll need for a good juicy opera like *La Traviata*.

As a *Regola*

To make a negative statement, as in "I don't understand," add the word *non* in front of the verb.

Non capisco la lezione.	I don't understand the lesson.
Antonio **non mangia** la carne.	Antonio doesn't eat meat.
Non partiamo per l'America.	We're not leaving for America.

Double negatives are acceptable in Italian, as in *No, non desidero niente*, which literally translates to "No, I don't want *nothing*." (Of course, in English you would say, "No, I don't want *anything*.")

Group II: -*ire* Verbs

Verb	Pronunciation	Meaning
aderire	*ah-deh-**ree**-reh*	to adhere
attribuire	*ah-tree-boo-**ee**-reh*	to attribute
capire	*kah-**pee**-reh*	to understand
colpire	*kol-**pee**-reh*	to hit/strike
costruire	*kohs-troo-**wee**-reh*	to construct
definire	*deh-fee-**nee**-reh*	to define
digerire	*dee-jeh-**ree**-reh*	to digest
diminuire	*dee-mee-noo-**wee**-reh*	to diminish
esaurire	*eh-zow-**ree**-reh*	to exhaust
fallire	*fah-**lee**-reh*	to fail/go bankrupt
finire	*fee-nee-reh*	to finish
garantire	*gah-rahn-tee-reh*	to guarantee
gestire	*jeh-**stee**-reh*	to manage/administrate
guarire	*gwah-**ree**-reh*	to heal/recover
impazzire	*eem-pah-**tsee**-reh*	to go crazy
istruire	*ee-stroo-**wee**-reh*	to instruct/teach
obbedire	*oh-beh-**dee**-reh*	to obey
preferire	*preh-feh-**ree**-reh*	to prefer
proibire	*pro-ee-**bee**-reh*	to prohibit/forbid
pulire	*poo-**lee**-reh*	to clean
punire	*poo-**nee**-reh*	to punish
riunire	*ree-yoo-**nee**-reh*	to reunite
spedire	*speh-**dee**-reh*	to send
stabilire	*sta-bee-**lee**-reh*	to establish
suggerire	*soo-jeh-**ree**-reh*	to suggest
tradire	*trah-**dee**-reh*	to betray/deceive
trasferire	*tras-feh-**ree**-reh*	to transfer
unire	*oo-**nee**-reh*	to unite

> **Attenzione!**
>
> Be careful of sounding like a robot when you read aloud. Say it like you mean it! When asking questions, be sure to change your intonation. Your voice should start out lower and gradually rise until the end of a sentence, as you do in English: *Parla l'italiano?* (Do you speak Italian?)

Asking Questions

No one knows everything. The curious mind wants to understand, so it needs to ask questions. In Italian, it is very easy to ask a question. This section shows you how to ask basic questions.

The Tags *Vero? No?* and *Giusto?*

Another way to ask a simple yes/no *domanda* (question) is to add the tags *vero?* (true? or right?), *no?* and *giusto?* (is that so? or is that correct?) to the end of a sentence:

Partiamo alle otto, no?   We're leaving at 8, no?

Capisci la lezione, vero?   You understand the lesson, right?

And the *Risposta* Is ...

To answer a question affirmatively (yes), use *sì* and give your *risposta* (response).

To answer a question negatively (no), use *no* attached to *non* before the conjugated verb form. This is equivalent to our *don't*, as in "No, I don't smoke."

Question	Affirmative Answer	Negative Answer
Lei fuma le sigarette?	Sì, fumo le sigarette.	**No, non** fumo le sigarette.
Do you smoke cigarettes?	Yes, I smoke cigarettes.	No, I don't smoke cigarettes.
Capisci la lezione?	Sì, capisco la lezione.	**No, non** capisco la lezione.
Do you understand the lesson?	Yes, I understand the lesson.	No, I don't understand the lesson.

A Whole Lot of *Niente*

If you are answering a question and starting your sentence with *no*, these negative expressions generally come directly after the conjugated verb. Try to determine the meaning of these examples. If you have difficulty determining the significance of the verbs, find the stem of the verb and use the charts to find the infinitive form.

Italiano	*English*	*Example*
mai	never	Non fumo **mai.**
niente	nothing	Non desidero **niente.***
nulla	nothing	Non compra **nulla.***
nessuno	no one	Nessuno **arriva.**

*Unlike English, Italian allows for double negatives.

Respira! Take a deep breath and let it out. Crack your spine, stretch your arms, and roll your *testa* around a couple of times.

If you're finding the lessons increasingly challenging, it's because you're in the thick of the *foresta* right now. Even if you went no further than this chapter, you would have enough Italian to get by. However, you might want to browse your bookstore for a good verb book, such as Barron's *501 Italian Verbs*, to deepen your understanding of them.

You might want to linger on verbs for a while. Later, after you've had time to digest this rather heavy meal, you can come back and review. Understanding the Italian verbs is the *chiave* (key) to your *successo! Buon appetito!*

The Least You Need to Know

♦ Determining the subject of a verb is essential to conjugation—and, therefore, speaking.

♦ Subject pronouns are used much less frequently in Italian than in English because the verb endings usually indicate the subject; however, you will sometimes hear subject pronouns used for clarity, emphasis, or courtesy.

♦ There are four forms of *you* in Italian: the second person plural, the second person singular, the third person singular, and the third person plural.

♦ Any verb that follows a subject noun or pronoun must be properly conjugated.

♦ There are three verb families: *-are*, *-ere*, and *-ire*. Each has its own set of conjugation rules.

♦ The verbs are the most essential aspect of learning a foreign language. Take your time and learn the verbs that you'll use the most.

Chapter 8

The Most Important *Verbi* You'll Ever Learn

In This Chapter

- The verbs *essere* and *stare* (to be)
- The verbs *avere* (to have) and *fare* (to do/make)
- Idiomatic expressions using *essere* and *avere*
- *Ci* and *vi* and *C'è* and *ci sono*
- *Ecco*

If you could only have four verbs to work with, they would be the ones covered in this chapter. If you ever thought of tattooing verb conjugations on your arm, these would be my first picks. *Perché?* You can be yourself with the verb *essere*. You can stay in a beautiful villa with the verb *stare*. You can have *gelato* for breakfast with *avere*. You can make money or love (and a whole lot more) with *fare*. That's the good news.

The bad news is that most of my favorite verbs happen to be highly irregular. (*Secondo me*, irregular verbs, like people, tend to be more interesting anyway.) Keep in mind that many irregular verbs are barely recognizable after they have been conjugated and consequently require old-fashioned memorization.

The Birds and the Bs

Two different *verbi* are used to express *to be* in Italian: *stare* and *essere*. When you ask someone, "*Come stai?*" (How are you?), you're using the verb *stare*. When you say, "*La vita è bella*" (Life is beautiful), you're using the verb *essere*. Because the two verbs mean the same thing, the difference between the two concerns usage.

Attenzione!

Don't be confused between *e* (and) and *è* (is): The accent tells you when it's the verb.

Fortunately, *stare* pretty much follows along the lines of the regular verbs you studied in Chapter 7.

Essere, on the other hand, has its own special way of being.

Both verbs can stand on their own, but they can also be used as *helping* or *auxiliary* verbs. You'll need helping verbs when you want to form compound tenses, including the past tense.

The Verb *Essere*

Look at how the highly irregular verb *essere* conjugates in the following table. You'll get a lot of mileage out of this one verb—learn it like the back of your hand.

The Verb *Essere*

Italian	English	Italian	English
io **sono**	I am	noi **siamo**	we are
tu **sei**	you are	voi **siete**	you are
lui/lei/Lei **è**	he/she (it)* is; You are	loro **sono**	they are

*Italian has no neuter it—*it uses the verb form alone to refer to things or animals.*

La Bella Lingua

The verb *essere* uses the same conjugation for the first person singular as the third person plural: *sono*. To ascertain the subject (I or they), look for clues such as a subject pronoun (*io* or *loro*), or infer the subject through the context of the statement by looking at the articles, nouns, or adjective endings (which must always reflect gender and plurality).

Sono una persona sincera.   I am a sincere person.

Sono persone sincere.   They are sincere people (persons).

The Verb *Stare*

The verb *stare* is easy to learn. Study the following table to see how it is conjugated.

The Verb *Stare*

Italian	English	Italian	English
io **sto**	I am	noi **stiamo**	we are
tu **stai**	you are	voi **state**	you are
lui/lei/Lei **sta**	he/she (it) is; You are	loro **stanno**	they are

As a *Regola*

You should always address a man as *Signore* (Mr. or Sir) and a woman as *Signora* (Mrs. or Ms.); young girls can be addressed as *Signorina* (Miss). When asking someone how they are, you should err on the side of formality and use the polite form of the verb *stare*, as follows:
     Come sta? (How are you?)
 The response will generally be this:
     Sto bene, grazie, e Lei? (I am well, thanks, and you?)

Essere vs. *Stare*: What's the *Differenza?*

Although the verbs *essere* and *stare* both mean *to be*, each verb follows specific rules of usage.

When to Use *Essere*

The verb *essere* is used in several different ways:

♦ To describe nationalities, origins, and inherent unchanging qualities:

Maurizio è di Verona.	Maurizio is from Verona.
*I Gambini **sono** italiani.*	The Gambinis are Italian.
La banana è gialla.	The banana is yellow.

♦ To identify the subject or describe the subject's character traits and physical attributes:

Maria è bionda.	Maria is blond.
Sono *io.*	It's me.

◆ To talk about the time (see Chapter 9):

*Che ore **sono?***	What time is it?
Sono *le tre e mezzo.*	It is 3:30.

◆ To talk about the date:

Natale è il 25 dicembre.	Christmas is December 25.
Che giorno è?	What day is it?
Oggi è lunedì.	Today is Monday.

◆ To indicate possession:

Questo è lo zio di Anna.	This is Anna's uncle.
Quella è la mia casa.	That is my house.

◆ For certain impersonal expressions:

È una bella giornata.	It is a beautiful day.
È molto importante studiare.	It is very important to study.

Come Sei Intelligente!

Now, prove how smart you are. Use the correct form of *essere* in the following phrases. (You can find the answers in Appendix A.)

1. Luisa _____ una bella persona.

2. Grazie per i fiori! Tu _____ romantico.

3. Abelardo e Antonella _____ di Firenze.

4. Gli occhi _____ le finestre dell'anima.

5. Voi _____ generosi.

When to Use *Stare*

You're already familiar with the most commonly used expression in Italian, *Come sta?* With few exceptions, the verb *stare* is also used in the following ways:

◆ To describe a temporary state or condition of the subject:

*Come **sta**?*	How are you?
***Sto** bene, grazie.*	I am well, thanks.

◆ To express a location:

***Stiamo** in albergo.*	We are staying in a hotel.
*Patrizia **sta** a casa.*	Patricia is at home.

◆ In many idiomatic expressions:

***Sta** attento!*	Pay attention!
***Sta** zitto!*	Be quiet!

◆ To form the progressive tenses (see Chapter 15):

***Stiamo andando** al cinema.*	We are going to the movies.
***Sto studiando** il mio libro.*	I am studying my book.

Chitchat

You're having a *conversazione* with the person sitting next to you on the plane. Should you use the verb *essere* or *stare?* Complete the following *frasi* with the correct form of the necessary *verbo*. (You can find the answers in Appendix A.)

1. Noi _____ nella pensione Paradiso per due giorni.

2. Come _____ Lei?

3. Io _____ bene, grazie.

4. Loro _____ turisti.

5. Il ristorante Caffè Greco _____ famoso.

6. Villa Borghese _____ molto bella.

> **As a *Regola***
>
> Use this formula to express *there is* or *is there ...?*: $ci + è = c'è$.

C'è and Ci sono (There Is, There Are)

The word *ci* used with the third person of *essere* indicates *there is* and *there are*. This important little adverb states the existence or presence of something or someone. When *ci* is used with the third person singular *è*, the contraction *c'è* is created:

C'è tempo; non c'è fretta.   There is time; there is no hurry.

Ci sono molti turisti a Roma.   There are many tourists in Rome.

Using *Ci* to Ask Questions

When using *c'è* in a question, the word order stays the same. Like in English, you should raise your voice at the end of the sentence:

C'è una banca?   Is there a bank?

Ci sono letti?   Are there beds?

Making a Negative Impression: *Non*

To make negative statements, simply add the word *non* in front of the adverb *ci*:

Non c'è problema.   There is no problem.

Non ci sono letti.   There are no beds.

Fill In the Blankety-Blanks

Study the following phrases and fill in the blanks with either *c'è* or *ci sono*. Translate the sentences. Don't forget to look at the endings to determine whether the subject is singular or plural. If you're unsure about the meaning of a word, consult the glossary in the back of the book.

Example: _____ un supermercato?
Answer: <u>C'è</u>   un supermercato?

1. _____ un museo?

2. _____ 58.000.000 abitanti in Italia.

3. _____ due piazze.

4. _____ un bagno privato in camera?

5. _____ molti ristoranti a Roma.

6. _____ quattro stagioni: la primavera, l'estate, l'autunno, e l'inverno.

7. _____ una festa stasera a casa di Alessandro.

8. Non _____ tempo.

Ci and *Vi*

Like the adverb *ci*, the word *vi* can also mean *here* or *there*. Modern Italian tends to use *ci* more often, although the two are interchangeable. Both adverbs often replace nouns or prepositional phrases preceded by *a*, *in*, and *su*, saving the speaker unnecessary repetition.

Denoting place:

Vai spesso in piazza?	Do you often go to the piazza?
*Sì, **ci** vado.*	Yes, I go there.
Abiti a New York?	Do you live in New York?
*No, non **ci** abito.*	No, I don't live there.

Denoting things or ideas:

Credi in Dio?	Do you believe in God?
*Sì, **ci** credo.*	Yes, I do [believe in God].
Pensi ai tuoi amici?	Do you think about your friends?
*Sì, **ci** penso.*	Yes, I do [think about them].

You'll hear these adverbs come up a lot. For now, familiarizing yourself with their existence is *sufficiente*.

It's Time to Have Some Fun: *Avere*

The irregular verb *avere* (to have) is used in myriad *situazioni* and idiomatic *espressioni* and is virtually unrecognizable from its infinitive when it has been conjugated. The following table outlines this useful verb.

La Bella Lingua
The verb *avere* is one of the few verbs with a silent letter that is used primarily to distinguish the conjugations from other Italian words. For example, take the *h* out of *ho* and you have *o*, meaning *or*. Take the *h* out of *hai* and you have the contraction *ai*, meaning *to the*. Take the *h* out of *ha* and you have the preposition *a*, meaning *to*; take the *h* out of *hanno* and you have the word *anno*, meaning *year*.

Avere

Italiano	English	Italiano	English
io **ho**	I have	noi **abbiamo**	we have
tu **hai**	you have	voi **avete**	you have
lui/lei/Lei **ha**	he/she has; You have	loro **hanno**	they have

Ho una fame da lupo! (I am hungry as a wolf!)

Aside from meaning *to have*, the verb *avere* is used in many idiomatic expressions to convey when you are hungry, when you feel cold, and when you want to talk about how old you are. You use *avere:*

> **Attenzione!** _____
>
> If you're feeling hot or cold, remember to use *avere* as in:
>
> *Ho freddo* (I *have* cold)
>
> *Ho caldo* (I *have* warm)
>
> Of course, it doesn't translate very well, but that's why we call these idiomatic expressions.

◆ To find out how old someone is. In Italian you ask how many years one has, as in *Quanti anni ha?*

◆ As an auxiliary—or helping—verb. Use this verb to form the present perfect tense, as in *Ho mangiato* (I have eaten). You'll learn more about this tense in Chapter 16.

◆ To express when you feel hot, cold, drowsy, hungry, and afraid, not to mention ashamed, sick, needy, and unlucky (and that's on a good day).

An Idiot's Guide to Idioms with *Avere*

Translations are not always literal. The idiomatic expressions in the following table will help you express your needs and feelings. The infinitive form of the verb is given in parentheses; it is up to you to conjugate it to reflect the subject of the verb.

Needs and Feelings

Italiano	English
(avere) l'abitudine di	to be in the habit of
(avere) ___ anni	to be ___ years old
(avere) bisogno di	to have need of
(avere) caldo	to feel hot

Italiano	English
(avere) colpa	to be at fault, to be guilty
(avere) fame	to be hungry
(avere) la s/fortuna di	to have the mis/fortune of
(avere) freddo	to feel cold
(avere) l'intenzione di	to have the intention of
(avere) mal di	to have pain/to be sick
(avere) l'occasione di	to have the chance to
(avere) l'opportunità di	to have the opportunity to
(avere) paura	to be afraid
(avere) la possibilità di	to have the possibility to
(avere) ragione	to be right
(avere) sete	to be thirsty
(avere) sonno	to be sleepy
(avere) torto	to be wrong
(avere) vergogna	to be ashamed
(avere) voglia di	to be in the mood, to feel like

La Bella Lingua

In Italian, you would never ask how *old* someone is. *Old* never enters the equation. Italians know that age is an attitude. Instead, ask how many years a person *has*: *Quanti anni hai?* (How many years do you have?)

Express Yourself

How can you ever be satisfied if you don't learn how to express your needs? Start by using either *ho* (I have) or *sono* (I am), and add the appropriate Italian word to say the following. (You can find the answers in Appendix A.)

Example:	When you are afraid, you say …
Answer:	*Ho paura.*

1. When you are hungry, you say … _____.

2. When the temperature drops below freezing and you don't have a coat, you say … _____.

3. When your legs feel like lead weights and you can't keep your eyes open, you say … _____.

4. When you want to indicate your age, you say … _____.

5. When you are embarrassed, you might say … _____.

What's What

A **helping verb** is used to form other tenses, including compound tenses such as the *present perfect* tense. In English, we usually use the auxiliary verb *to have*, as in *I have eaten*. In Italian, there are three helping verbs: *essere* (to be), *avere* (to have), and *stare* (to be), the latter being principally to create the *present progressive* tense (as in *I am leaving*).

Things to Do: The Verb *Fare*

If you are a doer, then this is your verb. You're really talking Italian when you get the hang of *fare*. The verb *fare* expresses when you want to make or do something. In addition, it is often used like the English verb *to take* and appears in many idiomatic expressions. For example, in Italian, you don't *take* a trip—rather, you *make* a trip (*fare un viaggio*). You don't *eat* breakfast, you *do* breakfast (*fare colazione*).

The verb *fare* is used to talk about the weather, or when you *take* that perfect picture (the one you always thought should be submitted to *National Geographic*). With this versatile verb, you can go shopping, pretend, or indicate where something hurts. You'll use it when you take a shower, a walk, or a spin. You'll see this verb a lot—and use it often during your travels. Because *fare* is irregular, you must memorize the different parts in the following table.

The Verb *Fare* (To Do; to Make)

Italiano	English	Italiano	English
io **faccio**	I do	noi **facciamo**	we do
tu **fai**	you do	voi **fate**	you do
lui/lei/Lei **fa**	he/she does; You do	loro **fanno**	they do

---

La Bella Lingua

Aside from its principal significance, *fare* is a verb used in many idiomatic *espressioni*, including when you talk about *il tempo* (the weather). Your Italian *dizionario* offers many of these idioms.

In English you *take* a shower, whereas in Italian you *make* a shower, as in *fare una doccia*.

Conversely, whereas in English you *make* a decision, in Italian you *take* a decision, as in *prendere una decisione*.

You may also see and hear the verb as *far*, as in *far le compere* (to go shopping).

Idiomatic Expressions Using *Fare*

The following table contains some idiomatic expressions using the verb *fare*. Remember that, like idiomatic expressions using the verbs *avere*, you must conjugate the verb in parentheses.

Expressions Using *Fare*

Italiano	English	Italiano	English
(fare) baccano	to make a ruckus	(fare) benzina	to get gas
(fare) colazione	to have lunch	(fare) del bene	to do good
(fare) finta	to pretend	(fare) il bagno	to take a bath
(fare) il pieno	to fill it up	(fare) la doccia	to take a shower
(fare) l'amore	to make love	(fare) l'autostop	to hitchhike
(fare) le spese	to go shopping	(fare) le valigie	to pack/prepare one's bags
(fare) male a qualcuno	to hurt someone	(fare) presto	to be early
(fare) tardi	to be late	(fare) un controllo	to get a tune-up
(fare) un giro	to take a spin	(fare) un regalo	to give a gift
(fare) un viaggio	to take a trip	(fare) una bella figura	to make a good impression
(fare) una brutta figura	to make a bad impression	(fare) una domanda	to ask a question
(fare) una fotografia	to take a picture	(fare) una passeggiata	to take a walk
(fare) vedere	to show		

Professionally Speaking

Many professional *titoli* (titles) are neuter (doctor, lawyer, teacher), with a few exceptions such as waiter/waitress and actor/actress. Modern Italian professionals, regardless of their gender, tend toward the once typically masculine titles: *avvocato* (lawyer), *dottore* (doctor), *attore* (actor), and *professore* (professor), to name a few. Other titles must reflect the gender of the subject. Exceptions include professions ending in *-a*, such as *dentista* (dentist) and *artista* (artist). In these cases, you will have to pay attention to the article preceding the *professione* to know whether the subject is *maschile* or *femminile*.

♦ Many professions ending in *-o* or *-e* often change to *-a* to reflect gender:

> *l'archeologo/l'archeologa* (archeologist)

> *lo scienziato/la scienziata* (scientist)

♦ Certain Italian professions have gender-specific endings such as *-ice* that may or may not be used, depending on the specific individual and regional influences.

> *l'attore/l'attrice* (actor/actress)

> *lo scrittore/la scrittrice* (writer)

As a *Regola*
Note that some words such as *il* (or *la*) *contabile* (accountant) and *il* (or *la*) *dentista* (dentist) can be used for either gender.

♦ Other professions may end in *-essa*:

> *il dottore/la dottoressa* (doctor)

> *il poeta/la poetessa* (poet)

> *il professore/la professoressa* (professor)

In My Professional Opinion

The following table lists several of the more common professions. If you have a *professione* that is atypical, such as a dog walker or floral designer, you may want to consult your *dizionario*. I have also indicated when there are separate words such as *attore* and *attrice* (actor and actress) for the same *professione*. Consult Chapter 20 for more work-related vocabulary.

Professions

Profession	Professione	Pronunciation
accountant	contabile (m./f.)	kon-*tah*-bee-leh
actor	attore (m./f.)	ah-*toh*-reh
actress	attrice (f.)	ah-*tree*-cheh
archeologist	archeologo (m.)	ar-keh-*oh*-loh-goh
	archeologa (f.)	ar-keh-*oh*-loh-gah
architect	architetto (m.)	ar-kee-*teh*-toh
	architetta (f.)	ar-kee-*teh*-tah
artist	artista (m./f.)	ar-*tees*-tah
banker	bancario (m.)	bahn-*kah*-ree-yoh
	bancaria (f.)	bahn-*kah*-ree-yah
barber	barbiere (m.)	bar-bee-*yeh*-reh
cashier	cassiere (m.)	kah-see-*yeh*-reh
	cassiera (f.)	kah-see-*yeh*-rah
consultant	consulente (m./f.)	kon-soo-*len*-teh
dentist	dentista (m./f.)	den-*tees*-tah
doctor	dottore (m.)	doh-*toh*-reh
	dottoressa (f.)	doh-toh-*reh*-sah
editor	editore (m.)	eh-dee-*toh*-reh
	editrice (f.)	eh-dee-*tree*-cheh
electrician	elettricista (m./f.)	eh-leh-tree-*chee*-stah
environmentalist	ecologo (m./f.)	eh-*koh*-loh-goh
	ecologa (m./f.)	eh-*koh*-loh-goh
firefighter	pompiere (m.)	pom-pee-*yeh*-reh
	vigile del fuoco (m./f.)	*vee*-jeh-leh del fwoh-koh
hair dresser	parrucchiere (m.)	pah-roo-kee-*yeh*-reh
	parrucchiera (f.)	pah-roo-kee-*yeh*-rah
housewife	casalinga (f.)	kah-zah-*leen*-gah
jeweler	gioielliere (m./f.)	joh-yeh-lee-*yeh*-reh
journalist	giornalista (m./f.)	jor-nah-*lee*-stah
lawyer	avvocato (m./f.)	ah-voh-*kah*-toh
manager	dirigente (m./f.)	dee-ree-*jen*-teh
mechanic	meccanico (m.)	meh-*kah*-nee-koh
musician	musicista (mf)	moo-zee-*chee*-stah

Profession	Professione	Pronunciation
nurse	infermiere (m.)	*een-fer-mee-**yeb**-reb*
	infermiera (f.)	*een-fer-mee-**yeb**-rah*
plumber	idraulico (m.)	*ee-**drow**-lee-koh*
police officer	agente di polizia (m./f.)	*ah-**jen**-teh dee poh-lee-**zee**-yah*
professor	professore (m.)	*proh-feh-**soh**-reb*
	professoressa (f.)	*proh-feh-soh-**reb**-sah*
scientist	scienziato (m.)	*shee-en-zee-**ah**-toh*
	scienziata (f.)	*shee-en-zee-**ah**-tah*
secretary	segretario (m.)	*seh-greh-**tah**-ree-oh*
	segretaria (f.)	*seh-greh-**tah**-ree-ah*
stock broker	agente di borsa (m./f.)	*ah-**jen**-teh dee bor-sah*
student	studente (m.)	*stoo-**den**-teh*
	studentessa (f.)	*stoo-den-**teh**-sah*
teacher	insegnante (m./f.)	*een-sen-**yahn**-teh*
waiter	cameriere (m.)	*kah-meh-ree-**yeh**-reb*
waitress/maid	cameriera (f.)	*kah-meh-ree-**yeh**-rah*
worker	operaio (m.)	*oh-per-**ay**-yoh*
	operaia (f.)	*oh-per-**ay**-yah*
writer	scrittore (m.)	*skree-**toh**-reb*
	scrittrice (f.)	*skree-**tree**-cheh*

So, What's Your Story?

To ask someone about their profession, try using the following:

*Qual è la **Sua** professione?*   What is Your profession?

If the other person is a peer and you feel comfortable enough to use the *tu* form, note how the possessive changes:

*Qual è la **tua** professione?*   What is your profession?

La Bella Lingua

If you're lucky enough to be self-employed, you can say, *Lavoro in proprio.*

Or, you can just ask them what they do using the verb *fare* (to do/make):

Che lavoro fa?	What work do You do?

Ecco! You Got It!

The word *ecco* is not what you hear when you scream into a canyon. I'm not talking about Nietzche's *Ecce Homo*, either. An adverb, *ecco* can mean *here* or *there*. *Ecco* can also be used to express understanding or agreement, and it is very similar to the French word *voilà*, meaning *Here it is! Got it!*

Ecco la stazione!	Here's the station!
Ecco Gabriella!	Here's Gabriella! (That's what my friends gleefully say when they see me.)
Eccomi!	Here I am! (That's what I say in response.)

The Least You Need to Know

- The verb *essere* is used to express various states of existence, usually permanent.

- The verb *stare* is generally used to describe a temporary condition such as *how y'all doing?*

- *Avere* (to have) is an important verb that can also be used to express expressions of luck, intention, and opportunity. It is also used as an auxiliary verb.

- *Fare* (to do or make) is used in many idiomatic expressions such as *fare una foto* (to take a photo), *fare un viaggio* (to take a trip) and *fare benzina* (to get gas). *Fare* also allows you to talk about the weather (see Chapter 9).

- Italian professions almost always reflect the gender of the subject.

- Use *ci* or *vi* in lieu of a prepositional phrase.

Chapter 9

Rain or Shine: It's Time to Talk About *Tempo*

In This Chapter

- Telling time
- Using the verb *fare* to talk about the weather and *il clima*
- Making appointments and scheduling time
- *L'astrologia*
- Using the verbs *sapere* and *conoscere*

Talking about *tempo* in Italian requires a little explanation. *Il tempo* refers to the weather, while *l'ora* refers to the hour. In this chapter, you'll learn everything you need to know about the weather, time, and dates. You'll develop the vocabulary you need to schedule an appointment and talk about the climate, the stars, the moon, and *l'astrologia*.

I've also thrown in a couple of extra verbs used to talk about what you know: *sapere* (to know something) and *conoscere* (to know someone, to be acquainted).

Keeping *Tempo*

Time is easy to learn. You need to remember the verb *essere* for asking what time it *is*. You use the verb *sapere* to ask if someone *knows* the time.

You can ask the time in several ways:

Che ore sono?	What time is it?
Che ora è?	What time is it?
Sa l'ora?	Do you know what time it is?

Use the third person of *essere* to respond.

Attenzione!

The Italian word *tempo*, although primarily used when talking about the weather (as in *temperatura*), can also refer to time.

È l'una.	It is 1 o'clock.
È mezzogiorno.	It is noon.
È mezzanotte.	It is midnight.
Sono *le due.*	It is 2 o'clock.
Sono *le nove e mezzo.*	It is 9:30.

If someone is already wearing *un orologio* (a watch) and asks you for the time, there may be a hidden motive behind their request. (Perhaps they want some of your time?) The following expressions will help talk about the time.

Time Expressions

English	Italiano	English	Italiano
What time is it?	Che ore sono? Che ora è?	The time is …	Sono le …
At what time?	A che ora?	an hour	un'ora
a half hour	una mezz'ora	a minute	un minuto
a quarter past	e un quarto	a quarter to	meno un quarto
a second	un secondo	ago	fa
and	e	before/after	prima/dopo
early/late	in anticipo/in ritardo	half past	e mezzo
in	fra	in the afternoon	di pomeriggio
… a while	… un po'	in the evening	di sera
… an hour	… un'ora	in the morning	di mattina
… a half hour	… una mezz'ora	less than/before	meno (le)
on time	in tempo	since	da

Use *è* when it is 1 o'clock. For all other times, because they are plural, use *sono*.

È l'una.	It is 1 o'clock.
Sono le tre.	It is 3 o'clock.

To express time after the hour, use *e* (without the accent, meaning *and*) plus the number of minutes past the hour:

Sono le quattro e dieci.	It is 4:10.
Sono le sei e cinque.	It is 6:05.
È l'una e un quarto.	It is 1:15.

> ### As a *Regola*
>
> When writing down the time, Italian uses a dot and not a colon:
>
> | English | Italian |
> |---|---|
> | 3:30 A.M. | 3.30 *del mattino* or *di mattina* |
> | 9:45 P.M. | 9.45 *di sera* |

To express time before the next hour (in English, we use *ten to*, *quarter to*, and so on), use the next hour + *meno* (less) + whatever time is remaining before the next hour:

Sono le otto meno un quarto.
It is a quarter to eight (literally, eight minus a quarter).

È l'una meno dieci.
It's ten to one (literally, one minus ten).

It is not unusual to hear the time expressed as follows:

Sono le sette e quarantacinque.   It is 7:45.

The following table spells out exactly how to tell the time minute by minute, hour by hour.

Telling Time

English	Italiano
It is 1:00.	È l'una.
It is 2:00.	Sono le due.
It is 2:05.	Sono le due e cinque.
It is 3:10.	Sono le tre e dieci.
It is 4:15.	Sono le quattro e un quarto.
It is 5:20.	Sono le cinque e venti.
It is 6:25.	Sono le sei e venticinque.
It is 6:30.	Sono le sei e trenta.

continues

Telling Time   (continued)

English	Italiano
It is 7:30.	Sono le sette e mezzo.
It is 8:40. (20 minutes to 9)	Sono le nove meno venti.
It is 9:45. (a quarter to 10)	Sono le dieci meno un quarto.
It is 10:50. (10 minutes to 11)	Sono le undici meno dieci.
It is 11:55. (5 minutes to noon)	È mezzogiorno meno cinque.
It is noon.	È mezzogiorno.
It is midnight.	È mezzanotte.

Time Will Tell

Answer the following questions as best you can using complete sentences. Remember that the answer is usually in the question. (You can find the answers in Appendix A.)

Example: *A che ora mangiamo?* (What time do we eat?)

Answer: *Mangiamo alle otto e mezzo.* (We're eating at eight thirty)

1. A che ora andiamo al cinema? (6:00 P.M.) _____

2. A che ora parte il volo? (8:25 A.M.) _____

3. A che ora inizia il programma? (7:00 P.M.) _____

4. Quando c'è l'autobus per Verona? (noon) _____

5. Che ore sono? (4:44 P.M.) _____

6. A che ora c'è il treno per Roma? (2:33 P.M.) _____

7. A che ora andiamo a fare colazione? (7:30 A.M.) _____

Talking About the Weather: *Che Tempo Fa?*

You can use several verbs to talk about *il tempo* (the weather). You'll need the verb *fare*, and you'll see the *ci + essere* combination here, too, as in *c'è il sole* (it's sunny). Some of the information in the following table might be review, and some is new.

Weather Expressions

Italiano	English
Che tempo fa?	What's the weather?
Fa caldo.	It's hot.
Fa freddo.	It's cold.
Fa fresco.	It's cool.
Quanto fa oggi?	What is the temperature today?
Fa trenta gradi.	It's 30° (Celsius).
C'è il sole.	It's sunny.
C'è nebbia.	It's foggy.
C'è un temporale.	There is a storm.
C'è vento.	It's windy.
È nuvoloso.	It's cloudy.
È umido.	It's humid.
È bello.	It's beautiful.
È brutto.	It's bad.
Grandina.	It's hailing.

As a *Regola*

The verbs *piovere* (to rain), *nevicare* (to snow), and *tuonare* (to thunder) are used only in the third person singular.

Piove.	It's raining.
Nevica.	It's snowing.
Tuona.	It's thundering.

Il Clima

There's a lot more out there than *la pioggia* (rain), *il sole* (sun), and *la neve* (snow). How about snowflakes? Rainbows? A personal favorite, *il tramonto* (sunset), literally breaks down to signify *between the mountains*. When it rains in Italy, there are no dogs or cats dropping from the sky; we say *Piove a catinelle*. (It's raining buckets.)

Che Tempo Fa?

English	Italiano	English	Italiano
air	l'aria	Centigrade	grado centigrado
atmosphere	l'atmosfera	climate	il clima (m.)
breeze	la brezza, il venticello	cloud	la nuvola
Fahrenheit	grado Fahrenheit	rainbow	l'arcobaleno
fog	la nebbia	sky	il cielo
frost	la brina	sleet	la pioggia ghiacciata, il nevischio
hail	la grandine	smog	lo smog
humidity	l'umidità	snow	la neve
ice	il ghiaccio	snowball	la palla di neve
lightning bolt	il fulmine, il lampo	snowflake	il fiocco di neve
mud	il fango	sun	il sole
nature	la natura	sunrise	l'alba
ozone	l'ozono	sunset	il tramonto
plain	la pianura	temperature	la temperatura
pollution	l'inquinamento	thermometer	il termometro
rain	la pioggia	wind	il vento

La Bella Lingua

What's the *previsioni del tempo* (forecast)? The next time you're hanging around the fatalists and doomsdayers, impress them with your knowledge of natural disasters, in Italian.

avalanche	*la valanga*	fire	*il fuoco*
calamity	*la calamità*	flood	*l'alluvione*
disaster	*il disastro*	pestilence	*la pestilenza*
earthquake	*il terremoto*	plague	*la peste*
famine	*la carestia*	vulcano	*il vulcano*

Dipinto di Blu

In the song *"Volare"* written by Domenico Modugno, the expression *dipinto di blu* refers to the sky painted blue. Some helpful adjectives used to talk about *il tempo* can be found in the following table.

Describing the Weather

English	Italiano	English	Italiano
calm	sereno	nice	bello
cloudy	nuvoloso	overcast	coperto
cold	freddo	rainy	piovoso
cool	fresco	sky blue	celeste, azzurro
dry	secco	starry	stellato
hot	caldo	tropical	tropicale
humid	umido	ugly	brutto
mild	mite		

La Temperatura: What's Hot and What's Not

To refer to *la temperatura* (the temperature), you use the verb *fare* in the third person, as you do with the weather.

If someone asks, *Quanto fa oggi?* what they're really asking is, "How many degrees (*gradi*) are there today?" The word *gradi* is implied and the use of *fare* in this case is idiomatic.

If it's 20° Centigrade, you simply reply *Fa venti gradi.* (It's 20°.)

If it's 10 *below*, you say *Fa dieci sotto zero.*

As a *Regola*

In Italy, as in all of Europe, the metric system is used to determine the temperature. To convert Centigrade to Fahrenheit, multiply the Centigrade temperature by 1.8 and add 32.

To convert Fahrenheit to Centigrade, subtract 32 from the Fahrenheit temperature and divide the remaining number by 2.

Here are some basic temperature reference points:

- ◆ Freezing: 32°F = 0°C
- ◆ Room temperature: 68°F = 20°C
- ◆ Body temperature: 98.6°F = 37°C
- ◆ Boiling: 212°F = 100°C

Le Quattro Stagioni

Ah! What's nicer than springtime in *Toscana* or a beautiful summer day lounging on the beaches of *Sicilia?* Before you start daydreaming about the seasons in which you'd like to travel, you first need to learn how to refer to *le quattro stagioni* (the four seasons) in Italian.

The Seasons

Italiano	English	Italiano	English
la primavera	spring	l'autunno	autumn
l'estate (f.)	summer	l'inverno	winter

> ### La Bella Lingua
>
> In Italy, *il ferragosto* refers to the mid-August holidays many Italians take during the hot, humid month. If you're planning a trip during this time, don't be surprised to find many of the smaller businesses closed for *le ferie* (the holidays).

When talking about *in* a particular season, Italian uses both the prepositions *in* and *di*.

Fa freddo **d'**inverno?   Is the winter cold?

Piove **in** primavera.   It rains in spring.

It's a Date!

To talk about the date requires a particular order. (Consult Chapter 3 for a review of the days of the week and months.) Often this simply means that, in Italian, you must place the day *before* the month—for example, *5 settembre* (September 5).

In addition, you should know that when Italians talk about *il Cinquecento* (literally, the five hundred), they are actually referring to the sixteenth century (and not the year 500).

Talking About *i Mesi*

With the exception of the *first* day of the month, dates in Italian require cardinal numbers (1, 2, 3, …). As indicated previously, in Italian the day must come before the month. This is not difficult to realize when you're talking about *il 25 dicembre* (December 25), but with some dates it can get tricky. For example, if you wrote the abbreviation 4/5, in Italian it would be read as the fourth of May. If you meant the fifth of April, you were off by almost a month! It's crucial that you remember to reverse the two numbers when dealing with any kinds of documents, such as a car lease or apartment contract. Or avoid this problem altogether and always be sure to write out the month.

In Italian, you must always put the definite article in front of the day, after which comes the month. Unless beginning a sentence, months are not capitalized.

il 25 (venticinque) giugno   June 25

il tre ottobre   October 3

What Century?

Talking about centuries can be confusing in both English and Italian. For example, in English when you talk about the *third century*, you're really talking about the century before (200–299). Additionally, you're using an *ordinal* number (first, second, third, …).

Italian, on the other hand, always uses cardinal numbers (1, 2, 3 …), unless referring to the *first* (day, month, year).

A.D.

The basis for today's calendar finds its roots in Christianity. As you probably know, the abbreviation A.D. comes from Latin and literally stands for *Anno Domini*, meaning *in the year of the Lord*. In writing, the Italian language uses both the Latin abbreviation A.D. and the Italian abbreviation D.C. (from *dopo Cristo*, meaning *after Christ*) to express time *after* the birth of Christ. (When speaking, the tendency is to use the words *dopo Cristo*.)

In Italian, to talk about dates from 1 A.D. *until* the year 1000 A.D., you must use cardinal numbers plus the words *dopo Cristo* (D.C.).

79 D.C.   *Il Vesuvio distrusse Pompei.*
79 A.D.   Vesuvius destroyed Pompei.

You might also see *anno domini* or the abbreviation A.D. written on monuments and tombstones.

121–180 D.C.   *Marco Aurelio, Imperatore*
121–180 A.D.   Marcus Aurelius, Emperor

As a general rule, you don't need to use A.D. for dates after the year 1000. Keep in mind that current terms used in English now include B.C.E. (before Common Era) and C.E. (in the Common Era).

B.C.

To express time *before* the birth of Christ (B.C.), as in 400 B.C., Italian uses the abbreviation *A.C.* (from *avanti Cristo*, meaning *before Christ*).

753 *A.C.*	*La fondazione di Roma*
753 B.C.	The foundation of Rome
106–43 *A.C.*	*Cicero, oratore*
106–43 B.C.	Cicero, orator

To talk about the year 1965, you would say it like any other number: *millenovecentosessantacinque* (one thousand nine hundred sixty-five).

1,000 Years Later

To express centuries *after* the year 1000, it gets a little tricky. To talk about the sixteenth century (1500–1599) like an Italian, you must omit the first thousand and say *il Cinquecento* (the five hundred). There is no need to indicate that this occurred after the birth of Christ.

However, it is also possible to use an ordinal number (first, second, third, …) when referring to centuries, as in *il quindicesimo secolo* (the fifteenth century).

In writing, the apostrophe before the number shows that it is after the year 1000.

'100—*La Crociata*	
1100—the Crusades	
'300–'600—*Il Rinascimento*	
1300–1600—the Renaissance	

Everything in Good Time

When discussing time, Italians often refer to the *periodo* as opposed to the specific date. I've included a few of the more important historical and artistic periods used when discussing *la storia* (history).

etrusco	Etruscan	*il Rinasciamento*	the Renaissance
ellenistico	Greek	*Barocco e Roccocò*	Baroque and Rococo
romano	Roman	*il Risorgimento*	Italy's unification
bizantino	Byzantine	*Novecento*	Twentieth century
Mediovale	Medieval		

Do You Have *un Appuntamento?*

In Italian, you make an *appuntamento* to meet people, whether it's social or business related. The following table offers some helpful time-related words. If you're planning a more romantic event, refer to the vocabulary in Chapter 19 for some up-to-date love lingo. I've given the Italian terms along with the appropriate definite articles. Remember to slide the different syllables together making sure to emphasize double consonants in words like *anno* (year).

It's a Date

English	Italiano	Pronunciation
afternoon	il pomeriggio	*eel poh-meh-**ree**-joh*
appointment	l'appuntamento	*lah-poon-tah-**men**-toh*
calendar	il calendario	*eel kah-len-**dah**-ree-yoh*
century	il secolo	*eel **seh**-koh-loh*
date	la data	*lah dah-tah*
day	il giorno	*eel jor-noh*
decade	il decennio	*eel deh-**chen**-nee-yoh*
evening	la sera	*lah seh-rah*
holiday	la festa	*lah fes-tah*
millennium	il millennio	*eel meel-**leh**-nee-yoh*
month	il mese	*eel meh-zeh*
morning	la mattina	*lah maht-**tee**-nah*
week	la settimana	*lah set-tee-**mah**-nah*
year	l'anno	*lahn-noh*

About Last Night

This year, last year, the day before, the day after—all of these times have significance. Was it good for you, too? The following table offers you some helpful *vocabolario* you'll find useful when talking about the past. You'll learn how to talk about the past in Chapter 16.

About Last Night

English	Italiano	Pronunciation
ago	fa	*fah*
every (day)	ogni (giorno)	*oh-nyee (jor-noh)*
in (two weeks)	fra (due settimane)	*frah (doo-weh seht-tee-__mah__-neh)*
last night	ieri notte	*yeh-ree noht-teh*
last year	l'anno scorso	*lahn-noh skor-soh*
next	prossimo	*__proh__-see-moh*
this evening	stasera*	*stah-__seh__-rah*
this morning	stamattina*	*stah-maht-__tee__-nah*
today	oggi	*oh-jee*
tomorrow	domani	*doh-__mah__-nee*
yesterday	ieri	*yeh-ree*
yesterday evening	ieri sera	*yeh-ree seh-rah*

*Note: The terms stamattina *and* stasera *are abbreviated from* questa mattina *and* questa sera.

La Bella Lingua

When referring to the day after tomorrow, Italians use *dopodomani* (literally, after tomorrow). To talk about the day before yesterday, Italians use *l'altro ieri* (literally, the other yesterday).

The Dating Game

How do you express the following? Remember that adjectives must agree with the nouns they modify. Nouns must always reflect number. (You can find the answers in Appendix A.)

Example: Last week   Answer: *La settimana scorsa*

Example: Three years ago   Answer: *Tre anni fa*

1. Last month_____

2. Last year _____

3. Next year _____

4. In 10 years _____

5. Last spring _____

6. Next winter _____

7. Seven years ago _____

8. Last night _____

9. Yesterday evening _____

10. This morning _____

How Often?

Some events occur once in a lifetime, whereas others reoccur, such as your birthday or getting your daily newspaper. The following terms may come in handy.

How Often?

English	Italiano	Pronunciation
annual	annuale	*ahn*-noo-ah-leh
biannual	biennale	bee-eh-*nah*-leh
bimonthly	bimestrale	bee-meh-*strah*-leh
biweekly	bisettimanale	bee-set-tee-mah-*nah*-leh
centennial	centenario	chen-teh-*nah*-ree-yoh
daily	quotidiano	kwoh-tee-dee-*ah*-noh
monthly	mensile	men-*see*-leh
quarterly	trimestrale	tree-meh-*strah*-leh
weekly	settimanale	set-tee-mah-*nah*-leh

Quando Quando Quando?

See how well you can answer the following questions. I've given you the first part.

1. *Quando è il tuo compleanno?* (When is your birthday?)

   Il mio compleanno è …

2. *Quando vai in vacanza?* (When are you going on vacation?)

   Vado in vacanza il …

3. *Quando è Natale?* (When is Christmas?)

   Natale è …

From What Realm Are You?

It is said by some that if you reach for *le stelle*, you might even arrive at *la luna*. But how would da Vinci or Galileo discuss such ethereal topics? Although it ends in *-a*, the Italian word for planet is masculine, as in *il pianeta*.

La Bella Lingua

Whether you're into *l'astronomia* or *l'astrologia*, the following words will help you stargaze from anywhere.

astrology	*l'astrologia*	sun	*il sole*
astronomy	*l'astronomia*	universe	*l'universo*
constellation	*la costellazione*	Big Dipper	*l'Orsa Maggiore*
galaxy	*la galassia*	Little Dipper	*l'Orsa Minore*
moon	*la luna*	Milky Way	*la Via Lattea*
star (stars)	*la stella (le stelle)*		

Planets

Planet	Il Pianeta	Planet	Il Pianeta
Mercury	Mercurio	Saturn	Saturno
Venus	Venere	Uranus	Urano
Earth	Terra	Neptune	Nettuno
Mars	Marte	Pluto	Plutone
Jupiter	Giove		

What's Your Sign?

If the weather isn't your thing, you can go to another planet and ask about someone's background—astrologically speaking. Find out if you are compatible by asking someone *Che segno sei?* (What's your sign?)

Astrological Signs

Simbolo	Segno	Elemento	Caratteristiche	Periodo	English
♈	ariete	fuoco	indipendente, aggressivo, impulsivo	21 marzo–19 aprile	Aries
♉	toro	terra	determinato, testardo, fedele, tollerante	20 aprile–20 maggio	Taurus
♊	gemelli	aria	intelligente, ambizioso, capriccioso	21 maggio–21 giugno	Gemini

Simbolo	Segno	Elemento	Caratteristiche	Periodo	English
♋	cancro	acqua	sensibile, simpatico, impressionabile	22 giugno–22 luglio	Cancer
♌	leone	fuoco	generoso, nobile, entusiasta	23 luglio–22 agosto	Leo
♍	vergine	terra	intellettuale, passivo, metodico	23 agosto–22 settembre	Virgo
♎	bilancia	aria	giusto, organizzato, simpatico	23 settembre–23 ottobre	Libra
♏	scorpione	acqua	filosofo, fedele, dominante	24 ottobre–21 novembre	Scorpio
♐	sagittario	fuoco	pragmatico, maturo, creativo	22 novembre–21 dicembre	Sagittarius
♑	capricorno	terra	ambizioso, fedele, perseverante	22 dicembre–19 gennaio	Capricorn
♒	acquario	aria	generoso, idealista, originale	20 gennaio–18 febbraio	Aquarius
♓	pesci	acqua	timido, simpatico, sensibile	19 febbraio–20 marzo	Pisces

It's Good to Know

Two verbs are equivalent to the English verb *to know*: *sapere* (to know something) and *conoscere* (to know someone; to be acquainted). You may already be familiar with the expression *non lo so* (I don't know).

La Bella Lingua

If someone asks you a question you don't know the answer to, shrug your shoulders and say, *"Chi sa?"* (Who knows?) or *"Non lo so."* (I don't know.)

Sapere: To Know Something

The irregular verb *sapere* is what you use to talk about all the information you have stuck inside that head of yours. Synonyms include *la sapienza* (knowledge) and consapevole (aware, conscious).

Sapere

Italiano	English	Italiano	English
io **so**	I know	noi **sappiamo**	we know
tu **sai**	you know	voi **sapete**	you know
lui/lei/Lei **sa**	he/she knows; You know	loro **sanno**	they know

Conoscere: To Know Someone/To Be Acquainted

The regular verb *conoscere* is generally used to talk about someone with whom you are acquainted, but you can also use it when referring to a city or place, or even *una lingua*. Even though it's regular, I think this verb is especially important. Synonyms include *conoscente* (acquaintance) and *conoscenza* (knowledge/acquaintance).

Conoscere

Italiano	English	Italiano	English
io **conosco**	I know	noi **conosciamo**	we know
tu **conosci**	you know	voi **conoscete**	you know
lui/lei/Lei **conosce**	he/she knows; You know	loro **conoscono**	they know

The Least You Need to Know

◆ To express the date, use the number of the day plus the month and the year.

◆ Use the words *dopo Cristo* to describe a historical event that occurred after the death of Christ but before the beginning of the second millennium; use *avanti Cristo* to describe an event before the birth of Christ. In English, to be P.C., however, you should use C.E. (common era) or B.C.E. (before common era).

- Telling time is easy; remember the key words *meno* (less than) and *e* (and).

- Use the third person of the verb *fare* (*fa*) to express weather conditions and the temperature, and use it for idiomatic expressions.

- The verb *sapere* is used to talk about *what* you know.

- The verb *conoscere* is used to talk about *who* you know. *Capisci?*

Chapter 10

Buon Viaggio: Travel Terms and the Imperative

In This Chapter

♦ The modes of transportation you'll use in *Italia*

♦ Asking what, when, where, and how much in Italian

♦ Essential travel terms, verbs, and *espressioni*

♦ Prepositions and contractions tie it all together

♦ Using the verbs *andare* (to go) and *salire* (to get on, go up)

This chapter gives you all the *vocabolario* you need to be as *indipendente* as *possibile* and the means to *navigare* through just about any travel challenge.

If you're in a major city like New York or Washington, you can visit your local Italian consulate, embassy, or tourist board to gather free maps, pamphlets, and travel guides. You can also find out who is doing business in your field. You may be permitted to leave your company's promotional materials with them.

I Mezzi Pubblici: Public Transportation

In Italy, public transportation is quite efficient, with buses, trains, and *la metro* (subway) to take you just about anywhere you want to go. It's a good idea to purchase bus tickets at a *cartoleria* or *tabacchi* to keep in your wallet because buses do not accept cash or coins. You can also buy *biglietti* (tickets) at train stations and from automated machines using your *carta di credito*. After you get on *l'autobus*, you must *convalidare* your ticket by punching it into a small box located on the back of the bus. Hold on to your ticket in case of a surprise check by stern-faced inspectors eager to find transgressions. When using *la metro*, you must also buy a ticket either from one of the automated machines or from a ticket booth. It's possible to buy daily, weekly, and monthly tickets.

Asking Questions

No one knows everything. The curious mind wants to understand, so it needs to ask questions. In Italian, it is very easy to ask a question. This section shows you how to ask basic questions. You'll also see more questions related to asking for directions in Chapter 12.

The Tags *Vero? No?* and *Giusto?*

Another way to ask a simple yes or no *domanda* (question) is to add the tags *vero?* (true? or right?), *no?* and *giusto?* (is that so? or is that correct?) to the end of a sentence:

Partiamo alle otto, no?	We're leaving at 8, no?
Capisci la lezione, vero?	You understand the lesson, right?

And the *Risposta* Is ...

To answer a question affirmatively (yes), use *sì* and give your *risposta* (response).

To answer a question negatively (no), use *no* attached to *non* before the conjugated verb form. This is equivalent to the English *don't*, as in *No, I don't smoke*.

Question	Affirmative Answer	Negative Answer
Lei fuma le sigarette? Do you smoke cigarettes?	*Sì, fumo le sigarette.* Yes, I smoke cigarettes.	*No, **non** fumo le sigarette.* No, I don't smoke cigarettes.
Capisci la lezione? Do you understand the lesson?	*Sì, capisco la lezione.* Yes, I understand the lesson.	*No, **non** capisco la lezione.* No, I don't understand the lesson.

A Whole Lot of *Niente*

If you are answering a question and starting your sentence with *no*, these negative expressions generally come directly after the conjugated verb. Try to determine the meaning of these examples. If you have difficulty determining the significance of the verbs, find the stem of the verb and use the charts to find the infinitive form.

Italiano	English	Example
mai	never	Non fumo **mai.**
niente	nothing	Non desidero **niente.***
nulla	nothing	Non compra **nulla.***
nessuno	no one	Nessuno **arriva.**

*Unlike English, Italian allows for double negatives.

Which One?

The interrogative pronoun and adjective *quale* means *which* or *what* and is also used to ask questions. There are two forms: *quale* (which one), and *quali* (which ones).

> *Ecco i libri; quale preferisce?*
> Here are the books; which do you prefer?
>
> *Quali sono gli autobus per il centro?*
> What are the buses (going) downtown?

Qual è …? expresses the question *What is …?*

> *Qual è il tuo numero di telefono?*
> What is your telephone number?

> **La Bella Lingua**
>
> *Quale* refers to a choice between two or more alternatives. *Che* (what) can be substituted for *quale* in almost any given situation: *Quale (che) ristorante avete scelto?* (Which restaurant did you choose?)

On the Road

Italy's *autostrade* are among the best in the world, but *le macchine* move pretty fast (often drivers do not abide by the speed limit), so keep in the right lane unless you're prepared to speed.

Inside la *Macchina*

English	Italiano	Pronunciation
accelerator	l'acceleratore	*lah-cheh-leh-rah-**toh**-reh*
air conditioning	l'aria condizionata	*lah-ree-yah kohn-dee-zee-oh-**nah**-tah*
brakes	i freni	*ee freh-nee*
dashboard	il cruscotto	*eel kroo-**skoh**-toh*
gear stick	il cambio	*eel **kahm**-bee-yoh*
glove compartment	il vano portaoggetti	*eel vah-noh por-tah-oh-**jeh**-tee*
handbrake	il freno a mano	*eel freh-noh ah mah-noh*
horn	il clacson	*eel klak-son*
ignition	l'accensione	*lah-**chen**-see-oh-neh*
keys	le chiavi	*leh kee-**ah**-vee*
radio	la radio	*lah **rah**-dee-oh*
rear-view mirror	il retrovisore	*eel reh-troh-vee-**zoh**-reh*
speed limit	il limite di velocità	*eel **lee**-mee-teh dee veh-loh-chee-**tah***
speedometer	il tachimetro	*eel tah-**kee**-met-roh*
steering wheel	il volante	*eel voh-**lahn**-teh*
turn signal	la freccia	*lah freh-chah*

Behind the Wheel

The following phrases will help you get some wheels:

Vorrei noleggiare una macchina.
I would like to rent a car.

Preferisco una macchina con il cambio automatico.
I prefer a car with automatic transmission.

Quanto costa al giorno (alla settimana/al chilometro)?
How much does it cost per day (per week/per kilometer)?

Quanto costa l'assicurazione per l'auto?
How much does automobile insurance cost?

Quale tipo di pagamento preferite?
What form of payment do you prefer?

Accettate carte di credito?
Do you accept credit cards?

La Bella Lingua

There are several types of roads in Italy:

- ◆ **L'autostrada:** Just like the throughway, expect to pay high tolls on these fast-paced lanes.

- ◆ **La superstrada:** Like a local highway, these roads are well maintained and can be quite scenic.

- ◆ **La statale:** This state road is slower than a *superstrada* but faster than the *strada comunale.*

- ◆ **La strada comunale:** On these local roads, watch out for slow-moving tractors and the occasional flock of sheep.

Automobile Parts

If you've decided to rent *una macchina*, carefully inspect it inside and out. Make sure there is *il cricco* or *cric* (a jack) and *la ruota di scorta* (a spare tire) in the trunk, in case you get a *gomma a terra* (flat tire)—and it doesn't hurt to check for any preexisting damages you could later be charged for.

The following table gives you the Italian words for car parts and predicaments. You never know—that cherry-red Ferrari you rent could turn out to be a *limone*.

Automobile Parts and Predicaments

English	Italiano	Pronunciation
antenna	l'antenna	*lahn-**teh**-nah*
battery	la batteria	*lah bah-teh-**ree**-yah*
breakdown	un guasto	*oon gwah-stoh*
carburetor	il carburatore	*eel kar-boor-ah-**toh**-reh*
door	la portiera	*lah por-tee-**yeh**-rah*
door handle	la maniglia	*lah mah-**nee**-lyah*
fan belt	la cinghia del ventilatore	*lah **cheen**-ghee-yah del ven-tee-lah-**toh**-reh*
fender	il parafango	*eel pah-rah-**fahn**-goh*
filter	il filtro	*eel feel-troh*
flat tire	una gomma a terra	*oo-nah goh-mah ah ter-rah*
	una ruota bucata	*oo-noh rwoh-tah boo-**kah**-tah*
fuse	un fusibile	*oon foo-**see**-bee-leh*
gas tank	il serbatoio	*eel ser-bah-**toy**-oh*

continues

Automobile Parts and Predicaments (continued)

English	Italiano	Pronunciation
headlights	i fari	*ee fah-ree*
hood	il cofano	*eel koh-**fah**-noh*
license	la patente	*lah pah-**ten**-teh*
license plate	la targa	*lah tar-gah*
motor	il motore	*eel moh-**toh**-reh*
muffler	la marmitta	*lah mar-**mee**-tah*
radiator	il radiatore	*eel rah-dee-yah-**toh**-reh*
sign	il segnale	*eel sen-**yah**-leh*
spark plug	la candela d'accensione	*lah kahn-**deh**-lah dah-chen-see-oh-neh*
tail light	la luce di posizione	*lah loo-cheh dee poh-zee-zee-**oh**-neh*
tire	la ruota	*lah rwoh-tah*
traffic officer	il/la vigile	*eel/lah **vee**-jee-leh*
trunk	il bagagliaio	*eel bah-gahl-**yiy**-yoh*
window	il finestrino	*eel fee-neh-**stree**-noh*
windshield	il parabrezza	*eel pah-rah-**breh**-zah*
windshield wiper	il tergicristallo	*eel ter-jee-kree-**stah**-loh*

The Road Less Traveled

The following table contains more useful verbs and expressions related to travel on the road.

La Bella Lingua
Tools are the last thing you think of when learning a second language, but if you're stranded, the following might be helpful:

Pliers (*le pinze*)   screwdriver (*il cacciavite*)

Hammer (*il martello*)   monkey wrench (*la chiave inglese*)

Macchina Speak

English	Italiano	English	Italiano
to break down	guastarsi	to get gas	fare benzina
to change a tire	cambiare la ruota	to get a ticket	prendere una multa
to check	controllare	to give a ride	dare un passaggio
… the water	… l'acqua	to go	andare
… the oil	… l'olio	to obey traffic signs	rispettare i segnali
… the tires	… le ruote	to park	parcheggiare
to drive	guidare	to run/function	funzionare
to fill it up	fare il pieno	to run out of gas	rimanere senza benzina

More Travel Verbs and Expressions

You'll be surprised to see how quickly you begin to understand the following, even if it all seems like a lot of gobbledygook.

La Bella Lingua	
Follow the signs!	
Deviazione	Detour
Divieto di Ingresso	No Entrance
Divieto di Sorpasso	No Passing
Divieto di Sosta	No Parking
Sosta Autorizzata	Parking Permitted
Doppio Senso	Two-Way Traffic
Senso Unico	One-Way Traffic

Viaggio Speak

English	Italiano	English	Italiano
to be (running) late	essere in ritardo	to leave	partire
to be (running) early	essere in anticipo	to miss, to lose	perdere
to be (running) on time	essere in orario	to return	tornare, ritornare
to change	cambiare	to stop	fermare
to commute	fare il pendolare	to take	prendere

continues

Viaggio Speak   (continued)

English	Italiano	English	Italiano
to get on	salire su	to turn around	tornare indietro
to get off	scendere da		

What, When, and How Much: Questions

In Italy, schedules are given in military time. If you are leaving at 2 P.M., for example, you are told 14:00 hours. This may be tricky at first, so confirm that you have understood correctly by asking if it is A.M. (*di mattino*) or P.M. (*di sera*).

The following table contains a list of words and expressions that will help you get what you want, find out where you want to go, and meet the people you would like to know.

Information Questions

English	Italiano	Pronunciation
how	come	*koh-meh*
how much	quanto	*kwahn-toh*
what	che cosa (can be broken up as *che* or *cosa*)	*kay koh-zah*
what time	a che ora	*ah kay oh-rah*
when	quando	*kwahn-doh*
where	dove	*doh-veh*
where is …?	dov'è …?	*doh-veh*
who	chi	*kee*
why	perché	*per-kay*

Questions, Questions

It's easy to ask questions in Italian. You don't even have to change the word order. Just take any phrase (following the usual rules of conjugation), and instead of making it sound like a statement, raise the intonation of your voice at the end of the phrase. Try practicing with the following two examples. Note that they are exactly the same phrase, but pronounced differently:

◆ As a statement:

Questo treno va a Roma. (This train goes to Rome.)

◆ As a question:

Questo treno va a Roma? (Does this train go to Rome?)

When asking a question using the word *dove* (where) with the third person of the verb *essere* (*è*), you must form a contraction, as in *dov'è* (where's), to avoid a double vowel and maintain the flow of the pronunciation.

Con chi viaggia Lei?	With whom are you traveling? (polite)
A che ora apre il museo?	At what hour does the museum open?
Quando c'è il treno per Roma?	When is the train for Rome?
Dov'è la fermata dell'autobus?	Where is the bus stop?
Quanto costa?	How much does this cost?
Di dov'è Lei?	Where are you from? (polite)
Di dove sei?	Where are you from? (informal)
Per quanto tempo state in Italia?	For how long are you in Italy? (you, plural)
C'è un ospedale qui vicino?	Is there a hospital nearby?
Ci sono molti turisti a quest'ora?	Are there many tourists at this hour?

Ask Away

What can you learn by reading the following biographical information about Cinzia and Signor Pesce? What questions might you ask someone to learn more about them? (The translation can be found in Appendix A.)

Mi chiamo Cinzia Bell e abito negli Stati Uniti. Sono una studentessa. Studio storia dell'arte. Viaggio in macchina con la mia amica in Italia. Passiamo un mese in Italia. Andiamo a visitare tutte le città importanti. Ritorno all'università a settembre.

Mi chiamo Mario Pesce e sono un bancario. Non parlo l'inglese molto bene. Abito a Milano con mia moglie. Abbiamo due figli, Giorgio e Isabella. A dicembre vado con mia moglie a New York.

All Aboard

You'll learn these terms quickly because they are essential to traveling through Italy.

Get Your *Biglietti* Ready

English	Italiano	Pronunciation
bus	l'autobus	*low-toh-bus*
bus stop	la fermata dell'autobus	*lah fer-**mah**-tah dow-toh-boos*
connection	la coincidenza	*lah koh-een-chee-**den**-zah*
information	l'ufficio informazioni	*loo-**fee**-choh een-for-mah-zee-**oh**-nee*
taxi	il tassì	*eel tah-**see***
train	il treno	*eel treh-noh*
... by train (railway)	... per ferrovia	*per feh-roh-**vee**-yah*
... train station	... la stazione ferroviaria	*lah stah-zee-**oh**-neh feh-roh-vee-**yah**-ree-ah*
ticket	il biglietto	*eel beel-**yeh**-toh*
... round-trip ticket	... il biglietto di andata e ritorno	*... dee ahn-**dah**-tah eh ree-**tor**-noh*
... one-way ticket	... il biglietto di corsa semplice	*... dee kor-sah **sem**-plee-cheh*
... first/second class	... di prima/seconda classe	*... dee pree-mah/seh-**kohn**-dah klah-seh*
ticket counter	la biglietteria	*lah beel-yeh-teh-**ree**-yah*
schedule	l'orario, la tabella	*loh-**rah**-ree-oh, lah tah-**beh**-lah*
track	il binario	*eel bee-**nah**-ree-oh*
waiting room	la sala d'aspetto	*lah sah-lah dah-**speh**-toh*
seat	il sedile/il posto	*eel seh-**dee**-leh/eel pohs-toh*
window	il finestrino	*eel fee-neh-**stree**-noh*

Here are some other handy phrases:

Vorrei un biglietto di andata e ritorno.	I would like a round-trip ticket.
Dov'è la fermata dell'autobus?	Where is the bus stop?
C'è la coincidenza?	Is there a connection?
A che ora parte il treno?	At what times does the train leave?
I voli sono in orario.	The planes (are running) on time.

Partiamo subito.	We're leaving immediately.
Da quale binario parte il treno?	On what track does the train leave?
Prenda quest'autobus.	Take this bus.
C'è un posto vicino al finestrino?	Is there a seat near the window?
Posso aprire il finestrino?	May I open the window?

La Bella Lingua

There's nothing more *romantico* than riding along *la costa* by *ferrovia* (railway, coming from *ferro*, meaning *iron*, and *via*, meaning *way*). Italian trains are generally well maintained, inexpensive, and comfortable. They are by far one of the best ways to get around and meet Italians (and practice your Italian!). There are several kinds of trains used within Italy, some of which require reservations:

◆ *Diretto:* This train actually takes the longest route because it makes the most local stops.

◆ *ES (Eurostar): Eurostar* is the fastest way to get between major European cities. Designed like a bullet, this train costs more and requires *una prenotazione*, but is well worth the extra money if time is an issue.

◆ *IC (Inter City):* This train offers passengers an economical way of getting from one *città* to another.

◆ *Regionale:* Like a *diretto*, this local train weaves its way into the smallest of villages.

Getting On with *Salire*

The irregular verb *salire* (to climb) is used to get on, mount, and go up. Use it to get on the bus or train.

CAUTION

Attenzione!

Remember to *validare* your ticket before boarding the train; otherwise, you could end up paying a fine.

The Verb *Salire*

Italiano	English	Italiano	English
io **salgo**	I climb	noi **saliamo**	we climb
tu **sali**	you climb	voi **salite**	you climb
lui/lei/Lei **sale**	he/she climbs; You climb	loro **salgono**	they climb

Going Crazy: The Verb *Andare*

The verb *andare* (to go) can come in handy as you make your way around. This is an irregular verb, so you will need to memorize the parts outlined in the following table. (You can cram on the seven-hour plane ride.)

The Verb *Andare*

Italiano	English	Italiano	English
io **vado**	I go	noi **andiamo**	we go
tu **vai**	you go	voi **andate**	you go
lui/lei/Lei **va**	he/she goes; You go	loro **vanno**	they go

Expressions of Leisure

Italiano	English
Andiamo …	Let's go … (see Chapter 10)
… al mare.	… to the seashore.
… all'estero.	… abroad.
… in giro.	… around, on tour.
… in campagna.	… to the country.
… in montagna.	… to the mountains.
… in vacanza.	… on vacation.

Andiamo al mare quest'estate.
We are going to the seashore this summer.

Siamo in vacanza il mese d'agosto.
We are on vacation for the month of August.

Facciamo il campeggio in montagna.
We are camping in the mountains.

Give Your Mind a Trip

You're familiar with all these words but may not have seen them used in these idiomatic expressions related to *la vacanza*. Match up the Italian and English sentences. (You can find the answers in Appendix A.)

1. essere in ferie	a) to take a cruise
2. essere in vacanza	b) to take a trip
3. fare il campeggio	c) to be on holiday
4. fare un viaggio	d) to party, to celebrate
5. fare una crociera	e) to be on vacation
6. fare una vacanza	f) to go camping
7. festeggiare	g) to take a vacation

> **As a *Regola***
>
> You use the preposition *a* when you want to express going to or staying in a city: *Vado a Roma.* (I'm going to Rome.)
>
> The preposition *in* is generally used when you are traveling to a country: *Andiamo in Italia.* (We are going to Italy.)

Andare is generally followed by the preposition *a* (to), as it usually is in English (I am going to …) when you want to say you're going somewhere or going to do something. Often, you must create a contraction when using the preposition *a* with a definite article. (You'll learn about contractions later in this chapter.)

> **Attenzione!**
>
> When using the verb *andare* to say you are going *by foot*, you use the preposition *a* (*not* in): *Vado a piedi.* (I am going by foot.)

Vado all'università.	I am going to the university.
Andiamo al ristorante.	We're going to the restaurant.
Andate a mangiare?	Are you going to eat?

Note that the Italians often say *Andiamo!* much in the same way we say *Let's go!*

Andare may also be followed by the preposition *in* (to) when describing means of transportation. Naturally, you'll still have to conjugate the infinitive verb:

andare in macchina	to go by car
andare in bicicletta	to go by bicycle
andare in treno	to go by train
andare in aeroplano	to go by plane

Going, Going, Gone

Fill in the appropriate form of *andare*. (You can find the answers in Appendix A.)

1. Luisa e Marta _____ in macchina all'aeroporto.

2. Io _____ a New York.

3. Tu _____ alla stazione.

4. Roberto ed io _____ a mangiare una pizza.

5. Voi _____ a piedi. Loro _____ in bicicletta.

All Verbed Up and Everywhere to Go

The regular verb *prendere* (to take) is used when traveling. If necessary, refer to Chapter 8 for a review of how to conjugate regular *-ere* verbs. Together with the irregular verb *andare*, use the two verbs in the following sentences. Remember that the gerund form in English is equivalent to the simple present in Italian. (You can find the answers in Appendix A.)

1. *(Io) _____ l'autobus per andare in centro. (prendere)*
   I am taking the bus to get downtown.

2. *(Noi) _____ in macchina in spiaggia. (andare)*
   We are going by car to the beach.

3. *(Loro) _____ il treno da Roma per arrivare a Milano. (prendere)*
   They are taking the train from Rome to get to Milan.

4. *(Tu) _____ a piedi al negozio. (andare)*
   You are going by foot to the store.

5. *(Voi) _____ la metro per arrivare alla piramide in Via Ostiense. (prendere)*
   You (plural) are taking the subway to get to the pyramid on Via Ostiense.

6. *(Lui) _____ in bicicletta a vedere la campagna. (andare)*
   He is going by bicycle to see the country.

Practice Those Conjugations

Try conjugating these travel-related regular verbs. You've been given the first person *(io)* to get you started:

andare (to go)	vado …
chiedere (to ask)	chiedo …
prendere (to take)	prendo …
prenotare (to reserve)	prenoto …
ritornare (to return)	ritorno …
salire (to get on; go up)	salgo …
scendere (to get off)	scendo …

Prepositions: Sticky Stuff

You've used these words thousands of times and probably never knew they were all prepositions. You've already seen a lot of prepositions because they are the glue of a *frase* and tie the words together. The following table provides a comprehensive list of Italian prepositions and their meanings.

What's What

The most commonly used prepositions follow:

a (to, at)	Andiamo a Roma.	We're going to Rome.
con (with)	Vado con Roberto.	I am going with Robert.
da (from, by)	Vengo da lontano.	I'm coming from far away.
di (of, from)	Di dove sei?	Where are you from?
in (in, to)	Viaggiano in Italia.	They are traveling to Italy.
per (for)	Questo regalo è per te.	This present is for you.
su (on)	Il libro sta sulla scrivania.	The book is on the table.

Prepositions

Italiano	English	Italiano	English
a	to, at, in	eccetto	except, save
accanto a	beside	fino a	until, as far as
attorno a	around	fra, tra	between, among, in, within
avanti	in front of, before, ahead	fuori di	outside
circa	about, around (when making an estimation)	in	in, into, by, on
con	with	lontano da	far from
contro	against, opposite to	oltre	besides, beyond
da	from, by	per	for, in order to
davanti a	before	senza	without
dentro a	inside	sopra	above
di	of, from, about	sotto	under
dietro a	behind	su	on, upon
dopo	after	vicino a	near

A Few Points on Prepositions

Prepositions in Italian can be a bit tricky. Does the Italian preposition *in* mean *to* or *by* or *in*? Does *a* mean *at* or *in*? Here are a few general rules about the most commonly used prepositions, all of which can be used to form contractions (I'll get to those next).

◆ The preposition *a* (at, to, in) is used with cities and towns. It is also used after many infinitive verbs

◆ The preposition *da* (from, at, by) is used to express when you've been *at* somewhere, whether an office, the doctor's, or far away.

◆ The preposition *di* (of, from, about) is also used to express possession and is used in many idiomatic expressions.

◆ The preposition *in* (at, in, to) is used before the names of countries, when talking about modes of transportation, and when talking about what street you live *on*.

La Bella Lingua

There is no equivalent to the preposition *on* before the names of days:

Arriviamo lunedì.	We are arriving (on) Monday.
Giuseppe arriva sabato.	Giuseppe is arriving (on) Saturday.

Contractions

No one is having a baby here. A *contraction*, in linguistic terms, is a single word made out of two words. The prepositions in the following table form contractions when followed by a definite article. Notice that the endings remain the same as the definite article. A contraction can be as simple as *alla* (to the) or *sul* (on the).

Contractions

	Masculine				Feminine			
Preposition	**Singular**		**Plural**		**Singular**		**Plural**	
	il	**lo**	**l'**	**i**	**gli**	**la**	**l'**	**le**
a	al	allo	all'	ai	agli	alla	all'	alle
in	nel	nello	nell'	nei	negli	nella	nell'	nelle

Preposition	Masculine				Feminine			
	Singular		Plural		Singular		Plural	
di	del	dello	dell'	dei	degli	della	dell'	delle
su	sul	sullo	sull'	sui	sugli	sulla	sull'	sulle
da	dal	dallo	dall'	dai	dagli	dalla	dall'	dalle

As a *Regola*

To express *in* with months, Italians use either the preposition *in* or *a*:

*Il mio compleanno è **a** giugno.*   My birthday is in June.

*Fa ancora freddo **in** marzo.*   It's still cold in March.

To express the notion of being *in* with seasons, Italians use either the preposition *in* or *di*:

*Andiamo in Italia **d'**inverno.*   We are going to Italy in the winter.

***In** primavera fa bello.*   It's beautiful in the spring.

Switcharoo

Replace the bold words with the words in parentheses, changing the preposition or contraction as necessary. Accommodate any changes in gender or plurality. (You can find the answers in Appendix A.)

1. Silvia ed io andiamo **al cinema.** (festa)

2. Il tassì va **in centro.** (piazza)

3. Andate **a piedi?** (macchina)

4. La giacca sta **sulla tavola.** (armadio)

5. Mangiamo **del riso.** (spaghetti)

As a *Regola*

The preposition *da* (from, by, of, or since) can mean "since" or can describe an amount of time. For example, use the present tense of the verb *essere* + *da* to create the following:

Da quanto tempo sei in Italia?	Literally, "You are in Italy from how much time?"
Sono in Italia da ottobre.	Literally, "I am in Italy since October."

You can use the preposition *di* plus an article to express an unspecified quantity or "some" of a greater amount:

Mangio della pasta.	I am eating some pasta.
Bevo del vino.	I am drinking some wine.
Vuole della frutta?	Do you want some fruit?

The Least You Need to Know

- Traveling in Italy using the *mezzi pubblici* (public transportation) is efficient and safe.

- *Che* and *quale* are used to ask *what?* and *which?*

- Ask questions by simply changing the intonation of your voice.

- Many idiomatic expressions are used in travel.

- It's important to familiarize yourself with the irregular verbs associated with travel. Some include *andare, fare,* and *salire.*

- Prepositions are the glue that ties words together and are frequently used with an article, forming a contraction.

Using the Modal Verbs at *l'Hotel*

In This Chapter

- ◆ The comfort zone: getting the most from your hotel
- ◆ Asking for what you need
- ◆ When things go wrong
- ◆ The modal verbs *volere*, *potere*, and *dovere*
- ◆ A review of irregular verbs

Whether you're willing to live on a shoestring or you want the best of the best, this chapter will help you get what you need when you want it. You'll also study the modal verbs *dovere* (to have to; must), *potere* (to be able to; can), and *volere* (to want), essential for expressing what you must, can, and want to do.

I've also thrown in a review of useful irregular verbs.

Una Grotta Will Do

For most people with limited vacation time, it's a good idea to make *prenotazioni* (reservations) in advance, especially during the busy season (called *alta stagione*), which lasts from *maggio* (May) through *agosto* (August).

For others, the fun of travel is the unexpected, the sense of living in the *momento*. You don't mind not knowing where you'll be next week because you want to go with the flow. In that case, it's a good idea to shop around before settling on a hotel or *pensione* (inn); prices may vary, and with a *sorriso* (smile) and a bit of wit, you might be able to get yourself a terrific deal.

Use the following *vocabolario* to help you find the place that's right for you. All Italian terms are given with the appropriate definite articles. Remember to emphasize double consonants, sliding the different syllables together. (Otherwise, you'll sound like an Italian robot.)

The Hotel and Nearby

Facilities	Italiano	Pronunciation
bar	il bar	*eel bar*
barber	il barbiere	*eel bar-bee-**eh**-reh*
cashier	la cassa	*lah kahs-sah*
doorman	il portiere	*eel por-tee-**eh**-reh*
dry cleaner	la tintoria	*lah teen-toh-**ree**-ah*
elevator	l'ascensore	*lah-shen-**soh**-reh*
gift shop	il negozio di regali	*eel neh-**goh**-zee-oh dee reh-**gah**-lee*
gym	la palestra	*lah pah-**leh**-strah*
hairdresser	il parrucchiere	*lah pah-roo-kee-**yeh**-reh*
hotel	l'albergo	*lahl-**ber**-goh*
	l'hotel	*loh-tel*
	la pensione	*lah pen-see-**yoh**-neh*
laundry service	la lavanderia	*lah lah-vahn-deh-**ree**-yah*
maid	la domestica	*lah doh-**mes**-tee-kah*
parking lot	il parcheggio	*eel par-**kej**-joh*
pharmacy	la farmacia	*lah far-mah-**chee**-ah*
room service	il servizio in camera	*eel ser-**vee**-zee-oh een **kah**-meh-rah*
sauna	la sauna	*lah sah-nah*
swimming pool	la piscina	*lah pee-**shee**-nah*
tailor	il sarto	*lah sar-toh-**ree**-yah*

A Room with a *Vista*

Unless you're staying in luxury digs, don't assume there will be *un bagno privato* (private bath) in your *camera*, the Italian word for *room;* you must ask. Start with *Vorrei …* (I would like …).

Your Room

Amenity	Italiano	Pronunciation
a room	una camera	*oo-nah **kah**-meh-rah*
a double room	una doppia	*oo-nah **dohp**-pee-yah*
… with a double bed	… con letto matrimoniale	*kohn leht-toh mah-tree-moh-nee-**ah**-leh*
a single room	una singola	*oo-nah **seen**-goh-lah*
… on the garden	… sul giardino	*sool jar-**dee**-noh*
… on the sea	… sul mare	*sool mah-reh*
with …	con …	*kohn*
… air conditioning	… l'aria condizionata	***lah**-ree-yah kohn-dee-zee-oh-**nah**-tah*
… (private) bathroom	… bagno (privato)	*kohn bah-nyoh pree-**vah**-toh*
… bathtub	… la vasca da bagno	*lah vah-skah dah bah-nyoh*
… refrigerator	… il frigorifero	*eel free-goh-**ree**-feh-roh*
… telephone	… il telefono	*eel teh-**leh**-foh-noh*
… television	… la televisione	*lah teh-leh-vee-zee-**oh**-neh*
… terrace	… terrazza	*kohn teh-**rah**-tsah*
… every comfort	… ogni confort	*kohn oh-nyee kohn-fort*
elevator	l'ascensore	*lah-shen-**soh**-reh*
fax	il fax	*eel fax*
heat	il riscaldamento	*eel ree-skahl-dah-**men**-toh*
key	la chiave	*lah kee-**yah**-veh*
safe deposit box	la cassaforte	*lah kah-sah-**for**-tay*
DVD	il DVD	*eel dee voo dee*
CD	il CD	*eel chee dee*
remote control	il telecomando	*eel teh-leh-koh-**man**-doh*

Simply Said

It's nice to understand how a language works, but it can take a while for it all to sink in. In the meantime, the following simple phrases will help you ask for what you need without breaking out your list of conjugated verbs:

Vorrei …	I would like …
Ho bisogno di …	I need …
Mi serve …	I need …

Get *Comodo*

The following table will help you find the word for whatever *amenità* you may be lacking.

Inside Your Room

Necessities	Amenità	Pronunciation
alarm clock	la sveglia	*lah sveh-lyah*
ashtray	il portacenere	*eel por-tah-**cheh**-neh-reh*
blanket	la coperta	*lah koh-**per**-tah*
blow-dryer	l'asciugacapelli	*lah-shoo-gah-kah-**peh**-lee*
	il fon	*eel fohn*
closet	il guardaroba	*eel gwar-dah-**rob**-bah*
cot	il lettino	*oon leh-**tee**-noh*
hanger	la gruccia	*lah groo-chah*
	la stampella	*lah stahm-**peh**-lah*
ice	il ghiaccio	*eel ghee-**ah**-choh*
matches	i fiammiferi	*ee fee-ah-**mee**-feh-reh*
mineral water	l'acqua minerale	*lah-kwah mee-neh-**rah**-leh*
pillow	il cuscino	*eel koo-**shee**-noh*
shampoo	lo shampoo	*loh sham-poo*
shower	la doccia	*lah doh-chah*
soap	il sapone	*eel sah-**poh**-neh*
stationery	la carta da lettere	*lah kar-tah dah **leh**-teh-reh*
tissues	i fazzoletti di carta	*ee fah-tsoh-**leh**-tee dee kar-tah*
toilet	la toilette	*lah toy-lett*
toilet paper	la carta igienica	*lah kar-tah ee-**jen**-ee-kah*

Necessities	Amenità	Pronunciation
towel	l'asciugamano	*lah-shoo-gah-**mah**-noh*
transformer	il trasformatore	*eel trah-sfor-mah-**toh**-reh*

As a *Regola*
When using the reflexive verb *servirsi*, the number of things you need must agree with the verb.

    Mi serve una coperta in più.   I need an extra blanket.

    Mi servono due cuscini in più.   I need two extra pillows.

You'll learn more about reflexive verbs in Chapter 18.

Room Service *Per Favore*

Ask the hotel for something from the previous list using one of the expressions you just learned. You might have to add the words *in più* after the item if you want an extra towel, blanket, and so on.

If you want to ask for *some* more, use the preposition *di* + the appropriate article, as in *del, della, dei,* and so on. (You can find the answers in Appendix A.)

    Example: un cuscino

    Answer: Vorrei un cuscino in più, per favore.

    Example: la carta igienica

    Answer: Mi serve della carta igienica.

1. carta da lettere _____
2. chiave _____
3. asciugamano _____
4. sveglia _____
5. saponetta _____

Una Camera, Per Favore

In a pinch, you can use the following phrases to express yourself and get the *informazione* you need.

Useful Expressions

English	Italiano
Do you have any rooms?	Avete delle camere?
I'd like to make a reservation.	Vorrei fare una prenotazione.
... for one night.	... per una notte
... for one week.	... per una settimana
At what time is check-out?	Qual è l'orario per lasciare la camera?
Is breakfast included?	Colazione compresa?
I'll take it (the room).	La prendo.
I need ...	Ho bisogno di ...
Compliments!	Complimenti!
Did I receive any messages?	Ho ricevuto dei messaggi?
May I leave a message?	Posso lasciare un messaggio?
Thank you so much.	Grazie tanto.
This room is too ...	Questa camera è troppo ...
... small.	... piccola.
... dark.	... buia.
... noisy.	... rumorosa.

When you check out, you may be given a *fattura* (invoice), *conto* (bill), or *ricevuta* (receipt).

Practice Makes *Perfetto*

Complete the following sentences with the appropriate Italian word. Don't forget to use the correct article when necessary; then translate the sentences. (You can find the answers in Appendix A.)

1. Mi servono _____ in più per favore. Fa freddo stasera! (two blankets)

2. Ho bisogno di un altro _____. (pillow)

3. Vorrei _____ per i miei capelli. (a hair dryer)

4. C'è un'altra _____ per la nostra camera? (key)

5. Ci sono dei buoni _____ qui vicino? (restaurants)

6. Vorrei _____ diversa. Questa non va bene. (a room)

7. Mi serve _____. (a bottle of mineral water)

Don't Forget *la Mancia*

While you were out catching the sights, some elves seem to have mysteriously neatened your room and made the bed.

Although *la mancia* (a tip) is optional, it's always nice to leave something extra to show your appreciation for good service. In restaurants, *il coperto e servizio* (cover and service) is included in the *conto* (bill). At *il bar* it's customary to leave a small token of appreciation. When staying for any length of time in a hotel, it's appropriate to leave a tip in an envelope or with the reception as you leave.

Help, I Lost My *Passaporto!*

Chances are the staff at your hotel will speak English. However, in the event you find yourself at the mercy of this book, the following expressions will help you get back on your *piedi*. You'll want to advise the *ambasciata* (embassy) as soon as *possibile*, and it wouldn't hurt to let *la polizia* know where you are staying in case the missing passport miraculously turns up.

Consult Chapter 19 for helpful telephone lingo you might need. (And *buona fortuna!*) I've used the American embassy as an example, but you can easily substitute the nationality to reflect your specific needs.

Don't Leave Home Without It (but If You Do ...)

English	Italiano
Where is ...	Dov'è ...
... the police station?	... la stazione di polizia?
... the (American) embassy?	... l'ambasciata (americana)?
... the (American) consul?	... il console (americano)?
I lost ...	Ho perso ...
... my passport.	... il passaporto.
... my wallet.	... il portafoglio.
... my purse.	... la borsa.
... my head.	... la testa.

Feeling Moody: The Modal Verbs

Do you *want* to learn Italian? You *can*, but you *must* study. The modal verbs *potere* (to be able to), *dovere* (to have to), and *volere* (to want) express a mood, such as when you say, "I want! I can! I must!"

Before you plunge in, take stock of what you've already learned—and be patient with yourself. Learning a language is a *processo*. It takes time—time to sink in, time to kick in—and when it does, there's nothing like it.

I Want What I Want!

An important verb you have already been using in its conditional form is the verb *volere*. When you say *Vorrei*, you are saying *I would like*. Because you *would like* to express your wants as delicately as possible, you use the conditional. Sometimes, however, you just want what you want and there's no doubt about it. The following table shows you how to express want, pure and simple, in the present tense.

Volere (To Want)

Italiano	English	Italiano	English
io **voglio**	I want	noi **vogliamo**	we want
tu **vuoi**	you want	voi **volete**	you want
lui/lei/Lei **vuole**	he/she wants; You want	loro **vogliono***	they want

Emphasis should be placed on the first syllable of the third person plural (loro).

I Think I Can, I Think I Can!

You use the verb *potere* (to be able to; can) to express your potential to do something. It's the same as what the little *treno* said as it puffed up the hill—and it's what you use to express that you *can* speak Italian. The *possibilità* are endless, as long as you think you can. The verb *potere* is always used with an infinitive.

Potere (To Be Able to/Can)

Italiano	English	Italiano	English
io **posso**	I can	noi **possiamo**	we can
tu **puoi**	you can	voi **potete**	you can
lui/lei/Lei **può**	he/she/You can	loro **possono***	they can

Emphasis should be placed on the first syllable of the third person plural (loro).

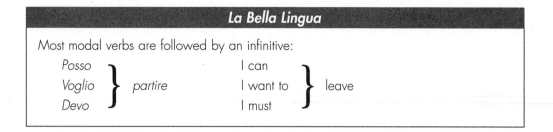

I Have to ...

The verb *dovere*, outlined in the following table, is what you use to express *to have to* and *must*, and is also used to express *to owe*. Like the verb *potere*, *dovere* is almost always used in front of an infinitive, such as when you say "I must study."

Dovere (To Have to/Must/To Owe)

Italiano	English	Italiano	English
io **devo**	I must	noi **dobbiamo**	we must
tu **devi**	you must	voi **dovete**	you must
lui/lei/Lei **deve**	he/she/You must	loro **devono***	they must

Emphasis should be placed on the first syllable of the third person plural (loro).

I'm in the Mood for ...

Read through the *frasi* and determine which *verbo* is most appropriate to each *situazione*. There may be more than one correct *risposta*. Don't forget to conjugate the verb according to the subject. The Italian pronouns are given in parentheses to help you determine the subject. Read the entire *frase* before giving your *risposta*. (You can find the answers in Appendix A.)

1. (Io) _____ studiare italiano ogni giorno.

2. Cinzia (tu), _____ venire alla festa domani sera?

3. Pino _____ fare una prenotazione.

4. (Io) _____ una camera singola per favore.

5. Tiziana e Maria _____ incontrare un'amica più tardi.

6. (Noi) _____ andare in macchina.

7. (Voi) _____ mangiare gli spaghetti al ristorante?

8. Giorgio _____ parlare il greco.

9. Leonardo non _____ mai studiare.

A Review of the Irregular Verbs

You've studied verbs until you thought you would go *matto* (crazy) trying to understand the different conjugations, stems, tenses, and persons. Don't try to rush through any of it. You'll learn Italian with perseverance and *pazienza*. Now is a good time to review the first two parts of this book to reinforce what you have studied. In the meantime, the following table offers a quick review of some of the more important *verbi* you have learned so far.

Irregular Verbs

Italian	Conjugation (Present Indicative)
andare (to go)	vado, vai, va, andiamo, andate, vanno
avere (to have)	ho, hai, ha, abbiamo, avete, hanno
dare (to give)	do, dai, dà, diamo, date, danno
*dovere** (to have to/must)	devo, devi, deve, dobbiamo, dovete, devono
essere (to be)	sono, sei, è, siamo, siete, sono
fare (to do/make)	faccio, fai, fa, facciamo, fate, fanno
potere (to be able to/can)	posso, puoi, può, possiamo, potete, possono
sapere (to know)	so, sai, sa, sappiamo, sapete, sanno
stare (to be/to stay)	sto, stai, sta, stiamo, state, stanno
volere (to want)	voglio, vuoi, vuole, vogliamo, volete, vogliono

*dovere *can also mean* to owe *as in the word* debt.

Practice with a friend and see if you have these verbs memorized. At first you'll probably fumble a bit, but after a while they'll come naturally. It's like doing scales on a musical instrument. After you can play them three times in a row with no mistakes, you've pretty much got them down pat.

Practice Makes *Perfetto* II

Conjugate and insert the correct verb where appropriate in each of these sentences. Note that not all verbs will be used. (You can find the answers in Appendix A.)

dovere	finire di
amare	fare
chiedere di	volere
aiutare a	credere di

1. Io _____ mangiare la pasta.

2. Enrico _____ fare la valigia.

3. Sandra e Filippo _____ preparare la cena.

4. Voi _____ essere poveri, ma siete ricchi—avete l'amore.

5. _____ pulire la tua camera!

6. Posso _____ una domanda?

The Least You Need to Know

♦ Important information, such as passport and credit card numbers, should be photocopied for safe keeping, just in case.

♦ The modal verbs *dovere* (to have to/must) and *potere* (to be able to/can) and *volere* (to want) are often followed by a verb.

♦ To express *I would like* … use *vorrei*, the conditional form of the modal verb *volere* (to want). You'll learn how to form the conditional in Chapter 20.

♦ Review the irregular verbs you have learned so far. These include *andare* (to go), *avere* (to have), *dare* (to give), *dovere* (to must/have to), *essere* (to be), *fare* (to do/make), *potere* (to be able to/can), *sapere* (to know), and *stare* (to be/to stay).

Chapter 12

Lezione di Geografia: Sightseeing

In This Chapter

- ◆ Verbs for sightseeing: *rimanere, venire, uscire,* and *dire*
- ◆ How to make suggestions and plans
- ◆ Asking for directions
- ◆ Geography terms
- ◆ Countries and nationalities

A lifetime wouldn't be long enough to see all there is in *Italia.* You can breeze through the boot from top to bottom or camp out in a corner and get intimate. There are so many things to see and do—but how? Read on; this chapter will give you the tools to set your own agenda.

Seeing Is Believing

There's a mystery to *Italia* and the people who live there that plucks at the strings of every heart. *Roma* wasn't built in *un giorno,* nor should it be seen in one. Because you can't do everything, think about what is most important to you and start from there.

Where to Go and What to Do

Il Luogo	L'Attività	The Place	The Activity
l'acquario	vedere i pesci	the aquarium	see the fish
l'azienda vinicola	fare un picnic	the winery	have a picnic
il castello	fare le foto	the castle	take pictures
la cattedrale	vedere le vetrate colorate	the cathedral	see the stained-glass windows
la chiesa	vedere l'architettura; accendere una candela	the church	see the architecture; light a candle
il cinema	vedere un film	the cinema	see a film
il circo	guardare lo spettacolo	the circus	watch the show
la discoteca	danzare/ballare	the discothèque	dance
l'enoteca	bere il vino	the wine bar	drink wine
il giardino	sentire i profumi dei fiori	the garden	smell the flowers
il mercato	fare la spesa	the market	go shopping
il museo	vedere le opere d'arte	the museum	see the art
il parco	fare una passeggiata	the park	take a stroll
la piazza	andare in giro	the public square	wander around
lo stadio	guardare una partita	the stadium	watch a game
il teatro	vedere una commedia	the theater	see a play
lo zoo	guardare gli animali	the zoo	look at the animals

Andiamo a Vedere ...

In one form or another, many of these verbs and expressions have been presented in earlier chapters and should sound familiar. Notice how some of the verbs require a preposition when followed by an infinitive. When a verb is used as part of an *espressione*, the verb in parentheses needs to be conjugated.

Verbs for Sightseeing

Verbi e Espressioni	Verbs and Expressions
andare	to go
(andare) a trovare	to go visit
(andare) a vedere	to go see
(fare) un giro	to take a spin/to go around

Verbi e Espressioni	Verbs and Expressions
(fare) una passeggiata	to take a walk
(fare) vedere	to show (literally, to make see)
girare	to go around
passeggiare	to stroll
passare a	to pass by
restare	to rest/stay
rimanere	to remain
ritornare	to return
uscire	to go out/exit
venire	to come
visitare	to visit

Critters

In Italy, even the animals have a saint: San Francesco d'Assisi (1182–1226). Italy's patron saint, this gentle man wrote *Il Cantico delle Creature* (Canticle of Created Things) praising all living things. You probably won't see too many *alligatori* in Italy, but you might see a *farfalla*, a lot of *gatti*, and the occasional *lucertola*.

Animal	L'Animale	Animal	L'Animale
alligator	l'alligatore	antelope	l'antilope
ant	la formica	bat	il pipistrello
bear	l'orso	lizard	la lucertola
bird	l'uccello	mole	la talpa
boar	il cinghiale	monkey	la scimmia
bull	il toro	mosquito	la zanzara
butterfly	la farfalla	mouse	il topo
cat	il gatto	ostrich	lo struzzo
chicken	la gallina	owl	la civetta, il gufo
cow	la mucca	pig	il maiale
crocodile	il coccodrillo	pigeon	il piccione
crow	il merlo	porcupine	il porcospino
deer	il cervo	rabbit	il coniglio

continues

continued

Animal	L'Animale	Animal	L'Animale
dog	il cane	raccoon	il procione
dolphin	il delfino	rooster	il gallo
donkey	l'asino	shark	il pescecane, lo squalo
duck	l'anatra	sheep	la pecora
eagle	l'aquila	skunk	la moffetta
elephant	l'elefante	snail	la lumaca
fish	il pesce	snake	il serpente
fly	la mosca	spider	il ragno
fox	la volpe	squirrel	lo scoiattolo
frog	la rana	swan	il cigno
giraffe	la giraffa	tiger	la tigre
goat	la capra	turtle	la tartaruga
gorilla	il gorilla	turkey	il tacchino
hare	la lepre	whale	la balena
hippopotamus	l'ippopotamo	wolf	il lupo
horse	il cavallo	worm	il baco, il bruco, il verme
leopard	il gattopardo	zebra	la zebra
lion	il leone		

La Bella Lingua

Ever see a *gregge* of *pecore?* Here are some other terms that express a group of a certain species: *gregge* (flock), *mandria* (herd), *banco* (shoal), and *sciame* (swarm).

Asking for *Indicazioni*

In Italian, when you add the pronoun *si* in front of the verb, you're using what's called the passive voice, as in *come si arriva* (how does one arrive). Review the imperatives in Chapter 10 to better understand what you'll be hearing in response to your questions. It helps to learn words in pairs, such as *sinistra/destra* (left/right).

You can use these words to get you pointed in the right *direzione:*

nord (north)   *est* (east)
sud (south)   *ovest* (west)

Useful Travel Terms

Italiano	English
Come si arriva a ...?	How does one arrive at ...?
Come si va ...?	How does one get to ...?
Dov'è ...?	Where is ...?
sempre diritto	"always straight"
lontano/vicino	far/near
sinistra/destra	left/right
diritto/dritto	straight
(sempre diritto)	(always straight)
giù in fondo	at the end of the street
di fronte a	opposite/in front of
dentro/fuori	inside/outside
fino a	until; up to
giù/su	down/up
sotto/sopra	below/above
prima/dopo	before/after

More Irregular Verbs

You may already be familiar with the following irregular verbs used to get around town.

Uscire

You're ready to paint the town red. The verb *uscire* (to go out or exit) will get you out of your hotel room and into the heart of the action.

Uscire (To Go Out/Exit)

Italiano	English	Italiano	English
io **esco**	I go out	noi **usciamo**	we go out
tu **esci**	you go out	voi **uscite**	you go out
lui/lei/Lei **esce**	he/she goes out; You go out	loro **escono**	they go out

Remember your pronunciation rules: The word *esco* is pronounced *es-koh*; *esci* is pronounced *eh-she*.

Venire

Eventually, you have to come down to Earth. The irregular verb *venire* (to come) might help you find your way.

Venire (To Come)

Italiano	English	Italiano	English
io **vengo**	I come	noi **veniamo**	we come
tu **vieni**	you come	voi **venite**	you come
lui/lei/Lei **viene**	he/she comes; You come	loro **vengono**	they come

Rimanere

The verb *rimanere* (to remain) has similar endings to the verb *venire*.

Rimanere (To Remain)

Italiano	English	Italiano	English
io **rimango**	I remain	noi **rimaniamo**	we remain
tu **rimani**	you remain	voi **rimanete**	you remain
lui/lei/Lei **rimane**	he/she remains; You remain	loro **rimangono**	they remain

La Bella Lingua
The verb *rimanere* can also be used idiomatically to express a state or condition, as in *rimanere male* (to be disappointed) or *rimanere soddisfatto* (to be satisfied). Among other things, it can also mean *to be situated*, as in *Dove rimane la stazione?* (Where is the station?) *Rimango in albergo stasera.* I'm remaining in the hotel this evening. *Rimangono in campagna.* They are remaining in the country.

Your Turn

How are you doing with the verbs? Check out your progress by filling in the appropriate conjugations for the following verbs. Keep in mind that some may be irregular. (You can find the answers in Appendix A.)

1. *Trovare* (to find/visit)

   io _____   noi _____

   tu _____   voi _____

   lui/lei/Lei _____   loro _____

2. *Andare* (to go; irregular)

   io _____   noi _____

   tu _____   voi _____

   lui/lei/Lei _____   loro _____

3. *Passare* (to pass)

   io _____   noi _____

   tu _____   voi _____

   lui/lei/Lei _____   loro _____

4. *Fare* (to do/make; irregular)

   io _____   noi _____

   tu _____   voi _____

   lui/lei/Lei _____   loro _____

5. *Ritornare* (to return)

io	_____	noi	_____
tu	_____	voi	_____
lui/lei/Lei	_____	loro	_____

Practice Makes *Perfetto*

You're no couch potato. Conjugate the highlighted verb in the present tense using the subject in parenthesis.

Example: **andare** a vedere il Colosseo (noi)
Answer: **Andiamo** a vedere il Colosseo.

1. **fare** una passeggiata in piazza (Pasquale) _____

2. **andare** a vedere un film (io) _____

3. **andare** ad ascoltare l'opera (noi) _____

4. **fare** una foto del castello (Giuseppe and Maria) _____

5. **fare** un giro in macchina (Voi) _____

6. **prendere** l'autobus (tu) _____

Dire

Dire (to say or tell) is another useful irregular verb. Note in the following table that the stem changes to *dic-* in all persons except the second plural.

Dire *(To Say/Tell)*

Italiano	English	Italiano	English
io **dico**	I say	noi **diciamo**	we say
tu **dici**	you say	voi **dite**	you say
lui/lei/Lei **dice**	he/she says; You say	loro **dicono**	they say

The Power of Suggestion

The gorgeous Italian you sat next to on the plane phoned you at your *albergo*, and you've made a date to go sightseeing. Although you haven't even left your hotel room, you've already planned your beautiful wedding. Sometimes a hint will not do; you have to come right out and make a suggestion.

Perché Non?

The easiest way to make a suggestion is to ask this simple question using the words *perché non* … (why not …):

> *Perché non* + the verb in the first person plural form (*noi*)?

For example:

> *Perché non andiamo in Italia?*
> Why don't we go to Italy?
>
> *Perché non partiamo domani?*
> Why don't we leave tomorrow?

La Bella Lingua

In English, you *make* a suggestion. In Italian, you *give* a suggestion, as in *dare un suggerimento.*

If you want to ask what someone thinks of the idea, use these phrases:

Che ne pensi/pensa?	What do you think (of it)?
Che ne dici/dice?	What do you say (about it)?

Let's …

To suggest the English *Let's* …, use the first person plural form (*noi*) of the verb:

andare (to go)	*Andiamo al cinema.*	Let's go to the movies.
mangiare (to eat)	*Mangiamo.*	Let's eat.
partire (to leave)	*Partiamo stasera.*	Let's leave this evening.
viaggiare (to travel)	*Viaggiamo in Italia.*	Let's travel to Italy.

La Bella Lingua

A quick *sommario* of question words includes …

chi	who	*perché*	why
che/cosa/che cosa	what; which	*come*	how
quando	when	*quanto*	how much
dove	where		

How About ...?

Shape the phrases in the following table to suggest doing whatever you want. After each *espressione*, simply add the infinitive of the verb that best expresses your suggestion.

Note how the object pronouns change, depending on who is being addressed. The pronouns most commonly used are *ti* (you, familiar), *Le* (You, polite), and *vi* (you, plural). You'll learn more about these in Chapter 16.

Getting Suggestive

Italiano	English
Le va di …?	Are you in the mood to …?
Ti interessa …?	Are you interested in …?
Vi piacerebbe …?	Would you like …?

Notice how the previous examples apply in the following suggestions:

> *Le va di andare al cinema?*
> Are you in the mood to go to the movies?

> *Ti interessa fare un viaggio in Italia?*
> Are you interested in taking a trip to Italy?

Using *Non* to Make Suggestions

Italians often add the word *non* in front of a suggestion. These examples use the third person form of the verb.

> *Non vi piacerebbe … vedere il castello?*
> Wouldn't you all like to see the castle?

> *Non Le interessa … guardare la partita?*
> Aren't you interested in seeing the game?

Yes or No

Respond to the suggestions offered by changing the object pronoun accordingly.
(You can find the answers in Appendix A.)

1. Ti va di andare al cinema?   No, non ___ va di andare al cinema.

2. Le interessa fare un viaggio in Italia. Sì, ___ interessa fare un viaggio in Italia.

3. Le piacerebbe vedere il castello.   No, non ___ piacerebbe vedere il castello.

4. Ti interessa accompagnarmi   No, non ___ interessa accompagnar
   al negozio?   ___ al negozio, grazie.

5. Ti piacerebbe mangiare un gelato?   Sì, ___ piacerebbe mangiare un gelato!

The Big, Blue Marble

As one of the world's smallest countries, *La Republica di San Marino*, is a land-locked independent city-state located on the slope of Mount Titano (near the Italian city of Rimini).
Like any self-respecting country, it has its own mint, postal system, and football team.

The following table tells you how to say the different countries and continents in Italian.

Countries

Country	Paese	Country	Paese
Belgium	Il Belgio	North Korea	La Corea del nord
China	La Cina	South Korea	La Corea del sud
Denmark	La Danimarca	Lebanon	Il Libano
Egypt	L'Egitto	Libya	La Libia
England	L'Inghilterra	Mexico	Il Messico
Ethiopia	L'Etiopia	Norway	La Norvegia
Finland	La Finlandia	Poland	La Polonia
France	La Francia	Portugal	Il Portogallo
Germany	La Germania	South Africa	Il Sud Africa
Great Britain	La Gran Bretagna	Spain	La Spagna
Greece	La Grecia	Sweden	La Svezia
Ireland	L'Irlanda	Switzerland	La Svizzera
Israel	Israele	Turkey	La Turchia
Italy	L'Italia	United States	Gli Stati Uniti d'America
Japan	Il Giappone	Vatican City	La Città del Vaticano

As a *Regola*
Some geographical terms, including continents, countries, states, and large islands, require the definite article:
Quest'estate, noi visitiamo l'Italia, la Spagna, la Francia, e la Grecia.
The only exception occurs when the term comes after the preposition *in:*
Noi andiamo in Italia, in Albania e in Africa.
All countries, regions, states, towns, and so on are capitalized. Nationalities are not capitalized.

We, the People

It's *impossibile* not to meet people from different nationalities and backgrounds when you are traveling. The first thing I notice about someone, like it or not, is his or her shoes. I can—with a fair amount of success—tell who is from where just by looking at their feet. (Note: The first example uses the polite form of address, the second example uses the familiar form.)

Lei è d'origine italiana?	*Sì, sono d'origine italiana.*
Are you of Italian origin?	Yes, I am of Italian origin.
Sei d'origine italiana?	*No, sono d'origine russa.*
Are you of Italian origin?	No, I am of Russian origin.

Nationalities

The following table provides a general list of nationalities. Nationalities are adjectives; gender must be reflected in the ending. Note also that in Italian, nationalities are *not* capitalized.

Nationalities

English	Italiano	Pronunciation
African	africano(a)	*ah-free-**kah**-noh(ah)*
American	americano(a)	*ah-meh-ree-**kah**-noh(ah)*
Belgian	belga	*bel-gah*
Canadian	canadese	*kah-nah-**deh**-zeh*
Chinese	cinese	*chee-**neh**-zeh*
Danish	danese	*dah-**neh**-zeh*
Dutch	olandese	*oh-lan-**deh**-zeh*

English	Italiano	Pronunciation
Egyptian	egiziano(a)	*eh-jee-zee-**ah**-noh(ah)*
English	inglese	*een-**gleh**-zeh*
European	europeo(a)	*eh-oo-roh-**peh**-oh(ah)*
French	francese	*frahn-**cheh**-zeh*
German	tedesco(a)	*teh-**des**-koh(ah)*
Greek	greco(a)	*greh-koh(ah)*
Indian	indiano(a)	*een-dee-**ah**-noh(ah)*
Israeli	israeliano(a)	*ees-rah-eh-lee-**yah**-noh(ah)*
Irish	irlandese	*eer-lahn-**deh**-zeh*
Italian	italiano(a)	*ee-tahl-**yah**-noh(ah)*
Japanese	giapponese	*jah-poh-**neh**-zeh*
Korean	coreano(a)	*koh-ree-**ah**-noh(ah)*
Mexican	messicano(a)	*meh-see-**kah**-noh(ah)*
Norwegian	norvegese	*nor-veh-**jeh**-zeh*
Polish	polacco(a)	*poh-**lah**-koh(ah)*
Russian	russo(a)	*roo-soh(ah)*
Spanish	spagnolo(a)	*spahn-**yoh**-loh(ah)*
Swedish	svedese	*sveh-**deh**-zeh*
Swiss	svizzero(a)	***svee**-tseh-roh(ah)*
Turkish	turco(a)	*toor-koh(ah)*

Religioni

You might be asked about your *religione;* some answers are provided in the following table.

Religions

English	Italiano	Pronunciation
agnostic	agnostico(a)	*ah-**nyoh**-stee-koh(ah)*
atheist	ateo(a)	*ah-**teh**-oh(ah)*
Buddhist	buddista	*boo-**dees**-tah*
Catholic	cattolico(a)	*kah-**toh**-lee-koh(ah)*
Christian	cristiano(a)	*kree-stee-**ah**-noh(ah)*

continues

Religions (continued)

English	Italiano	Pronunciation
Jewish	ebreo(a)	*eh-**breh**-oh(ah)*
Hindu	indù	*een-**doo***
Muslim	mussulmano(a)	*moo-sool-**mah**-noh(ah)*
Protestant	protestante	*proh-tes-**tahn**-teh*

CAUTION

Attenzione!

Use the preposition *in* before the name of a country and the preposition *a* before the name of a city: *Andiamo in Italia a Venezia.*

I Continenti

As air travel becomes more common, the world shrinks exponentially. How many continents have you hopped?

L'Africa	L'Asia	L'Antartide
L'America del Nord	L'Australia	
L'America del Sud	L'Europa	

Once Upon a Time

In 1492, *Cristoforo Colombo* bumped into North America, thinking he had found a route to India. Ten years later, the Florentine *Amerigo Vespucci*—a skilled navigator and cartographer—was commissioned by King Ferdinand of Spain to do some fact checking. In addition to the colorful letters he wrote that described his findings, Vespucci's well-charted maps became the rage all over Florence, leading the new continent to be named in his honor. Until his dying day, Columbus refused to accept the possibility that he had not reached India.

Before its unification in 1862, the peninsula now known as Italy was once a cluster of city-states ruled by powerful families. Although Italy is now a unified state, each of its 20 regions has a distinctive character.

The regions of Italy are …

L'Abruzzo	Il Molise	Il Friuli-Venezia Giulia	La Toscana
La Basilicata	Il Piemonte	Il Lazio	Il Trentino-Alto Adige
La Calabria	La Puglia	La Liguria	L'Umbria
La Campania	La Sardegna	La Lombardia	La Val d'Aosta
L'Emilia-Romagna	La Sicilia	Le Marche	Il Veneto

A Refresher

Tell someone you are from the following countries and what your nationality is. To say you have a particular origin, you must use *sono d'origine* + the nationality in its feminine form.

Sono d'origine italiana.	I'm of Italian origin.
Sono d'origine tedesca.	I'm of German origin.
Sono d'origine irlandese.	I'm of Irish origin.

Your turn. (You can find the answers in Appendix A.)

Example: *Italia*

Answer: *Sono italiano. Sono d'origine italiana.*

1. Gli Stati Uniti d'America _____

2. La Francia _____

3. La Spagna _____

4. La Grecia _____

5. L'Irlanda _____

The Least You Need to Know

◆ To suggest an activity (*Let's …*), use the first person plural (*noi*) form of the verb.

◆ Countries and some geographical locations always take the definite article and are capitalized. Nationalities are not capitalized.

◆ The verbs *venire* (to come), *uscire* (to go out), *rimanere* (to remain), and *dire* (to say or tell) are all irregular.

◆ To say you have a particular origin, you must use *sono d'origine* + the nationality in its feminine form.

Part 3

La Dolce Vita

Part 3 celebrates the things that made you want to learn Italian in the first place. You'll learn how to shop for your dinner, make a simple *zuppa* (soup) using an Italian recipe from the Tuscan countryside, and order a *bottiglia* of *vino* from a *ristorante*. You'll also learn how to express your pleasure with the verb *piacere* (to be pleasing). Finally, you'll take your verb skills into the past and learn about the *passato prossimo* and the *imperfetto*.

Of course, there's a lot more to *la bella lingua* than verbs. Aside from the food chapters, I love this phase of language learning because we can begin to discuss the things that make us fall in love over and over again with Italy: *lo sport*, *l'arte*, *la musica*, and *il cinema*. Ah, *la dolce vita!*

Chapter 3

Pane, Vino, e Cioccolata: Expressing Your Pleasure

In This Chapter

- ◆ Different foods and where to buy them
- ◆ Using *ne* and expressing quantity
- ◆ Food-related verbs and idiomatic expressions
- ◆ The verb *piacere* (to be pleasing to)

Food. Italy. The two are inseparable. It's *gastronomia* brought to the level of *arte*. What makes Italy so special is the *attenzione* it gives to the everyday elements of successful living; it's *naturale* that food plays an important *ruolo* in the Italian lifestyle. Italians know that fine cuisine is a precursor to living *la dolce vita*.

Many different kinds of stores cater to food, although a great deal of crossover occurs. Make sure you eat something before reading this chapter, or you won't be able to *concentrare* on anything. *Buon appetito!*

To Market! To Market!

Imagine that you are staying with your *famiglia* in a rented villa for a month. The tomatoes are ripe and the *basilico* is fresh. Maybe you want to *fare un picnic*. Whatever your *preferenza*, in Italy there's something *delizioso* for everyone.

Some food-oriented verbs you might find useful include the following:

assaggiare (to taste)   *fare* colazione* (to have breakfast, lunch)

cenare (to dine)   *mangiare* (to eat)

comprare (to buy)   *pranzare* (to eat lunch)

cucinare (to cook)   *preparare* (to prepare)

The idiomatic expression *fare la prima colazione* (to eat breakfast) differs slightly from *fare colazione*. Both can be used to eat breakfast, while the latter can also be used to eat lunch. Don't forget *fare la spesa* (to go food shopping).

B Is for *Bere*

You'll definitely need to use the irregular verb *bere* (to drink) if you plan on enjoying any number of the fine beverages, from *il vino* to *un bicchiere d'acqua* (a glass of water).

Italiano	English	Italiano	English
io bevo	I drink	noi beviamo	we drink
tu bevi	you drink	voi bevete	you drink
lui/lei/Lei beve	he/she drink; You drink	loro bevono	they drink

Dal Negozio

The words in the following table should help you on your next shopping expedition. To tell someone you would like to take something, use the verb *prendere* (to take), as in *Prendo un chilo di pomodori*. (I'll take a kilo of tomatoes.)

Dal Negozio (At the Store)

Negozio	Store	Il Prodotto	The Product
il bar	bar	il caffè, i liquori, gli alcolici	coffee, liquors, alcohol
la drogheria	grocery store	tutto	everything

Negozio	Store	Il Prodotto	The Product
l'enoteca	wine bar	il vino	wine
il fornaio	bakery	il pane	bread
la gelateria	ice cream shop	il gelato	ice cream
la latteria	dairy store	il formaggio, il latte, le uova	cheese, milk, eggs
la macelleria	butcher	la carne, il pollo	meat, chicken
il mercato	market	tutto	everything
il fruttivendolo	green grocer	la frutta, le verdure, i legumi	fruit, vegetables, legumes
la pasticceria	pastry shop	la pasta, i dolci	pastry, sweets
la pescheria	fish store	il pesce	fish
il supermercato	supermarket	tutto	everything
il vinaio	wine store	il vino	wine

I Love Olives

L'agriturismo is an increasingly popular way for families to vacation abroad. Guests stay in the countryside on working farms or vineyards and eat the cheeses, meats, and vegetables produced at the establishment.

Why not take a cooking vacation? Eat, live, and drink Italian as you go from the market to the kitchen to the vineyard to the table!

The following table gives you the terms to express your needs.

Le Verdure

Vegetable	La Verdura	Pronunciation
anise	l'anice	*lah-nee-cheh*
artichoke	il carciofo	*eel kar-choh-foh*
asparagus	gli asparagi	*ylee ah-spah-rah-jee*
beans	i fagioli	*ee fah-joh-lee*
cabbage	il cavolo	*eel kah-voh-loh*
carrots	le carote	*leh kah-roh-teh*
cauliflower	il cavolfiore	*eel kah-vol-fyoh-reh*
corn	il mais	*eel mais*

continues

Le Verdure (continued)

Vegetable	La Verdura	Pronunciation
eggplant	la melanzana	*lah meh-lan-**zah**-neh*
garlic	l'aglio	*lah-lyoh*
green beans	i fagiolini	*ee fah-joh-**lee**-nee*
legumes	i legumi	*ee leh-**goo**-mee*
lettuce	la lattuga	*lah lah-**too**-gah*
mushrooms	i funghi	*ee foon-ghee*
olive	l'oliva	*loh-**lee**-vah*
onion	la cipolla	*lah chee-**poh**-lah*
peas	i piselli	*ee pee-**zeh**-lee*
potato	la patata	*lah pah-**tah**-tah*
rice	il riso	*eel ree-zoh*
spinach	gli spinaci	*ylee spee-**nah**-chee*
tomato	il pomodoro	*ee poh-moh-**doh**-roh*
vegetable/greens	la verdura	*lah ver-**doo**-rah*
zucchini	gli zucchini	*ylee zoo-**kee**-nee*

La Frutta

In Rome, a favorite summertime treat is *il cocomero*, also called *l'anguria* (watermelon), which can be bought at brightly lit *bancarelle* (stands). It's so sweet your teeth will hurt, and as wet as a waterfall (get extra napkins). Somehow, the Italians manage to eat the thickly sliced pieces with a plastic spoon (good luck!). Another fruit fact: Italians rarely bite into an apple. They peel it with a knife in one long curl and then slice it into bite-sized chunks to share with everyone at the table. The following table provides a list of the Italian for various fruits and nuts.

La Frutta e La Nocciola

English	Italiano	Pronunciation
almond	la mandorla	*lah **mahn**-dor-lah*
apple	la mela	*lah meh-lah*
apricot	l'albicocca	*lal-bee-**koh**-kah*
banana	la banana	*lah bah-**nah**-nah*
cherry	la ciliegia	*leh cheel-**yeh**-jah*

English	Italiano	Pronunciation
chestnut	la castagna	*lah kah-__stah__-nyah*
date	il dattero	*eel __dah__-teh-roh*
figs	i fichi	*ee fee-kee*
fruit	la frutta	*lah froo-tah*
grapefruit	il pompelmo	*eel pom-__pehl__-moh*
grapes	l'uva	*loo-vah*
hazelnut	la nocciola	*lah __noh__-choh-lah*
lemon	il limone	*eel lee-__moh__-neh*
melon	il melone	*eel meh-__loh__-neh*
orange	l'arancia	*lah-__rahn__-chah*
peach	la pesca	*lah pes-kah*
pear	la pera	*lah peh-rah*
pineapple	l'ananas	*__lah__-nah-nas*
pistachio nut	il pistacchio	*eel pee-__stah__-kee-yoh*
pomegranate	la melagrana	*lah meh-lah-__grah__-nah*
raisin	l'uva passa	*loo-vah pah-sah*
raspberry	il lampone	*eel lam-__poh__-neh*
walnut	la noce	*lah noh-cheh*

In Macelleria

Italian food is fresh. Most perishables are bought and cooked immediately. You will find the terms for different types of meat in the following table.

La Macelleria (At the Butcher)

Meat and Poultry	La Carne e Pollame	Pronunciation
beef	il manzo	*eel mahn-zoh*
chicken	il pollo	*eel poh-loh*
cold cuts	i salumi	*ee sah-__loo__-mee*
cutlet	la costoletta	*lah koh-stoh-__leh__-tah*
duck	l'anatra	*__lah__-nah-trah*
fillet	il filetto	*eel fee-__leh__-toh*
ham	il prosciutto	*eel proh-__shoo__-toh*

continues

La Macelleria (At the Butcher)   (continued)

Meat and Poultry	La Carne e Pollame	Pronunciation
lamb	l'agnello	*lah-**nyeh**-loh*
liver	il fegato	*eel **feh**-gah-toh*
meat	la carne	*lah kar-neh*
meatballs	le polpette	*leh pol-**peh**-teh*
pork	il maiale	*eel mah-**yah**-leh*
pork chop	la braciola	*lah brah-**choh**-lah*
quail	la quaglia	*lah kwah-lyah*
rabbit	il coniglio	*eel koh-**neel**-yoh*
salami	il salame	*eel sah-**lah**-meh*
sausage	la salsiccia	*lah sal-**see**-chah*
steak	la bistecca	*lah bee-**steh**-kah*
tripe	la trippa	*lah tree-pah*
turkey	il tacchino	*eel tah-**kee**-noh*
veal	il vitello	*eel vee-**teh**-loh*
veal shank	lo stinco di vitello	*lo stin-ko vee-**teh**-loh*

Got Milk? *La Latteria*

The only real *parmigiano* comes from Parma, Italy. There are so many wonderful cheeses in Italy that you'll want to *fare un picnic*. Nothing beats fresh *pane, una bottiglia di vino*, and good company. Most *supermercati* carry a wide selection of cheeses and wines, but you can check your neighborhood stores as well for the products described in the following table.

La Latteria

Dairy Product	Il Prodotto	Pronunciation
butter	il burro	*eel boo-roh*
cheese	il formaggio	*eel for-**mah**-joh*
cream	la panna	*lah pah-nah*
eggs	le uova	*leh woh-vah*
milk	il latte	*eel lah-teh*
yogurt	lo yogurt	*loh yoh-gurt*

Di Bocca Buona

The Italians have a saying for everything. Read the idiomatic expressions related to food and eating, and draw a line connecting them to the appropriate translation. (You can find the answers in Appendix A.)

1. Bere come una spugna.

2. Di bocca buona.

3. Una ciliegia tira l'altra.

4. Non me ne importa un fico secco.

5. Fare la frittata.

6. Fino al midollo.

7. Liscio come l'olio.

8. Un osso duro.

9. Dire pane al pane e vino al vino.

10. Mangiare pane e cipolla.

11. Togliersi il pane di bocca.

12. Di pasta buona.

13. Avere lo spirito di patata.

14. Essere un sacco di patate.

15. Fare polpette di …

16. Rosso come un peperone.

A. A good mouth (a good eater).

B. A hard bone.

C. I don't care one dry fig's worth.

D. Of good pasta (good-natured).

E. One cherry pulls the other. (One thing leads to another.)

F. Red as a pepper.

G. Smooth as oil.

H. To be a sack of potatoes.

I. To call bread bread and wine wine (to call a spade a spade).

J. To drink like a sponge (to drink like a fish).

K. To eat bread and onion (to live on bread and water).

L. To give bread from your mouth.

M. To have a potato's sense of humor.

N. To make an omelette of things.

O. To make meatballs of …

P. To the marrow.

Fruit of the Sea: *La Pescheria*

Ahh, *i frutti di mare!* Go to any seaside village in Italy, and you're guaranteed to eat some of the best seafood you've ever had. The following table gives you a little taste.

La Pescheria

Fish and Seafood	I Pesci e Frutti di Mare	Pronunciation
anchovies	le acciughe	*leh ah-**choo**-gheh*
cod	il merluzzo	*eel mer-**loo**-tsoh*
crab	il granchio	*eel **gran**-kee-yoh*
fish	il pesce	*eel peh-sheh*
flounder	la passera	*lah **pah**-seh-rah*
halibut	l'halibut	***lah**-lee-boot*
herring	l'aringa	*lah-**reen**-gah*
lobster	l'aragosta	*lah-rah-**gohs**-tah*
mussel	la cozza	*lah koh-tsah*
oyster	l'ostrica	***loh**-stree-kah*
salmon	il salmone	*eel sahl-**moh**-neh*
sardines	le sardine	*leh sar-**dee**-neh*
scallop	la cappasanta	*lah kah-pah-**sahn**-tah*
shrimp	i gamberetti	*ee gahm-beh-**reh**-tee*
sole	la sogliola	*lah sohl-**yoh**-lah*
squid	i calamari	*ee kah-lah-**mah**-ree*
swordfish	il pesce spada	*eel peh-sheh spah-dah*
trout	la trota	*lah troh-tah*
tuna	il tonno	*eel toh-noh*

What's in a Name?

When you're talking about food, what often sounds slightly exotic almost invariably derives from a simple description of its shape or taste. Look at the word *capellini*, referring to a type of spaghetti that is as thin as *capelli* (in English, you call this angel-hair pasta), or *orecchiette*, which literally means *little ear*. And what about those wonderful ricotta-filled *calzoni* you treat yourself to at the local pizza parlor? When you bite into one, you're not really eating pants for dinner!

The pasta known as *conchiglie* are named after the seashells they resemble. *Bombarde* describe the huge "bomblike" tubes of pasta that are stuffed with cheese and meat fillings. The word for the popular *ziti* may find its origins in the word *zitellone*, referring to an old bachelor. (*Zitella* was used to describe a spinster.) And let's not forget the corkscrew-shaped pasta *fusilli*, perhaps finding its origins in the word *fusello*, meaning *spindle* or *bobbin*. Finally, note the similarities between the words *lasagna* and *lenzuolo* (bed sheet). Ah ha!

This Drink's on Me

As is the Italian way, certain times befit certain beverages. *Il cappuccino* is generally consumed in the morning with a *cornetto* (similar to a croissant). *L'espresso* can be consumed any time of the day, but is usually taken after meals (never *cappuccino*).

To whet your appetite, you can have an *aperitivo*, and to help you digest, a *digestivo* or *amaro*. As an afternoon pick-me-up, you can indulge in a *spremuta* (freshly squeezed juice). The following table lists different beverages. You should be able to pronounce these words without the guide—just sound them out like you see them.

Le Bibite

Drinks	Le Bibite
beer	la birra
coffee	il caffè
drink	la bibita, la bevanda
freshly squeezed juice	la spremuta
freshly squeezed grapefruit juice	la spremuta di pompelmo
freshly squeezed orange juice	la spremuta d'arancia
fruit juice	il succo di frutta
hot chocolate	la cioccolata calda
iced tea	il tè freddo
lemon soda	la limonata
milk	il latte
mineral water	l'acqua minerale
nonalcoholic beverage	l'analcolico
noncarbonated mineral water	l'acqua minerale naturale
orange soda	l'aranciata
sparkling mineral water	l'acqua minerale gassata/frizzante
sparkling wine	lo spumante
tea	il tè
wine	il vino

Dolcezza!

The word *dolcezza* is a term of endearment meaning *sweetheart*. Do you have a sweet tooth? Italians love their *caramelle*, and if you're a chocolate addict, you definitely want to check out Perugina's *Baci* (kisses), which come in a silver wrapper and always include a *fortuna* about love in different languages. The following table lists a number of *dolci*.

For Your Sweet Tooth

The Candy	La Caramella
chocolate	la cioccolata
cough drop	una caramella per la tosse
gum	la gomma americana
licorice	la liquirizia
mint	la menta

Expressing *Quantità*

You want a little of this and a little of that. You'll take some olives, a loaf of bread, and a couple of boxes of pasta. Maybe you'll also get a slice of cheese, and since you're there, why not a chicken cutlet or two? Once you're out there shopping, you'll need to know how to express how much you want of something. There are a few ways of doing this.

It's the *Quantità* That Counts

The following table will help make the metric system much easier to follow. These comparisons are approximate but close enough to get roughly the right amount.

Measuring

Solid Measures		Liquid Measures	
U.S. System	**Metrico**	**U.S. System**	**Metrico**
1 oz.	28 grammi	1 oz.	30 millilitri
1/4 lb.	125 grammi (un etto)*	16 oz. (1 pint)	475 millilitri
1/2 lb.	250 grammi	32 oz. (1 quart)	circa un litro

Solid Measures		Liquid Measures	
U.S. System	**Metrico**	**U.S. System**	**Metrico**
3/4 lb.	375 grammi	1 gallon	3.75 litri
1.1 lbs.	500 grammi		
2.2 lbs.	1 chilogrammo (un chilo)		

Prices are often quoted by the etto *(a hectogram).*

It might be just as easy to indicate a little of this, a little of that, and then say when enough is enough using the expression, *Basta così.* Italy uses the metric system; instead of asking for *a dozen,* you can also ask for *ten of.* Some helpful ways of expressing quantity are listed in the following table.

Quantities

Amount	La Quantitì	Amount	La Quantitì
a bag of	un sacchetto di	a kilo of	un chilo di
a bottle of	una bottiglia di	a pack of	un pacchetto di
a box of	una scatola di	a piece of	un pezzo di
a can of	una lattina di	a quarter pound of	un etto di
a container of	un barattolo di	a sack (lot) of	un sacco di
a dozen of	una dozzina di	a slice of	una fetta di
a drop of	una goccia di	a ten of	una decina di
a jar of	un vasetto di		

Give Me Some!

To indicate that you would like *some of* a larger quantity, you can use the preposition *di* + the noun (with its appropriate definite article) to create the partitive. (Refer to Chapter 11 to refresh your memory of contractions.) Take a look at the following examples:

*Vorrei **del** pane.*	I'd like some bread.
*Prendo **della** frutta.*	I'll take some fruit.
*Ho anche bisogno **dello** zucchero.*	I also need some sugar.

La Bella Lingua

Try to make sense of this *indovinello toscano* (Tuscan riddle) and determine the identity of *"la bella del palazzo."*

Son la bella del palazzo; Casco in terra e non mi ammazzo; Faccio lume al gran Signore, Son servita con amore.

(Hint: I'm edible and listed somewhere in this chapter.)

Some or Any: The Partitive *Ne*

Imagine that someone asks you whether you want some ice cream. You're stuffed to the gills, though. If you eat one more bite, you'll explode, so you say, "Nah, I don't want any, thanks." It is assumed that *any* refers to the ice cream.

You've learned how to indicate some or any by using the preposition *di* plus *l'articolo*. The partitive pronoun *ne* comes in handy when used to ask for a part of or some of a greater quantity. It can be translated to mean *some, any, of it, of them, some of them, any of it,* and *any of them.* It is especially used in response to a question, when the object has already been indicated.

Like most object pronouns, *ne* usually precedes the verb but attaches itself to the infinitive form (minus the final *-e*).

Vuole della frutta?	Would you like some fruit?
No grazie, non ne voglio.	No, thanks; I don't want any.
Non voglio mangiarne.	I don't want to eat any.

Some Practice

Answer the following questions with the pronoun *ne* using the affirmative and the negative. (You can find the answers in Appendix A.)

Example: *Vuole un frutto?* (Do you want a piece of fruit?)
Answer: *No, non ne voglio.* (No, I don't want any.)

1. *Hanno dei soldi?* (Do they have money?) *Sì,* _____.

2. *Avete del pane?* (Do you [all] have some bread?) *Sì,* _____.

3. *Bevi vino?* (Do you drink wine?) *Sì,* _____.

4. *C'è del gelato?* (Is there any ice cream?) *No,* _____.

What's Your Pleasure? The Verb *Piacere*

One of the first things an Italian will ask is *Le piace l'Italia?* (Do you like Italy?) What's not to like?

You need to understand the verb *piacere* (to be pleasing to) to express your likes and dislikes in Italian. In Italian, you don't say, "I like pizza." Using the verb *piacere*, you would say the equivalent of, "Pizza is pleasing to me," as in *"Mi piace la pizza."* If you were talking about *gli spaghetti*, because the word *spaghetti* is plural in Italian, you would say, *"Mi piacciono gli spaghetti."*

Unlike English, in Italian, the thing that is pleasing is the subject of the sentence. The person who is pleased is the indirect object.

Because the subject of the sentence dictates how the verb is conjugated, *piacere* is rarely used in anything other than the third person singular and plural. Those two forms are shown here:

piace (it is pleasing/it pleases)

piacciono (they are pleasing/they please)

On rare occasions, you might find it necessary to use the verb in the first or second persons, in which case it is conjugated as shown in the following table.

Piacere (To Please)

Italiano	English	Italiano	English
io **piaccio**	I am pleasing	noi **piacciamo**	we are pleasing
tu **piaci**	you are pleasing	voi **piacete**	you are pleasing
lui/lei/Lei **piace**	he/she (it) is pleasing; You are pleasing	loro **piacciono**	they are pleasing

Using *Piacere*

Expressing your likes and dislikes in Italian is much easier if you reprogram your brain. Instead of saying, "I like …," reword the expression to say "… is pleasing to me."

Some rules about the verb *piacere* are outlined here. In the first few examples, the **indirect object** (or pronoun) is in **bold** and the <u>subject</u> is <u>underlined</u>:

◆ *Piacere* is almost always used in third person (singular and plural) and is always used with an indirect object or indirect object pronoun. (Refer to Chapter 16 to review your indirect objects and their pronouns):

Mi piace <u>la pizza</u>.	I like pizza. (<u>Pizza</u> is pleasing **to me.**)
Mi piacciono <u>gli spaghetti</u>.	I like spaghetti. (<u>Spaghetti</u> is pleasing **to me.**)
*Bambini, **vi** piace <u>la pizza</u>?*	Children, do you like pizza? (Is <u>pizza</u> pleasing **to you?**)
*Sì, **ci** piacciono la pizza e gli spaghetti!*	Yes, we like pizza and spaghetti. (Yes, pizza and spaghetti are pleasing **to us.**)

◆ When used as the subject, the <u>infinitive</u> is singular.

Mi piace <u>mangiare</u> la pizza.	I like <u>eating</u> pizza.
Ti piace <u>studiare</u>?	Do you like <u>to study</u>?

◆ When you're not using an indirect object pronoun, you must use the preposition *a* (or its contraction, *a* + the article) before the noun.

A Marcello piace bere il vino.	Marcello likes to drink wine. (Drinking wine is pleasing **to Marcello.**)

Ai bambini piace la cioccolata.　　　The children like chocolate.
　　　　　　　　　　　　　　　　　　(Chocolate is pleasing **to the** children.)

◆ The word order is somewhat flexible. The indirect object (the recipient of the verb's action) of the verb can come before or after the conjugated form of *piacere*.

*A **Giovanni** piace il pane.*　　　To Giovanni, bread is pleasing.

*Piace il pane **a Giovanni?***　　　Is bread pleasing to Giovanni?

◆ To make a negative statement, *non* goes in front of the indirect object pronoun.

***Non** mi piace il fegato.*　　　I don't like liver.

However, when the indirect object of the verb is a noun (and not a pronoun), *non* goes in front of the conjugated form of *piacere*.

*Ai bambini **non** piace il fegato.*　　　The children don't like liver.

◆ The indirect object pronoun *loro* (to them) generally precedes the verb.

*A **loro** piacciono le caramelle.*　　　They like the candies.

◆ The verb *dispiacere* means *to be sorry* (not *to be displeasing*) as well as *to mind*. It is used exactly like the verb *piacere*:

Mi dispiace.　　　I'm sorry.

As a *Regola*

The indirect object pronouns are …

Singular	Plural
mi (to me)	*ci* (to us)
ti (to you)	*vi* (to you)
gli (to him)	*a loro* (to them)
le (to her)	
Le (to You [polite])	

Using the Verb *Piacere*

Ask someone if he or she likes the following. Remember that the thing that is liked is the subject and that the verb *piacere* must reflect number. (You can find the answers in Appendix A.)

> Example: Le _____ il vino bianco?
> Answer: Le piace il vino bianco?

1. Ti _____ la frutta?

2. Signora, Le _____ il vino?

3. Vi _____ gli spaghetti?

4. Ti _____ cucinare?

5. Mamma, ti _____ le caramelle?

6. L'Italia _____ loro?

Using the Verb *Piacere* II

Imagine that you are asking your partner if he or she likes something from the following list. Give both an affirmative and a negative response. (You can find the answers in Appendix A.)

> Example: Ti piacciono i biscotti?
> Answer: Sì, mi piacciono i biscotti.
>   No, non mi piacciono i biscotti.

1. i dolci _____

2. la pasta _____

3. gli spaghetti _____

4. le acciughe _____

5. i fichi _____

6. il fegato _____

A Special Treat

There's nothing like good old-fashioned cooking. Here's an opportunity to apply your new Italian skills with a special recipe. The following words will help your dish turn out *perfetto:*

aggiungere	to add	*girare*	to mix
bollire	to boil	*mettere*	to put
cuocere	to cook	*versare*	to pour

Minestra di Riso e Limone

Ingredienti:

8 tazze di brodo	¼ tazza formaggio Parmigiano Reggiano, grattugiato
1 tazza di riso Arborio	1 cucchiaino di scorza di limone grattugiata
3 tuorli di uova	1 cucchiaino di succo di limone

1. Mettete il brodo in un tegame e portatelo al punto di ebollizione. Aggiungete il riso, coprite il tegame e fatelo cuocere 20 minuti.

2. Nel frattempo battete le uova, aggiungete il formaggio, il limone grattugiato e il succo di limone.

3. Quando il riso è cotto, versate le uova nella minestra, sbattendo in continuazione. Riscaldate la minestra e servitela subito.

Per 4 persone.

The Least You Need to Know

◆ You need to do two things to eat well in Italy: Work up a good appetite and learn a few gastronomical verbs, such as *mangiare* (to eat), *bere* (to drink), *assaggiare/gustare* (to taste), *cenare* (to dine), *comprare* (to buy), *cucinare* (to cook), *pranzare* (to eat lunch), and *preparare* (to prepare).

◆ The pronoun *ne* is used to express that you want a *part of* or *some of* a greater quantity.

◆ To say that you like something, you must use the verb *piacere* (to be pleasing).

◆ You must use indirect object pronouns with *piacere*.

14

Buon Appetito: Dining Out

In This Chapter

◆ First things first: ordinal numbers

◆ Ordering in a restaurant

◆ Eating out and special diets

◆ Infinitive verbs and prepositions

◆ Making comparisons

◆ The present progressive tense

You're on vacation and don't want to do dishes. Why not take a break? Sit back, relax, and let someone else do the running around for a change. If you want to understand the menu, or if you have special needs, this chapter will help you ask for what you want.

Who's on First?

When you *ordini* your dinner in a *ristorante*, you start with your *primo piatto* (first course). Maybe you order *pasta primavera* (which means *springtime* and translates literally as *first green*). You move along to your *secondo piatto* (second course), and afterward, you might have *per ultimo* (for last)—a nice *tiramisù*, so sweet and light and lovely that you feel like you died and went to heaven.

What do all these things have in common (other than they are *delizioso*)? They all use ordinal numbers.

The Ordinal Numbers

Ordinal numbers specify the order of something in a series. The word *primo* is similar to the English word primary, *secondo* is like secondary, *terzo* is like tertiary, *quarto* is like quarter, *quinto* is like quintuplets, and so on. The following table gives you a rundown of useful ordinal numbers you need and how to recognize them in both the masculine and feminine abbreviated forms.

Ordinal Numbers

English	Italian	Masc.	Fem.	Pronunciation
first	primo	1°	1ª	*pree-moh*
second	secondo	2°	2ª	*seh-kohn-doh*
third	terzo	3°	3ª	*ter-zoh*
fourth	quarto	4°	4ª	*kwahr-toh*
fifth	quinto	5°	5ª	*kween-toh*
sixth	sesto	6°	6ª	*sehs-toh*
seventh	settimo	7°	7ª	*seh-tee-moh*
eighth	ottavo	8°	8ª	*oh-tah-voh*
ninth	nono	9°	9ª	*noh-noh*
tenth	decimo	10°	10ª	*deh-chee-moh*
eleventh	undicesimo	11°	11ª	*oon-dee-cheh-zee-moh*
twelfth	dodicesimo	12°	12ª	*doh-dee-cheh-zee-moh*
twentieth	ventesimo	20°	20ª	*ven-teh-zee-moh*
twenty-first	ventunesimo	21°	21ª	*ven-too-neh-zee-moh*
twenty-third*	ventitreesimo	23°	23ª	*ven-tee-treh-eh-zee-moh*
sixty-sixth*	sessantaseiesimo	66°	66ª	*seh-sahn-tah-seh-eh-zee-moh*
seventy-seventh	settantasettesimo	77°	77ª	*seh-tahn-tah-seh-teh-zee-moh*
hundredth	centesimo	100°	100ª	*chen-teh-zee-moh*
thousandth	millesimo	1000°	1000ª	*mee-leh-zee-moh*

Note: The final vowel of the cardinal number is not dropped with numbers ending in 3 (-tre) and 6 (-sei).

There are some basic rules for using ordinal numbers in Italian:

♦ Like any adjective, ordinal numbers must agree in gender and number with the nouns they modify. As in English, they precede the nouns they modify. Notice how they are abbreviated, as in 1° (1st), 2° (2nd), and 3° (3rd)—much easier than the English. The feminine abbreviation reflects the ending *-a*, as in 1ª, 2ª, and 3ª.

la prima volta (1ª)	the first time
il primo piatto (1°)	the first course

♦ The first 10 ordinal numbers all have separate forms, but after the tenth ordinal number, they simply drop the final vowel of the cardinal number and add the ending *-esimo.*

tredici	tredicesimo	13th
venticinque	venticinquesimo	25th
ventisei	ventiseiesimo	26th

♦ You need to use ordinal numbers whenever you reference a Roman numeral, as in Enrico V (*quinto*) or Papa Giovanni Paolo II (*secondo*).

♦ Unlike in English, dates in Italian require cardinal numbers, unless you are talking about the first day of a month, as in *il primo ottobre*. June 8th is *l'otto (di) giugno* because the day always comes before the month. The use of the preposition *di* is optional. Therefore, it's important to remember that in Italian, 8/6/98 is actually June 8, 1998 (and not August 6, 1998).

La Bella Lingua

In Italian, the word for floor is *piano* (just like the instrument). The *primo piano* (first floor) is actually the floor above the *pianterreno* (ground floor) and equal to what is considered the second floor in the United States. So if someone says he lives on the *terzo piano*, he is actually living on the fourth floor.

So Many Restaurants

You don't need to go to a five-star restaurant to eat well in Italy—there are restaurants for every palate and every pocket. Some of the smaller, family-run joints have the best food in town. Choose the place that best fits your needs:

Il bar. Apart from serving drinks of all kinds, bars serve *i panini* (sandwiches), snacks, and assorted *paste* (pastries).

La caffeteria. Pick and choose from whatever you see behind the glass counter, find an empty table, and eat. The food here is inexpensive and nourishing.

La mensa. Like a cafeteria, here you'll find wholesome food on a fixed-price basis; these places are usually frequented by *gli studenti* or *i lavoratori.*

L'osteria. No different from a *taverna*, it's often family-run and frequented by locals.

La paninoteca. Here you can order sandwiches and beverages, good "on-the-go" food.

Attenzione!

Words ending in *à* (as in *specialità* and *città*) always remain in the singular form. In these cases, the article reflects plurality.

La pizzeria. Just like it sounds, at the *pizzeria* you can get your own personal pizza the size of a dinner plate, or a square cut from a large tray. Whatever the shape, the taste is unbeatable.

Il ristorante. This can range in *qualità* and *costo;* usually it has a more formal *ambiente.*

Self-service. Increasingly popular with young people; like a cafeteria, here you grab a tray and pick your *piatto.*

La tavola calda. Literally, this is a "hot table"—ready-to-eat food that you can take out as well.

La trattoria. Similar to *la taverna*, this local establishment offers home-style cooking in an intimate environment.

Two for Dinner, Please

The next time you are in an Italian *ristorante*, you may hear the following:

A che ora vorrebbe* mangiare?	At what time would you like to eat?
Vuole prenotare?	Would you like to make a reservation?
Per quante persone?	For how many people?
Va bene questo tavolo?	Is this table all right?
Tutto bene?	Is everything all right?
Le specialità del giorno sono	Today's specials are ....
Si accomodi.	Make yourself comfortable.

*Third person conditional tense of volere *(to want).*

What's the House Special?

The following expressions will help you ask for what you want at a restaurant or eatery.

Dal Ristorante

L'Espressione	Expression
Cameriere!	Waiter!
Vorrei prenotare ...	I'd like to make a reservation ...
... per stasera.	... for this evening.
... per domani sera.	... for tomorrow evening.
... per sabato sera.	... for Saturday evening.
... per due persone.	... for two people.
... alle otto.	... for 8:00.
Possiamo sederci ...	May we sit ...
... vicino alla finestra?	... near the window?
... sul terrazzo?	... on the terrace?
C'è una zona per non fumatori?	Is there a nonsmoking section?
Quanto tempo si deve aspettare?	How long is the wait?
Qual è la specialità della casa?	What is the house special?
Qual è il piatto del giorno?	What is the special for the day?
Che cosa ci consiglia?	What do you recommend?
Vorrei una porzione di	I'd like one portion of ....
Il conto, per favore.	The check, please.
Abbiamo mangiato* molto bene.	We ate very well.

Past participle of mangiare.

La Bella Lingua

Il tavolo refers to a table in a restaurant; *la tavola* refers to a table at home. You may already be familiar with the term *Buon appetito!*

When you want to make a toast (*fare un brindisi*) you say: *Alla salute!* or *Cincin!* (pronounced *cheen-cheen*)

A Table Setting

Prior to the fifteenth century, most food was eaten with *le mani* (the hands) or from the point of a knife. Although it did not come to be commonly used until the seventeenth century, it appears that *i napoletani* created the four-pronged *forchetta* to aid them in eating *gli spaghetti*. Nowadays, it is considered *maleducato* (rude) to eat with your hands unless you're eating *il pane* (bread). The following table provides terms for the eating implements and other useful items.

At the Table

At the Table	Al Tavolo	Pronunciation
bowl	la ciotola	*lah **choh**-toh-lah*
	la scodella	*lah skoh-**dehl**-lah*
carafe	la caraffa	*lah kah-**raf**-fah*
cup	la tazza	*lah tah-tsah*
dinner plate	il piatto	*eel pee-**ah**-toh*
fork	la forchetta	*lah for-**keh**-tah*
glass	il bicchiere	*eel bee-kee-**yeh**-reh*
knife	il coltello	*eel koh-**tel**-loh*
menu	il menù	*eel meh-**noo***
napkin	il tovagliolo	*eel toh-vah-**lyoh**-loh*
oil	l'olio	***lohl**-yoh*
pepper	il pepe	*eel peh-peh*
pitcher	la brocca	*lah broh-kah*
salad bowl	l'insalatiera	*leen-sah-lah-tee-**yeh**-rah*
salt	il sale	*eel sah-leh*
silverware	l'argenteria	*lar-jen-teh-**ree**-ah*
spoon	il cucchiaio	*eel koo-kee-**ay**-yoh*
sugar bowl	la zuccheriera	*lah zoo-keh-ree-**yeh**-rah*
table	il tavolo	*eel **tah**-voh-loh*
tablecloth	la tovaglia	*lah toh-**vah**-lyah*
teapot	la teiera	*lah teh-**yeh**-rah*
teaspoon	il cucchiaino	*eel koo-kee-**ay**-ee-noh*
vinegar	l'aceto	*lah-**cheh**-toh*

In the Kitchen

There's no better way than to eat your way to fluency! Why not tape the following kitchen-related terms to your refrigerator?

Nella Cucina (In the Kitchen)

English	Italiano	English	Italiano
basket	il cesto	oven	il forno
bowl	la ciotola	oven mitt	il guanto da forno
box/container	la scatola	pitcher	la caraffa
can opener	l'apriscatole	recipe	la ricetta
canister	il barattolo	recipe book	il libro di cucina
colander	il colapasta	refrigerator	il frigorifero
counter	il piano di lavoro	rolling pin	il matterello
cupboard	l'armadietto	sauce pan	la padella
curtains	le tende, le tendine	saucer	il piattino
cutting board	il tagliere	sink	il lavandino
dishwasher	la lavastoviglie	stove	la cucina a gas o elettrica
faucet	il rubinetto	stove burner	il fornello
frying pan	la padella	straw	la cannuccia
funnel	l'imbuto	toaster	il tostapane
grill	la griglia	tray	il vassoio
measuring cup	il misurino	vase	il vaso
microwave oven	il forno a microonde		

Il Bar

In Italy, the bar is a very different place than it is in other countries. At *il bar*, you can meet friends, have a *caffè*, grab a *panino* (sandwich, which literally comes from the word *pane*, meaning *little bread*), or sip an *amaro* after dinner. You must go to the *cassa* (cashier), pay for your choice, take your *scontrino* (receipt) to the bar, and pick up your order. It is customary to leave *una mancia* of 20 *centesimi* or so as a gesture of goodwill.

> ### *La Bella Lingua*
>
> Traditionally, Italians drink their coffee *in piedi* (standing up). Anytime you sit down for service, you're going to pay up to four times the amount you would otherwise. Some smaller, local establishments have courtesy tables—it's polite to bring your *tazza* back up to the bar after you've finished drinking.

Il bar is usually well lit and very clean. No Italian bar would be the same without the familiar sound of milk being steamed for *il cappuccino*.

Il Caffè

In Italy, people take their *caffè* very seriously, and it is served in a variety of manners. If you must drink American coffee, which by Italian standards is considered weak and without flavor, ask for *un caffè americano*. If you are in a small town, you should indicate this as *un caffè molto lungo*.

The following table illustrates the different kinds of *caffè* you can order. My preference is for *caffè corretto* ("corrected coffee"). Practice reading your Italian. Remember to use the verb *prendere* (to take) to ask for what you want, as in *Prendo un espresso*.

Coffee, Coffee Everywhere

Il Tipo di Caffè	La Descrizione
un espresso	caffè normale
un espresso lungo	caffè con molta acqua
un espresso ristretto	caffè concentrato
un cappuccino	un espresso con latte vaporizzato (steamed)
un latte macchiato	molto latte, poco caffè
un caffè macchiato	caffè con una goccia (a drop) di latte
un caffèlatte	caffè fatto (made) a casa con latte
un caffè corretto	caffè con un liquore
un caffè decaffeinato	caffè senza caffeina
un caffè Hag	caffè senza caffeina come (like) la Sanka
un caffè freddo	caffè freddo

Etiquette for Idiots

Italians are not big snackers; when they eat, they really eat. Although nothing is written in stone, to enhance your dining *esperienza*, a few guidelines won't hurt.

For example, in Italy, almost everything is *alla carta*—that is, ordered individually. If you want *un contorno* (a side) of veggies, you'll get a separate *piattino* because Italians almost never have more than one kind of food on a plate unless you're eating from a buffet, usually referred to as either *la tavola fredda* or *la tavola calda*.

What's What

Contrary to popular belief, Marco Polo wasn't the first to introduce *gli spaghetti* to Italy. Evidence that the Romans had various forms of pasta predates Marco Polo's adventure, although tomatoes weren't introduced to Italy until the fifteenth century from South America. It was believed that the yellow and red fruit (yes, the tomato is a fruit—the Italian word *pomodoro* literally means *golden apple*) was poisonous unless cooked for a long time.

The order of the meal is important. Generally, you order a *primo piatto* (first course), which is usually a pasta dish or soup, and then you eat your *secondo piatto* (main course). *L'insalata* is usually eaten with *il secondo piatto*. Finally, when you order *un caffè*, it is assumed that you mean *espresso*. (Remember, Italians drink espresso [and not cappuccino] after a meal, and grated cheese is never offered for pasta dishes that include fish.)

The Courses

Be creative; unless you're in a formal establishment, why not order several *antipasti* or a bunch of *contorni* and give everything *un assaggio* (a taste)? The following table outlines the different courses.

Courses

Italiano	La Definizione	English	The Definition
l'antipasto	un assaggio per stimolare l'appetito	appetizer	a taste to stimulate the appetite
il primo piatto	la pasta, il risotto, o la zuppa	first course	a pasta, risotto, or soup
il secondo piatto	la carne, il pollo, o il pesce	second course	meat, chicken, or fish
il contorno	di solito le verdure: gli spinaci, i fagioli, le melanzane, ecc.	side dish	usually vegetables: spinach, beans, eggplant, and so on

What's on the Menu?

Il cibo italiano (Italian food) can be found in *ristoranti* all over the world. You are probably already familiar with a lot of *piatti*. The following three tables help you interpret some of what you might find, although I doubt you'll have much *difficoltà* communicating your needs when it comes to eating.

I Primi Piatti

Il Primo Piatto	What It Is
brodo	broth
gnocchi al sugo di pomodoro	potato pasta with tomato sauce
lasagne	lasagna
linguine alle vongole	spaghetti in clam sauce
minestrone	vegetable soup
orecchiette ai broccoli e aglio	ear-shaped pasta with broccoli and garlic
pasta e fagioli	pasta with beans
penne alla vodka	tubes of pasta with tomato, vodka, cream, and hot peppers
ravioli di zucca e ricotta	pumpkin ravioli with ricotta cheese
risotto di mare	seafood risotto
spaghetti alla bolognese	spaghetti in meat sauce
spaghetti alla carbonara	spaghetti with bacon, egg, and Parmesan
stracciatella	egg-drop soup
tortellini prosciutto e piselli	tortellini with prosciutto and peas
zuppa di verdura toscana	Tuscan country soup

I Secondi Piatti

Il Secondo Piatto	What It Is
pollo al limone	lemon chicken
pollo ai funghi	chicken with mushrooms
polpette al ragù	meatballs in tomato sauce
cotoletta alla milanese	breaded cutlet
pollo alla francese	chicken cooked in wine and lemon sauce
involtini di vitello	veal rolls cooked in wine with mushrooms
calamari alla marinara	squid in tomato sauce
salsiccia affumicata	smoked sausage
pollo alla griglia	grilled chicken
bistecca	steak
ossobuco alla milanese	veal shanks with lemon, garlic, and parsley
agnello arrosto al rosmarino	roast lamb spiced with rosemary
anatra con vinsanto	duck with holy wine (sherry)
coda di rospo con carciofi	monkfish with artichokes

I Contorni e Gli Antipasti

Il Contorno e L'Antipasto	What It Is
la bruschetta lucchese	bruschetta with tomatoes, beans, and herbs
calamari fritti	fried calamari
cuori di carciofo marinati	marinated artichoke hearts
fagioli alla veneziana	beans, anchovies, and garlic
finocchi al cartoccio	baked fennel (literally "fennel in a bag")
formaggi vari	various cheeses
funghi trifolati	sautéed mushrooms, garlic, onion, and parsley
prosciutto con melone	prosciutto with melon
insalata	salad
insalata di pomodoro e cipolla	tomato and onion salad
insalata verde	green salad
melanzane alla griglia	grilled eggplant
patate bollite	boiled potatoes
spiedini di gamberi alla griglia	skewered, grilled shrimp
spinaci saltati	spinach tossed with garlic
zucchini fritti	fried zucchini

Ristorante Gabriella

There's no better way to understand what's on a menu than to look at one. Take a look and see how much you can understand. These are a few of my personal favorites. *Buon appetito!*

Ristorante Gabriella

La Lista

Antipasti:

Insalata di sedano, funghi e formaggio 8

Insalata di frutti di mare 10

Bruschetta al pomodoro 4

Insalata di carciofi e Parmigiano 8

Carpaccio con rucola e Parmigiano 11

Primi Piatti:

Vermicelli alle vongole 12

Polenta con porcini 10

Spaghetti alla Bolognese 10

Minestrone 8

Carni:

Spiedino misto 15

Bistecca marinata alla griglia 20

Coniglio alla contadina 18

Pesci:

Gamberi e cannellini alla Toscana 19

Filetti di Sogliola fritti 19

Lumache alla Ligure 23

Contorni:

Insalata Mista 6

Melanzane alla Griglia 8

Fiori di Zucca Ripieni 6

Dolci:

Granita al limone 3

Tiramisù 5

Zabaglione 6

Gelati o sorbetti 4

Pane e Coperto 3

Per gruppi di oltre sei persone sarà aggiunto l'8 percento di servizio.

What's What _____

In Italy, each region has its own bread. For example, *il pane toscano* is found throughout Tuscany and Umbria; here the bread has no salt, stemming back to the thirteenth century when a salt tax was imposed on the people.

La Pizza e il Formaggio

Italians like to have their own pizza, which are about as big as a plate and ordered individually. The crust is crunchy, and the pizza is lightly covered with melted cheeses ranging from *gorgonzola*, a sharp cheese; *mozzarella*, a soft delicate cheese made from the milk of water buffalo; *Parmigiano Reggiano*, a sharp cheese and one of Italy's finest; *pecorino*, a sharp cheese made from sheep milk; *provolone*, a sharp cheese often grated; and *ricotta* (literally meaning *recooked*), which is made from the whey produced in the cheese-making process, resulting in a soft, almost sweet cheese. The following table describes some of the pizza you can order.

Le Pizze

La Pizza	English Description
bianca	"white" pizza; plain (no tomato, no cheese; just crust)
ai funghi	tomato, mozzarella, and mushrooms
margherita*	tomato, mozzarella, basil
napoletana	tomato, mozzarella, anchovies
quattro formaggi	four cheeses: mozzarella, fontina, swiss, and gorgonzola
quattro stagioni	represents the four seasons: artichokes (spring), olives (summer), mushrooms (autumn), prosciutto (winter)
alle verdure	vegetables: tomato, mozzarella, zucchini, spinach, eggplant, and mushrooms

Pizza margherita was created in 1889 as a tribute to the Queen of Italy, Margherita di Savoia. Its colori, not so coincidentally, resemble those of the Italian flag.

That's the Way I Like It

Do you want your eggs scrambled or poached? Your meat cooked rare, or well done? A poached egg is called *le uova in camicia* because the white of the egg surrounds the yolk, like a shirt. Italians generally eat eggs for lunch or dinner as a *secondo piatto*. The terms in the following table will allow you to express exactly how you would like your meats and vegetables prepared.

Cooked to Order

Preparation	La Preparazione	Pronunciation
baked	al forno	*ahl for-noh*
boiled	bollito	*bohl-**lee**-toh*
breaded	impanato	*eem-pah-nah-toh*
fried	fritto	*freet-toh*
grilled	alla griglia	*ah-lah gree-lyah*
marinated	marinato	*mah-ree-**nah**-toh*
medium	normale	*nor-**mah**-leh*
poached	in camicia	*een kah-**mee**-chah*
rare	al sangue	*ahl sahn-gweh*
steamed	al vapore	*ahl **vah**-poh-reh*
well done	ben cotto	*ben koh-toh*
fried (eggs)	le uova fritte	*leh woh-vah freet-teh*
hard-boiled (eggs)	le uova bollite	*leh woh-vah boh-**lee**-teh*
poached (eggs)	le uova in camicia	*leh woh-vah een kah-**mee**-chah*
scrambled (eggs)	le uova strapazzate	*leh woh-vah strah-pah-**tsah**-teh*
soft-boiled (eggs)	le uova alla coque	*leh woh-vah ah-lah koh-kay*
omelette	la frittata	*lah freet-**tah**-tah*

Spice Up Your Life

Italian food is generally flavored with a variety of *spezie* (spices) that are subtly blended to create the dishes you love. If you want it hot, as in "spicy hot," ask for *piccante*. Need a little salt, ask for *il sale*. The following table describes some of the spices you'll encounter while eating Italian cuisine.

Spices and Seasonings

Spices	Le Spezie	Spices	Le Spezie
basil	il basilico	caper	il cappero
bay leaf	la foglia di alloro	chive	l'erba cipollina
dill	l'aneto	oregano	l'origano
garlic	l'aglio	paprika	la paprika
ginger	lo zenzero	parsley	il prezzemolo

Spices	Le Spezie	Spices	Le Spezie
honey	il miele	pepper	il pepe
ketchup	il ketchup	rosemary	il rosmarino
mint	la menta	saffron	lo zafferano
mustard	la senape	salt	il sale
nutmeg	la noce moscata	sugar	lo zucchero

Special People Have Special Needs

You're in great shape and have eliminated certain things from your *dieta*. There's no reason to destroy all your hard work with one visit to Italy. The phrases in the following table will help you stick to your *dieta*.

Special Needs

Phrase	La Frase
I am allergic to …	Sono allergico/a a …
I am on a diet.	Faccio la dieta/Sto in dieta.
I'm a vegetarian.	Sono vegetariano(a).
Do you serve Kosher food?	Servite del cibo Kosher?
I can't have any …	Non posso prendere …
… dairy products.	… i latticini.
… alcohol.	… l'alcol.
… saturated fat.	… i grassi saturi.
… shellfish.	… i frutti di mare.
I'm looking for a dish …	Cerco un piatto …
… high in fiber.	… con molta fibra.
… low in cholesterol.	… con poco colesterolo.
… low in fat.	… con pochi grassi.
… low in sodium.	… poco salato.
… without preservatives.*	… senza conservanti.

Be sure to use the Italian word conservanti *and not the false cognate* preservativi, *which means prophylactics!*

You Call This Food?

You asked for a rare steak, but you received what looks like a *scarpa*; there's a small nail in your pizza (don't worry, you won't be charged extra), and a hair in your spaghetti. The following table gives you the terms.

Take It Away!

English	Italiano
This is ...	Questo è ...
... burned.	... bruciato.
... dirty.	... sporco.
... overcooked.	... troppo cotto.
... spoiled.	... andato a male.
... too cold.	... troppo freddo.
... too rare.	... troppo crudo.
... too salty.	... troppo salato.
... too spicy.	... troppo piccante.
... too sweet.	... troppo dolce.
... unacceptable.	... inaccettabile.

Fine Wine

Italian wines are among the best in the world, fulfilling one fifth of the total production. Wine talk is presented in the following table.

Bottle o' Wine, Fruit of the Vine

Wine	Il Vino
red wine	il vino rosso
rosè wine	il vino rosè
white wine	il vino bianco
dry wine	il vino secco
sweet wine	il vino dolce
sparkling wine	lo spumante

> ### As a *Regola*
>
> Italian standards for wine are very high. The next time you go for a *degustazione vini* (wine tasting), it might help you to know a little about how Italian wines are classified.
>
> Finer wines are classified as *denominazione di origine controllata* (DOC) or *denominazione di origine controllata e garantita* (DOCG), which you'll see on the wine label.
>
> Other wines are simply classified as *vino da tavola* (table wine), which range in quality and are served by many restaurants as *il vino della casa* (the house wine).

A *Bellini* Please

One of Italy's most popular cocktails is the *Bellini*, created by Giuseppe Cipriani of Harry's Bar in Venice. This light, refreshing drink is perfect before a meal. You can find the translation in Appendix A.

> *Bellini*
>
> ²/₃ tazza (160 ml.) di purè di pesca
> 1 cucchiaino di purè di lampone
> 1 bottiglia di Prosecco (o Asti Spumante o champagne)
>
> In ogni bicchiere di vino o spumante, versate 7 cucchiaini di purè di pesca. Aggiungete 2–3 goccie di purè di lampone. Aggiungete il vino e servite subito.

What's Your Fancy?

Gli aperitivi (aperitifs) and *gli amari* (digestives) are a lovely part of a meal. Try something new, and bring back a bottle of Cynar (made from artichokes) to share with your friends. A common practice is to drink Sambuca with a couple of coffee beans (*grani di caffè*). In some parts, they are called *le mosche* (flies) because of their resemblance to the little pests. Word has it that this controls garlic breath (and you're going to be eating *a lot* of garlic). You'll find many drinks to try in the following table.

Gli Alcolici

Gli Aperitivi	Gli Amari
Aperol	Fernet
Campari (bevuto con/senza acqua mineralle frizzante)	Jeigermeister (Germania)
Cynar (di carciofo)	Lucano

continues

Gli Alcolici   (continued)

Gli Aperitivi	Gli Amari
Martini (bianco o rosso)	Petrus (Olanda)
Negroni	Averna

I Dolci

Italians don't fool around when it comes to dessert. Many *dolci* are peculiar to a particular region and cannot be found elsewhere.

The following list mentions some of the sweets you can find in Italy. If baked goods, such as *biscotti* (cookies, literally meaning *twice-baked*) and *torte* (cakes), don't trip your trigger, dip into *un gelato* (ice cream) at a *gelateria* where you are given up to three flavors in any *porzione* (portion). If you're not sure of a flavor, ask for *un assaggio* (a taste).

Bavarese (as in Bavarian)	*Panettone*
Biscotti di mandorle (almond cookies)	*Panforte* (Tuscan)
Cannolo (Sicilian)	*Profiterole*
Colomba	*Ricciarelli* (Tuscan)
Cornetto	*Sfogliatella della Nobiltà* (noble's pastry)
Danese (Danish)	*Torta di Frutta Fresca*
Diplomatico (literally, diplomat)	*Tiramisù* (literally, pick me up)
Macedonia di frutta (mixed fruit)	*Ventaglio*
Maritozzo	*Zuppa Inglese* (English trifle)
Millefoglie (literally, 1,000 leaves)	

Comparatives and Superlatives

In Chapter 6 you learned all about adjectives and adverbs. In addition to describing nouns and verbs, you use adjectives and adverbs to compare things. Often, you can add *-er* or *-est* to an adjective in English to indicate that something is more (or less) beautiful, big, sweet, tall, and so on, as in *She is sweeter than honey; in fact, she is the sweetest person I have ever met.* Use the following table to help you compare things.

Comparison of Adjectives: Inequality

	Italiano	**English**
Adjective	dolce	sweet
Comparative	più dolce	sweeter
	meno dolce	less sweet
Superlative	il/la* più dolce	the sweetest
	il/la* meno dolce	the least sweet

Note: The same rules apply using the plural articles i, gli, *and* le.

♦ To compare one thing as being either more or less than another, place the word *più* (more) or *meno* (less) before the adjective:

> *Questo ristorante è più caro.*
> This restaurant is more expensive.
>
> *Quel ristorante è meno caro.*
> That restaurant is less expensive.

♦ To express the English *than,* use the preposition *di* (or its contraction) in front of nouns and pronouns:

> *Ho più amici di te.*
> I have more friends than you.
>
> *Il gatto è più piccolo del cane.*
> The cat is smaller than the dog.
>
> *I cani sono più grandi dei gatti.*
> Dogs are bigger than cats.

♦ The comparative and superlative forms of the adjectives must agree in gender and number with the nouns they describe:

> *La luna è meno grande della terra.*
> The moon is smaller than the earth.
>
> *I tuoi occhi sono i più belli.*
> Your eyes are the most beautiful.

♦ *Che* is used when making comparisons of quantity, when comparing two qualities pertaining to the same person or thing, or when comparing two infinitive verbs:

> *più ... di (che)*
> more ... than

meno ... di (che)
less ... than

Tu sei più alto di me.
You are taller than I.

Io sono meno alta di te.
I am less tall than you.

Di sera fa più freddo che di giorno.
The evening is colder than the day.

Meglio tardi che mai.
Better late than never.

È più facile giocare che studiare.
It's easier to play than study.

CAUTION

Attenzione!

You've seen *che* used as an interrogative adjective meaning *what*. It is also used with the subjunctive signifying *that* and *than*. Look for clues in a sentence that can help you determine its meaning. The following examples illustrate the different uses of this word:

Che significa?
What does it mean?

*È più bello cantare **che** urlare.*
Singing is more beautiful **than** shouting.

*Penso **che** Giulia sia simpatica.*
I think **that** Giulia is nice.

◆ To make a relative comparison between two things, simply add *più* (more) or *meno* (less) before the adjective or adverb:

> *Questo è il ristorante più caro.*
> This restaurant is the most expensive.
>
> *Quello è il ristorante meno caro.*
> That restaurant is the least expensive.

Better Than the Best

In addition to having regular forms, some adjectives have irregular comparative and superlative forms. Are you good? Getting better? Or the best?

Irregular Adjective Comparatives and Superlatives

Adjective	Comparative	Relative Superlative
buono (good)	*migliore* (better)	*il/la migliore* (the best)
cattivo (bad)	*peggiore* (worse)	*il/la peggiore* (the worst)
grande (big/great)	*maggiore* (bigger/greater)	*il/la maggiore* (the biggest/greatest)
piccolo (small)	*minore* (smaller/lesser)	*il/la minore* (the smallest/least)

What's What

Maggiore and *minore* are often used to reference family members, such as younger sister or older brother. The superlative is used to indicate *the oldest* or *the youngest*.

> *Mio fratello minore si chiama Roberto.*
> My younger brother is called Robert.

The superlatives migliore, peggiore, maggiore, and minore drop the final -e before nouns, except with nouns beginning with s + consonant or z:

> *Tu sei la mia miglior amica!*
> You are my best friend!

Irregular Comparisons

How are you doing? Well? A perfect illustration of an irregular adverb is the English word *well*. In Italian, irregular adverbs are easily learned. The following table outlines some of the most commonly used adverbs.

Irregular Adverb Comparatives and Superlatives

Adverb	Comparative	Absolute Superlative
bene (well)	*meglio* (better)	*benissimo* (best)
male (badly)	*peggio* (very badly)	*malissimo* (worse)
molto (much/a lot)	*più, di più* (more)	*moltissimo* (very much)
poco (little)	*meno, di meno* (less)	*pochissimo* (very little)

La Bella Lingua

Give all that you have to give! To say this in Italian, use the following *espressione: Farò del mio meglio.* (I will do my best.)

To make the relative superlative, simply add the definite article in front of the comparative:

> *Arrivo il più presto possibile.*
> I'm arriving as soon as possible.

> *Faccio del mio meglio.*
> I'm doing my best.

Comparisons of Equality

To say that something is as good as another is called a comparison of equality.

♦ To say that two things are equal:

> *tanto … quanto* + adjective or adverb
> as … as + adjective or adverb

> *così … come* + adjective or adverb
> as … as + adjective or adverb

As a *Regola*

Ottimo is often used in addition to *buonissimo* when something is really great, as in the best. *Pessimo* is used to describe something that is as bad as bad can get, as in *Questo ristorante è pessimo.* (This restaurant is the worst.)

> *Jessica è tanto alta quanto Gabriella.*
> Jessica is as tall as Gabriella.

> *Tu sei così bello come tuo padre.*
> You are as handsome as your father.

> *Mi piace sciare tanto quanto giocare a tennis.*
> I like skiing as much as playing tennis.

> *L'insegnante impara tanto quanto insegna.*
> The teacher learns as much as she teaches.

♦ Personal pronouns following *come* or *quanto* are always stressed:

> *Io sono intelligente come te.*
> I am as intelligent as you are.

> *Tu sei come me.*
> You are like me.

Absolutely, Totally Superlative

If something is really extraordinary, you can use the adverb *veramente* (truly) or *molto* (very) in front of your adjective or adverb. Or, to show the extreme of something, a poetic, commonly used ending is *-issimo*. The following table lists a few adjectives (which must always reflect gender and number) used in this manner.

Above Average

Adjective	Very	Extremely
bello	molto bello	bellissimo
buono	molto buono	buonissimo/ottimo*
cattivo	molto cattivo	cattivissimo/pessimo*
grande	molto grande	grandissimo
piccolo	molto piccolo	piccolissimo
vecchio	molto vecchio	vecchissimo
veloce	molto veloce	velocissimo

*Irregular.

Infinitive Verbs and Prepositions

The infinitive of a verb, as you know, is a verb before it has been conjugated, or the *to* form of a verb, as in *to study*, *to laugh*, and *to cry*. Sometimes an infinitive takes a different form, as in this sentence: I plan on *studying* a lot this summer.

In Italian, when a verb does not have a subject, it is usually in its infinitive form, even if this form resembles the gerund (*-ing* form) of the verb.

Some Italian verbs are preceded by a preposition, others are followed by a preposition, and some take none at all. Knowing when to use a preposition is often a question of usage, because the meaning of a verb can change when used with one. This applies in English as well; compare these two sentences and see how the meaning changes by changing the preposition:

I want to go *on* the plane.   I want to go *to* the plane.

Italian prepositions sometimes change while their English counterparts do not:

(*pensare di*)	*Penso **di** andare in italia.*
	I am thinking **of** going to Italy.
(*pensare a*)	*Penso **a** te.*
	I'm thinking **of** you.

Memorization might work for the few who have a photographic memory, but for the rest of us, practice and usage are the only way to remember which verb takes what. After you have repeated something three times, you generally remember it.

CAUTION

Attenzione! _____

It is important to avoid literally translating from one language to another—context is key—because you might get caught up in details that cannot be completely "decoded." For example, in Italian you must use the preposition *in* when visiting a country and *a* for cities. In English, you simply use *to*. When translating from Italian to English, there is no distinction between the two.

Alone at Last

For some verbs, you don't have to worry about the preposition at all. The following verbs can be followed by an infinitive without a preposition.

Verbs Without a Preposition

Italiano	English	Italiano	English
amare	to love	potere	to be able
bastare	to suffice	preferire	to prefer
desiderare	to desire	sapere	to know (something)
dovere	to have to	sembrare	to seem
fare	to do/make	sentire	to listen
lasciare	to leave (something behind)	vedere	to see
occorrere	to be necessary	volere	to want
parere	to seem		

Oddballs

There are always going to be peculiarities that cannot be translated. The verbs and idiomatic expressions used in the following table require the preposition *di* when followed by an infinitive.

Verbs and Idiomatic Expressions Taking di Before an Infinitive

English	Italiano	English	Italiano
to accept from	accettare di …	to hope to	sperare di …
to admit to	ammettere di …	to intend to	avere intenzione di …
to ask for	chiedere di …	to offer to	offrire di …
to be afraid of	avere paura di …	to order to	ordinare di …

English	Italiano	English	Italiano
to be in the mood for	avere voglia di …	to permit to	permettere di …
to be right about	avere ragione di …	to pray to	pregare di …
to believe in	credere di …	to remember to	ricordare di …
to decide to	decidere di …	to repeat to	ripetere di …
to dream of	sognare di …	to respond to	rispondere di …
to expect to	aspettare di …	to say to	dire di …
to finish	finire di …	to speak of	parlare di …
to forget to	dimenticare di …	to think of	pensare di …
to have need of	avere bisogno di …	to search for	cercare di …
		to stop/quit	smettere di …

The Preposition *a*

Some verbs, as in the following table, take the preposition *a* before an infinitive. Pay attention to how the preposition in the English changes from one verb to the next. While you *help* **to** *protect someone*, you *succeed* **at** *your job*. (This flexible nature of prepositions is what makes them as annoying as fruit flies.)

The Preposition *a* Before an Infinitive

English	Italiano	English	Italiano
to be at	stare a …	to help to	aiutare a …
to be careful to	stare attento a …	to invite to	invitare a …
to be ready to	essere pronto a …	to learn to	imparare a …
to begin to	cominciare a …	to pass to	passare a …
to bring to	portare a …	to prepare for/to	preparare a …
to come to	venire a …	to return to	tornare a …
to enter into	entrare a …	to run to	correre a…
to exit to	uscire a …	to succeed at	riuscire a …
to go to	andare a …	to teach to	insegnare a …

Learning by Example

Complete the sentences using the subjects provided. Translate the sentences. (You can find the answers in Appendix A.)

Example:	_____ essere brava. (io/cercare di)
Answer:	Cerco di essere brava. (I try to be good.)

1. _____ studiare. (voi/avere bisogno di)

2. _____ parlare l'italiano. (tu/imparare a)

3. _____ lavorare mentre studia. (Cristoforo/continuare a)

4. _____ dormire presto. (noi/andare a)

5. _____ fumare le sigarette. (io/smettere di)

6. _____ mangiare alle 8.00. (Loro/finire di)

Present Progressive Tense (-ing)

In Italian, the present progressive tense is used to describe an action in progress.

Because the Italian present tense can serve as both the simple present and the progressive, native Italian, French, and Spanish speakers have difficulty distinguishing the difference between *I am going to the store now* and *I go to the store now*. In English, we use the present progressive much more often than the simple present tense.

To form the present progressive, you'll need the verb *stare* (to be; to stay). This helping verb does most of the work because the present participle does not change.

To create the present participle, simply slice off the infinitive ending of the verb and add the progressive endings in the following table.

Notice how the *-ere* and the *-ire* progressive tense endings are the same.

Present Progressive

Infinitive Verb		Present Progressive	English
studi**are**	→	studi**ando**	studying
scriv**ere**	→	scriv**endo**	writing
fin**ire**	→	fin**endo**	finishing

The following table takes the verb *studiare* and shows what happens when we attach the auxiliary verb *stare* to the present progressive.

Forming the Present Progressive

Studiare	To Study
io sto studiando	I am studying
tu stai studiando	you are studying
lui/lei/Lei sta studiando	he/she is studying
noi stiamo studiando	we are studying
voi state studiando	you are studying
loro stanno studiando	they are studying

Making Progress

Turn the following sentences into the present progressive. (Hint: You need to determine the infinitive of the verb before you can find the appropriate progressive form. You can find the answers in Appendix A.)

1. Guardiamo il film.
2. Scrivi una lettera.
3. Nicola cucina la cena.
4. I bambini dormono.
5. Leggo il libro.
6. Pulisco la camera.

The Least You Need to Know

♦ Ask to make a reservation using the expression *Vorrei fare una prenotazione* or *Vorrei prenotare un tavolo*. Do not use the cognate *riservare*, which means *to keep* or *to put aside*.

♦ There are several parts to an Italian meal: *gli antipasti, i contorni, i primi piatti, i secondi piatti,* and *i dolci*.

♦ Use *meno* (less) or *più* (more) before adjectives and adverbs to make comparisons or express the superlative.

♦ Use *(tanto) quanto* or *(così) come* to express that things are equal.

♦ Use the ending *-issimo* to form the absolute superlative of adverbs and adjectives.

♦ The present progressive tense is used to indicate an action that is occurring in the moment. It requires the use of the present participle (the verb form ending in *-ing*).

Made in *Italia:* Using Object Pronouns and Shopping

In This Chapter

- ◆ Stores and their wares
- ◆ Bejeweled and bedazzled—Italian style
- ◆ Clothing: colors, sizes, and materials
- ◆ Direct and indirect object pronouns
- ◆ Double object and disjunctive pronouns

The word *Italian* is synonymous with style, and whether you bring back hand-blown wine glasses from the famous Venetian island Murano, a Fendi bag from Milano, or an expressive cameo made in Florence, Italy is a place you definitely want to shop.

Stores Galore

As you meander through the *strade* of Italia, you might find some *liquirizia* lozenges in a small *tabaccheria*, a silk scarf gently blowing in the wind at the *mercato*, or a hand-painted porcelain doll staring blankly in a *vetrina*. Whatever you discover, there's no question about it: Shopping for new delights is one of life's greatest pleasures.

Most stores will ship major purchases for you. Some purchases made with a credit card will be covered for loss or damage. The I.V.A. (value-added tax) is a sales tax attached to all major purchases. Save your receipts—non-European travelers receive I.V.A. refunds when they leave the country.

> *Posso avere la ricevuta, per favore?*
> May I have a receipt, please?

The following table will help you find your way to the stores that carry the merchandise you're looking for. Italian terms are given with the appropriate definite article.

Stores

Il Negozio	La Merce	The Store	The Merchandise
la bottega	tutto	shop	everything
la cartoleria	la carta, le cartoline, i giochi, le sigarette	stationery store	paper, postcards, toys, cigarettes
la farmacia	le medicine	pharmacy	medicine
il fioraio	i fiori, le piante	florist	flowers, plants
la gioielleria	i gioielli	jewelry store	jewelry
il giornalaio	i giornali, le riviste, le cartoline	newspaper stand	newspapers, magazines, postcards
il grande magazzino	i gioielli, i giochi, le riviste, i mobili, i profumi, i vestiti	department store	jewelry, toys, magazines, furnishings, perfumes, clothing
la libreria	i libri	bookstore	books
il mercato	tutto	market	everything
il negozio d'abbigliamento	l'abbigliamento, i vestiti	clothing store	clothing
il negozio d'arredamento	i mobili	furniture store	furniture
il negozio di scarpe	le scarpe	shoe store	shoes
la pasticceria	le paste, le torte, i biscotti	pastry shop	pastries, cakes, cookies
la pelletteria	le giacche, le borse, le valigie	leather store	jackets, purses, luggage

Il Negozio	La Merce	The Store	The Merchandise
la profumeria	i profumi, i cosmetici	cosmetics shop	perfumes, cosmetics
la tabaccheria	le sigarette, i sigari, i fiammiferi	tobacco shop	cigarettes, cigars, matches

La Cartoleria

In addition to office supplies, stationery, candy, and cigarettes, *la cartoleria* often sells stamps and bus tickets. It's also a good place to find inexpensive gift items.

La Cartoleria (The Stationary Store)

Stationery	La Cartoleria	Pronunciation
candy	le caramelle	*leh kar-ah-**mehl**-leh*
cigarettes	le sigarette	*leh see-gah-**reht**-teh*
cigars	i sigari	*ee **see**-gah-ree*
gift	il regalo	*eel reh-**gah**-loh*
a guidebook	una guida	*oo-nah gwee-dah*
lighter	l'accendino	*lah-chen-**dee**-noh*
map	la pianta, la cartina, … la mappa	*lah pee-**ahn**-tah, lah kar-**tee**-nah, … lah mah-pah*
matches	i fiammiferi	*ee fee-ahm-**mee**-feh-ree*
notebook	il quaderno	*eel kwah-**der**-noh*
paper	la carta	*lah kar-tah*
pen	la penna	*lah pehn-nah*
pencil	la matita	*lah mah-tee-tah*
postcard	la cartolina	*lah kar-toh-**lee**-nah*
stamp	il francobollo	*eel fran-koh-**boh**-loh*
ticket	il biglietto	*eel beel-**yeh**-toh*
… for the bus	… per l'autobus	*… per **lau**-toh-boos*
… for the metro	… per la metro	*… per lah meh-troh*

La Profumeria

We all need a little help now and then. Makeup isn't called *il trucco* (the trick) for nothing! Many toiletries, cosmetics, and perfume can be found at *la profumeria*. Other sundries can be found at *la farmacia*. Refer to Chapter 18 for a comprehensive list.

La Profumeria (The Cosmetics Store)

English	Italiano	English	Italiano
blush	il fard	eye shadow	l'ombretto
body lotion	la crema per il corpo	nail polish	lo smalto per le unghie
brush	la spazzola	perfume	il profumo

Diamonds Are a Girl's Best Friend

It could be a sapphire ring, a gold watch, or a silver chain that catches your eye. Throughout Italy, you'll find a *tradizione* of fine gold- and silversmithing, with some of the most exquisite jewelry in the world. The following table shows you how to ask for it. I've given you the definite articles.

Jewelry

Object	Oggetto	Pronunciation
amethyst	l'ametista	*lah-meh-**tees**-tah*
aquamarine	l'acquamarina	*lah-kwah-mah-**ree**-nah*
bracelet	il braccialetto	*eel brah-chah-**leh**-toh*
cameo	il cammeo	*eel kahm-**meh**-oh*
chain	la catena	*lah kah-**teh**-nah*
cufflinks	i gemelli	*ee jeh-meh-lee*
diamond	il diamante	*eel dee-ah-**mahn**-teh*
earrings	gli orecchini	*ylee oh-reh-**kee**-nee*
enamel	lo smalto	*loh smal-toh*
gold	l'oro	*loh-roh*
jade	la giada	*lah jah-dah*
jewelry	i gioielli	*ee joy-**yeh**-lee*
mother-of-pearl	la madreperla	*lah mah-dreh-**per**-lah*
onyx	l'onice	***loh**-nee-cheh*

Object	Oggetto	Pronunciation
pearls	le perle	*leh per-leh*
pendant	il ciondolo	*eel **chon**-doh-loh*
pewter	il peltro	*eel pel-troh*
platinum	il platino	*il **plah**-tee-noh*
precious stone	la pietra preziosa	*lah pee-eh-trah pre-zee-**oh**-zah*
ring	l'anello	*lah-**neh**-loh*
... engagement ring	... l'anello di fidanzamento	*... lah-**neh**-loh dee fee-**dahn**-zah-men-toh*
... wedding ring	... la fede	*... lah feh-deh*
ruby	il rubino	*eel roo-**bee**-noh*
sapphire	lo zaffiro	*loh zah-**fee**-roh*
silver	l'argento	*lar-**jen**-toh*
topaz	il topazio	*eel toh-**pah**-zee-oh*
turquoise	il turchese	*eel toor-**keh**-zeh*

La Bella Lingua

Is your watch fast? Tell the repair person *Va avanti.* Is it slow? Tell him *Va indietro.*

battery	*la batteria, la pila*	watch	*l'orologio*
chain	*la catena*	watch band	*il cinturino*
clasp	*il gancio*		

Say "Mozzarella"

You bought what you thought was enough film for your camera, but now you need more. You want to buy a cap for your lens before it gets scratched—and it could also use a good cleaning.

Dal Negozio di Fotografia (At the Camera Shop)

English	Italiano	English	Italiano
battery	la batteria, la pila	flash	il "flash"
camera	la macchina fotografica	lens	l'obiettivo
exposure	l'esposizione	transformer	il trasformatore
film	la pellicola, il film	to develop	sviluppare
filter	il filtro		

It's in the Jeans

Italians seem to be born knowing how to dress. If the body is a blank canvas, they sure know how to paint! Maybe it's in part because Italians are used to being watched—and to watching each other. Some would say it's all in *le scarpe* (the shoes), the finely woven fabrics, and the tailoring. Whatever the reason, *la moda* is a refined *eleganza* that has deep and powerful roots, permeating Italian culture. If you're hoping some of that Italian style will rub off on you, the following table gives you some helpful words to get you started.

L'Abbigliamento (Clothing)

Clothing Item	Italiano	Pronunciation
article	l'articolo	*lahr-tee-koh-loh*
bathing suit	il costume di bagno	*eel kohs-too-meh dee bahn-yoh*
bra	il reggiseno	*eel reh-jee-seh-noh*
clothing	l'abbigliamento	*lah-beel-yah-men-toh*
… women's	… per donna	*per dohn-nah*
… men's	… per uomo	*per woh-moh*
… children	… per bambini	*per bam-bee-nee*
coat	il cappotto/il giubbotto	*eel kah-poht-toh/eel joob-boht-toh*
dress	l'abito	*lah-bee-toh*
… evening dress	… l'abito da sera	*lah-bee-toh dah seh-rah*
jeans	i jeans	*ee jeens*
jacket	la giacca	*lah jahk-kah*
lining	la fodera	*lah foh-deh-rah*
model	il modello	*eel moh-dehl-loh*
pajamas	il pigiama	*eel pee-jah-mah*
pants	i pantaloni	*ee pahn-tah-loh-nee*
pullover	il golf	*eel golf*
raincoat	l'impermeabile	*leem-per-mee-ah-bee-leh*
robe	l'accappatoio	*lah-kahp-pah-toh-yoh*
skirt	la gonna	*lah gohn-nah*
suit	il completo	*eel kom-pleh-toh*
sweat suit	la tuta da ginnastica	*lah too-tah dah jee-nah-stee-kah*
sweater	la maglia	*lah mah-lyah*
t-shirt	la maglietta	*lah mah-lyeh-tah*

Clothing Item	Italiano	Pronunciation
undershirt	la canottiera	*lah kan-oht-tee-**yeh**-rah*
underwear	gli slip	*ylee sleep*
... panties	... le mutandine	*leh moo-tahn-**dee**-neh*
... briefs	... le mutande	*leh moo-**tahn**-deh*

La Bella Lingua

Note the subtle shift in meaning when the noun (and its article) is made plural:

> Fare **la** spesa (singular) generally means you are shopping for the household (groceries).

> Fare **le** spese (plural) refers to shopping in general, as in "shop 'til you drop!"

Accessories

By adding *gli accessori* that best complement your wardrobe, you can look like a million bucks without spending a million *euros*.

Accessories

Clothing Item	Italiano	Pronunciation
accessories	gli accessori	*ylee ah-chess-**oh**-ree*
belt	la cintura	*lah cheen-**too**-rah*
boots	gli stivali	*ylee stee-**vah**-lee*
cosmetics	i cosmetici	*ee kos-meh-**tee**-chee*
gloves	i guanti	*ee gwahn-tee*
handkerchief	il fazzoletto	*eel fah-tsoh-**leht**-toh*
hat	il cappello	*eel kahp-**pehl**-loh*
lingerie	la biancheria intima	*lah bee-an-keh-**ree**-yah **een**-tee-mah*
pantyhose	i collant	*ee kohl-lant*
purse	la borsa	*lah bor-sah*
sandals	i sandali	*ee **sahn**-dah-lee*
scarf	la sciarpa	*lah shar-pah*
shoes	le scarpe	*leh skar-peh*
slippers	le pantofole	*leh pahn-**toh**-foh-leh*

continues

Accessories (continued)

Clothing Item	Italiano	Pronunciation
sneakers	le scarpe da tennis	*leh skar-peh dah teh-nees*
socks	le calze*, i calzini	*leh kal-zeh, ee kal-zee-nee*
stockings	le calze	*leh kal-zeh*
umbrella	l'ombrello	*lohm-breh-loh*

*Do you see this word in calzone *(the kind you eat)?*

How Do I Look?

The helpful expressions in the following table will make your shopping even more enjoyable.

Phrases for Shopping 'Til You Drop

Espressione	Expression
Che taglia porta?	What size do you wear?
Porto la misura …	I wear size …
Che numero di scarpe?	What size shoe?
Porto il numero …	I wear a size …
Dov'è il camerino?	Where is the fitting room?
Sto solo dando un'occhiata.	I'm just looking.
Questo è (troppo) …	This is (too) …
… caro.	… expensive, dear.
… classico.	… classical.
… corto.	… short.
… di moda.	… in fashion.
… economico.	… inexpensive.
… fuori stagione.	… out of season.
… grande.	… big.
… lungo.	… long.
… stretto.	… tight.
il commesso/la commessa	the sales clerk
la misura, la taglia**	the size
il numero di scarpe	the shoe size

Espressione	Expression
il prezzo	the price
lo sconto	discount
la svendita	sale
la taglia: piccola, media, grande	size: small, medium, large
la vetrina	shop window

****Like the word* tagliatelle.

One Size Does Not Fit All

The following table will help you determine what *misura* you are.

Conversion Tables for Clothing Sizes

Italy	United States	Italy	United States
Women—Clothing		Men—Clothing	
38	4	44	34
40	6	46	36
42	8	48	38
44	10	50	40
46	12	52	42
48	14	54	44
50	16	56	46
52	18	58	48
		60	50
Women—Shoes		Men—Shoes	
35	5	38	5
36	6	39	6
37	7	40	7
38	8	41	8
39	9	42	9
40	10	43	10
41	11	44	11
		45	12
		46	13

To convert centimeters into inches, divide by .39. To convert inches into centimeters, multiply by 2.54.

Smooth as *Seta*

Fine Italian cloth, such as silks, cashmeres, wools, cottons, and chiffons, are practically a national treasure. Rather than spend a *fortuna* on designer clothing, you might consider buying the fabrics and having a *sarto* (tailor) sew something custom-made to your style and fit. The following table will give you the *vocabolario* to describe *esattamente* what you want. For an unforgettable tale of love and adventure, check out the book *Seta* written by Alessandro Baricco (Rizzoli, 1998).

Fabric

Fabric	Italiano	Pronunciation
acetate	l'acetato	*lah-cheh-**tah**-toh*
cashmere	il cachemire	*eel kah-sheh-**mee**-reh*
chiffon	lo chiffon	*loh shee-fohn*
cotton	il cotone	*eel koh-**toh**-neh*
flannel	la flanella	*lah flah-**nehl**-lah*
gabardine	il gabardine	*eel gah-bar-**dee**-neh*
knit	la maglia	*lah mah-lyah*
lace	il merletto	*eel mer-**leht**-toh*
	il pizzo	*eel pee-tsoh*
leather	il cuoio	*eel kwoy-yoh*
	la pelle	*lah pehl-leh*
linen	il lino	*eel lee-noh*
nylon	il nylon	*eel ny-lon*
rayon	il rayon	*eel ray-on*
silk	la seta	*lah seh-tah*
taffeta	il taffettà	*eel tahf-feh-**tah***
velvet	il velluto	*eel vehl-**loo**-toh*
wool	la lana	*lah lah-nah*

If the Shoe Fits ...

You've never walked this much before, and every step takes you deeper into the mystery of *Italia*. Maybe you want to have your *scarpe* stretched, a heel replaced, or a new shoelace added. The phrases in the following table will help you.

Dal Calzolaio (At the Shoemaker's)

English	Italiano	English	Italiano
boot	lo stivale	sole	la suola
heel	il tacco	to stretch	allargare
shoe	la scarpa	to shine	lucidare
shoelace	il laccio da scarpe	to repair	riparare
shoemaker	il calzolaio		

The Dirt on Dirt (and Other Mishaps)

Perhaps you went out *ieri sera*, and now your favorite silk shirt has a *macchia* (stain) on it. Then there's that grass smudge on your pants from the picnic you had in the *parco* the other day. Having fun, aren't we? Here's the lingo you'll need to keep your pants on straight.

In Tintoria (At the Dry Cleaner's)

English	Italiano
There is ...	C'è ...
... a stain.	... una macchia.
... a missing button.	... un bottone che manca.
... a tear.	... uno strappo.
Can you dry-clean this (these ...) for me?	Mi potete lavare a secco questo (questi ...)?
Can you mend this (these ...) for me?	Mi potete rammendare questo (questi ...)?
Can you iron this (these ...) for me?	Mi potete stirare questo (questi ...)?
Can you starch this (these ...) for me?	Mi potete inamidare questo (questi ...)?
When will it be ready?	Quando sarà pronto?
I need it as soon as possible.	Ne ho bisogno il più presto possibile.

The Florist

Flowers are often associated with particular occasions or with certain emotions. For example, red roses are traditionally used to make a declaration of love. Chrysanthemums are given at funerals. Regardless of whether you're giving flowers, reading about them, or just stopping to smell the roses, the following table will give you some sweet-smelling help.

Flowers

Flower	Il Fiore	Flower	Il Fiore
carnation	il garofano	orchid	l'orchidea
chrysanthemum	il crisantemo	pansy	la viola del pensiero
daffodil	la giunchiglia	petunia	la petunia
dandelion	il dente di leone	poppy	il papavero
daisy	la margherita	rose	la rosa
flower	il fiore	sunflower	il girasole
lily	il giglio	violet	la violetta

Sock It to Me!

Imagine you're shopping for clothes and see the following items in the shop window. See how many you can identify and write in Italian. (You can find the answers in Appendix A.)

La Bella Lingua

Whether you need to raise, lower, loosen, or tighten your clothes, a visit to *il sarto* or *la sarta* (tailor) may be required. Start with *Vorrei* (I would like) + the appropriate expression + the item you want mended.

aggiustare	to mend
cucire	to sew
fare l'orlo a	to hem
modificare	to alter
rammendare	to mend

Pants: _____

Belt: _____

Pullover: _____

Shoes: _____

Socks: _____

Umbrella: _____

Coat: _____

Scarf: _____

Skirt: _____

Gloves: _____

Hat: _____

Shoes: _____

Stockings: _____

Purse: _____

Objection!

In this chapter, you've learned all about shopping and how to ask for what you want. Since we're on the subject of precious objects, this is as good an *opportunità* as any to introduce objects and object pronouns. Although not as exciting as shopping for new shoes, understanding object pronouns can certainly help you purchase them (I want those and those and these and those …).

A Little Review

As a reminder: An object pronoun sits in place of the object in a sentence. In Italian, it must agree in gender and number with the noun it is replacing. There are direct and indirect object pronouns. The key is to understand what an object is.

A direct object indicates who or what is affected by the verb's action. When you say, "I love *my mother,*" the object of your love (and the verb) is Mommie Dearest. You can replace the object *my mother* with a direct object pronoun and simply say, "I love *her.*"

An indirect object answers the question *to whom* or *for whom.* Indirect objects refer only to people (and pets) and are generally preceded by the preposition *to* or *for.*

When you say, "I talk *to my parents* every week," you could replace *to my parents* with an indirect object pronoun, as in "I talk *to them* every week."

In Italian, you also use double object pronouns, like when you say, "Give it to her." These pronouns are covered in Chapter 18.

Stressed pronouns are used to emphasize and highlight certain nouns or pronouns. These are briefly covered in Chapter 20.

Objectify Me, Baby

The object pronouns may be confusing for the non-native speaker because of their similarity to each other as well as to the articles and other words in Italian. This is why it is so important to listen to the context of a sentence. One trick is to remember that direct and indirect object pronouns are all the same except in the third person singular and plural forms. As shown in the following table, *gli* is commonly used to replace *loro* primarily in the spoken language.

The following table outlines the object pronouns in Italian. It might help you to see how the direct and indirect object pronouns correspond to the subject pronouns.

Direct and Indirect Object Pronouns

Subject Pronouns	Direct Object Pronouns		Indirect Object Pronouns	
io	**mi**	me	**mi**	to me
tu	**ti**	you	**ti**	to you
lui	**lo**	he/it	**gli**	to him
lei	**la**	she/it	**le**	to her
Lei	**La**	You	**Le**	to You
noi	**ci**	us	**ci**	to us
voi	**vi**	you	**vi**	to you
loro	**li/le**	them (m./f.)	**a loro/gli**	to them

Follow the Rules

The following rules will make it easier to understand Italian object pronouns. Study the examples:

1. All Italian object pronouns agree in gender and number with the nouns they replace. The referred object is given in parentheses:

Direct object pronouns:

La vedo ogni giorno. (Maria)
I see **her** every day. (Maria)

Li vedo ogni settimana. (i ragazzi)
I see **them** every week. (the boys)

Indirect object pronouns:

Gli offro una mano. (a mio fratello)
I offer **him** a hand. (to my brother)

Le mando un bacio. (alla ragazza)
I send **her** a kiss. (the girl)

2. Both direct and indirect object pronouns are usually placed immediately before a conjugated verb.

*Leopoldo compra il giornale e **lo** legge a Mario.*
Leopoldo buys the newspaper and reads **it** to Mario. (direct)

*Giulia **gli** legge una storia.*
Giulia reads **him** a story. (indirect)

3. When an infinitive verb depends on the verbs *dovere* (to have to, to must), *potere* (to be able to), or *volere* (to want), the object pronoun can come before the conjugated verb. You'll also see it attached to the end of the infinitive (minus the final *-e*):

Ti voglio accompagnare al cinema.
I want to accompany **you** to the movies.

Voglio accompagnarti al cinema.
I want to accompany **you** to the movies.

What's What

Are you confused over whether to use a direct or an indirect object pronoun? Remember that most indirect object pronouns are preceded by a preposition. Think of the preposition as a little bridge that must be crossed to get to the object. There is no "direct" way to get there—you must take the "indirect" way, over the bridge.

When to Use the Direct Object Pronoun

"The next time I go to Italy, my friend Sofia asked me to buy a book for Sofia." You would probably never say something so awkward. You'd say something like, "The next time I go to Italy, my friend Sofia asked me to buy a book for *her*." As you can see, direct object pronouns can make your life a lot easier when you use them to replace the direct object in a sentence:

*Bacio **il ragazzo**.*	➔	***Lo** bacio.*
I kiss **the boy**.	➔	I kiss **him**.
*Leggo **i libri**.*	➔	***Li** leggo.*
I read **the books**.	➔	I read **them**.

Easy, right? You don't even have to add a preposition (as in to look *at* or to wait *for*). In Italian, the commonly used verbs *guardare* (to look at), *cercare* (to look for), and *aspettare* (to wait for) have a built-in preposition:

*Cerco **il teatro**.*	➔	***Lo** cerco.*
I am searching for **the theatre**.	➔	I am searching for **it**.
*Guardo **la ragazza**.*	➔	***La** guardo.*
I am looking at **the girl**.	➔	I am looking at **her**.

Whenever you hear someone use the expression *Non lo so* (I don't know it), the speaker is using the direct object pronoun *lo*.

When to Use Indirect Object Pronouns

"Congratulations! If you have the winning number, a check for $1 billion will be sent *to you!*" Lucky you—you're the indirect object of the billion-dollar sweepstakes. As you can see here, the indirect object of a sentence tells to whom or for whom the action is done. Indirect objects are often replaced by indirect object pronouns:

*Marco offre un bicchiere di vino **a Marina**. ➔ Marco **le** offre un bicchiere di vino.*
Marco offers a glass of wine **to Marina**. ➔ Marco offers **her** a glass of wine.

*Elisabetta scrive **a Francesco** una lettera. ➔ Elisabetta **gli** scrive una lettera.*
Elisabetta writes a letter **to Francesco**. ➔ Elisabetta writes **him** a letter.

Verbs That May Use an Indirect Object

Some verbs that take a direct object in English take an indirect object in Italian:

*Telefono a **Dario** stasera. ➔ **Gli** telefono stasera.*
I am calling **Dario** this evening. ➔ I am calling **him** this evening.

The following Italian verbs may use an indirect object or its pronoun in Italian:

chiedere	to ask	*parlare*	to speak
dare	to give	*portare*	to bring
dire	to say	*preparare*	to prepare
domandare	to question	*presentare*	to present
donare	to give	*prestare*	to lend
fare sapere	to let know	*regalare*	to give
insegnare	to teach	*rendere*	to render
leggere	to read	*rispondere*	to respond
mandare	to send	*scrivere*	to write
mostrare	to show	*telefonare*	to telephone
offrire	to offer	*vendere*	to sell

*Joel telefona **ai suoi amici**. → Joel telefona a **loro**.*
Joel telephones **his friends.** → Joel telephones **them.**

*Faccio sapere **a Silvia** la data. → **Le** faccio sapere la data.*
I'm letting **Silvia** know the date. → I'm letting **her** know the date.

Attenzione!

The indirect object pronoun *loro* is often replaced with *gli* in modern spoken Italian:

> Giovanni telefona *loro.* → Giovanni *gli* telefona.

> Chiede *loro* di uscire. → *Gli* chiede di uscire.

> In an imperative, *gli* is attached to the end of the verb:

> Telefona *loro!* → Telefona*gli!*

Who's in Command?

The indirect object pronoun follows the imperative (a command) when you use the *tu, noi,* or *voi* form of the verb and can usually be attached to the end of the verb to form one word.

*Compra il libro per **Giovanni**! → **Compragli** il libro!*
Buy the book for **Giovanni**! → Buy **him** the book!

*Invitate **la vostra amica** a casa!* → *Invitatela a casa!*
Invite your **friend** home! → Invite **her** home.

The exception is *loro*, which must always remain separate.

*Telefona ai tuoi **amici**!* → *Telefona a **loro**.*
Call your **friends!** → Call **them!**

*Non date una risposta a **Carlo e Maria**.* → *Non date **loro** una risposta.*
Don't give a response to **Carlo and Maria.** → Don't give **them** a response.

As a *Regola*

Remember that all object pronouns agree in gender and number with the nouns they replace. Keep the following in mind:

- In a negative sentence, the word *non* always comes before the object pronoun:

  *Non **la** voglio.*   I don't want it.
  *Non **lo** bacio.*   I don't kiss him.

- When object pronouns are attached to the end of an infinitive, the final *-e* of the infinitive is omitted:

  *Devo **darti** un bacio.*   I must give you a kiss.
  *Vorrei **invitarli** alla festa.*   I'd like to invite them to the party.

- Singular object pronouns can be contracted in front of verbs that begin with a vowel:

  L'ascolto. (la musica)   I'm listening to it. (the music)

- In certain cases, such as with the verbs *dire* and *fare*, you add an extra *m* when using the familiar form (*tu*) of the imperative with an object pronoun:

  Dimmi!   Tell me!
  Fammi sapere!   Let me know!

What's What

Verbs that take a direct object are called **transitive** (I eat an *apple*, you *speak* Italian). Verbs that do not take a direct object are called **intransitive** (I *go*, you *return*).

Who's Who

Replace the direct object in each sentence with the direct object pronoun. Translate the sentences. (You can find the answers in Appendix A.)

Example: Leggo il giornale.
Answer: Lo leggo.

1. Mangiamo la pasta. _____

2. Dante e Boccaccio vogliono mangiare la pizza. _____

3. Prendo l'autobus. _____

4. Mario scrive un libro. _____

5. Vedo Giuseppe e Mario. _____

6. Giovanni bacia la sua ragazza. _____

7. Comprate una macchina. _____

8. Lei capisce la materia? _____

Who's Who II

Replace the indirect object with its appropriate pronoun. (You can find the answers in Appendix A.)

Example: Beatrice scrive una lettera a Dante.
Answer: Beatrice gli scrive una lettera.

1. Desideriamo parlare a voi. _____

2. Maria e Giorgio danno un regalo a te. _____

3. Carlo telefona ad Anna. _____

4. Lo studente fa una domanda al professore. _____

5. Offro un caffè a Caterina. _____

6. I nonni danno le caramelle ai bambini. _____

7. Offro una birra a Domenico. _____

8. Augurano a noi una buona notte. _____

Who's Who—Final Round

Determine which kind of object pronoun should go in the following sentences where it is bold. (You can find the answers in Appendix A.)

1. Guardate **il film.** _____

2. Regalo a Lorenzo **un mazzo di fiori.** (bunch of flowers) _____

3. Vede la **bella ragazza?** _____

4. Regalo **a Lorenzo** un mazzo di fiori. _____

5. Danno i libri **ai bambini.** _____

6. Conosco **il signor Spadone** molto bene. _____

7. Danno **i libri** ai bambini. _____

8. Accettiamo **l'invito** con piacere. _____

Double Object Pronouns

You've learned your object pronouns and remember that they must reflect the gender and number of the objects they replace.

In Italian, unlike English, it is possible to join the object pronouns together to form one word. In the following table, notice how the indirect object pronouns *mi, ti, ci, vi,* and *si* change to *me, te, ce, ve,* and *se*. Also note that the indirect object pronouns *gli, le,* and *Le* change to *glie-* before direct object pronouns, creating one word.

Double Object Pronouns

	Indirect Object		Direct Object		
Pronoun	**lo**	**la**	**li**	**le**	**ne**
mi	me lo	me la	me li	me le	me ne
ti	te lo	te la	te li	te le	te ne
gli, le, Le	glielo	gliela	glieli	gliele	gliene
ci	ce lo	ce la	ce li	ce le	ce ne
vi	ve lo	ve la	ve li	ve le	ve ne
si	se lo	se la	se li	se le	se ne

Keep in mind the following:

◆ When the same verb has two object pronouns, the indirect object always precedes the direct object:

Mandi la lettera al signor Rossi? Sì, **gliela** *mando.*
Are you sending the letter to Mr. Rossi? Yes, I'm sending it to him.

Restituiscono i soldi alla signora? Sì, **glieli** *restituiscono.*
Are they giving back the money to the woman? Yes, they are giving it back to her.

◆ After an infinitive, the final -*e* is dropped and the double object pronoun is attached to the end of the infinitive forming one word:

Posso spedirtela?
Can I send it to you?

Vuole darcelo.
He wants to give it to us.

◆ When dealing with double object pronouns, it is assumed that the speaker has already referred to the object of the sentence. In certain cases, the gender of the indirect object is not always obvious:

Presti la macchina a Silvia? Sì, gliela presto.
Are you lending the car to Silvia? Yes, I'm lending it to her.

Stressed Out

As if you haven't had enough of pronouns, here are a few more. Disjunctive, or stressed, pronouns—called *i pronomi tonici* in Italian—must follow a preposition or verb. They are also used to emphasize certain facts and highlight or replace certain nouns or pronouns. Study how they correspond to the object pronouns you have learned so far.

Disjunctive Pronouns

Subject	Direct Object	Indirect Object	Disjunctive (Stressed)
io	mi	mi	**me** (me)
tu	ti	ti	**te** (you)
lui	lo	gli	**lui/esso** (him/it)
lei	la	le	**lei/essa** (her/it)
Lei	La	Le	**Lei** (You)
			sè (himself, herself, itself, oneself, yourself)
noi	ci	ci	**noi** (us)
voi	vi	vi	**voi** (you)
loro	li/le	a loro/gli	**loro** (them)
			sè (yourselves, themselves)

The following points might help you remember when to use a disjunctive pronoun:

◆ Disjunctive pronouns must always follow a verb or preposition:

*Vuoi venire **con** me?*
Do you want to come with me?

*Sono fiero **di** te.*
I am proud of you.

*Aspetto una telefonata **da** lei.*
I am waiting for a phone call from her.

*Questi fiori sono **per** voi.*
These flowers are for you.

Lui parte prima di me.
He is leaving before me.

◆ The disjunctive pronoun *sè* is used to indicate *oneself, himself, herself,* and *themselves* as well as *itself*:

*Caterina parla sempre di **sè**.*
Caterina always talks about herself.

*Anna lavora per **sè**.*
Anna works for herself.

*La luce si spegne da **sè**.*
The light goes out by itself.

◆ The disjunctive pronoun is most commonly used when there are two direct or indirect objects in a phrase:

*Daniela scrive **a me** e **a te**.*
Daniela writes to me and to you.

*Telefonano **a lui** e **a lei**.*
They are telephoning him and her.

◆ Disjunctive pronouns are used after a verb to emphasize the object (direct or indirect).

Emphatic	Unemphatic	English
*Aspetto **lui**.*	**Lo** *aspetto.*	I'm waiting **for him.**
*Do un regalo **a te**.*	**Ti** *do un regalo.*	I give **you** a gift.
*Telefona **a me**.*	**Mi** *telefona.*	Call (telephone) **me.**

Stressful Exercise

Use the appropriate stressed pronoun in the following sentences. (You can find the answers in Appendix A.)

1. Senza di _____, non posso vivere. (you, informal)

2. Mario parla sempre di _____. (himself)

3. Vuole parlare a _____? (me)

4. Questa lettera è per _____. (Cristina)

5. Passiamo la sera a casa di _____. (Robert)

6. Viene con _____ o con _____? (me, her)

The Least You Need to Know

♦ Italians use the metric system, so make sure you know what your proper *misura* is.

♦ The verb *portare* is used to express *to wear*.

♦ A direct object answers the question *what* or *whom* is the subject acting upon.

♦ An indirect object answers the question *to what* or *to whom* is the subject acting for.

♦ Use object pronouns to replace the object in a sentence. Object pronouns are usually placed before the conjugated verb, except in an affirmative command, when they come after the verb.

♦ When dealing with double object pronouns, the indirect object pronoun always precedes the direct object pronoun.

♦ Use stressed pronouns when you want to emphasize a point or after the preposition *a*.

Chapter 16

Life's a Carnevale:
Il Passato Prossimo

In This Chapter

◆ Sports and games

◆ Italian holidays, pastimes, and *feste*

◆ Italian critters

◆ The present perfect tense

◆ Using double object pronouns in the past

This chapter covers many of the pastimes that make up the Italian lifestyle. Whether you are a sports buff, a film fanatic, an opera lover, or an art appreciator, there's a little bit of everything and something for everyone.

In addition, you'll learn a very important new verb tense: *il passato prossimo* (called the present perfect tense in English). Use of this tense allows you to talk about your sordid past.

Name Your Game

In Italian, *il football*—also known as *il calcio*—refers to soccer. The touchy-feely version played in the Super Bowl is aptly called *football americano*. Italians refer to baseball, golf, hockey, tennis, and windsurfing, however, in English.

There are three things you should never dare take away from an Italian: *la mamma*, *la pasta*, and *il calcio*. Expect anarchy if you dare. (For more on anarchy, try reading the translated works of Nobel Prize winner Dario Fo.)

Keep in mind that the Italian terms in the following table are offered with the appropriate definite articles.

La Bella Lingua

If you like to play *scacchi* (chess), you might get a rise out of playing one of the many accomplished players you'll find in some local establishments. You'll need a little chess terminology to get you started understanding *i pezzi* (the pieces) on your *scacchiera* (chessboard):

Check!	*Scacco!*	the rook	*la torre* (the tower)
Checkmate!	*Scacco Matto!*	the bishop	*l'alfiere*
the king	*il re*	the knight	*il cavallo* (the horse)
the queen	*la regina*	the pawn	*il pedone*

Game Time

Sport	Lo Sport	Pronunciation
aerobics	l'aerobica	*lay-eh-**roh**-bee-kah*
basketball	la pallacanestro	*lah pah-lah-kah-**neh**-stroh*
bicycling	il ciclismo	*eel chee-**kleez**-moh*
boating	il canottaggio	*eel kah-noh-**tah**-joh*
boxing	il pugilato	*eel poo-jee-**lah**-toh*
fencing	la scherma	*lah sker-mah*
fishing	pescare	*peh-**skah**-reh*
game	la partita	*lah par-**tee**-tah*
horseback riding	l'equitazione	*leh-kwee-tah-zee-**oh**-neh*
karate	il karatè	*kah-rah-**teh***

Sport	Lo Sport	Pronunciation
rock climbing	l'alpinismo	*lahl-pee-**nee**-zmoh*
sailing	la vela	*lah veh-lah*
score	il punteggio	*eel poon-**teh**-joh*
skating	il pattinaggio	*eel pah-tee-**nah**-joh*
skiing	lo sci	*loh shee*
… cross-country skiing	… lo sci di fondo	*loh shee dee fon-doh*
… water skiing	… lo sci acquatico	*loh shee ak-**wah**-tee-koh*
soccer	il calcio, il football	*eel kahl-choh*
swimming	il nuoto	*eel nwoh-toh*
team	la squadra	*lah skwah-drah*
volleyball	la pallavolo	*lah pah-lah-**voh**-loh*
wrestling	la lotta libera	*lah loh-tah **lee**-beh-rah*

You're Playing with My Head

If you're looking for less exertion, a few games allow you to use more brain power than brawn. *Briscola* and *Scopa* are two popular card games. *Giochiamo!*

Games for the Brain

English	Italiano	English	Italiano
backgammon	backgammon	dominoes	domino
briscola	briscola	hide-and-seek	cu-cù
cards	carte	poker	poker
checkers	dama	scopa (a popular card game)	scopa
chess	scacchi	tarot	tarocchi
dice	dadi		

Festeggiamo!

The word *carnevale* (meaning *carnival* and source of the English word *carnal*) is no different from the infamous Mardi Gras (in Italian, *Martedì Grasso*—literally, *fat Tuesday*). This was the last night one was permitted to eat *la carne* (meat) before beginning the period of Lent (called *la quaresima* in Italian).

What's What

Here's a who's who of mythological archetypes. The Romans and Greeks shared many of the same gods. The Greek equivalents are in parentheses.

The Gods	The Goddesses
Apollo (Apollo)	Ceres (Demeter)
Jupiter (Zeus)	Diana (Artemis)
Mars (Ares)	Juno (Hera)
Mercury (Hermes)	Minerva (Athena)
Neptune (Poseidon)	Venus (Aphrodite)
Vulcan (Hephaistos)	Vesta (Hestia)

In Italy, two of the most famous *carnevale* celebrations take place in Venice and Viareggio, where tens of thousands show up to participate in the festivities and watch the parades.

Many of the more important Christian holidays coincide with the major Roman celebrations of Bacchanalia and Saturnalia.

Out in Left Field

Each sport or activity has its own particular playing field, as shown in the following table. Whether you are pitching or out in left field, there's a place for everyone in the game of life.

Beach-Blanket Bingo

The Place	Il Posto	Pronunciation
the beach	la spiaggia	*lah **spee**-ah-jah*
the casino	il casinò	*eel kah-see-**noh***
the court/field	il campo	*eel kam-poh*
the golf course	il campo da golf	*eel kam-poh dah golf*
the gym	la palestra	*lah pah-**leh**-strah*
the mountain	la montagna	*lah mon-**tahn**-yah*
the ocean	l'oceano	*loh-sheh-**ah**-noh*
the park	il parco	*eel par-koh*
the path	il sentiero	*eel sen-tee-**eh**-roh*
the pool	la piscina	*lah pee-**shee**-nah*
the rink	la pista di pattinaggio	*lah pees-tah dah pah-tee-**nah**-joh*

The Place	Il Posto	Pronunciation
the sea	il mare	*eel mah-reh*
ski slope	la pista da sci	*lah pees-tah dah shee*
stadium	lo stadio	*loh stah-dee-yoh*
track	la corsa	*lah kor-sah*

Don't Play with Me!

In Italian, there are many ways of expressing *to play*:

- The verb *giocare* (to play) is used when playing sports or games. (Think of the English word *joker*.)

- The verb *suonare* (to play) is used when playing an instrument. (Think of the English word *sound*.)

- The verbs *andare* (to go) and *fare* (to do/to make) are often used when participating in a sport or activity.

- The idiomatic expression *prendere in giro* (to take for a spin; to tease) is especially useful if you want to play with someone's head.

Buon'Idea

In Italy, in addition to making a big deal out of birthdays, many people celebrate also their *onomastico* (Saint's Day), or one's name day. Pick up an Italian calendar and see if there's a day for you!

Il Passato Prossimo

The *passato prossimo* (present perfect) is used to say *I forgot, I ate,* and *I was.* In addition, the *passato prossimo* expresses *I have forgotten, I have eaten,* and *I have been.*

A compound tense, the *passato prossimo* requires the use of the helping verbs *avere* and *essere* (see Chapter 8). In Italian, all *transitive verbs* (verbs that take a direct object) require the use of the auxiliary verb *avere.* All *intransitive verbs* (verbs taking an indirect object) require the use of *essere.*

As a *Regola*

When to use *avere:*

♦ When forming compound tenses, most *transitive verbs* (verbs that take a direct object) use *avere* as an auxiliary verb.

♦ Transitive verbs answer the question *what?* and include verbs such as *lavare* (to wash), *mangiare* (to eat), and *studiare* (to study). Transitive verbs also answer the question of *whom?* and include the verbs *cercare* (to look for), *conoscere* (to be acquainted with), and *invitare* (to invite).

When to use *essere:*

♦ *Intransitive verbs* use *essere* as an auxiliary verb and include verbs of locomotion such as *andare* (to go), *arrivare* (to arrive), *entrare* (to enter), *uscire* (to go out/exit), and *venire* (to come). Other intransitive verbs include *morire* (to die) and *nascere* (to be born).

Constructing the Past Participle

When you use the *passato prossimo,* you need a past participle. For example, in English you use the helping verb *have* plus the participle (wished/finished/studied). Most of the time this is regular, but English also has several irregular past participles (had/been/sang). The same goes for Italian.

As you recall from Chapter 8, Italian has three principal verb families (*-are, -ere,* and *-ire*). To form the past participle from an infinitive, you hold on to the stem and add the appropriate ending, as shown in the following table.

Regular Endings for the Past Participle

Endings			Infinitive		Participle
-are	→	*-ato*	lavare	→	lavato
-ere	→	*-uto*	potere	→	potuto
-ire	→	*-ito*	capire	→	capito

Forming the Past with *Avere*

It's easy to construct the *passato prossimo.* After you understand how this works, you'll have no trouble learning all of the other compound tenses. It all starts with the helping verb *avere.* When you've determined your subject, you only have to conjugate *avere* in the present tense. The past participle stays the same, regardless of the subject (unless accompanied by a direct object pronoun, which will be discussed in a bit). Study the verb *lavare* (to wash) to better understand how this works.

The Present Perfect of *Lavare*

Italian	English
io **ho lavato**	I have washed
tu **hai lavato**	you have washed
lui/lei Lei **ha lavato**	he/she has washed; You have washed
noi **abbiamo lavato**	we have washed
voi **avete lavato**	you have washed
loro **hanno lavato**	they have washed

Notice that the participle *lavato* did not change; the helping verb is the only thing you need to conjugate.

In their efforts to determine the subject, and create the past participle from the infinitive, many of my students forget to use their helping verbs. You can learn from their mistakes and always remember to use your helping verb. (*Capisco* … there's a lot to remember!)

Irregular Past Participles Used with *Avere*

Some commonly used irregular past participles are shown in the following table. All of these are generally used with the helping verb *avere*.

Commonly Used Irregular Past Participles with *Avere*

Verb	Past Participle	Meaning
accendere	acceso	to turn on, to light
aprire	aperto	to open
ardere	arso	to burn
bere	bevuto	to drink
chiedere	chiesto	to ask
chiudere	chiuso	to close
conoscere	conosciuto	to know someone
correggere	corretto	to correct

continues

Commonly Used Irregular Past Participles with *Avere*   (continued)

Verb	Past Participle	Meaning
correre	corso	to run
decidere	deciso	to decide
dire	detto	to say
leggere	letto	to read
mettere	messo	to put, to place, to wear
offrire	offerto	to offer
perdere	perso	to lose
permettere	permesso	to permit
prendere	preso	to take
rispondere	risposto	to respond
rompere	rotto	to break
scrivere	scritto	to write
spegnere	spento	to turn off, to extinguish
spendere	speso	to spend
togliere	tolto	to take from
vedere	visto	to see
vincere	vinto	to win

Abbiamo vinto la partita.	We won the game.
Hai scritto alla mamma?	Did you write to Mom?
Il ristorante ha chiuso presto.	The restaurant closed early.
Ci hanno chiesto un favore.	They asked us for a favor.

Forming the Past with *Essere*

Some verbs, called *intransitive verbs*, always require the use of *essere* as their auxiliary. How can you remember what those verbs are? Think of a *scoiattolo* (squirrel) living in a tree, and imagine all the motions he does in and around his home, high up in the branches of a great old *quercia* (oak): he comes and he stays awhile before he goes again, then he returns, departs, and so on.

Whenever *essere* is used as the auxiliary verb, the participle is still formed by adding the appropriate ending to the stem of the verb. However, in addition to conjugating your helping verb *avere*, your past participle must reflect both gender and number of the subject. Participles act very much like adjectives in this case.

You'll understand better by studing the verb *andare* (to go) in the following table.

The Present Perfect Using *Essere: Andare (To Go)*

Andare	English
io sono andato(a)	I have gone
tu sei andato(a)	you have gone
lui/lei Lei è andato(a)	he/she has gone; You have gone
noi **siamo andati(e)**	we have gone
voi **siete andati(e)**	you have gone
loro **sono andati(e)**	they have gone

Oriana è andata all'università di Bologna.
Oriana went to the university of Bologna.

As a *Regola*
When forming the *passato prossimo* (present perfect, the verb *avere* takes itself as an auxiliary verb. *Ho avuto un'idea.* (I had an idea.) Likewise, the verb *essere* also takes itself as an auxiliary verb. *Sono stato in Italia.* (I was in Italy.)

Verbs Taking *Essere*

The following table contains a list of the most commonly used intransitive verbs conjugated with *essere*. Irregular participles are indicated with an asterisk.

Intransitive Verbs Commonly Used with *Essere*

Verb	Past Participle	Meaning
andare	andato	to go
apparire	apparso*	to appear
arrivare	arrivato	to arrive

continues

Intransitive Verbs Commonly Used with *Essere* (continued)

Verb	Past Participle	Meaning
bastare	bastato	to be enough
cadere	caduto	to fall
dimagrire	dimagrito	to lose weight
dispiacere	dispiaciuto*	to be sorry
diventare	diventato	to become
entrare	entrato	to enter
esistere	esistito	to exist
essere	stato*	to be
ingrassare	ingrassato	to gain weight
morire	morto*	to die
nascere	nato*	to be born
partire	partito	to leave
piacere	piaciuto*	to be pleasing
restare	restato	to stay
rimanere	rimasto*	to remain
ritornare	ritornato	to return
salire	salito	to go up/to get on
scendere	sceso*	to get off
sembrare	sembrato	to seem
stare	stato*	to stay
succedere	successo*	to happen
tornare	tornato	to return
uscire	uscito	to go out
venire	venuto	to come
vivere	vissuto*	to live

Irregular participle.

Additional Applications of the *Passato Prossimo*

There are a few instances when you might find juggling all of these new concepts a bit confusing. Keep in mind the following rules when using the *passato prossimo:*

◆ Although considered transitive, all *reflexive verbs* require *essere* as their auxiliary verb. Reflexives are most easily identified by their endings, and include the verbs *alzarsi* (to get up), *arrabbiarsi* (to get angry), and *chiamarsi* (to call oneself). You'll learn all about reflexive verbs in Chapter 18.

Reflexive verbs always take *essere* as their auxiliary verb:

Il bambino si è divertito. (The baby enjoyed himself.)

Mi sono alzata prestissimo. (I woke up very early.)

Ci siamo baciati. (We kissed each other.)

◆ When forming compound tenses, the verb *piacere* always takes the helping verb *essere*. Refer to Chapter 13 for a review of the verb *piacere*.

Ti piace lo spettacolo?	*Ti **è piaciuto** lo spettacolo?*
Mi piacciono gli animali.	*Mi **sono piaciuti** gli animali.*
Le piace l'Italia?	*Le **è piaciuta** l'Italia?*
Vi piacciono le macchine.	*Vi **sono piaciute** le macchine.*

Adverbs in Compound Tenses

In this beautiful *sinfonia* (symphony) of words, it's time to add a few more notes. Refer to Chapter 6 for a review of your adverbs. For now, keep in mind the following:

◆ Most adverbs are placed after the past participle in compound sentences, such as in the *passato prossimo*:

*Abbiamo mangiato **bene.***	We ate **well.**
*Isabella ha studiato **regolarmente.***	Isabella studied **regularly.**

◆ Adverbs related to time, such as *ancora*, *già*, *mai*, and *sempre*, are placed between the auxiliary verb and the past participle:

*Ha **già** mangiato?*	Have you **already** eaten? (formal)
*Hai **mai** visto un leone?*	Have you **ever** seen a lion? (informal)
*Abbiamo **sempre** passato l'estate al mare.*	We **always** passed the summer by the sea.

◆ When negating something in the past, the word *non* comes before the helping verb:

Non ho mangiato molto.　　　　　I did **not** eat much.

◆ Unlike English, double negatives are acceptable in Italian:

*Non ho **mai** visto un leone.*　　　I have never seen a lion

Direct Object Pronouns in Compound Tenses

Transitive verbs take a direct object and are conjugated with the verb *avere*. When using direct object pronouns in compound tenses, including the *passato prossimo*, the ending of the participle must reflect gender and plurality of the direct object. Note that the singular direct object pronouns meaning *it* (*lo/la*) drop the final vowel and elide with the auxiliary verb *avere*. The plural object pronouns don't change.

The following table illustrates this for you. The direct object and direct object pronouns (DOPs) are in bold.

Passato Prossimo with Direct Object Pronouns

Question	DOP	Answer
*Hai spedito **la lettera?***	*la*	*Sì, **l'ho** spedita.*
Did you send the letter?	it	Yes, I sent it.
*Hai mangiato **il pane?***	*lo*	*Sì, **l'ho** mangiato.*
Did you eat the bread?	it	Yes, I ate it.
*Hai ricevuto **le lettere?***	*le*	*No, non **le** ho ricevute.*
Did you receive the letters?	them	No, I didn't receive them.
*Hai letto **i libri?***	*li*	*Sì, **li** ho letti.*
Did you read the books?	them	Yes, I read them.

Indirect Object Pronouns and the *Passato Prossimo*

Both transitive and intransitive verbs can take an indirect object pronoun. In compound tenses, to distinguish the indirect and direct object pronouns from one another, the gender and number of indirect object pronouns—unlike the direct object pronouns—do not affect the participle. In the following table, the indirect object and indirect object pronouns (IOPs) are in bold.

Passato Prossimo with Indirect Object Pronouns

Question	IOP	Answer
Hai parlato alla ragazza?	*le*	*Sì, le ho parlato.*
Did you speak to the girl?	to her	Yes, I spoke to her.
Hai spedito la lettera a Paolo?	*gli*	*Sì, gli ho spedito la lettera.*
Did you send the letter to Paolo?	to him	Yes, I sent him the letter.
Hai offerto ai signori un caffè?	*loro/gli*	*Sì, ho offerto loro un caffè.* *
		Sì, gli ho offerto un caffè. *
Did you offer the men coffee?	to them	Yes, I offered them coffee.
Hanno mandato un pacco a noi?	*ci*	*Sì, ci hanno mandato un pacco.*
Did they send a package to us?	to us	Yes, they sent us a package.

*Both of these are correct. If you recall, loro *can be replaced with the pronoun* gli.

The *Passato Prossimo* and Double Object Pronouns

Everything here is detail. If you don't always remember to make things agree, you won't be locked into a tower and fed stale *pane*. However, if you want to be a master, you've got to pay special attention to the little things.

When the same verb has two object pronouns, the indirect object pronoun always precedes the direct object pronoun. The following examples illustrate how double object pronouns work with the *passato prossimo*. Notice how the participle ending reflects the number and gender of the direct object.

> **Attenzione!**
>
> When dealing with double object pronouns, it is necessary to infer the gender of the indirect object (to him/to her).
>
> | | |
> |---|---|
> | *Hai dato la lettera alla signora?* | *Sì gliel'ho data.* |
> | Did you give the letter to the lady? | Yes, I gave it to her. |
> | *Hai dato la lettera al ragazzo?* | *Sì gliel'ho data.* |
> | Did you give the letter to the boy? | Yes, I gave it to him. |

Double Object Pronouns

Question	Answer
Hai mandato la lettera al signor Rossi?	*Sì, gliel'ho mandata.*
Did you send the letter to Mr. Rossi?	Yes, I sent it to him.
Hanno restituito i soldi alla signora?	*Sì, glieli hanno restituiti.*
Did they give back the money to the woman?	Yes, they gave it back to her.

The Least You Need to Know

◆ The verbs *andare* and *fare* are often used to describe participation in a sport. Use the verb *giocare* to play games and the verb *suonare* to play an instrument.

◆ The past participle is created by adding the appropriate ending to the stem of a verb. The three regular forms are *-ato*, *-uto*, and *-ito*.

◆ Many past participles are irregular, such as *chiuso* (closed) and *stato* (was).

◆ The two helping verbs used to form the *passato prossimo* are *essere* and *avere*.

◆ Intransitive verbs and reflexive verbs require *essere* as their auxiliary verb.

◆ The past participle must agree in gender and number with the preceding direct object pronoun. Double object pronouns often form one word and are used to refer to something already mentioned.

Chapter 17

The Arts and the *Imperfetto*

In This Chapter

◆ Cinema, music, and art

◆ Using the Imperfect

◆ Imperfect versus the present perfect

◆ Using double object pronouns in the past

In this chapter, you'll learn about the arts and the imperfect tense, another way to talk about the past. You may not feel up to learning yet another tense, and ask, "When does it end?"

Mai, I say. Never.

Scherzavo! I was just kidding! You'll get it, I promise.

The Arts

Ah, *la Madre Patria!* The Italians have an emotional relationship to *la politica, la famiglia,* and *l'amore.* It is no surprise that their art reflects these powerful forces.

Il Cinema

There's no better way to practice your Italian than by watching films (next to visiting Italy, that is). Italy started as one of the world's major film producers. *Cinecittà* (the Hollywood of Italy), in *Roma*, has spawned some of the best filmmakers in the world, including Bernardo Bertolucci, Vittorio De Sica, Federico Fellini, Pier Paolo Pasolini, and Luchino Visconti, to name a few.

Movie Talk

The Cinema	Il Cinema	The Cinema	Il Cinema
actor	l'attore	plot	la trama
actress	l'attrice	producer	il produttore
camera	la cinepresa, la macchina fotografica	scene	la scena
cinema	il cinema	screen	lo schermo
close-up	il primo piano	theater	la sala cinematografica
director	il/la regista	to hear	sentire, udire
dissolve	la dissolvenza	to listen	ascoltare
film	il film, la pellicola	to see	vedere
long-shot	il campo lungo	to watch/look	guardare
panning	panoramica	video camera	la telecamera

La Musica

Nothing soothes the savage beast like music. The great violin maker Antonio Stradivari (1644–1747) came from Cremona. Is there a musical instrument that makes you swoon every time you hear it? Find it in the following table, or find your favorite Italian composer in the timeline.

The Venetian composer Giovanni Gabrielli (1557–1612) was one of the first to use the term *concerto* (bringing into agreement), a classical term describing music that uses many different voices to form one.

The Sound of Musica

Instrument	Lo Strumento	Instrument	Lo Strumento
accordion	la fisarmonica	oboe	l'oboe
cello	il violoncello	piano	il pianoforte
clarinet	il clarinetto	piccolo	il piccolo
drum	il tamburo, la batteria	saxophone	il sassofono
flute	il flauto	trombone	il trombone
guitar	la chitarra	trumpet	la tromba
harp	l'arpa	viola	la viola
horn	il corno	violin	il violino

A Note on *Opera*

Opera. It's an Italian word—some would say the most beautiful Italian word. By the time Giuseppe Verdi (1813–1901)—who at the age of 20 was already performing at Milano's famous opera house *La Scala*—came onto the scene, opera had spread across Europe. During the course of his long career, the patriotic composer wrote 26 operas, including *Otello, Rigoletto,* and *La Traviata* (meaning "*the corrupted*").

It's All About *il Libretto*

Opera has as much drama as any Spielberg film, and the stories told are filled with unrequited love, betrayal, and revenge. To fully appreciate any opera, you need to understand the plot behind the rolled *R*'s and high *C*'s.

That's where *il libretto* comes in. Literally meaning *little book* in Italian, *il libretto* tells the story, outlines the plot, and paints the picture that will be so passionately expressed by the singers. Without *il libretto*, opera loses half its meaning.

Sing It to Me!

You don't need to speak Italian to appreciate opera, but a quick glossary of terms might help:

a cappella   Voices without music; no instruments

aria   A song or melody sung by a single voice

belcanto   *Beautiful song* in Italian

cadenza   A passage toward the end of a song designed for the singer alone to strut his or her stuff *canzone*   Literally *song* in Italian

coloratura   Describes the *color* in a passage, including those difficult trills and sparkling arpeggios that singers train all their lives to sing

duetto   Two people singing simultaneously, often with different words and melodies

forte/mezzo forte   Loud/not so loud

piano/mezzo piano   Soft/not so soft

falsetto   The high part for a man's voice

fuga   A baroque style passage in which three or more distinct musical lines are tossed from voice to voice

libretto   Literally *little book* in Italian, the script for the piece

opera buffa   Comic, *buffoon* opera

opera seria   Serious, more formal opera

operetta   A cross between *opera buffa* and *opera seria*; usually very light

overture   An instrumental composition introducing the entire opera

prelude   A shorter overture

prima donna   A female opera star

recitativo   Sung dialogue between arias, to help advance the story

vibrato   A slight wavering in pitch used to enhance notes

Life Imitates Art

Le belle arti attempt to interpret the real world, glorify God (or gods), or express something without words. As ideas about the world have changed, so has the *arte* that depicts these notions. Ultimately, you know what you like and what you don't, and that is often the only criterion necessary to appreciate a piece.

You may have seen countless reproductions of Botticelli's *Birth of Venus* on everything from greeting cards to coffee mugs, but there's still nothing like seeing her up close. If you want to be an artist, these verbs can help: *disegnare* (to draw/to design), *dipingere* (to paint), and *scolpire* (to sculpt).

Adding to Your Palette

English	Italiano	English	Italiano
abstract	astratto	masterpiece	il capolavoro
acrylic	acrilico	the Middle Ages	il Medioevo
architecture	l'architettura	mosaic	il mosaico
background	lo sfondo	oil	olio
Baroque	il Barocco	painter	il pittore
bronze	il bronzo	painting	il quadro
ceramic	la ceramica	pencil	la matita
classical	classico	pen	la penna
cubism	il cubismo	perspective	la prospettiva
depth	la profondità	picture	la pittura, il quadro
drawing	il disegno	pigments	i colori
Etruscan	etrusco	portrait	il ritratto
figure	la figura	realism	il realismo
foreground	il primo piano	the Renaissance	il Rinascimento
fresco	l'affresco	restoration	il restauro
futurism	il futurismo	sculpture	la scultura
geometric	geometrico	shadow	l'ombra
granite	il granito	sketch	lo schizzo
human figure	la figura umana	statue	la statua
landscape	il paesaggio	still-life painting	la natura morta
light	la luce	symbol	il simbolo
marble	il marmo	visual arts	le belle arti
master	il maestro	work of art	un'opera d'arte

I Was What I Was: The Imperfect

L'imperfetto (the imperfect) tense describes repeated actions that occurred in the past. Whenever you refer to something that used to be or describe a habitual pattern, you use the imperfect. *Mentre* (while), *quando* (when), *sempre* (always), *spesso* (often), and *di solito* (usually) are all key words you can look for to identify when the imperfect is being used.

The imperfect also expresses actions we were doing when something else happened. For example, I was studying when the telephone rang. The phone interrupted your studies, which you had been doing for an indefinite amount of time.

As a *Regola*

Which tense should you use? The *present perfect* expresses an action that was completed at a specific time in the past; you did it once and now it's over and done with. The *imperfect* represents an action that continued to occur, that was happening, that used to happen, or that would (meaning used to) happen: *Andavamo al mare ogni estate.* (We used to go to the sea every summer.)

Formation of the Imperfect

The imperfect tense is one of the easiest tenses to remember. With the exception of the verb *essere*, there are hardly any irregularities—and when there are, they are usually consistent with stem changes in the present. The best part is that the endings are the same for all three verb families. Just drop the final *-re* from the infinitive and add the endings in the following table.

Imperfect Endings

Subject	Imperfect Endings	Subject	Imperfect Endings
io	*-vo*	noi	*-vamo*
tu	*-vi*	voi	*-vate*
lui/lei/Lei	*-va*	loro	*-vano*

The verbs *parlare* (to speak), *leggere* (to read), and *capire* (to understand) all share the same endings. Take a look at them in the following table.

Imperfect Examples

Subject	Parlare	Leggere	Capire
io	parla**vo**	legge**vo**	capi**vo**
tu	parla**vi**	legge**vi**	capi**vi**
lui/lei/Lei	parla**va**	legge**va**	capi**va**

Subject	Parlare	Leggere	Capire
noi	parla**vamo**	legge**vamo**	capi**vamo**
voi	parla**vate**	legge**vate**	capi**vate**
loro	parla**vano**	legge**vano**	capi**vano**

The only verb that completely changes form in the imperfect is the highly irregular verb *essere*, shown in the following table.

Essere (To Be)

Italiano	English	Italiano	English
io **ero**	I was	noi **eravamo**	we were
tu **eri**	you were	voi **eravate**	you were
lui/lei/Lei **era**	he/she was; You were	loro **erano**	they were

Fill in the Spazio

Take a look at these stem-changing verbs and fill in the rest of the chart using the endings you just learned. (You can find the Answers in Appendix A.)

	Dire (To Say)	*Fare* (To Do/Make)	*Bere* (To Drink)
io	_____	facevo	_____
tu	dicevi	_____	_____
lui/lei/Lei	_____	_____	beveva
noi	dicevamo	_____	_____
voi	_____	facevate	_____
loro	_____	_____	bevevano

La Pratica

Fill in the blanks with the verb in parenthesis, using the imperfect. (You can find the Answers in Appendix A.)

1. Quando hai telefonato, (io) _____ (guardare) la televisione.

2. Quando (noi) _____ (essere) bambini, _____ (andare) spesso al mare.

3. Mentre Maria _____ (lavorare), Luigi _____ (preparare) la cena.

4. Mi _____ (piacere) ascoltare la radio ogni notte.

5. Quando Katerina _____ (avere) 18 anni, è andata in Italia per la prima volta.

6. (Loro) _____ (abitare) in Via Condotti quando è nata loro figlia.

7. Mio nonno _____ (fare) una passeggiata ogni giorno della sua vita. Lui _____ (essere) un uomo forte.

8. (Io) _____ (tornare) a casa quando ho visto l'incidente.

9. (Noi) Ci _____ (vedere) spesso al lavoro.

10. Maurizio si _____ (alzare) sempre tardi la mattina.

What's Done Is Done

It's awkward trying to speak in the present tense all the time. Replace the underlined verbs with the appropriate form of the past tense (present perfect or imperfect). (You can find the Answers in Appendix A.)

Arriviamo il 21 settembre, il primo giorno d'autunno. Il sole brilla e fa bel tempo. Viaggiamo spesso ma questa è la nostra prima volta in Italia. Prima andiamo a Roma dove vediamo il Vaticano, il Foro Romano e il Colosseo. Poi andiamo a Firenze per una settimana.

A Review

You've seen these verbs before and should know them pretty well by now. Each verb has its participle in parentheses. Conjugate each verb in both the present perfect (simple past) and the imperfect tense using the helping verb *avere*. (You can find the Answers in Appendix A.)

1. Scrivere (scritto)

Subject	Present Perfect	Imperfect
io	_____	_____
tu	_____	_____
lui/lei/Lei	_____	_____
noi	_____	_____

voi	_____	_____
loro	_____	_____

2. Spedire (spedito)

Subject	Present Perfect	Imperfect
io	_____	_____
tu	_____	_____
lui/lei/Lei	_____	_____
noi	_____	_____
voi	_____	_____
loro	_____	_____

3. Leggere (letto)

Subject	Present Perfect	Imperfect
io	_____	_____
tu	_____	_____
lui/lei/Lei	_____	_____
noi	_____	_____
voi	_____	_____
loro	_____	_____

4. Mandare (mandato)

Subject	Present Perfect	Imperfect
io	_____	_____
tu	_____	_____
lui/lei/Lei	_____	_____
noi	_____	_____
voi	_____	_____
loro	_____	_____

The Least You Need to Know

♦ The imperfect tense is used to indicate something that occurred in the past over a period of time or something that you *used to do*. It is also used to talk about a mental, emotional, or physical condition that happened in the past.

♦ The present perfect is used to indicate an isolated event that occurred in the past.

♦ Intransitive verbs and reflexive verbs require *essere* as their auxiliary verb.

♦ The past participle must agree in gender and number with the preceding direct object pronoun.

♦ Double object pronouns often form one word and are used to refer to something already mentioned.

Part 4

Minutiae

In this part, you'll learn practical *vocabolario* related to your body and what to say if (God forbid) you need to visit the *dottore* when you are in Italy. You'll learn how to make a telephone call and deal with *l'ufficio postale*, and how to use the future and conditional tenses, the subjunctive mood, and *il passato remoto*, a highly irregular tense used to talk about the distant past. Finally, to sweeten up the lesson, I'll help you develop your romantic skills (when in Rome…) with some useful *terminologia* related to *l'amore*.

Remember, at this point, your primary objective should still be to simply and effectively communicate with others in Italian. And if you've paid attention so far, you should have no problem expressing yourself in *la bella lingua*. Off to your next *avventura*. *In bocca al lupo!*

A presto!

Chapter 18

Using the Body to Test Your *Riflessivi:* Reflexive Verbs

In This Chapter

◆ Naming your body parts

◆ Talking to *il medico* about what ails you

◆ Visiting the *ottica*

◆ Visiting the *dentista*

◆ La *profumeria*

◆ Reflexive verbs and pronouns

You're probably more prone to getting sick while in a foreign country than any other time. You're in a new environment, you're eating different foods, your daily rituals have been altered, and you're having a great time. Those little bugs know just when to crash a party. In this chapter, you'll learn how to feed your cold, starve your fever, and get back on your feet. You'll also learn about the imperfect tense, another way to talk about the past.

What a Bod!

You've only got one, so you might as well love it. Just like people, the names of body parts (and their plurals) are often irregular. Start at your toes and work up.

The Sum of Your Parts

The Body	Il Corpo	The Body	Il Corpo
ankle	la caviglia	hand	la mano (le mani)
appendix	l'appendice	head	la testa
arm	il braccio (le braccia)	heart	il cuore
back	la schiena	joint	l'articolazione
bladder	la vescica	knee	il ginocchio (le ginocchia)
blood	il sangue	leg	la gamba
body	il corpo	ligament	il legamento
bone	l'osso (le ossa)	mouth	la bocca
brain	il cervello	muscle	il muscolo
breast	il seno	nail	l'unghia
buttock	il sedere	neck	il collo
chest	il petto	nose	il naso
chin	il mento	skin	la pelle
ear	l'orecchio	shoulder	la spalla
elbow	il gomito	stomach	lo stomaco
eye	l'occhio	throat	la gola
face	il viso	toe	il dito (le dita)
finger	il dito (le dita)	tongue	la lingua
foot	il piede	tooth	il dente
gland	la ghiandola	wrist	il polso

La Bella Lingua

A little schmoozing can go a long way. To give someone a compliment, use the word *che* + the appropriate form of *bello* + the body part, as in *Che begli occhi!* (What beautiful eyes!)

Farsi

The reflexive and highly idiomatic verb *farsi* comes from the verb *fare* (to do/to make) and can be used in several manners. *Farsi* is used to talk about when something hurts. In this case, the subject of the sentence is the troublesome body part (or parts). If what is hurting you is singular—for example, your head—so is your verb; if your feet hurt you, because they are plural, your verb must also be plural.

Mi fa male la testa.	My head hurts. (My head is hurting me.)
Mi fanno male i piedi.	My feet hurt. (My feet are hurting me.)

A doctor or pharmacist will ask you what hurts by changing the indirect object pronoun. The verb stays the same.

Ti fa male il braccio?	Does your arm hurt?
Le fa male lo stomaco?	Does your stomach hurt?
Le fanno male i piedi?	Do your feet hurt?

Express Yourself

When talking about your body, you use the verb *avere* to describe any kind of ache, whether it's in your head or your stomach. You'll also use the reflexive verb *sentirsi* (to feel) to describe your various ailments, as in, *Mi sento male* (I feel bad). When using the idiomatic expression *avere mal di*, the final *-e* is dropped from the word *male*. The following expressions will help you describe your discomfort or pain.

Ho ...	I have ...
... *mal di testa.*	... a headache.
... *mal di stomaco/pancia.*	... a stomachache.
... *mal di gola.*	... sore throat.
Mi fa male ...	(The body part) ... hurts me.
Mi fa male il ginocchio.	My knee hurts.
Mi fanno male i piedi.	My feet hurt.
Mi sento male.	I feel bad.
Non mi sento bene.	I don't feel well.

What Ails You?

Sickness can be especially exasperating in a foreign country where you don't know the names of your medicines and you have to explain to a *dottore* or *farmacista* exactly what the problem is.

There's no need to be shy about what you're experiencing. Italians have the same kinds of ailments you do. The doctor will ask you a few questions. Naturally, the *Lei* form of the verb is used to maintain a professional relationship.

Qual è il problema?	What is the problem?
Come si sente?	How do you feel?
Quanti anni ha?	How old are you?
Da quanto tempo soffre?	(For) How long have you been suffering?
Prende delle medicine?	Are you taking any medications?
Ha delle allergie?	Do you have any allergies?
Soffre di …?	Do you suffer from …?
Ha avuto …?	Have you had …?
Che cosa Le fa male?	What hurts you?

Tell Me Where It Hurts

Imagine that you are telling a doctor what your aches and pains are. If you are using the expression *mi fa male*, don't forget to account for number if what hurts you is plural.

Example: your head
Answer: *Mi fa male la testa* or *Ho mal di testa*.

1. your knee _____
2. your shoulders _____
3. your feet _____
4. your throat _____
5. your tooth _____
6. your ankle _____

This Isn't Funny Anymore

If you have a serious medical condition that warrants immediate attention, don't hesitate to contact a doctor should you feel the need for one.

The following table will help you describe what's going on.

Symptoms and Conditions

Symptom	Il Sintomo	Symptom	Il Sintomo
abscess	l'ascesso	bump	la tumefazione
blister	la vescica	burn	la scottatura
broken bone	un osso rotto	chills	i brividi
bruise	il livido	constipation	la stitichezza
cough	la tosse	headache	il mal di testa
cramps	i crampi	indigestion	l'indigestione
diarrhea	la diarrea	insomnia	l'insonnia
dizziness	le vertigini	lump (on the head)	il bernoccolo
exhaustion	l'esaurimento	migraine	l'emicrania
fever	la febbre	nausea	la nausea
fracture	la frattura	pain	il dolore
rash	un'irritazione	swelling	il gonfiore
sprain	la distorsione	toothache	il mal di denti
stomachache	il mal di stomaco	wound	la ferita

CAUTION

Attenzione!

You may think you've taken care of everything by bringing your own little medicine chest filled with leftover pills from prescriptions for one thing or another, but self-medicating could make things worse, especially in a foreign country.

Feeling *Strano*

Some particularly unattractive verbs and other useful phrases describing conditions are outlined in the following table. I've conjugated the first one for you. With idiomatic expressions, the verb in parentheses needs to be conjugated.

How Are You Feeling?

Italian	English	Example	English
(avere) la febbre	to have a fever	Ho la febbre.	I have a fever.
(avere) la nausea	to be nauseous	Ho la nausea.	I am nauseous.
(avere) la tosse	to cough	Ho la tosse.	I am coughing.
(avere) mal di	to have pain	Ho mal di ….	I have pain in my ….
(essere) esaurito	to be exhausted	Sono esaurito/a.	I am exhausted.
sanguinare	to bleed	Sanguino.	I am bleeding.
(soffrire) di	to suffer from	Soffro di ….	I am suffering from ….
starnutire	to sneeze	Starnutisco.	I am sneezing.
vomitare	to vomit	Vomito.	I am vomiting.

This Is What You Have

The word *disease* literally means *not at ease*. Here again, you'll see the Italian terms given with the appropriate definite articles.

Conditions and Diseases

Illness	La Malattia	Illness	La Malattia
angina	l'angina	hemophilia	l'emofilia
appendicitis	l'appendicite	hepatitis	l'epatite
asthma	l'asma	measles	il morbillo
bronchitis	la bronchite	mumps	gli orecchioni
cancer	il cancro	pneumonia	la polmonite
cold	il raffreddore	polio	la poliomielite
diabetes	il diabete	smallpox	il vaiolo
drug addiction	la tossicodipendenza	stroke	il colpo apoplettico
dysentry	la dissenteria	sunstroke	il colpo di sole
flu	l'influenza	tetanus	il tetano
German measles	la rosolia	tuberculosis	la tubercolosi
gout	la gotta	whooping cough	la pertosse
heart attack	l'infarto		

Your doctor may give you *una ricetta medica* (prescription) to be filled at the *farmacia*.

Al Dente?

Ouch, there's nothing like a *mal di denti* to ruin a perfectly good holiday. Hopefully, you won't need a dentista when you go to Italy, but should you need to, the vocabulary in the following table will help. Similar to the words *artista, musicista,* and *poeta,* the word *dentista* is used to describe both boy dentists and girl dentists.

Il Dentista

English	Italiano	English	Italiano
braces	l'apparecchio	gums	le gengive
bridge	il ponte	jaw	la mascella
cavity	la carie	nerve	il nervo
crown	la corona	tooth	il dente
dentist	il/la dentista (m./f.)	toothache	il mal di denti
denture	la dentiera	widsom tooth	il dente del giudizio

La Farmacia

A visit to the *farmacia* (pharmacy) will provide you with prescriptions, vitamins, and assorted sundries. Pick up some *vitamina C* to get your system back in sync, buy some *aspirina* for your head, or smooth some moisturizer all over your body.

Drugstore Items

English	Italian	English	Italian
ace bandage	la fascia elastica	mirror	lo specchio
antibiotics	gli antibiotici	needle and thread	ago e filo
antiseptic	l'antisettico	nose drops	le gocce per il naso
aspirin	l'aspirina	pacifier	il ciuccio
Band-Aids	i cerotti	pills	le pastiglie
body lotion	la lozione	prescription	la ricetta medica
baby bottle	il biberon	razor	il rasoio
castor oil	l'olio di ricino	safety pin	la spilla di sicurezza
condoms	i preservativi, i profilattici	sanitary napkins	gli assorbenti
cotton balls	i batuffoli di ovatta	scissors	le forbici
cotton swabs (for ears)	i tamponi per le orecchie	shaving cream	la crema da barba
cough syrup	lo sciroppo per la tosse	sleeping pill	il sonnifero
deodorant	il deodorante	soap	il sapone
depilatory wax	la ceretta depilatoria	syringe	la siringa
diapers	i pannolini	talcum powder	il talco
eye drops	le gocce per gli occhi	tampons	i tamponi
floss	il filo interdentale	thermometer	il termometro
gauze bandage	la fascia	tissues	tovaglioli di carta
heating pad	l'impacco caldo	toothbrush	lo spazzolino da denti
ice pack	la borsa del ghiaccio	toothpaste	il dentifricio
laxative	il lassativo	tweezers	le pinzette
		vitamins	le vitamine

Dall'Ottico

I once forgot my only pair of driving glasses on a table in a restaurant in Roma's Piazza Navona. By the time I had remembered them, they were long gone, gracing someone else's face, and I was forced to go order a new pair. If you need to go to *l'ottico* (the optician), these terms will help. By the way, if you're blind as a *pipistrello* (bat) and depend on your glasses, for your sake, *per favore* remember to bring an extra *paio!*

The Better to See You With

English	Italiano	English	Italiano
astigmatism	l'astigmatismo	glasses	gli occhiali
contact lens	le lenti a contatto	lens	le lenti
eyes	gli occhi	near-sighted	miope
far-sighted	presbite	prescription	la ricetta medica
frame	la montatura	sunglasses	gli occhiali da sole

Make Me Look Like That: Hair

All of this language about diseases and toothaches. It's time to take care of yourself and get a new look. Women in Italy tend to go to *la parrucchiera,* whereas men visit *il barbiere.*

Getting Gorgeous (the Italian Way)

English	Italiano
to blow-dry	asciugare i capelli
to color	tingere i capelli
to curl	fare i riccioli
to cut	tagliare
to get a haircut	farsi tagliare i capelli
to get a manicure	farsi fare la manicure
to get a pedicure	farsi fare il pedicure
to get a permanent	farsi la permanente
to shampoo	farsi lo shampoo
to shave	farsi la barba
to wax	farsi la ceretta

Build up your grooming vocabulary with the terms in the following table.

Well Groomed

English	Italiano	English	Italiano
bald	calvo	hairspray	la lacca
bangs	la frangia	head	la testa
beard	la barba	mud	il fango
brush	la spazzola	mustache	i baffi
comb	il pettine	nail	l'unghia
conditioner	il balsamo	nail file	la limetta
cut	il taglio	nail polish	lo smalto per le unghie
face	il viso	razor	il rasoio
gel	il gel	shampoo	lo shampoo
hair	i capelli		

You've Got Good Reflexes

Whenever you tell someone *Mi chiamo* (I call myself), you are using a reflexive verb. In Italian, when you enjoy yourself, get dressed, or comb your hair, you are using a reflexive verb.

Reflexive verbs are easily identified by the *-si* attached at the end of the infinitive. Conjugation of the reflexive verbs follows the same rules as any other Italian verb, with one exception: Reflexive verbs require the use of reflexive pronouns. These pronouns show that the subject is performing (or reflecting back) an action upon itself. In other words, the subject and the reflexive pronoun both refer to the same persons or things, as in the phrases *We enjoyed ourselves* and *I hurt myself.*

The reflexive pronouns differ only from the direct object pronouns in the third person singular and plural. Study the following reflexive pronouns.

Reflexive Pronouns

Reflexive Pronoun	English Equivalent
mi	myself
ti	yourself
si	himself/herself; Yourself
ci	ourselves
vi	yourselves
si	themselves

I Call Myself

Look at the reflexive verb *chiamarsi* in the following table to see how the reflexive pronouns work with the conjugated verb.

Chiamarsi (To Call Oneself)

Italiano	English
mi chiamo	I call myself
ti chiami	you call yourself
si chiama	he/she calls him/herself; You call yourself
ci chiamiamo	we call ourselves
vi chiamate	you call yourselves
si chiamano	they call themselves

Come ti chiami?	How do you call yourself?
Mi chiamo Gabriella.	I call myself Gabriella.

Attenzione!

In Italian, you are responsible for your own boredom because the verb *annoiarsi* (to be bored) is reflexive, literally translating to *I bore myself*.

The verb *truccarsi* is the verb used *to put on makeup*. It's interesting to note that the noun *trucco* means *trick* in Italian.

Flexing Those Muscles

Look at some common reflexive verbs in the following table.

Reflexive Verbs

Il Verb Riflessivo	Meaning	Il Verb Riflessivo	Meaning
accorgersi	to notice	lavarsi	to wash
addormentarsi	to fall asleep	mettersi	to put on
alzarsi	to get up	pettinarsi	to comb one's hair
annoiarsi	to be bored	rendersi	to realize
arrabbiarsi	to get angry	ricordarsi	to remember/to remind

continues

Reflexive Verbs (continued)

Il Verb Riflessivo	Meaning	Il Verb Riflessivo	Meaning
conoscersi	to know each other	sentirsi	to feel
chiamarsi	to call	sposarsi	to get married
diplomarsi	to obtain a diploma	svegliarsi	to get up
divertirsi	to enjoy	truccarsi	to make up
fermarsi	to stop	vestirsi	to dress oneself
laurearsi	to graduate		

Vi conoscete da molto tempo?	Do you know each other for a long time?
Federico si laurea a giugno.	Federico is graduating in June.
Ricorda di lavarti la faccia!	Remember to wash your face!
I bambini si divertono al parco.	The children enjoy themselves in the park.
Come ti chiami?	What do you call yourself?

A Little Reflection

Some rules applying to reflexive verbs might make them easier to master:

1. When talking about parts of the body or clothing, a possessive adjective is not required when using a reflexive verb:

Mi lavo il viso.	I wash my face.
Si toglie la giacca.	He/she takes off the jacket.

2. The reflexive pronoun can be placed before the verb or after the infinitive when preceded by a form of the verb *potere*, *dovere*, or *volere*:

Non voglio alzarmi troppo presto.	I don't want to wake up too early.
Devo lavarmi i capelli.	I must wash my hair.

Mirror, Mirror

Some verbs greatly change their meaning when made reflexive. The regular verb *sentire* can mean *to hear* or *to smell*.

Sento la musica.	I hear the music.
Sento il profumo.	I smell the perfume.

As a reflexive verb, *sentirsi* means *to feel*.

Mi sento bene.	I feel well.
Come si sente?	How do you feel?

The verbs in the following table exemplify the pliable nature of these flexible reflexives.

What's in a Name

Verb	English	Reflexive Verb	English
annoiare	to annoy	annoiarsi	to get bored
arrabbiare	to become rapid	arrabbiarsi	to get angry
arrestare	to arrest	arrestarsi	to pause, to stop
battere	to beat	battersi	to fight
chiedere	to ask	chiedersi	to wonder
comportare	to entail	comportarsi	to behave
giocare	to play	giocarsi	to risk
lamentare	to mourn	lamentarsi	to complain
licenziare	to dismiss/to fire	licenziarsi	to resign/to quit
offendere	to offend	offendersi	to take offense (at)
onorare	to honor	onorarsi	to take pride (in)
perdere	to lose	perdersi	to get lost
scusare	to excuse	scusarsi	to apologize
sentire	to hear/to smell	sentirsi	to feel

Mi perdo nelle città nuove.	I get lost (I lose myself) in new cities.
Giovanni si annoia quando va all'opera.	Giovanni is bored when he goes to the opera.

Test Your Reflexes

Use the reflexive verbs in parentheses in the following sentences with the appropriate reflexive pronoun. (You can find the answers in Appendix A.)

Example:	Noi _____ spesso. (vedersi)
Answer:	Noi ci vediamo spesso.

1. Io _____ alle nove. (alzarsi)

2. Luciano e Marcello _____ da nove anni. (conoscersi)

3. Tu _____ in palestra? (divertirsi)

4. Giulia deve _____ i capelli ogni giorno. (lavarsi)

5. Tu, come _____ ? (chiamarsi)

6. Noi _____ una volta la settimana. (telefonarsi)

7. Come _____ la nonna di Sandra? (sentirsi)

8. Antonella e Marco _____ lunedì prossimo. (sposarsi)

Reciprocity

Every time you say to someone *Arrivederci!* you are using a reflexive. The expression literally translates as to *re-see each other.* (Ah-hah!) The same goes for the expression *Ci vediamo!* (We'll see one another), which comes from the infinitive *vedersi.*

You have seen all of the verbs in the following table as nonreflexive verbs. By simply being made reflexive, these verbs can all express reciprocity.

Do Unto Others

Reflexive Verb	English
abbracciarsi	to hug one another
baciarsi	to kiss one another
capirsi	to understand one another
conoscersi	to know one another
guardarsi	to look at one another
incontrarsi	to meet one another/to run into
salutarsi	to greet each other
vedersi	to see one another

Ci abbracciamo ogni volta che ci vediamo.
We hug one another every time we see each other.

Madre e figlia si capiscono senza parole.
Mother and daughter understand one another without words.

The Least You Need to Know

◆ To tell someone that a certain part of your body doesn't feel well, use *Mi fa male* plus the body part.

◆ Certain body parts are irregular in the plural.

◆ Reflexive verbs, identified by the pronoun *-si* attached to the end of the infinitive, require the use of one of the reflexive pronouns: *mi, ti, si* (singular), *ci, vi,* and *si* (plural).

◆ Many regular verbs can become reflexive. In some cases, the meaning changes dramatically.

Che Sarà, Sarà: Communicating in the *Futuro*

In This Chapter

- ◆ Using *il telefono*
- ◆ Visiting *l'ufficio postale*
- ◆ Writing *una lettera*
- ◆ *Amore* Italian style
- ◆ *Il futuro*

The twentieth century has brought us to levels of *comunicazione* that a *Romano* living during the poet Virgilio's time could not fathom. Satellites are beaming down signals through space. You drop a package off today, and it clears the *continente* by tomorrow.

You've become accustomed to these *servizi* and may require them in Italy. This chapter shows you how to make *una telefonata* (telephone call), send a fax, deal with the *ufficio postale* (post office), and write *una lettera*. You'll also take a look at what's to come in the *futuro*.

Love and Consequences

A *roman* was originally a medieval tale whose origins derive from the ancient epic poems that told of adventure and conquest. Later, as love ballads (told by the traveling storytellers, the medieval equivalent of today's comedians) swept through Europe in the twelfth and thirteenth centuries, the "romantic" tales began to take on the meaning we now associate with the word *romance*.

> ### La Bella Lingua
>
> *Quel che l'occhio vede, il cuor crede.* (What the eye sees, the heart believes.)

Were we duped into thinking such tales could exist in real time? *Assolutamente!* And we'll never be the same.

I'm a hopeless romantic, which is probably why I love languages so much; they allow us to express the realm that lives within our minds and hearts. Sigh.

Sei sposato/a?	Are you married?
Non ho un fidanzato/a.	I don't have a boyfriend/girlfrend.
Vuoi andare a cena insieme stasera?	What about dinner tonight?
Tu sei bellissimo/a.	You are beautiful.
Sei affascinante.	You are fascinating.
Posso darti un bacio sulla guancia?	Can I give you a kiss on your cheek?
Posso baciarti?	Can I kiss you?
Possiamo vederci ancora?	Can we meet again?
Ti amo.	I love you.
Ti voglio bene.	I care for you.
Mi vuoi sposare?	Will you marry me?

> ### La Bella Lingua
>
> *L'amore* seems to bring out the best and the worst in all of us. Many of the most colorful terms are as "off-color" as they are expressive and are commonly used among friends. Those fit for print here include:
>
> *affamato* (starved)
>
> *allupato* (hungry as a wolf)
>
> *arrapare,* as in *quella ragazza m'arrapa un casino* (I crave that girl)
>
> Also: *m'attizza, m'acchiappa, mi tira, m'ispira, mi prende, mi gusta, ce n'è.*

Il Telefono

Most telephone numbers in Italy start with 0 + the area code followed by the number. To get an operator, you must dial 15; to get an international operator, dial 170. Your best option is to use a prepaid telephone card called a *scheda telefonica,* and most public telephones still accept coins.

Types of Phone Calls

When speaking to an international operator, you can probably speak in English. What happens if you're in a small village and need to call back home? The *vocabolario* in the following table should help you reach out and touch someone. Review Chapter 3 to remember how to spell your name in Italian.

Types of Calls

Type of Call	La Telefonata
collect call	una telefonata a carico del destinatario
credit-card call	una telefonata con carta di credito
intercontinental call	una telefonata intercontinentale
international call (Europe)	una telefonata internazionale
local call	una telefonata urbana
long-distance call	una telefonata interurbana
person-to-person call	una telefonata con preavviso

Attenzione!

In case of an emergency, keep these helpful contact numbers handy:

General SOS (free from any telephone): 113

Carabinieri (police; free): 112

Automobile Club d'Italia (car accidents and breakdowns): 116

Reach Out

Le pagine gialle (the Yellow Pages) are a handy reference for more than phone numbers—check here for listings of museum hours, places to go, and things to do. Familiarize yourself with the terms related to the *telefono* in the following table.

The Telephone

The Telephone	Il Telefono
800 number (free)	il numero verde
answering machine	la segreteria telefonica
area code	il prefisso
booth	la cabina telefonica
cellular phone	il telefonino/il cellulare
coin return	la restituzione monete
cordless phone	il telefono senza fili
keypad	la tastiera
line	la linea
message	il messaggio
operator	l'operatore
phone card	la scheda telefonica
public phone	il telefono pubblico
receiver	il ricevitore/la cornetta
telephone book	l'elenco telefonico
telephone call	la telefonata
token	il gettone*
touch-tone phone	il telefono a tastiera
Yellow Pages	le pagine gialle

Some of you may remember using gettoni *(telephone tokens) to make* una telefonata.

As a *Regola*

When calling any establishment open to the public, it is appropriate to use the second person plural (*voi*) form of the verb:

Avete …?	Do you have …?
Potete …?	Are you able to …?
A che ora aprite?	At what time do you open?
A che ora chiudete?	At what time do you close?

Call Me Sometime!

Some useful verbs and expressions related to the telephone might come in handy. (Bonus: You've probably seen most of these verbs by now!)

Phone Phrases and Verbs

The Verb	Il Verbo
to call back	richiamare
to dial	comporre il numero
to drop a line/to buzz someone	dare un colpo di telefono (idiomatico)
to hang up	attaccare, riagganciare
to hold	attendere
to insert the card	introdurre la carta
to leave a message	lasciare un messaggio
to make a call	fare una telefonata
to pick up	alzare il ricevitore/la cornetta/rispondere al telefono
to press	premere
to receive a call	ricevere una telefonata
to ring	suonare/squillare
to speak to an operator	parlare con un operatore
to telephone	telefonare

Say What?

The following words and phrases should help you get your point across.

Icebreakers

English	Italiano
Hello!	Pronto!
With whom do I speak?	Con chi parlo?
I would like to make a phone call.	Vorrei fare una telefonata.
Do you sell telephone cards?	Vendete schede telefoniche?
Is ... there?	C'è ...?
It's ... (your name).	Sono ... (il tuo nome).
I'd like to speak with	Vorrei parlare con ....
I'll call back later.	Richiamo più tardi.

Hello, Operator?

You can run into many problems when you're making a phone call. You may dial the wrong number or hear a recording telling you the number is no longer in service. The following are some phrases you might hear or want to say to an operator. They may be in the past tense, so keep an ear out for the auxiliary verbs and their participles.

What you might say:

È caduta la linea.	The line was disconnected.
La linea è sempre occupata.	The line is always busy.
Mi scusi, ho sbagliato numero.	Excuse me, I dialed the wrong number.
Non posso prendere la linea.	I can't get a line.
Posso parlare con un operatore internazionale?	May I speak with an international operator?
Mi può mettere in communicazione con …?	Can you connect me with …?

What the operator might say:

Attendere.	Hold.
Che numero ha fatto?	What number did you dial?
Non risponde.	No one is answering.
Questo (quel) numero di telefono è fuori servizio.	This (that) number is out of service.
Questo (quel) numero non funziona.	This (that) number does not work.

La Bella Lingua

When calling back home from Italy, it's always cheaper to charge your calls to your home phone. To contact MCI from anywhere in Italy, dial 172-1022. To contact AT&T, dial 172-1011. Although this is a toll-free call, you'll still need to use a calling card or 0.1 euro to get a line. Make sure you get your password *before* you leave for Italy.

Just the Fax

You might have some business to attend to while you are away or need directions to your next destination point. The following terms all relate to sending messages electronically or through the telephone lines.

Faxing Lingo

English	Italiano
fax/fax machine	il facsimile/il fax
fax number	il numero di fax
to send a fax	inviare un fax/"faxare"
fax modem	il fax modem
Internet	l'internet
e-mail	la posta elettronica
e-mail address	l'indirizzo elettronico/internet

Rain or Shine: The Post Office

A visit to *l'ufficio postale* (the post office) can bring the most reasonable person to the verge of insanity. All you want is a stamp, but you've got to wait in *la fila* (line) just like everyone else. If you want to send a *pacco*, you wait in one line only to find out you need to go to the other *sportello* (counter).

Take a deep breath and remember: You're not just in the post office, you're in the post office in *Italy*. Things could be worse.

The Post Office

English	Italiano
addressee	il recipiente
cardboard box	la scatola di cartone
counter/window	lo sportello
envelope	la busta
extra postage	la soprattassa postale
letter	la lettera
line	la fila
mail	la posta
mail carrier	il postino
mailbox	la buca da lettere, la cassetta della posta
money transfer	il vaglia postale, il vaglia telegrafico
package	il pacco

continues

The Post Office (continued)

English	Italiano
packing paper	la carta da pacchi
post office	l'ufficio postale
post office box	la cassetta postale
postage	la tariffa postale
postal worker	l'impiegato(a) postale
postcard	la cartolina
receipt	la ricevuta
to send	spedire, mandare
sender	il mittente
stamps	i francobolli
telegram	il telegramma

Rain or Shine

There are many different ways to send something—some costing more, some taking longer than others. If you don't indicate how you want something to be shipped, chances are good that it will take the longest route. *Vorrei mandare questa lettera …* (I'd like to send this letter …).

Letter Perfect

English	Italiano
by airmail	per posta aerea/per via aerea
by C.O.D.	con pagamento alla consegna
by express mail	per espresso
by special delivery	per corriere speciale
by registered mail	per posta raccomandata

Dear Gianni

Pick up some beautiful handmade marbleized paper from a *cartoleria* in Firenze. You don't have to write a lot; a couple of lines letting someone know you appreciate him or her goes a long way.

La Lettera

Letter	La Lettera
Dear (informal)	Caro/a
Dear (formal)	Egregio/a
Affectionately (informal)	Affettuosamente
Cordially (formal)	Cordialmente
Yours (formal)	il Suo/la Sua
Yours (informal)	il tuo/la tua
Sincerely (formal)	Sinceramente
A hug (informal)	Un abbraccio
A big kiss (informal)	Un bacione
Soon! (informal)	A presto!

Che Sarà Sarà: The Future

The future tense is quite easy. It is used in Italian in exactly the same manner as in English. Some irregular verbs may change their stem (such as *potere*, *fare*, and *andare*), but future endings are all the same for all three verb families.

Unlike most verb conjugations, where you add the appropriate conjugated ending to the infinitive stem, the future endings are added to the end of the infinitive minus its final *-e*. Regular *-are* verbs must also change the final *-a* of the future stem to *-e*, except the verbs *dare*, *fare*, and *stare*.

Future Endings

Subject	Future Endings	Subject	Future Endings
io	*-ò*	noi	*-emo*
tu	*-ai*	voi	*-ete*
lui/lei/Lei	*-à*	loro	*-anno*

The following illustrates how the future works in all three verb families. Pay attention to what happens to the *-are* verb *parlare*.

Future Examples

Subject	Parlare	Scrivere	Capire
io	parlerò	scriverò	capirò
tu	parlerai	scriverai	capirai
lui/lei/Lei	parlerà	scriverà	capirà
noi	parleremo	scriveremo	capiremo
voi	parlerete	scriverete	capirete
loro	parleranno	scriveranno	capiranno

Ti parlerò domani. — I'll speak to you tomorrow.

Durante la sua vacanza, — During her vacation,
Maria scriverà molte lettere. — Maria will write many letters.

What Will Be Will Be

You may already be familiar with the old Italian adage *Che sarà sarà!* (What will be, will be!) The following table shows how you talk about the future. As usual, the irregular verb *essere* has its own set of rules.

Essere (To Be)

Italiano	English	Italiano	English
io **sarò**	I will be	noi **saremo**	we will be
tu **sarai**	you will be	voi **sarete**	you will be
lui/lei/Lei **sarà**	he/she/(it)* will be; You will be	loro **saranno**	they will be

*Italian has no neuter it *but uses the verb form alone to refer to things and animals.*

As a *Regola*

In Italian, you can express the probability of something by using the future tense.

Dov'è Roberto? — Where is Robert?

Sarà in giro. — He must be around.

What Will You Have?

The following table shows how the irregular verb *avere* is conjugated in the future.

Avere (To Have)

Italiano	English	Italiano	English
io **avrò**	I will have	noi **avremo**	we will have
tu **avrai**	you will have	voi **avrete**	you will have
lui/lei/Lei **avrà**	he/she/You will have	loro **avranno**	they will have

Look for the Pattern

Verbs that end in *-care* or *-gare* (such as *cercare*, *giocare*, and *pagare*) add an *-h* before the *-er* base in order to maintain the original sound of their infinitives.

Verb		Stem	Future Conjugations
cercare	→	cercher-	cercherò, cercherai, cercherà …
giocare	→	giocher-	giocherò, giocherai, giocherà …
pagare	→	pagher-	pagherò, pagherai, pagherà …

Many verbs that end in *-iare* (such as *cominciare*, *lasciare*, *mangiare*, and *noleggiare*) change *-ia* to *-e*.

Verb		Stem	Future Conjugations
cominciare	→	comincer-	comincerò, comincerai, comincerà …
lasciare	→	lascer-	lascerò, lascerai, lascerà …
mangiare	→	manger-	mangerò, mangerai, mangerà …

As a *Regola*

Often it is not the endings that are irregular in the future tense, but the stems of the infinitives. After you have memorized the stem, you will have no problem conjugating a verb into the future.

Irregular Stems

The following table shows a list of commonly used verbs with irregular future stems. However, after the stem has been changed, these verbs use regular future endings.

Verb	Stem	Future
andare (to go)	*andr-*	andrò, andrai ...
bere (to drink)	*berr-*	berrò, berrai ...
dare (to give)	*dar-*	darò, darai ...
dovere (to have to)	*dovr-*	dovrò, dovrai ...
fare (to do/make)	*far-*	farò, farai ...
giocare (to play)	*giocher-*	giocherò, giocherai ...
potere (to be able to)	*potr-*	potrò, potrai ...
rimanere (to remain)	*rimarr-*	rimarrò, rimarrai ...
sapere (to know)	*sapr-*	saprò, saprai ...
stare (to stay)	*star-*	starò, starai ...
tenere (to hold)	*terr-*	terrò, terrai ...
vedere (to see)	*vedr-*	vedrò, vedrai ...
vivere (to live)	*vivr-*	vivrò, vivrai ...

Ti darò i soldi fra una settimana.
I'll give you the money in a week.

Staremo in vacanza per dieci giorni.
We will be on vacation for 10 days.

Back to the *Futuro*

Fill in the blanks with the proper future conjugation of the following verbs. Look at the stems to determine the rest. (You can find the answers in Appendix A.)

	Andare	Dovere	Potere	Sapere	Vedere
io	andrò	dovrò	potrò	saprò	vedrò
tu	_____	_____	_____	_____	_____
lui/lei/Lei	_____	_____	potrà	_____	_____
noi	andremo	_____	_____	_____	_____
voi	_____	_____	_____	_____	vedrete
loro	_____	_____	_____	sapranno	_____

Verbs such as *bere, rimanere, tenere, venire,* and *volere* double the final *-r* before the endings. See if you can fill in the conjugation for them:

	Bere	Rimanere	Tenere	Venire	Volere
io	berrò	rimarrò	terrò	verrò	vorrò
tu	berrai	_____	_____	_____	_____
lui/lei/Lei	_____	_____	_____	_____	_____
noi	_____	rimarremo	_____	_____	_____
voi	_____	rimarrete	_____	_____	_____
loro	_____	_____	_____	verranno	_____

Now let's put it all together. Replace the underlined verbs with the future tense.

Domani <u>ho</u> molto da fare. <u>Devo</u> fare la spesa per la cena. Prima <u>devo</u> comprare la frutta al mercato, poi <u>compro</u> il pane alla panetteria. <u>Vado</u> al supermercato per comprare la pasta e poi <u>vado</u> alla pescheria per comprare del pesce. Probabilmente <u>sono</u> stanca; allora <u>prendo</u> l'autobus per tornare a casa. I miei amici <u>arrivano</u> alle otto.

The Future Perfect

When you have finished this book, *you will have learned* the Italian language. The future perfect is a compound tense that indicates something *will have happened* in the future before another future action. You form the future perfect by using either the auxiliary verb *avere* or *essere* in the future and the past participle of a verb.

Per l'anno prossimo avrò imparato l'italiano.

I will have learned Italian by next year.

Sarai tornato dal lavoro alle otto?

Will you have returned from work by 8:00?

The Future Perfect Examples

Ah, the future. So many possibilities. Study the following tables to see how the future perfect works.

Parlare (To Speak)

Italiano	English
io **avrò parlato**	I will have spoken
tu **avrai parlato**	you will have spoken
lui/lei/Lei **avrà parlato**	he/she/You will have spoken
noi **avremo parlato**	we will have spoken
voi **avrete parlato**	you will have spoken
loro **avranno parlato**	they will have spoken

Tornare (To Return)

Italiano	English
io **sarò tornato/a**	I will have returned
tu **sarai tornato/a**	you will have returned
lui/lei/Lei **sarà tornato/a**	he/she/(it)/You will have returned
noi **saremo tornati/e**	we will have returned
voi **sarete tornati/e**	you will have returned
loro **saranno tornati/e**	they will have returned

The Least You Need to Know

- Although true love may be difficult to find, it's worth the effort.

- The future endings are the same for all three verb families.

- Many verbs have irregular stems in the future tense.

- The verbs *avere* and *essere* are irregular in the future and must be memorized (as usual).

- To create the future perfect, use the helping verb in the future + the participle.

Chapter 20

There's No Place Like *Casa* to Learn the *Condizionale*

In This Chapter

- ◆ Apartments and houses
- ◆ Rooms, furnishings, and amenities
- ◆ The conditional tense

We all share a basic need for a safe haven. This chapter gives you the language to discuss the place you call *casa*. Interestingly, there is no Italian equivalent to the English word *home*; *casa* works for both *house* and *home*.

In addition, we'll be looking at the conditional, a verb form that allows you to express things as you *would like* them to be. If you're a dreamer, or simply deluded (like me), the conditional *could* be your tense.

Your Home Away from Home

Pick up a local paper and comb through the real estate section to search for your perfect home. How many bedrooms does it have? Is there a balcony? The following table lists the various features people look for in a home. Use the expression *Ce l'ha …?* (Does it have …?) to ask if it has what you're looking for.

Internal Affairs

English	Italiano	English	Italiano
air conditioning	l'aria condizionata	hallway	il corridoio
apartment	l'appartamento	heating	il riscaldamento
attic	la soffitta	electricity	l'elettricità, la corrente
balcony	il balcone	gas	il gas
basement	la cantina	house	la casa
bathroom	il bagno	kitchen	la cucina
bathtub	la vasca da bagno	laundry room	la lavanderia
bedroom	la camera da letto	lease	il contratto di affitto
building	il palazzo, l'edificio	living room	il soggiorno
ceiling	il soffitto	maintenance	la manutenzione
closet	l'armadio, il guardaroba	owner	il padrone di casa
condominium	il condominio	rent	l'affitto
courtyard	il cortile	roof	il tetto
day room	il soggiorno	room	la stanza, la camera
dining room	la sala da pranzo	security deposit	il deposito cauzionale
entrance	l'ingresso	shower	la doccia
elevator	l'ascensore	stairs	le scale
fireplace	il camino	storage room	la cantina
floor	il pavimento	tenant	l'inquilino, l'affittuario
floor (story)	il piano	terrace	la terrazza
garden	il giardino	villa	la villa
garage	il garage	window	la finestra
ground floor	il pianterreno		

Inside Your Home

Is the house furnished, or do you have to provide your own bed? Is there an eat-in kitchen? Curtains for the windows? Clothes dryers are quite uncommon in Italy; you'll have to *stendere* your clothes on a line just like the Italians do. The following table gives you the names of the basics you need to live comfortably.

Furniture and Accessories

Furniture	I Mobili	Furniture	I Mobili
armchair	la poltrona	carpet	il tappeto
bed	il letto	chair	la sedia
bookcase	la libreria	chest of drawers	il cassettone
desk	la scrivania	refrigerator	il frigorifero
dishwasher	la lavapiatti, la lavastoviglie	rug	il tappeto
dresser	la cassettiera	sideboard	la credenza
freezer	il freezer	sofa	il divano
furniture	i mobili	stereo	lo stereo
glass case	la cristalliera	stove	la macchina del gas
lamp	la lampada	table	il tavolo
microwave oven	il forno a microonde	television	la televisione, il televisore
mirror	lo specchio	trunk	il baule
night table	il comodino	VCR	il videoregistratore
oven	il forno	washing machine	la lavatrice

Useful Verbs

It's always good to know your verbs. The following table contains a few you might find useful when shopping around for a home.

Verbs for Renting (or Buying)

Verb	Il Verbo	Verb	Il Verbo
to buy	comprare	to sell	vendere
to lease	noleggiare	to share	condividere
to move	cambiare casa	to transfer	trasferirsi
to rent	affittare/prendere in affitto		

Bright, Spacious, and Cheap

Is your concern light or space? Do you want something modern or old? The adjectives in the following table can help you describe just what you're looking for.

It Looks Like ...

Adjective	L'Aggettivo	Adjective	L'Aggettivo
antique	antico	new	nuovo
big	grande	noisy	rumoroso
bright	luminoso	old	vecchio
luxurious	lussuoso	quiet	silenzioso
modern	moderno	restored	ristrutturato, restaurato
modest	modesto	small	piccolo

How's Your Italian?

Read the following *annunci* (ads) in the real estate section of a Roman *giornale* (newspaper) and see how much you understand. If you're staying for a couple of weeks somewhere, why not rent a room in someone's *appartamento*? Usually there's a maximum stay of three weeks, but if an owner likes you, you may be able to stay longer. Many ads indicate when you should call: *Ore pasti* refers to lunch and dinner hours. Other ads will tell you not to waste any time: *No perditempo*. Keep in mind that Italians use the metric system. *Metri quadrati* refers to square meters.

Trastevere
Appartamento in affitto. 40 mq. Secondo piano. Luminoso, ristrutturato.
Referenze. No perditempo.
06-34-56-32

Testaccio
Palazzo in vendita. 4 piani, 8 appartamenti: da ristrutturare. No agenzie.
06-45-16-22

Via Flaminia
Casa in vendita o affitto. Totale mq. 180. Giardino mq. 1500 con alberi alto
fusto. Migliore offerente. Dilazioni. Tel. ore pasti
06-78-53-10

Centro
Camera affittasi a turisti in ampio appartamento. Uso cucina. Massimo 3
settimane—1 settimana di deposito.
06-99-45-12

That Would Be Nice: The Conditional Tense

When *should* you use the conditional tense? You *would* use it whenever you *would* like to express what *would* happen or what you *would* do under certain circumstances.

Forming the Conditional Tense

The conditional tense follows easy, idiot-proof rules that make it one of the easier tenses to learn. Verbs that are irregular in the present tense tend to be regular in the conditional. The same stems you learned for the future tense apply to the conditional tense.

As you saw with the future tense, simply drop the final *-e* of the infinitive and add the endings. Regular *-are* verbs, except the verbs *dare*, *fare*, and *stare*, must again change the final *-a* of their base to *-e*.

The conditional tense is often used in conjunction with another tense, the subjunctive. You'll see how that works in Chapter 21.

Conditional Endings

Subject	Conditional Endings	Subject	Conditional Endings
io	*-ei*	noi	*-emmo*
tu	*-esti*	voi	*-este*
lui/lei/Lei	*-ebbe*	loro	*-ebbero*

The following examples illustrate how the conditional works.

Conditional Examples

Subject	Parlare	Vendere	Capire
io	parler**ei**	vender**ei**	capir**ei**
tu	parler**esti**	vender**esti**	capir**esti**
lui/lei/Lei	parler**ebbe**	vender**ebbe**	capir**ebbe**
noi	parler**emmo**	vender**emmo**	capir**emmo**
voi	parler**este**	vender**este**	capir**este**
loro	parler**ebbero**	vender**ebbero**	capir**ebbero**

The consistently irregular verb *essere* maintains the same stem as it did for the future tense.

Essere (To Be)

Italiano	English	Italiano	English
io **sarei**	I would be	noi **saremmo**	we would be
tu **saresti**	you would be	voi **sareste**	you would be
lui/lei/Lei **sarebbe**	he/she/You would be	loro **sarebbero**	they would be

---

As a *Regola*

The conditional tense uses the same stems as the future. After you have learned the stems, you simply add the appropriate conditional ending. Note that the first person plural in the future should not be confused with the conditional, which has an extra *-m:*

- Future: *Vorremo* (we will want)
- Conditional: *Vorremmo* (we would like)

What Would You Have?

The following table shows how the verb *avere* is conjugated in the conditional.

Avere (To Have)

Italiano	English	Italiano	English
io **avrei**	I would have	noi **avremmo**	we would have
tu **avresti**	you would have	voi **avreste**	you would have
lui/lei/Lei **avrebbe**	he/she/You would have	loro **avrebbero**	they would have

Look for the Pattern II

Just like you saw in the future tense, verbs that end in *-care* or *-gare* (such as *cercare*, *giocare*, and *pagare*) add an *-h* before the *-er* base to maintain the original sound of their infinitives:

Verb		Stem	Conditional Conjugations
cercare	→	cercher-	cercherei, cercheresti, cercherebbe …
giocare	→	giocher-	giocherei, giocheresti, giocherebbe …
pagare	→	pagher-	pagherei, pagheresti, pagherebbe …

Many verbs that end in *-iare* (such as *cominciare*, *lasciare*, *mangiare*, and *noleggiare*) change *-ia* to *-e*.

Verb		Stem	Conjugations
cominciare	→	comincer-	comincerei, cominceresti, comincerebbe …
lasciare	→	lascer-	lascerei, lasceresti, lascerebbe …
mangiare	→	manger-	mangerei, mangeresti, mangerebbe …

The conditional tense of the verbs *dovere*, *potere*, and *volere* express *should*, *could*, and *would like*.

Stem-Changing Verbs

Let's look at some of those stem-changing verbs again. Try finishing the conjugations.

Verb	Stem	Conditional
andare (to go)	*andr-*	andrei, andresti …
bere (to drink)	*berr-*	berrei, berresti …
dare (to give)	*dar-*	darei, daresti …
fare (to do/make)	*far-*	farei, faresti …
rimanere (to remain)	*rimarr-*	rimarrei, rimarresti …
sapere (to know)	*sapr-*	saprei, sapresti …
stare (to stay)	*star-*	starei, staresti …
tenere (to hold)	*terr-*	terrei, terresti …
vedere (to see)	*vedr-*	vedrei, vedresti …
venire (to come)	*verr-*	verrei, verresti …

As a *Regola*

The verb *piacere* is used in the conditional to indicate that something would be pleasing to you.

> *Ti piacerebbe andare al cinema?* (Would you like to go to the movies?)
>
> *Sì, mi piacerebbe andarci.* (Yes, I'd like to go [there].)

Coulda, Shoulda, Woulda

The verbs *dovere* (to have to), *potere* (to be able to), and *volere* (to want) are often used in the conditional tense. When you should do something, you use the verb *dovere*. When you could do something, use the verb *potere*. When you would like something, use *volere*. These verbs in the conditional are often used with the infinitive form of another verb.

Dovere, *Potere*, and *Volere*

Subject	Dovere	Potere	Volere
io	dovrei	potrei	vorrei
tu	dovresti	potresti	vorresti
lui/lei/Lei	dovrebbe	potrebbe	vorrebbe
noi	dovremmo	potremmo	vorremmo
voi	dovreste	potreste	vorreste
loro	dovrebbero	potrebbero	vorrebbero

La Bella Lingua

To form the conditional past tense, as in *I would have gone* or *He would have eaten*, simply use the conditional form of the appropriate helping verb *avere* or *essere* + the past participle. The past conditional is most often used in conjunction with the subjunctive mood.

Avrei telefonato ma non c'era tempo. (I would have called but there wasn't time.)
Sarebbe stato un disastro! (It would have been a disaster!)

Practice Makes *Perfetto*

Translate the following sentences into Italian. (You can find the answers in Appendix A.)

1. I'd like to go to Italy for the summer.

2. We should leave; it's getting late.

3. I could come later.

4. Sofia, would you like to see a film?

5. I'd like a big house in the country.

6. I would be rich with a million dollars.

The Least You Need to Know

♦ The conditional is formed by adding the conditional endings to the stem of the verbs.

♦ Many irregular stems are the same as used in the future tense.

♦ To express that you should, could, or would like, you must use the conditional form of the verbs *dovere*, *potere*, and *volere*.

♦ The verb *piacere* is used in the conditional to indicate that something would be pleasing to you and is used like the verb *volere*, as in *would like*.

Brass Tacks: Money, Business, and *Tecnologia*

In This Chapter

- *Il computer*
- Banking terms
- Business lingo and titles
- *Il congiuntivo:* the subjunctive
- *Il passato remoto:* the past absolute

Money can't buy you *l'amore*, but you sure can have fun spending it. For people doing *business* in Italy and for those fortunate enough to have the *fortuna* to stay in Italy for an extended *periodo*, this chapter gives you the terms you need to open a bank account, take out a mortgage, or make an investment.

To round out your studies, I've also added a computer section to give you the latest terminology. I've included a few of the more entertaining and commonly used emoticons Italians use when they are *ciattando* (chatting) online.

This chapter also deals with the *subjunctive*, a somewhat unique tense (actually, it's called a mood) used to express hypothetical situations (such as, you guessed it, living in Italy).

Finally, readers are given a crash course on the *passato remoto*, known as the past definite, or preterit, a form of the past used to describe events that are considered "over and done with." Except for particular regions (generally in the south), you'll rarely hear the *passato remoto* used in spoken Italian. Keep in mind that, although you will probably not need to use this tense it is nevertheless *molto importante* to be able to recognize it, because it is often used in Italian *fiabe* (fables) and history books.

Il Computer

Computer terms in Italian are *per la maggiore parte* borrowed from English and often *un salto* (jump) from their English counterparts. Take *daunloddare*, for instance. To look at it, you might not immediately recognize it as *to download*, yet it becomes quite obvious once you say it.

The following terms should get you *navigando/surfando sulla rete* (surfing on the Internet) in no time.

Vocabulary for the Information Superhighway

English	Italiano
adapter	l'adattatore
address	l'indirizzo
at (@)	la chiocciola
battery	la batteria, la pila
computer	il computer
dialogue box	la finestra di dialogo
disks	i dischetti
e-mail	la posta elettronica
folder	la cartella
icon	l'icona
Internet	la rete
keyboard	la tastiera
laptop computer	il computer portabile
mouse	il mouse
online	in linea
page	la pagina
password	la parola d'acceso/codice
printer	la stampante

English	Italiano
screen	lo schermo
search engine	il motore di ricerca
website	il sito internet; il sito

Computer- and Internet-Related Verbs

In the constant *evoluzione* and intermingling of languages, many of these computer-related verbs have been assimilated from English and Italianized.

to back up a file	*backuppare*
to burn (a CD or DVD)	*masterizzare*
to chat online	*ciattare*
to click	*cliccare*
to compact	*compattare*
to compress a series of files	*zippare*
to connect	*connettersi*
to crash	*andare in bomba*
to debug	*debuggare*
to download	*daunloddare*
to format	*formattare*
to scan	*scannare or scandire*
to surf the web for fun	*surfare/navigare*

Italian Emoticons

Tell them you heard it here first. Italians are no strangers to chatting, and the Internet provides no exception. Try using the following emoticons to express yourself the next time you're online:

:-(*Triste* (sad)

:-) *Contento* (content)

:-/ *Indeciso, hummm …* (undecided)

%-) *Confuso* (confused)

:-c *Molto dispiaciuto* (very disappointing)

:-O *Molto stupito* (very surprised)

:-? *Non capisco* (I don't get it.)

:~i *Fumando* (smoking)

:~j *Fumando e sorridendo* (smoking and smiling)

(:-* *Bacio* (kiss)

;*) *Bacio sulla punta del naso* (kiss on the point of your nose)

'-) *Strizzatina d'occhio* (wink of an eye)

:-B *Dire sciocchezze (o cose strane)* (to talk nonsense)

:---) *Grossa bugia* (a really big lie)

:^) *Piccola bugia* (a little lie)

:*) *Forse ho bevuto troppo* (maybe I drank too much)

(:-) *Sono calvo* (I am bald)

8-) *Porto gli occhiali* (I wear glasses)

:/i *Vietato fumare* (no smoking)

@--- *Una rosa* (a rose)

*<|:-) *Babbo Natale* (Santa Claus)

Bank On It

Founded in 1472, Monte dei Paschi di Siena is one of the oldest banks in the world. The official currency used at the time was the *florin* (named after Florence), but credit as we know it today was an alien concept until the creation of the *cambiale*—the first example of an official document stating one's debt to another. In today's world, we call this a check.

Let's face it, banking terms are neither sexy nor fun, but they are absolutely *necessario*. Money talks, and so do you.

Mini Dictionary of Banking Terms

The Bank	La Banca
account	il conto
… checking account	… il conto corrente
… savings account	… il conto di deposito

The Bank	La Banca
amount due (balance)	corrispettivo non pagato
amount paid	corrispettivo riscosso
automated teller machine	Bancomat/lo sportello
balance	l'estratto conto
bank	la banca
… savings bank	… la cassa di risparmio
bank account	il conto bancario
bill	la bolletta, il conto, la fattura
bill of sale	l'atto di vendita
bills payable	gli effetti passivi
bills receivable	gli effetti attivi
to borrow	prendere in prestito
branch	la filiale
cash	i contanti
cashier	il cassiere
change	gli spiccioli/il resto
change (transaction)	il cambio
check	l'assegno
checkbook	il libretto degli assegni
coins	le monete
credit	il credito
currency (foreign)	la valuta
customer	il cliente
debt	il debito
deposit	il deposito
down payment	l'anticipo
employee	l'impiegato
endorsement	la girata
exchange rate	il tasso di scambio
final payment	il saldo
guarantee	la garanzia
holder	il titolare
installment plan	il piano di pagamento

continues

Mini Dictionary of Banking Terms (continued)

The Bank	La Banca
interest	l'interesse
… compound	… composto
… rate	… tasso di
investment	l'investimento
invoice	la fattura
loan	il prestito
long term	a lungo termine
monthly statement	l'estratto conto
mortgage	il mutuo
overdrawn account	il conto scoperto
overdrawn check	l'assegno scoperto
payment	il pagamento
percentage	la percentuale
pin	codice
promissory note	la cambiale
quarter	il trimestre
rate	la rata
receipt	la ricevuta
revenue	i ricavi
safe	la cassaforte
sale	la vendita
savings book	il libretto di risparmio
short term	a breve termine
signature	la firma
stock	l'azione
sum	la somma
teller	l'impiegato di banca
total	il totale
traveler's check	travel check
window	lo sportello

Do you need to cancel a check? Open an account? Take out a loan to continue your fabulous Italian vacation? You may need to know the verbs in the following table. Verbs used in idiomatic expressions are in parenthesis to remind you they need to be conjugated.

Banking Lingo

Verb	Il Verbo
to annul/cancel	annullare
to balance the accounts	(fare) tornare i conti
to cash	incassare
to change money	(cambiare) i soldi
to close an account	(chiudere) il conto
to deposit	depositare
to do the accounting	(tenere) i conti
to endorse	girare
to fill out (a form)	riempire, compilare
to go to the bank	(andare) in banca
to invest	investire
to loan	prestare
to manage	occuparsi
to open an account	(aprire) un conto
to pay by check	(pagare) con assegno
to pay cash	(pagare) in contanti
to save	risparmiare
to sign	firmare
to take out a loan	(prendere) in prestito
to transfer	trasferire
to withdraw	ritirare

The Wheel of Life

These days, with multitasking as the norm, it's more difficult to pinpoint professions. The terms in the following table will help you talk about where you fit in.

Trades

Trade	Attività	Trade	Attività
banking	banca	insurance	assicurazioni
communications	comunicazioni	law	legge
computers	computer	manufacturing	produzione
construction	costruzioni	marketing	marketing
design	design	medicine	medicina
development	sviluppo	public relations	pubbliche relazioni
education	istruzione, pedagogia	publishing	editoria
engineering	ingegneria	real estate	immobiliari
fashion	moda	retail	vendita al dettaglio
finance	finanza	sales	vendite
food services	alimentazione	software	software
government	governo		

Everyone Has Needs: *Il Congiuntivo*

Il congiuntivo is not pink eye; it's the subjunctive. The subjunctive is a mood, not a tense, and it expresses wishes, feelings, and doubt. It's the mood you use to express your hunches, your dreams, and your musings. As opposed to describing what is, the subjunctive describes what might be.

> **La Bella Lingua**
>
> Several English business terms have made their way into Italian, including the words *business, computer, software,* and *fax.*

> **What's What**
>
> The **present subjunctive** can be used to refer to either the present or the future. The **past subjunctive** talks about things you "wished had happened."

You use the subjunctive every time you express your opinion or describe a hypothetical situation. When the fiddler on the roof starts singing, he's using the subjunctive mood in the imperfect tense: "If I *were* a rich man ...."

Using the Subjunctive

The subjunctive is most often used in dependent clauses introduced by *che* (meaning *that*, as in *I think that ...* or *It's important that ...*).

> *Penso che Marcello arrivi domani.*
> I think that Marcello is arriving tomorrow.

> *È importante che lui parli con un dottore.*
> It's important that he speaks to a doctor.

The present subjunctive is formed by adding the subjunctive endings to the stem of the verb. Unlike future and conditional stems, most subjunctive stems change little from the infinitive.

Unless you are using a proper noun, you need to use the singular subject pronouns (*io, tu, lui/lei/Lei*) to distinguish the singular forms from one another. The pronouns are not necessary for the plural forms. The examples presented in the following three tables are given with *che* to familiarize you with this construction.

Present Subjunctive Examples

Parlare	Vendere	Offrire	Capire
che io parli	che io venda	che io offra	che io capisca
che tu parli	che tu venda	che tu offra	che tu capisca
che lui/lei/Lei parli	che lui/lei/Lei venda	che lui/lei/Lei offra	che lui/lei/Lei capisca
che parliamo	che vendiamo	che offriamo	che capiamo
che parliate	che vendiate	che offriate	che capiate
che parlino	che vendano	che offrano	che capiscano

È difficile che lui venda la casa a quel prezzo.
It's difficult for him to sell the house at that price.

Non penso che Maria capisca.
I don't think that Maria understands.

As a *Regola*

The subjunctive is used when:

1. Two different clauses exist (dependent and independent) pertaining to two different subjects.
2. Those clauses are joined by *che*.
3. One of these clauses expresses need, emotion, doubt, or an opinion:

   Need. *È necessario che lui vada da un dottore.* (It's necessary for him to go to the doctor.)

   Doubt. *Dubito che vinca la nostra squadra.* (I doubt that our team will win.)

   Opinion. *Credo che tu sia la più bella donna del mondo.* (I think that you are the most beautiful woman in the world.)

   Emotion. *Ho paura che sia troppo tardi per andarci.* (I am afraid it's too late to go there.)

The verbs *essere* and *avere* are both irregular.

Essere (To Be)

che io **sia**	che noi **siamo**
che tu **sia**	che voi **siate**
che lui/lei/Lei **sia**	che loro/essi **siano**

Penso che Luisa sia bella.
I think that Luisa is beautiful.

Credo che siano a casa.
I believe that they are at home.

Avere (To Have)

che io **abbia**	che noi **abbiamo**
che tu **abbia**	che voi **abbiate**
che lui/lei/Lei **abbia**	che loro/essi **abbiano**

*Penso che Tiziana **abbia** ragione.*
I think that Tiziana is right.

*È un peccato che non **abbiano** il tempo di venire.*
It's a shame that they don't have time to come.

Oh, So Moody

Oh, those irregularities. It should be no surprise at this point that there are several verbs with irregular subjunctive forms.

Irregular Verbs in the Present Subjunctive

Verb	Irregular Present Subjunctive
andare	vada, vada, vada, andiamo, andiate, vadano
dare	dia, dia, dia, diamo, diate, diano
dire	dica, dica, dica, diciamo, diciate, dicano
dovere	debba, debba, debba, dobbiamo, dobbiate, debbano
fare	faccia, faccia, faccia, facciamo, facciate, facciano

Verb	Irregular Present Subjunctive
mantenere	mantenga, mantenga, mantenga, manteniamo, manteniate, mantengano
piacere	piaccia, piaccia, piaccia, piacciamo, piacciate, piacciano
potere	possa, possa, possa, possiamo, possiate, possano
rimanere	rimanga, rimanga, rimanga, rimaniamo, rimaniate, rimangano
salire	salga, salga, salga, saliamo, saliate, salgano
sapere	sappia, sappia, sappia, sappiamo, sappiate, sappiano
stare	stia, stia, stia, stiamo, stiate, stiano
tenere	tenga, tenga, tenga, teniamo, teniate, tengano
venire	venga, venga, venga, veniamo, veniate, vengano
volere	voglia, voglia, voglia, vogliamo, vogliate, vogliano

Dependent Clauses and the Subjunctive

The following expressions are all dependent clauses requiring the subjunctive mood. *I think …* is the independant (main) clause that works closely with the dependent clause *… that it is raining.* You use the subjunctive when you're not sure of something. It could be raining or not.

Express Yourself

Expression	L'Espressione
Expressions of Wishing, Emotion, Need, and Doubt	
I am happy that …	Sono contento che …
I am sorry that …	Mi dispiace che …
I believe that …	Credo che …
I desire that …	Desidero che …
I doubt that …	Dubito che …
I imagine that …	Immagino che …
I think that …	Penso che …
I want that …	Voglio che …
Impersonal Expressions and Conjunctions	
although …	sebbene …
before …	prima che …

continues

Express Yourself (continued)

Expression	L'Espressione
even though …	benché …
in case …	nel caso che …
It seems that …	Sembra che …
It's difficult that …	È difficile che …
It's easy that …	È facile che …
It's good/bad that …	È bene/male che …
It's important that …	È importante che …
It's incredible that …	È incredibile che …
It's likely (probable) that …	È probabile che …
It's necessary that …	Bisogna che …
It's not important that …	Non importa che …
It's possible/impossible that …	È possibile/impossibile che …
It's strange that …	È strano che …
provided that …	purché …
so that …	affinché …
unless …	a meno che …
until …	finché non …
without …	senza che …

Mi sembra che tu sia intelligente.
It seems to me that you are intelligent.

Sebbene io non possa suonare il violino, mi piace ascoltarlo.
Although I can't play the violin, I like listening to it.

Attenzione!

You can avoid the subjunctive altogether when the subject is the same for both the dependent and independent clauses by using *di* plus the infinitive:

Penso di andare al cinema. (I'm thinking of going to the movies.)

Cara Silvia–Practice Makes *Perfetto*

Paola hopes she can go to Italy this summer to study the language. She wants her friend Silvia to join her on an excursion. Fill in the blanks with the appropriate form of the subjunctive. (You can find the answers in Appendix A.)

1 aprile
Cara Silvia:
Spero che tu _____(stare) bene.

Ho ricevuto la tua lettera. È probabile che io _____(venire) in Italia quest'estate. Penso che _____(essere) una buon'idea per imparare la lingua e voglio che tu _____(venire) con me in Sardegna. Mi dicono che l'isola _____(essere) molto bella. Ti piace l'idea? Che cosa ne pensi? Basta che tu mi _____(scrivere) la tua risposta. Sono contenta che la tua famiglia _____(stare) bene. Scrivimi!

Un abbraccio forte,
Paola

Silvia d'Argento
Via Flaminia 23
00100   Roma
Italia

The Past (Present Perfect) Subjunctive

To make the past subjunctive (*passato del congiuntivo*), you'll need to use the present subjunctive form of the auxiliary verbs *avere* or *essere* + the past participle of your verb. Remember that verbs requiring *essere* as their auxiliary reflect gender and number in the participle. You use the past (or perfect) subjunctive when the action expressed by the verb of the dependent clause occurred before the action expressed by the verb in the independent clause. Study the following examples.

Past Subjunctive

Avere + Telefonare	Essere + Andare
che io abbia telefonato	che io sia andato(a)
che tu abbia telefonato	che tu sia andato(a)
che lui/lei/Lei abbia telefonato	che lui/lei/Lei sia andato(a)

continues

Past Subjunctive (continued)

Avere + Telefonare	Essere + Andare
che noi abbiamo telefonato	che siamo andati(e)
che voi abbiate telefonato	che siate andati(e)
che loro abbiano telefonato	che siano andati(e)

Sono contenta che tu abbia telefonato.
I am happy that you telephoned.

Sembra che lui sia diventato pazzo.
It seems that he has gone crazy.

Purely Speculation: The Imperfect Subjunctive

By the time you're comfortable using this tense, you probably won't need me anymore. In any case, the imperfect subjunctive (*imperfetto del congiuntivo*) is most often used when someone is talking about what they *would have done if*.

Imperfetto

Parlare	Vendere	Offrire	Capire
che io parlassi	che io vendessi	che io offrissi	che io capissi
che tu parlassi	che tu vendessi	che tu offrissi	che tu capissi
che lui/lei/Lei parlasse	che lui/lei/Lei vendesse	che lui/lei/Lei offrisse	che lui/lei/Lei capisse
che parlassimo	che vendessimo	che offrissimo	che capissimo
che parlaste	che vendeste	che offriste	che capiste
che parlassero	che vendessero	che offrissero	che capissero

The Past Was Perfect

The possibilities are endless when you start mixing and matching auxiliary verbs in compound tenses. The past perfect subjunctive (*trapassato del congiuntivo*) is created by using the imperfect subjunctive of your auxiliary verb (*avere* or *essere*) + the past participle of the verb you are conjugating.

Trapassato

Parlare	Partire
che io avessi parlato	che io fossi partito(a)
che tu avessi parlato	che tu fossi partito(a)
che lui/lei/Lei avesse parlato	che lui/lei/Lei fosse partito(a)
che avessimo parlato	che fossimo partiti(e)
che aveste parlato	che foste partiti(e)
che avessero parlato	che fossero partiti(e)

Once Upon a Time: *Il Passato Remoto*

The *passato remoto* (also called the past definite and the past absolute) is a tense that goes so far back that it doesn't even have an equivalent in English. Although it translates to the simple past, as in *I went*, the *passato remoto* requires you to look at time differently.

The *passato remoto* is the tense you hear when a story begins, "Once upon a time ...." It is the tense used in literature, fables, and historical references to describe an event that took place at a specific time in the distant past. A highly irregular verb tense, at times it is difficult to determine the infinitive of a conjugation. Although rarely used in daily speech, an understanding of the *passato remoto* is necessary in order to read Italian literature and poetry (which you definitely don't want to miss!).

Past Absolute Examples

Subject	Parlare	Vendere	Capire
io	parlai	vendei	capii
tu	parlasti	vendesti	capisti
lui/lei/Lei	parlò	vendè	capì
noi	parlammo	vendemmo	capimmo
voi	parlaste	vendeste	capiste
loro	parlarono	venderono	capirono

Dante scrisse La Divina Commedia *nel 1307.*
Dante wrote *The Divine Comedy* in 1307.

Ci Fu Una Volta (Once Upon a Time)

The *passato remoto* is used in *fiabe* (fables) and *racconti* (stories). These ancient forms of the verbs *essere* and *avere* are virtually unrecognizable from the present-tense conjugations.

Essere (To Be)

Italiano	English	Italiano	English
io **fui**	I was	noi **fummo**	we were
tu **fosti**	you were	voi **foste**	you were
lui/lei/Lei **fu**	he/she was; You were	loro **furono**	they were

Avere (To Have)

Italiano	English	Italiano	English
io **ebbi**	I had	noi **avemmo**	we had
tu **avesti**	you had	voi **aveste**	you had
lui/lei/Lei **ebbe**	he/she/You had	loro **ebbero**	they had

Cose Da Vedere

The following has been excerpted from a travel brochure promoting *la bellissima città di San Gimignano*. See if you can identify the use of the *passato remoto*. (You can find the answers in Appendix A.)

Cose da vedere

San Gimignano prende il nome dal vescovo di Modena morto nel 387. Nel 1099 divenne libero Comune. Combattè contro i vescovi di Volterra e le città vicine. La peste del 1348 e la successiva crisi portarono San Gimignano nel 1353 alla sottomissione a Firenze.

Well, that's it. I hate to leave you hanging but hope that you have enjoyed the *viaggio*. It's time for you to fly away, *i miei uccellini*. Fly high, live well, love with a full heart, and drop me a line once in a while. Just make sure it's in *italiano!*

The Least You Need to Know

◆ Use the Italian emoticons to express yourself the next time you're *surfando* the Internet.

◆ If you need to open a bank account or deal with money matters, it's helpful to have the terms.

◆ The subjunctive is a mood, not a tense, and it is used to express opinions, thoughts, feelings, and desires.

◆ The absolute past is used primarily in the written language and is very irregular.

◆ Learning Italian will improve your life. Enjoy the process—it's a short *viaggio*.

Answer Key

Chapter 2

Name That Subject

1. The stars (they)
2. Jessica (she)
3. Leslie (she)
4. My mother (she)
5. Louis (he)
6. The food (it)
7. Italian (it)
8. Anna (she)

Practice Makes *Perfetto*

1. dentro
2. stomaco
3. entro
4. informazioni riservate
5. interno

Chapter 4

How *Intelligente* You Are

1. posizione
2. incredibile
3. nazione
4. presenza
5. identità
6. pessimismo
7. prudente
8. continente
9. religioso
10. differenza

Masculine Nouns

1. the airplane
2. the anniversary
3. the arch
4. the actor
5. the bus
6. the coffee
7. the color
8. the communism
9. the continent
10. the cotton
11. the director
12. the dictionary
13. the doctor
14. the elephant
15. the fact
16. the group
17. the idiot
18. the lemon
19. the mechanic
20. the motor
21. the museum
22. the nose
23. the odor
24. the paradise
25. the president
26. the perfume
27. the program
28. the respect
29. the salary
30. the service
31. the socialism
32. the spirit
33. the student
34. the taxi
35. the tea
36. the telephone
37. the train

Feminine Nouns

1. the art
2. the bicycle
3. the carrot
4. the guitar
5. the class
6. the condition
7. the conversation
8. the culture
9. the curiosity
10. the depression
11. the diet
12. the difference
13. the discussion
14. the emotion
15. the experience
16. the expression
17. the holiday, party, festivity
18. the figure
19. the fountain
20. the form
21. the fortune
22. the idea
23. the identity
24. the inflation
25. the salad
26. the lamp
27. the letter
28. the list
29. the medicine
30. the music
31. the nation
32. the person
33. the possibility
34. the probability
35. the profession
36. the region
37. the religion
38. the rose
39. the sculpture
40. the temperature
41. the tourist
42. the university
43. the violence

How Much Do You Understand Already?

1. The city is beautiful.
2. The restaurant is terrible.
3. The jacket is big.
4. The museum is interesting.
5. The service is good.
6. The mountain is tall.

Your Turn

1. Il dottore è elegante.
2. Il presidente è famoso.
3. La banca è ricca.
4. La violenza è terribile.
5. La discussione è importante.
6. L'idiota è stupida.

Verbi

to study
to assist
to sleep

Traduzione, Per Favore

1. Italy is part of the continent of Europe.
2. The student studies mathematics and history.
3. The actor is very famous in the movies.
4. The mechanic repairs the automobile.
5. The cook prepares a salad and an appetizer.
6. The doctor speaks with the patient.
7. The family desires a modern and big apartment.
8. The Japanese tourist visits the museum and the cathedral.
9. The president presents the plan (the program).
10. Robert prefers classical music.

What's Your Take?

1. La cioccolata è deliziosa.
2. Il ristorante è eccellente.
3. La città è splendida e magnifica.
4. Il profumo è elegante.
5. La conversazione è interessante.
6. Il dottore è sincero.
7. Lo studente è intelligente.
8. Il museo è importante.
9. La cattedrale è alta.
10. Il treno è veloce.

Are You Well Read?

Barzini, *The Italians*
Eco, *The Name of the Rose*
Morante, *History*

Pirandello, *6 Characters in Search of an Author*
Dante, *The Divine Comedy*
Machiavelli, *The Prince*

Chapter 5

Practice Makes *Perfetto*

1. la casa (f.)
2. il cane (m.)
6. l'estate (f.)
7. la chiesa (f.)

3. l'albero (m.)
4. il piatto (m.)
5. la lezione (f.)

8. lo straniero (m.)
9. la cattedrale (f.)
10. il pianeta (m./irregular)

La Pratica

1. i libri
2. i gatti
3. le ragazze

4. le stazioni
5. gli amici
6. le amiche

Practice Those Plurals

1. Cerco le cartoline.
2. Cerco le riviste.
3. Cerco le collane.

4. Cerco i profumi.
5. Cerco le cravatte.
6. Cerco le penne.

What Have You Learned About Gender?

1. Mature actress (40 to 50 years old) sought with the ability to speak English and French for interpreting the role of countess. Distinct look. Send resumé with photo to Via Garibaldi 36, Roma.

2. Strong actor, athletic, young with light hair sought to interpret the role of Caesar. Present yourself on June 25 at 9:00 at Superforte gym, second floor.

3. Very sexy men and women sought to appear nude in beach scene: various ages. No experience necessary. Telephone 06/040357.

Chapter 6

A Sense of Belonging

1. la sua casa
2. la mia scuola
3. i suoi libri

4. i suoi libri
5. il tuo amico

One Yellow Banana, Please

1. *bianca; pulita* (The white house is clean.)
2. *vecchio* (The Colisseum is very old.)
3. *alte* (The mountains in Switzerland are high.)
4. *chiuso* (The store is closed on Sundays.)
5. *economico* (This hotel is inexpensive.)
6. *facile* (The Italian language is easy.)

Make the Connection

Definite Article	Translation	Quello	Translation
1. il libro	the book	quel libro	that book
2. i libri	the books	quei libri	those books
3. la penna	the pen	quella penna	that pen
4. le penne	the pens	quelle penne	those pens
5. l'articolo	the article	quell'articolo	that article
6. gli articoli	the articles	quegli articoli	those articles
7. lo studente	the student	quello studente	that student
8. gli studenti	the students	quegli studenti	those students

The More Things Change

1. dolcemente
2. sinceramente
3. intelligentemente
4. necessariamente
5. velocemente
6. regolarmente
7. difficilmente
8. probabilmente
9. solamente
10. gentilmente

Chapter 7

Hey You!

1. tu
2. voi
3. voi
4. voi
5. tu
6. tu
7. Lei

Practice Makes *Perfetto*

1. lavora
2. aspettiamo
3. abiti
4. parlo
5. passate
6. preparano

Practice Makes *Perfetto* II

1. spendono
2. scrivo
3. accendi
4. vediamo
5. risolve
6. prendete

Chapter 8

Come Sei Intelligente!

1. è
2. sei
3. sono
4. sono
5. siete

Chitchat

1. stiamo
2. sta
3. sto
4. sono
5. è
6. è

Fill In the Blankity-Blanks

1. C'è
2. Ci sono
3. Ci sono
4. C'è
5. Ci sono
6. Ci sono
7. Ci sono
8. c'è

Express Yourself

1. ho fame
2. ho freddo
3. sono stanco, sono stanca, ho sonno
4. ho ___ anni
5. ho vergogna

Chapter 9

Time Will Tell

1. Andiamo al cinema alle sei.
2. Il volo parte alle otto e venticinque di mattino.
3. Inizia il programma alle sette.
4. C'è l'autobus per Verona a mezzogiorno.
5. Sono le quattro e quarantaquattro. (That's a mouthful, isn't it?)
6. C'è il treno per Roma alle due e trentatrè.
7. Andiamo a fare la colazione alle sette e mezzo.

The Dating Game

1. Il mese scorso
2. L'anno scorso
3. L'anno prossimo
6. L'inverno prossimo
7. Sette anni fa
8. Ieri notte

4. Fra dieci anni
5. La primavera scorsa

9. Ieri sera
10. Stamattina

Quando Quando Quando?

1. Il mio compleanno è …
2. Vado* in vacanza … (*the verb *andare* (to go) is irregular)
3. Natale è il venticinque di dicembre.

Chapter 10

Ask Away

My name is Cinzia Bell and I live in the United States. I am a student. I am studying art history. I am traveling by car with my friend in Italy. We're passing a month in Italy. We're going to visit all of the important cities. I return to the university in September.

My name is Mario Pesce and I am a banker. I don't speak English very well. I live in Milan with my wife. We have two children, Giorgio and Isabella. In December I am going with my wife to New York.

Give Your Mind a Trip

1. b
2. e

3. f
4. b

5. a
6. g

7. d

Going, Going, Gone

1. vanno
2. vado

3. vai
4. andiamo

5. andate; vanno

All Verbed Up and Everywhere to Go

1. prendo
2. andiamo

3. prendono
4. vai

5. prendete
6. va

Practice Those Conjugations

to go: (andare) vado, vai, va, andiamo, andate, vanno
to ask: (chiedere) chiedo, chiedi, chiede, chiediamo, chiedete, chiedono
to take: (prendere) prendo, prendi, prende, prendiamo, prendete, prendono
to reserve: (prenotare) prenoto, prenoti, prenota, prenotiamo, prenotate, prenotano
to return: (ritornare) ritorno, ritorni, ritorna, ritorniamo, ritornate, ritornano
to get off/go down: (scendere) scendo, scendi, scende, scendiamo, scendete, scendono

Switcharoo

1. alla festa
2. alla piazza
3. in macchina
4. sull'armadio
5. degli spaghetti

Chapter 11

Room Service, *Per Favore*

(Remember: There are several ways to express needs. ***Mi serve*** comes from the reflexive verb ***sentirsi,*** covered in more depth in Chapter 18.)

1. Mi serve della carta da lettera.
   Ho bisogno della carta da lettera.
   Vorrei la carta da lettera

2. Mi serve la chiave.
   Ho bisogno della chiave.
   Vorrei la chiave.

3. Mi serve un asciugamano in più.
   Ho bisogno di un asciugamano in più.
   Vorrei un asciugamano in più.

4. Mi serve la sveglia.
   Ho bisogno di una sveglia.
   Vorrei la sveglia.

5. Mi serve una saponetta in più.
   Ho bisogno di una saponetta in più.
   Vorrei una saponetta in più.

Practice Makes *Perfetto*

1. due coperte
2. cuscino
3. un asciugacapelli, un fon
4. chiave
5. ristoranti
6. una camera, una stanza
7. una bottiglia d'acqua minerale

I'm in the Mood for ...

Any one of the answers given is sufficient.

1. voglio, devo, posso
2. vuoi
3. deve, vuole
4. voglio
5. vogliono, devono
6. possiamo, vogliamo, dobbiamo
7. volete
8. può
9. vuole, deve

Practice Makes *Perfetto* II

1. voglio
2. finisce di
3. aiutano a
4. credete di
5. devi
6. fare

Chapter 12

Your Turn

1. (to find) trovare: trovo, trovi, trova, troviamo, trovate, trovano
2. (to go) andare: vado, vai, va, andiamo, andate, vanno
3. (to pass) passare: passo, passi, passa, passiamo, passate, passano
4. (to do/make) fare: faccio, fai, fa, facciamo, fate, fanno
5. (to return) ritornare: ritorno, ritorni, ritorna, ritorniamo, ritornate, ritornano

Practice Makes *Perfetto*

1. fa
2. vado
3. andiamo
4. fanno
5. fate
6. prendi

Yes or No

1. mi
2. mi
3. mi
4. mi, ti
5. mi

A Refresher

1. Sono americano(a). Sono d'origine americana.
2. Sono francese. Sono d'origine francese.
3. Sono spagnolo(a). Sono d'origine spagnola.
4. Sono greco(a). Sono d'origine greca.
5. Sono irlandese. Sono d'origine irlandese.

Chapter 13

Di Bocca Buona

1. Bere come una spugna.
2. Di bocca buona.
3. Una ciliegia tira l'altra.
4. Non me ne importa un fico secco.
5. Fare la frittata.
6. Fino al midollo.
7. Liscio come l'olio.

j. To drink like a sponge.
a. A good mouth (a good eater).
e. One cherry pulls the other.
c. I don't care one dry fig's worth.
n. To make an omelette of things.
p. To the marrow.
g. Smooth as oil.

8. Un osso duro.

b. A hard bone.

9. Dire pane al pane e vino al vino.

i. To call bread bread and wine wine (to call a spade a spade).

10. Mangiare pane e cipolla.

k. To eat bread and onion. (To live on bread and water.)

11. Togliersi il pane di bocca.

l. To give bread from your mouth.

12. Di pasta buona.

d. Of good pasta (good natured).

13. Avere lo spirito di patata.

m. To have the spirit of a potato. (a bore)

14. Essere un sacco di patate.

h. To be a sack of potatoes. (lazy)

15. Fare polpette di …

o. To make meatballs of …

16. Rosso come un peperone.

f. Red as a pepper.

La Bella del Palazzo

The following is an adaptation of the poem, altered slightly to re-create the rhym:.

> I am the beauty of the palace;
> I fall on the ground without malaise;
> I shine for the Grand Lord above,
> I am always served with love.

What am I?—*un'oliva* (an olive)

Some Practice

1. Sì, ne hanno. No, non ne hanno.

2. Sì, ne abbiamo. No, non ne abbiamo.

3. Sì, ne bevo. No, non ne bevo.

4. Sì, c'è ne. No, non c'è ne.

Using the Verb *Piacere*

1. piace
2. piace
3. piacciono
4. piace
5. piacciono
6. piace

Using the Verb *Piacere* II

1. Ti piacciono i dolci?
   Sì, mi piacciono i dolci.
   No, non mi piacciono i dolci.

2. Ti piace la pasta?
   Sì, mi piace la pasta.
   No, non mi piace la pasta.

3. Ti piacciono gli spaghetti?
   Sì, mi piacciono gli spaghetti.
   No, non mi piacciono gli spaghetti.

4. Ti piacciono le acciughe?
   Sì, mi piacciono le acciughe.
   No, non mi piacciono le acciughe.

5. Ti piacciono i fichi?
   Sì, mi piacciono i fichi.
   No, non mi piacciono i fichi.
6. Ti piace il fegato?
   Sì, mi piace il fegato.
   No, non mi piace il fegato.

Minestra di Riso e Limone

Ingredients

8 cups of broth	¼ cup of grated Parmigiano-Reggiano
1 cup of Arborio rice	1 teaspoon of grated lemon rind
3 egg yolks	1 teaspoon of lemon juice

1. Place broth in pan and bring to boil point. Add the rice; cover the pan and allow it to cook for 20 minutes.
2. In the meantime, beat the eggs, add the cheese, grated lemon rind, and lemon juice.
3. When the rice is cooked, mix the eggs into the soup, beating continually. Warm the soup and serve immediately. (Serves four people.)

(Recipe used courtesy of Anne Bianchi from her book *Tuscan Women*.)

Chapter 14

A *Bellini* Please

⅔ cup (160 ml.) of peach purée
1 teaspoon of raspberry purée
1 bottle of Prosecco (or Asti Spumante or champagne)

In every glass of wine or sparkling wine, mix 7 teaspoons of the peach purée. Add 2 to 3 drops of the raspberry purée. Add wine and serve immediately.

Learning by Example

1. Avete bisogno di
2. Impari a
3. Cristoforo continua a
4. Andiamo a
5. Smetto di
6. Finiscono di

Making Progress

1. Stiamo guardando.
2. Stai scrivendo.
3. Sta cucinando.
4. Stanno dormendo.
5. Sto leggendo.
6. Sto pulendo.

Chapter 15

Sock It to Me!

Man

1. i pantaloni
2. la cintura
3. la maglia, il golf
4. le scarpe
5. l'ombrello

Woman

1. il cappotto, il giubotto
2. la sciarpa
3. la gonna
4. i guanti
5. il cappello
6. le scarpe
7. le calze
8. la borsa

Who's Who

1. **La** mangiamo.
2. Dante e Boccaccio vogliono mangiar**la**.
3. **Lo** prendo.
4. Mario **lo** scrive.
5. **Li** vedo.
6. **La** bacia.
7. **La** comprate.
8. **La** capisce?

Who's Who II

1. Desideriamo parlar**vi**.
2. Mario e Giorgio **ti** danno un regalo.
3. Carlo **le** telefona.
4. Lo studente **gli** fa una domanda.
5. **Le** offro un caffè.
6. I nonni danno le caramelle **a loro.**
7. **Gli** offro una birra.
8. **Ci** augurano una buona notte.

Who's Who: Final Round

1. **Lo** guardate.
2. **Lo** regalo a Lorenzo.
3. **La** vede?
4. **Gli** regalo un mazzo di fiori.
5. Danno i libri **a loro.**
6. **Lo** conosco molto bene.
7. **Li** danno ai bambini.
8. **Lo** accettiamo con piacere.

Stressful Exercise

1. te (Without you, I cannot live.)
2. sè (Mario always talks about himself.)
3. me (Do you want to speak to me?)
4. lei (This letter is for her.)
5. lui (We're spending the evening at Robert's house.)
6. me, lei (Are you coming with me or her?)

Chapter 17

Fill in the *Spazio*

dire: dicevo, diceva, dicevate, dicevano

fare: facevi, faceva, facevamo, facevano

bere: bevevo, bevevi, bevevamo, bevevate

La Pratica

1. guardavo
2. eravamo, andavamo
3. lavorava, preparava
4. piaceva
5. aveva
6. abitavano
7. faceva, era
8. tornavo
9. vedevamo
10. alzava

What's Done Is Done

(Remember: Sometimes it is possible to use either the *passato prossimo* or the *imperfetto*. I've provided my answers, but your answers might be just as appropriate, whichever tense you use!)

siamo arrivati, brillava, faceva, viaggiavamo, era, siamo andati, abbiamo visto, siamo andati

A Review

1. Scrivere

ho scritto	scrivevo
hai scritto	scrivevi
ha scritto	scriveva
abbiamo scritto	scrivevamo
avete scritto	scrivevate
hanno scritto	scrivevano

2. Spedire

ho spedito	spedivo
hai spedito	spedivi
ha spedito	spediva
abbiamo spedito	spedivamo
avete spedito	spedivate
hanno spedito	spedivano

3. Leggere

ho letto	leggevo
hai letto	leggevi
ha letto	leggeva
abbiamo letto	leggevamo
avete letto	leggevate
hanno letto	leggevano

4. Mandare

ho mandato	mandavo
hai mandato	mandavi
ha mandato	mandava
abbiamo mandato	mandavamo
avete mandato	mandavate
hanno mandato	mandavano

Chapter 18

Tell Me Where It Hurts

1. Mi fa male il ginocchio.
2. Mi fanno male le spalle.
3. Mi fanno male i piedi.
4. Mi fa male la gola/Ho mal di gola.
5. Mi fa male il dente/Ho mal di denti.
6. Mi fa male la caviglia.

Test Your Reflexes

1. mi alzo
2. si conoscono
3. ti diverti
4. lavarsi
5. ti chiami
6. ci telefoniamo
7. si sente
8. si sposano

Chapter 19

Look for the Pattern

cercare (to look for/search): cercherò, cercherai, cercherà, cercheremo, cercherete, cercheranno

giocare (to play): giocherò, giocherai, giocherà, giocheremo, giocherete, giocheranno

pagare (to pay): pagherò, pagherai, pagherà, pagheremo, pagherete, pagheranno

cominciare (to begin): comincerò, comincerai, comincerà, cominceremo, comincerete, cominceranno

lasciare (to leave behind): lascerò, lascerai, lascerà, lasceremo, lascerete, lasceranno

mangiare (to eat): mangerò, mangerai, mangerà, mangeremo, mangerete, mangeranno

Back to the *Futuro*

andrai, andrà, andrete, andranno

dovrai, dovrà, dovremo, dovrete, dovranno

potrai, potremo, potrete, potranno

saprai, saprà, sapremo, saprete

vedrai, vedrà, vedremo, vedranno

berrà, berremo, berrete, berranno

rimarrai, rimarrà, rimarranno

terrai, terrà, terremo, terrete, terranno
verrai, verrà, verremo, verrete
vorrai, vorrà, vorremo, vorrete, vorrano

Chapter 20

How's Your Italian?

Trastevere. Apartment for rent. 40 square meters. Second floor. Lots of light, renovated. References required. Don't waste time.

Testaccio. Building for sale. 4 floors, 8 apartments: needs restoration. No agencies.

Via Flaminia. House for sale or rent. Total square meters 180. Shaded garden 1,500 square meters. Best offer. Installment plan. Call during meal times.

Downtown. Room for rent for tourists in large apartment. Use of kitchen. Maximum stay 3 weeks—1 week deposit.

Practice Makes *Perfetto*

1. Vorrei andare in Italia per l'estate.
2. Dovremmo partire; è tardi.
3. Potrei venire più tardi.
4. Sofia, vorresti vedere un film?
5. Vorrei una grande casa in campagna.
6. Sarei ricco(a) con un milione di dollari.

Chapter 21

Cara Silvia

1. stia
2. venga
3. sia
4. venga or venissi (the imperfect subjunctive)
5. sia
6. scriva
7. stia

April 1

Dear Silvia:

I hope that everything is going well.

I received your letter. I will probably come to Italy this summer. I think it's necessary for learning the language. I would be so pleased if you came with me to Sardegna. They tell me the island is very beautiful. What do you think? Do you like the idea? It's enough if you write me your response. I am happy your family is well.

Write me!

A big hug,

Paola

Cose Da Vedere

San Gimignano took its name from the Bishop of Modena who died in 387 A.D. In 1099 it became a free township. It fought against the bishops of Volterra and bordering cities. The plague of 1348 and successive crisis brought San Gimignano to the submission of Florence in 1353.

Verb Tables

Think of your verb tables as the scales on a piano. The more you practice, the less you have to think about what you are doing. If nothing else, verb tables can also serve as an effective sleeping aid during *le ore piccole. Buona Notte!*

Reflexive Verbs (*Verbi Reflessivi*)

All reflexive verbs use *essere* in compound tenses such as the *passato prossimo* (present perfect). Reflexive verbs are conjugated according to regular rules and include the following reflexive pronouns:

mi (myself)   *ci* (ourselves)
ti (yourself)   *vi* (yourselves)
si (himself, herself, yourself)   *si* (themselves)

Commonly Used Reflexive Verbs Include:

Italiano	*English*	*Italiano*	*English*
alzarsi	to get up	lavarsi	to wash oneself
annoiarsi	to become bored	mettersi	to put on
arrabbiarsi	to become angry	radersi	to shave
chiamarsi	to call oneself	sentirsi	to feel
conoscersi	to know each other	sposarsi	to get married
divertirsi	to enjoy	svegliarsi	to wake up
fermarsi	to stop	vestirsi	to dress oneself
laurearsi	to graduate		

Regular Verbs

After you have mastered the following verbs, you will be ready to use all of the tenses. Consult Barron's *501 Italian Verbs* for a more comprehensive list.

Infinito (Infinitive)	Presente (Present)	Passato Prossimo (Present Perfect)	Imperativo (Imperative)	Imperfetto (Imperfect)	Futuro (Future)	Condizionale (Conditional)	Congiuntivo (Subjunctive)	Passato Remoto (Past Definite/Absolute)
parlare (to speak)	parlo	ho parlato	*	parlavo	parlerò	parlerei	parli	parlai
	parli	hai parlato	parla, non parlare	parlavi	parlerai	parleresti	parli	parlasti
	parla	ha parlato	parli	parlava	parlerà	parlerebbe	parli	parlò
	parliamo	abbiamo parlato	parliamo	parlavamo	parleremo	parleremmo	parliamo	parlammo
	parlate	avete parlato	parlate	parlavate	parlerete	parlereste	parliate	parlaste
	parlano	hanno parlato	parlino	parlavano	parleranno	parlerebbero	parlino	parlarono
scrivere (to write)	scrivo	ho scritto	*	scrivevo	scriverò	scriverei	scriva	scrissi
	scrivi	hai scritto	scrivi, non scrivere	scrivevi	scriverai	scriveresti	scriva	scrivesti
	scrive	ha scritto	scriva	scriveva	scriverà	scriverebbe	scriva	scrisse
	scriviamo	abbiamo scritto	scriviamo	scrivevamo	scriveremo	scriveremmo	scriviamo	scrivemmo
	scrivete	avete scritto	scrivete	scrivevate	scriverete	scrivereste	scriviate	scriveste
	scrivono	hanno scritto	scrivano	scrivevano	scriveranno	scriverebbero	scrivano	scrissero
partire (to depart)	parto	sono partito/a	*	partivo	partirò	partirei	parta	partii
	parti	sei partito/a	parti, non partire	partivi	partirai	partiresti	parta	partisti
	parte	è partito/a	parta	partiva	partirà	partirebbe	parta	partì
	partiamo	siamo partiti/e	partiamo	partivamo	partiremo	partiremmo	partiamo	partimmo
	partite	siete partiti/e	partite	partivate	partirete	partireste	partiate	partiste
	partono	sono partiti/e	partano	partivano	partiranno	partirebbero	partano	partirono

Infinito (Infinitive)	Presente (Present)	Passato Prossimo (Present Perfect)	Imperativo (Imperative)	Imperfetto (Imperfect)	Futuro (Future)	Condizionale (Conditional)	Congiuntivo (Subjunctive)	Passato Remoto (Past Definite/Absolute)
capire (to understand)	capisco	ho capito	*	capivo	capirò	capirei	capisca	capii
	capisci	hai capito	capisci, non capire	capivi	capirai	capiresti	capisca	capisti
	capisce	ha capito	capisca	capiva	capirà	capirebbe	capisca	capì
	capiamo	abbiamo capito	capiamo	capivamo	capiremo	capiremmo	capiamo	capimmo
	capite	avete capito	capite	capivate	capirete	capireste	capiate	capiste
	capiscono	hanno capito	capiscano	capivano	capiranno	capirebbero	capiscano	capirono

Essere (To Be), *Avere* (To Have)

As usual, the verbs *essere* and *avere* stand in a class all their own.

Infinito (Infinitive)	Presente (Present)	Passato Prossimo (Present Perfect)	Imperativo (Imperative)	Imperfetto (Imperfect)	Futuro (Future)	Condizionale (Conditional)	Congiuntivo (Subjunctive)	Passato Remoto (Past Definite/Absolute)
essere (to be)	sono	sono stato/a	*	ero	sarò	sarei	sia	fui
	sei	sei stato/a	sii, non essere	eri	sarai	saresti	sia	fosti
	è	è stato/a	sia	era	sarà	sarebbe	sia	fu
	siamo	siamo stati/e	siamo	eravamo	saremo	saremmo	siamo	fummo
	siete	siete stati/e	siate	eravate	sarete	sareste	siate	foste
	sono	sono stati/e	siano	erano	saranno	sarebbero	siano	furono
avere (to have)	ho	ho avuto	*	avevo	avrò	avrei	abbia	ebbi
	hai	hai avuto	abbi, non avere	avevi	avrai	avresti	abbia	avesti
	ha	ha avuto	abbia	aveva	avrà	avrebbe	abbia	ebbe
	abbiamo	abbiamo avuto	abbiamo	avevamo	avremo	avremmo	abbiamo	avemmo
	avete	avete avuto	abbiate	avevate	avrete	avreste	abbiate	aveste
	hanno	hanno avuto	abbiano	avevano	avranno	avrebbero	abbiano	ebbero

Irregular Verbs

The more you read through the myriad irregularities that make *la bella lingua* so special, the sooner you'll begin to recognize these forms.

Infinito (Infinitive)	Presente (Present)	Passato Prossimo (Present Perfect)	Imperativo (Imperative)	Imperfetto (Imperfect)	Futuro (Future)	Condizionale (Conditional)	Congiuntivo (Subjunctive)	Passato Remoto (Past Definite/Absolute)
andare (to go)	vado	sono andato/a	*	andavo	andrò	andrei	vada	andai
	vai	sei andato/a	va, non andare	andavi	andrai	andresti	vada	andasti
	va	è andato/a	vada	andava	andrà	andrebbe	vada	andò
	andiamo	siamo andati/e	andiamo	andavamo	andremo	andremmo	andiamo	andammo
	andate	siete andati/e	andate	andavate	andrete	andreste	andiate	andaste
	vanno	sono andati/e	vadano	andavano	andranno	andrebbero	vadano	andarono
dire (to say)	dico	ho detto	*	dicevo	dirò	direi	dica	dissi
	dici	hai detto	di', non dire	dicevi	dirai	diresti	dica	dicesti
	dice	ha detto	dica	diceva	dirà	direbbe	dica	disse
	diciamo	abbiamo detto	diciamo	dicevamo	diremo	diremmo	diciamo	dicemmo
	dite	avete detto	dite	dicevate	direte	direste	diciate	diceste
	dicono	hanno detto	dicano	dicevano	diranno	direbbero	dicano	dissero
dovere (to have to/must)	devo	ho dovuto	--	dovevo	dovrò	dovrei	debba (deva)	dovei/dovetti
	devi	hai dovuto	--	dovevi	dovrai	dovresti	debba (deva)	dovesti
	deve	ha dovuto	--	doveva	dovrà	dovrebbe	debba (deva)	dové/dovette
	dobbiamo	abbiamo dovuto	--	dovevamo	dovremo	dovremmo	dobbiamo	dovemmo
	dovete	avete dovuto	--	dovevate	dovrete	dovreste	dobbiate	doveste
	devono	hanno dovuto	--	dovevano	dovranno	dovrebbero	debbano (devano)	doverono/dovettero
fare (to do/make)	faccio	ho fatto	*	facevo	farò	farei	faccia	feci
	fai	hai fatto	fa', fai, non fare	facevi	farai	faresti	faccia	facesti
	fa	ha fatto	faccia	faceva	farà	farebbe	faccia	fece
	facciamo	abbiamo fatto	facciamo	facevamo	faremo	faremmo	facciamo	facemmo
	fate	avete fatto	fate	facevate	farete	fareste	facciate	faceste
	fanno	hanno fatto	facciano	facevano	faranno	farebbero	facciano	fecero

Infinito (Infinitive)	Presente (Present)	Passato Prossimo (Present Perfect)	Imperativo (Imperative)	Imperfetto (Imperfect)	Futuro (Future)	Condizionale (Conditional)	Congiuntivo (Subjunctive)	Passato Remoto (Past Definite/Absolute)
morire (to die)	muoio	sono morto/a	*	morivo	morirò	morirei	muoia	morii
	muori	sei morto/a	muori, non morire	morivi	morirai	moriresti	muoia	moristi
	muore	è morto/a	muoia	moriva	morirà	morirebbe	muoia	morì
	moriamo	siamo morti/e	moriamo	morivamo	moriremo	moriremmo	moriamo	morimmo
	morite	siete morti/e	morite	morivate	morirete	morireste	moriate	moriste
	muoiono	sono morti/e	muoiano	morivano	moriranno	morirebbero	muoiano	morirono
nascere (to be born)	nasco	sono nato/a	*	nascevo	nascerò	nascerei	nasca	nacqui
	nasci	sei nato/a	nasci, non nascere	nascevi	nascerai	nasceresti	nasca	nascesti
	nasce	è nato/a	nasca	nasceva	nascerà	nascerebbe	nasca	nacque
	nasciamo	siamo nati/e	nasciamo	nascevamo	nasceremo	nasceremmo	nasciamo	nascemmo
	nascete	siete nati/e	nascete	nascevate	nascerete	nascereste	nasciate	nasceste
	nascono	sono nati/e	nascano	nascevano	nasceranno	nascerebbero	nascano	nacquero
potere (to be able)	posso	ho potuto	--	potevo	potrò	potrei	possa	potei
	puoi	hai potuto	--	potevi	potrai	potresti	possa	potesti
	può	ha potuto	--	poteva	potrà	potrebbe	possa	poté
	possiamo	abbiamo potuto	--	potevamo	potremo	potremmo	possiamo	potemmo
	potete	avete potuto	--	potevate	potrete	potreste	possiate	poteste
	possono	hanno potuto	--	potevano	potranno	potrebbero	possano	poterono
rimanere (to remain)	rimango	sono rimasto/a	*	rimanevo	rimarrò	rimarrei	rimanga	rimasi
	rimani	sei rimasto/a	rimani, non rimanere	rimanevi	rimarrai	rimarresti	rimanga	rimanesti
	rimane	è rimasto/a	rimanga	rimaneva	rimarrà	rimarrebbe	rimanga	rimase
	rimaniamo	siamo rimasti/e	rimaniamo	rimanevamo	rimarremo	rimarremmo	rimaniamo	rimanemmo
	rimanete	siete rimasti/e	rimanete	rimanevate	rimarrete	rimarreste	rimaniate	rimaneste
	rimangono	sono rimasti/e	rimangano	rimanevano	rimarranno	rimarrebbero	rimangano	rimasero
salire (to go up)	salgo	sono salito/a	*	salivo	salirò	salirei	salga	salii
	sali	sei salito/a	sali, non salire	salivi	salirai	saliresti	salga	salisti
	sale	è salito/a	salga	saliva	salirà	salirebbe	salga	salì
	saliamo	siamo saliti/e	saliamo	salivamo	saliremo	saliremmo	saliamo	salimmo

continues

continued

Infinito (Infinitive)	Presente (Present)	Passato Prossimo (Present Perfect)	Imperativo (Imperative)	Imperfetto (Imperfect)	Futuro (Future)	Condizionale (Conditional)	Congiuntivo (Subjunctive)	Passato Remoto (Past Definite/ Absolute)
	salite	siete saliti/e	salite	salivate	salirete	salireste	saliate	saliste
	salgono	sono saliti/e	salgano	salivano	saliranno	salirebbero	salgano	salirono
sapere (to know)	so	ho saputo	*	sapevo	saprò	saprei	sappia	seppi
	sai	hai saputo	sappi, non sapere	sapevi	saprai	sapresti	sappia	sapesti
	sa	ha saputo	sappia	sapeva	saprà	saprebbe	sappia	seppe
	sappiamo	abbiamo saputo	sappiamo	sapevamo	sapremo	sapremmo	sappiamo	sapemmo
	sapete	avete saputo	sappiate	sapevate	saprete	sapreste	sappiate	sapeste
	sanno	hanno saputo	sappiano	sapevano	sapranno	saprebbero	sappiano	seppero
venire (to come)	vengo	sono venuto/a	*	venivo	verrò	verrei	venga	venni
	vieni	sei venuto/a	vieni, non venire	venivi	verrai	verresti	venga	venisti
	viene	è venuto/a	venga	veniva	verrà	verrebbe	venga	venne
	veniamo	siamo venuti/e	veniamo	venivamo	verremo	verremmo	veniamo	venimmo
	venite	siete venuti/e	venite	venivate	verrete	verreste	veniate	veniste
	vengono	sono venuti/e	vengano	venivano	verranno	verrebbero	vengano	vennero
volere (to want)	voglio	ho voluto	*	volevo	vorrò	vorrei	voglia	volli
	vuoi	hai voluto	vuoi, non volere	volevi	vorrai	vorresti	voglia	volesti
	vuole	ha voluto	voglia	voleva	vorrà	vorrebbe	voglia	volle
	vogliamo	abbiamo voluto	vogliamo	volevamo	vorremo	vorremmo	vogliamo	volemmo
	volete	avete voluto	vogliate	volevate	vorrete	vorreste	vogliate	voleste
	vogliono	hanno voluto	vogliano	volevano	vorranno	vorrebbero	vogliano	vollero

Commonly Used Irregular Past Participles

If you don't know what the following infinitive forms refer to in English, may I suggest a *dizionario?* This chart is for those of you looking for a quick review of the irregular past participles used in compound tenses such as the *passato prossimo*.

Infinitive	Past Participle	Infinitive	Past Participle
accludere	accluso	nascere	nato
aprire	aperto	offendere	offeso
assumere	assunto	offrire	offerto
chiedere	chiesto	piacere	piaciuto
chiudere	chiuso	piangere	pianto
convincere	convinto	prendere	preso
correre	corso	rendere	reso
cuocere	cotto	ridere	riso
decidere	deciso	rimanere	rimasto
dipendere	dipeso	rispondere	risposto
dipingere	dipinto	rompere	rotto
dire	detto	scegliere	scelto
discutere	discusso	scendere	sceso
distinguere	distinto	scoprire	scoperto
dividere	diviso	succedere	successo
esprimere	espresso	tradurre	tradotto
fare	fatto	uccidere	ucciso
leggere	letto	vedere	visto/veduto
mettere	messo	venire	venuto
morire	morto	vincere	vinto
muovere	mosso	vivere	vissuto

Idiomatic Expressions

There are more *espressioni idiomatiche* than I could ever offer here, but I've provided a few of my favorites along with the more commonly used.

Common Idioms

The following two tables provide a sample of the most commonly used Italian idioms.

The Italian verb *andare* is used in a number of expressions, including *andare matto* (to go crazy)!

Va Bene: Idioms with *Andare* (To Go)

Italiano	English
Come va?	How's it going?
Va bene/male	It's going well/badly.
andare all'altro mondo	to go to the other world
andare in giro	to go around; to take a spin
andare matto	to go crazy
andare in pezzi	to go to pieces
lasciare andare	to let something go
Ma va!	Get out of here! You're kidding!

In Italian, you use the verb *fare* (to do or make) most often when you would use the English verb *to take*. You take a shower in English, but you *do a shower* (*fare la doccia*) in Italian.

Fa Freddo: Idioms with *Fare* (To Do/To Make)

Italiano	English
fare alla Romana	to go Roman (to go Dutch)
fare finta	to pretend (to fake)
fare il furbo	to be clever; sly
fare l'amore	to make love
fare il compito	to do homework
fare la doccia	to take a shower
fare le ore piccole	to do the wee hours (to burn the midnight oil)
fare lo spiritoso	to be spirited (to be a wise-guy)
fare un freddo cane	to be dog cold
fare una foto	to take a picture
fare una vita da cani	to live like a dog
Fatti gli affari tuoi!	Mind your business!

Idioms Expressing Your Opinion

The following table summarizes the idioms you can use to express yourself and your opinion.

Secondo Me

Italiano	English	Italiano	English
al contrario	on the contrary	Lascia correre	Forget it
allora	now then, well	Lascia perdere	Forget it
Basta!	That's enough!	Lascia stare	Forget it
Che barba!	How boring	Meglio così.	It is better this way.
Che cavolata!	What cabbage!	Meno male!	Luckily!
Che macello!	What a mess	naturalmente	naturally
Che mattone!	How boring	Non importa.	It doesn't matter.
Che noia!	How boring	Parole d'oro.	Amen, you said it.
Che peccato!	What a shame!	Penso di sì/no.	I think so/not.
Che roba!	I can't believe it	Per carità!	No way! God forbid!
Che schifo!	How disgusting!	per dire la verità	to tell the truth
comunque	anyhow	Roba da matti!	That's crazy!
Credo di sì/no.	I believe so/not.	Santa pace!	My goodness!
d'accordo	agreed	Santo cielo!	Holy heaven! Good heavens!
Davvero?	Really?	secondo me	in my opinion
dunque	now then/so	senza dubbio	without a doubt
È una parola!	Easy to say!	senz'altro	certainly
Fra l'altro …	Among other things …	Sul serio?	Really?
Hai torto.	You are wrong. (fam.)	tanto meglio/peggio	so much the better/worse
in ogni modo	anyway; or at any cost	tutt'altro	on the contrary
in parole povere	in a few words	Vale la pena.	It's worth it.
in poche parole	in a few words		

Idioms Involving Time

The following table lists time-related idioms.

Un'ora Buona

Italiano	English
Alla buon'ora!	It was about time!
a tutte le ore	at any time
di buon ora	early
essere in orario	to be on time
Il tempo è denaro.	Time is money.
in un batter d'occhio	in no time
l'ora di punta	rush hour
le ore piccole	the wee hours
nelle prime ore	in the early hours
ora legale	daylight savings time
per il momento	for the time being
un'ora buona	a full hour
un'oretta	about an hour

Italian Colloquialisms

Whether lonely dogs, hungry wolves, or depressed potatoes, Italian possesses thousands of idiomatic expressions and colloquialisms.

In Bocca al Lupo!

Italiano	English
a tutti i costi	at any cost—no matter what
Affare fatto.	It's a deal.
Altro che!	Of course; You can bet your life!
Amen	Amen
Bella roba!	Very nice! (ironic)
Bell'affare!	That's really good! (ironic)
Buon per te!	Lucky you!
caschi il mondo	no matter what
C'è modo e modo!	There are ways and ways.
Che ti passa per la testa?	What's the matter with you?
Chi dorme non piglia pesci.	Those that sleep won't catch fish. The early bird gets the worm.
Ci mancherebbe altro!	God forbid!
Ci vuole altro!	It takes much more than that!
come mamma l'ha fatto	like mamma made him naked as a jay bird

continues

In Bocca al Lupo! (continued)

Italiano	English
Con rispetto parlando.	Excuse my French.
Cose dell'altro mondo.	It is out of this world.
costare un occhio della testa	to cost an eye from your head
	to cost an arm and a leg
da morire	a lot
d'altro canto	on the other hand
dare una mano	to give a hand
Di mamma c'è n'è una sola.	Of mothers, there is only one.
Dio ce la mandi buona!	Let's hope for the best.
Due gocce d'acqua	two drops of water (two peas in a pod; one and the same)
essere al settimo cielo	to be in seventh heaven
essere nei guai	to be in trouble; to have problems
essere nelle nuvole	to be in the clouds
essere solo come un cane	to be alone as a dog
essere un pesce fuor d'acqua	to be a fish out of water
fuori moda	out of fashion
Gatta ci cova.	I smell a rat.
girare la testa	to spin one's head
Lasciami stare.	Leave me alone.
Le bugie hanno le gambe corte.	Lies have short legs.
mancino	southpaw
manco per sogno!	in your dreams
mangiare come una bestia	to eat like a beast
meglio di nulla	better than nothing
nemmeno per sogno!	in your dreams
Non c'è altro.	That's all.
Non ne posso più.	I can't stand it anymore.
nudo e crudo	nude and crude (the plain truth)
Padronissimo!	As you like! All right then!
prendere in giro	to tease or joke
sfumare nel nulla	to fade into nothing (to go up in smoke)
sogni d'oro	sweet dreams
stanco da morire	dead tired
toccare ferro	to touch iron (to knock on wood)
volere la botte piena e	to want the bottle full and the
la moglie ubriaca	wife drunk

Tongue Twisters

Get your mouth around a *scioglilingua* (literally, tongue melter) and see how well you do.

◆ A quest'ora il questore in questura non c'è!

◆ Al pozzo dei pazzi una pazza lavava le pezze. Andò un pazzo e buttò la pazza con tutte le pezze nel pozzo dei pazzi.

◆ Andavo a Lione cogliendo cotone, tornavo correndo cotone cogliendo.

◆ Apelle figlio d'Apollo fece una palla di pelle di pollo tutti i pesci vennero a galla per vedere la palla di pelle di pollo fatta d'Apelle figlio d'Apollo.

◆ Caro conte chi ti canta tanto canta che t'incanta.

◆ Chi ama chiama chi ama, chiamami tu che chi ami chiami. Chi amo chiameró se tu non chiami.

◆ Figlia, sfoglia la foglia sfoglia la foglia, figlia.

◆ Sopra la panca la capra campa sotto la panca la capra crepa.

Appendix D

Italian *Grammatica* at a Glance

If I could give you an intravenous transfer of knowledge, I would. Since I can't, I've provided you with a quick summary of some of the more important elements related to Italian grammar that you'll need to know.

Basic Grammar

The Definite Articles

	Sg.	Pl.	Examples
Masculine	il	i	*il libro* (the book) ➔ *i libri* (the books)
	lo	gli	*lo scienziato* (the scientist) ➔ *gli scienziati* (the scientists)
	l'	gli	*l'albero* (the tree) ➔ *gli alberi* (the trees)
Feminine	la	le	*la casa* (the house) ➔ *le case* (the houses)
	l'	le	*l'italiana* (the Italian woman) ➔ *le italiane* (the Italian women)

Noun and Adjective Endings

	Sg.		Pl.
Masculine	-o	→	-i
Feminine	-a	→	-e
M/F	-e	→	-i

Commonly Used Prepositions

Italian	English	Italian	English
a	at, in, to	in	at, in, to
con	with	per	for
da	from	tra/fra	between, among
di	of, from		

Contractions

Preposition	Masculine				Feminine			
	Singular		Plural		Singular		Plural	
	il	lo	l'	i	gli	la	l'	le
a	al	allo	all'	ai	agli	alla	all'	alle
in	nel	nello	nell'	nei	negli	nella	nell'	nelle
di	del	dello	dell'	dei	degli	della	dell'	delle
su	sul	sullo	sull'	sui	sugli	sulla	sull'	sulle
da	dal	dallo	dall'	dai	dagli	dalla	dall'	dalle

Additional Useful Prepositions

Italian	English	Italian	English
attraverso	through, across	lontano	far
dentro	inside	sopra	above
fino a	until	sotto	below
fuori	outside	verso	toward
insieme	together	vicino	close

Commonly Used Adjectives

Italian	English	Italian	English
alto	tall	giovane	young
basso	short	grande	big
bello	beautiful	lungo	long
brutto	ugly	piccolo	small

Italian	English	Italian	English
buono	good	povero	poor
cattivo	bad	ricco	rich
difficile	difficult	vecchio	old
facile	easy		

Possessive Adjectives

	Singular		Plural	
Possessive	Masculine	Feminine	Masculine	Feminine
my	il mio	la mia	i miei	le mie
your (informal)	il tuo	la tua	i tuoi	le tue
his/her	il suo	la sua	i suoi	le sue
Your (polite)	il Suo	la Sua	i Suoi	le Sue
our	il nostro	la nostra	i nostri	le nostre
your	il vostro	la vostra	i vostri	le vostre
their	il loro	la loro	i loro	le loro

Commonly Used Adverbs

You can form many adverbs by adding *-mente* to the feminine singular adjective. Adjectives ending in *-e* (*dolce, intelligente, verde,* and so on) remain the same:

> *allegra* (happy) ➜ *allegramente* (happily)
> *dolce* (sweet) ➜ *dolcemente* (sweetly)
> *sincera* (sincere) ➜ *sinceramente* (sincerely)

Commonly Used Irregular Adverbs

Italian	English	Italian	English
abbastanza	enough	molto	very, a lot
adesso	now	sempre	always
assai	very	spesso	often
bene	well	subito	immediately
mai	never, ever	tanto	so
male	badly	troppo	too much

Asking Questions

Italian	English	Italian	English
che cosa?	what?	dove?	where?
cosa?	what?	perché?	why?
che?	what?	quale/i?	which?
chi	who?	quando	when?
come?	how?	quanto/a/i/e?	how much?
di chi?	whose?		

Italian *Sinonimi*

Can you tell me the difference between *finestra*, *critallo*, *vetrina*, and *vetro?* What do the words *roccia* and *rocca*, *pietra* and *sasso* have in common? They all refer to a rock in one form or another. Try this: *gabinetto*, *bagno*, *toilette*, *cesso*, *water*; not to mention *latrina*, *ritirata*, and *servizi*; these are all words commonly used to describe the lavatory, bathroom, restroom, outhouse, toilet (also called "the office" in certain circumstances).

In all of these cases, we're talking about *sinonimi* (synonyms), words that mean the same, or almost the same, as another word in the same language. In a sense, by learning synonyms your brain is "batching" information. After you have created a connection between two words, your ability to remember them is enhanced. The following list offers *lettori* (readers) the chance to improve their language learning with some of the more commonly used Italian synonyms. This is especially helpful for improving reading skills. Due to space restrictions, and assuming you have plenty of verbiage to work with, I've focused on nouns, adjectives, adverbs, and helpful expressions you might hear used or want to try using yourself. Curious minds may want to consult a *dizionario* (also called *lessico*, *grammatica*, and *vocabolario*) for more in-depth definitions.

> *KEY*
> *f* = feminine noun
> *fpl* = feminine plural noun
> *m* = masculine noun
> *mpl* = masculine plural noun
> *mf* = masculine/feminine noun (usually an adjective or title)
> *abb* = abbreviation
> (pejor) = pejorative or derogatory
> (vulg) = vulgar and/or pejorative, often colloquial
> (coll) = colloquial

Italiano	English	Sinonimi
abbastanza	enough	bastante, sufficiente
abitudine *f*	habit, practice	consuetudine *f*, convenzione *f*, costume *m*, tradizione *f*, usanza *f*
accordo	agreement	concordanza *f*, consenso, convenzione *f*, intesa *f*, patto
adatto	suitable	adeguato, appropriato, buono, giusto, opportuno
adesso	now	appena, ora (coll), subito
affare *m*	business, matter	avvenimento *m*, caso *m*, episodio *m*, evento *m*, faccenda *f*, incidente *m*, vicenda *f*
agricoltore *m*	farmer	contadino/a *m/f*, coltivatore *m*, coltivatrice *f*, fattore *m*, paesano/a *m/f*, terrone *m* (pejor)
albergo *m*	hotel	hotel *m*, locanda *f*, ostello *m*, pensione *f*
allenatore/ istruttore *m*	trainer, coach, manager	mister *m*, ct *m abb* commissario tecnico, tecnico *m*
ambiente	environment	atmosfera *f*, clima *m*
amico/a *m/f*	friend	confidente *mf*, camerata *mf*, compagno/a *m/f*, conoscenza *f*
amministrazione *f*	administration, office, department	burocrazia *f*, direzione *f*, gestione *f*
anche	also, even	ancora, addirittura, d'altronde, del resto, inoltre, in più, per di più, perfino, persino, poi, pure
anello *m*	ring	fede *f*, vera *f*
antiquato	out of date	arretrato, retrivo, retrogrado, superato
apposta	on purpose	deliberatamente, di proposito, intenzionalmente, volutamente
argomento *m*	subject	discorso *m*, materia *f*, problema *m*, questione *f*, soggetto *m*, tema *m*
arma *f*	weapon	cannone *m*, carabina *f*, fucile *m*, mitra *m*, pistola *f*, revolver *m*, rivoltella *f*
aspetto	appearance	apparenza *f*, aria *f* atteggiamento *m*, espressione *f*, look *m* (coll)
assassino *m*	murderer	killer *m* (coll), omicida *m*, sicario *m*, uccisore *m*
associazione	association, club	circolo *m*, club *m*, ritrovo *m*, società *f*
attivo	active	assiduo, diligente, dinamico, energico
attraverso	through (by means of)	per mezzo di, tramite
aumento *m*	increase	allargamento *m*, ampliamento *m*, crescita *f*, espansione *f*, incremento *m*, sviluppo
autobus *m*	bus	bus *m*, corriera *f*, filobus *m*, pullman *m*, pulmino *m*, tram *m*
avaro	miserly, stingy	gretto, meschino, taccagno (coll), tirato, tirchio (coll)
avvocato *mf*	lawyer	legale *mf*, giudice *m*, magistrato *m*, notaio *m*, procuratore *m*
bagno *m*	bathroom, toilet	cesso *m*, gabinetto *m*, latrina *f*, lavandino *m*, ritirata *f*, servizi *mpl*, toilette *f*, water *m*

Italiano	English	Sinonimi
bambino/a *m/f*	child	bimbo/a *m/f*, bebé, creatura *f*, marmocchio *m* (coll), neonato/a *m/f*, piccino/a *m/f*, piccolo/a *m/f*, pupo/a *m/f* (coll), ragazzino/a *m/f*
banco *m*	counter, stall	bancarella *f*, chiosco *m*, edicola *f*, stand *m*
barca *f*	boat	aliscafo *m*, barcone *m*, battello *m*, canotto *m*, chiatta *f*, nave *f*, panfilo *m*, traghetto *m*
bello/a *m/f*	beautiful, nice	affascinante, attraente, avvenente, bellino, bellissimo, carino, gradito, grazioso, piacevole, simpatico
bevanda *f*	drink/beverage	bibita *f*, cicchetto *m*, drink
biglietto *m*	ticket	cartolina *f*, nota *f*
blu	blue	azzurro, celeste
borsa *f*	bag	borsetta *f*, sacchetto *m*, zaino *m*
brillante	brilliant, shiny	lucente, luminoso, radioso, splendente, vivace, vivo
brutto	bad, ugly	cattivo, pessimo, sgradito, spiacevole
buffo	funny	burlesco, comico, divertente, giocoso, scherzoso, umoristico
bugia *f*	lie	balla *f*, falsità *f*, fandonia *f*, finzione *f*, frottola *f*, invenzione *f*, panzana *f*, storia *f*
buono	good, nice	bravo, in gamba (coll), fico (coll), figo (coll), ganzo (coll)
calma *f*	calm, stillness	armonia *f*, concordia *f*, quiete *f*, pace *f*, serenità *f*, tranquillità *f*
calza *f*	sock, stocking	calzino *m*, collant *mpl*, calzamaglia *f*
cambiamento *m*	change	alterazione *f*, cambio *m*, conversione *f*, modificazione *f*, scambio *m*, variazione *f*
camino *m*	fireplace	caminetto *m*, ciminiera *f*, focolare *m*, fumaiolo *m*
camion *m*	truck	autocarro *m*, furgone *m*, furgoncino *m*
canzone *f*	song	aria *f*, arietta *f*, canto *m*, canzonetta *f*, melodia *f*, motivo *m*
capacità *f*	ability	abilità *f*, attitudine *f*, facilità *f*, talento *m*
caro	dear, expensive	costoso, prezioso, salato
carta *f*	card, document, paper, map	bollettino *m*, certificato *m*, documento *m*, formulario *m*, mappa *f*, modulo *m*, passaporto *m*, pianta *f*, scheda *f*
casa *f*	house, home	alloggio *m*, appartamento *m*, casolare *m*, condominio *m*, domicilio *m*, dimora *f*, indirizzo *m*, palazzo *m*, residenza *f*, villa *f*, caseggiato *m*
casalinga *f*	housewife	donna di casa *f*, massaia *f* (coll)
causa *f*	cause, reason	cagione *f*, motivo *m*, occasione *f*, opportunità *f*, perché *m*, ragione *f*
cavatappi *m*	corkscrew	cavataraccioli *m*, apribottiglie *m*
celibe *m*/nubile *f*	unmarried, single	scapolo *m*, single *mf*, signorina *f*, zitella *f* (pejor)
certo	certain, sure	chiaro, indubbio, ovvio, sicuro
cesto *m*	basket	canestro *m*, cesta *f*, cestello *m*, cestino *m*, paniere *m*
che	which, who, that	cui, il/la quale, i/le quali

continues

continued

Italiano	English	Sinonimi
che cosa	what	che, ciò che, cosa
chiacchierone	talkative	ciarliero, garrulo, pettegolo, verboso, prolisso
chiesa *f*	church	abbazia *f*, basilica *f*, cappella *f*, cattedrale *f*, moschea *f*, santuario *f*, sinagoga *f*, tempio *m*
cibo *m*	food	alimentari *mpl*, alimento *m*, mangiare *m*, piatto *m*, pietanza *f*, vettovaglie *fpl*, viveri *m*
cima *f*	top	cresta *f*, culmine *m*, picco *m*, sommità *f*
cioè	that is	ossia, vale a dire
circa	about, approximately	intorno a, più o meno, pressappoco, pressoché, quasi, su per giù
collina *f*	hill	altura *f*, colle *m*, montagna *f*, monte *m*, poggio *m*
colpo *m*	blow	botta *f*, percossa *f*, pugno *m*, schiaffo *m*, urto *m*
commerciante *mf*	shopkeeper, trader	bottegaio/a *m/f*, commercialista *mf*, mercante *mf*, negoziante *mf*, venditore *m*
completo	complete	assoluto, integrale, intero, puro
comunque	anyway	in ogni caso, lo stesso, ugualmente
confusione *f*	confusion	caos *m*, bordello *m* (vulg), casino (vulg), disordine *m*, macello *m* (coll), pasticcio *m*
conoscenza *f*	knowledge	cognizione *f*, consapevolezza *f*, erudizione *f*, sapere *m*
consapevole	aware	cosciente, conscio
contento	glad, happy	allegro, beato, felice, gioioso, lieto
conto *m*	bill, account	bolletta *f*, canone *m*, fattura *f*, nota *f*, pigione (coll)
contrario	opposite	inverso, opposto
conversazione *f*	conversation	colloquio *m*, dialogo *m*, diceria *f*, discussione *f*, pettegolezzo *m*
coraggioso	courageous	ardito, audace, gagliardo, valoroso
corda *f*	cord, rope	cavo *m*, filo *m*, fune *f*, spago *m*
cosa *f*	thing	fatto *m*, oggetto *m*, roba *f*
così	so, therefore	allora, dunque, perciò, pertanto, quindi
costo *m*	cost	importo *m*, prezzo *m*, spesa *f*, tariffa *f*, tassa *f*, valore *m*
cura *f*	cure, treatment	farmaco *m*, guarigione *f*, rimedio *m*, terapia *f*, trattamento *m*
dappertutto	everywhere	dovunque, ovunque
davanti a	in front of	di fronte a, dinanzi a, fuori di
delinquente *mf*	scoundrel, rascal	birbante *mf*, briccone/a *m/f*, brigante *m*, furfante *m*, malandrino, stronzo (vulg) fuori legge *m*
delitto *m*	crime	crimine *m*, infrazione *f*, reato *m*
denaro *m*	money	contanti *mpl*, grana *f* (coll), lucro *m*, moneta *f*, quattrini *mpl*, resto *m*, soldi *mpl*, spiccioli *mpl*, valuta *f*
detto *m*	saying, expression, slogan	adagio *m*, massima *f*, motto *m*, proverbio *m*, sentenza *f*
difficoltà *f*	difficulty	guaio *m*, problema *m*, svantaggio *m*

Italiano	English	Sinonimi
dirigente *mf*	manager, executive, leader	direttore *m*, direttrice *f*, direzione *f*, manager *mf*
ditta *f*	firm, company	azienda *f*, casa *f*, commercio *m*, impresa *f*, società
donna *f*	woman	signora *f*, signorina *f*
eccetto	except	a parte, escluso, fuorché, tranne
edificio *m*	buildng	costruzione *f*, fabbricato *m*, palazzo *m*
emozionato	excited, moved	appassionato, commosso, eccitato
errore *m*	mistake	gaffe *f*, sbaglio *m*
esame *m*	exam, test	concorso *m*, prova *f*, test *m*
esercizio *m*	exercise, practice	addestramento *m*, allenamento *m*, esercitazione *f*, pratica *f*
esperto	expert, capable	abile, bravo, capace, competente, destro, dotato, forte, pratico
esperto/a *m/f*	expert, specialist	dotto, erudito, intenditore/intenditrice *m/f*, maestro/a *m/f*, specialista *mf*
est *m*	east	levante *m*, oriente *m*
fabbrica *f*	factory	officina *f*, opificio *m*, stabilimento *m*
faccia *f*	face	muso *m* (coll), viso *m*, volto *m*
falso	false	erroneo, inesatto, sbagliato
famiglia *f*	family	discendente *mf*, discendenza *f*, lignaggio *m*, progenie *f*
fattoria *f*	farm	podere *m*, tenuta *f*
fede *f*	faith	credo *m*, culto *m*, dogma *m*, fiducia *f*, religione *f*
fidanzato/a *m/f*	fiancé, fiancée, boy/girl friend	amante *mf*, ragazzo/a *m/f*
figlio/a *m/f*	son/daughter	bambino/a *m/f*, figliolo/a *m/f*, femminuccia *f*, maschietto *m*
fila *f*	line, row	coda *f*, sequenza *f*, serie *f*
finestra *f*	window	cristallo *m*, vetrina *f*, vetro *m*
fiume *m*	river	rivoletto *m*, ruscello *m*, torrente *m*
foresta *f*	forest	bosco *m*, selva *f*
freddo	cold	congelato, frigido, gelido, ghiacciato
furbo (coll.)	cunning, sly	accorto, astuto, perspicace, scaltro, sveglio
futuro *m*	future	avvenire *m*, domani *m*
gara *f*	contest	competizione *f*, corsa *f*, incontro *m*, match *m*
gente *f*	people	abitanti *mpl*, folla *f*, persone *fpl*, popolazione *f*, società *f*
giornale *m*	newspaper	mensile *m*, periodico *m*, quotidiano *m*, rassegna *f*, rivista *f*, settimanale *m*
grande	big, large	enorme, gigantesco, grosso, immenso, robusto, vasto
ignorante	ignorant	analfabeta, ignaro, incolto
imbroglio *m*	swindle, trick	fregatura *f*, frode *f*, inganno *m*, presa in giro *f*, racket *m*, tiro *m*, trucco *m*, truffa *f*
impegno *m*	commitment	dovere *m*, obbligo *m*

continues

continued

Italiano	English	Sinonimi
importante	important	notevole, significativo
incidente *m*	accident	collisione *f*, scontro *m*, tamponamento *m*
incinta	pregnant	gravida, in stato interessante, pregna, in attesa
incrocio *m*	intersection, crossroads	bivio *m*, crocevia *m*, crocicchio *m*
indagine *f*	investigation	inchiesta *f*, investigazione *f*, rassegna *f*, ricerca *f*, sondaggio *m*
infatti	in fact, really	anzi, difatti, in effetti, in realtà, in verità, veramente, per dire la verità
informazione *f*	information	annuncio *m*, avviso *m*, comunicato *m*, comunicazione *f*, indicazione *f*, notizia *f*
ingresso *m*	entrance	anticamera *f*, atrio *m*, entrata *f*
insegnante *mf*	teacher	docente *mf*, maestro/a *m/f*, pedagogo/a *m/f*, professore *mf*[*]
insieme	together	assieme, allo stesso tempo, contemporaneamente
insomma	all in all, in sum	dopotutto, in fin dei conti, alla fin fine, in tutto
intanto	meanwhile, in the meantime	nel frattempo, per ora, mentre, nello stesso momento
intenzione *f*	intention	intento *m*, mira *f*, obiettivo *m*, scopo *m*, goal *m*
intorno	around	attorno a, circostante
ladro/a *m/f*	thief	borsaiolo/a *m/f*, delinquente *mf*, rapinatore *m*, scassinatore *m*
largo	wide	ampio, capace, spazioso
lavoro *m*	work	attività *f*, carica *f*, compito *m*, mestiere *m*, occupazione *f*, professione *m*
legame *m*	connection, relationship	connessione *f*, collegamento *m*, rapporto *m*, relazione *f*, unione *f*
legge *f*	law	decreto *m*, diritto *m*, editto *m*, giurisprudenza *f*
lento	slow	a poco a poco, adagio, passo passo, pian piano
libro *m*	book	testo *m*, opera *m*, tomo *m*
linea *f*	line	riga *f*, striscia *f*, tratto *m*
lista *f*	list, menu	elenco *m*, menù *m*
locale *m*	place, establishment	bar *m*, caffè *m*, luogo *m*, mensa *f*, osteria, posto *m*, ristorante *m*, tavola calda *f*, trattoria *f*, pub *m*,
luce *f*	light	lume *m*, lampione *m*, lampada *f*, lampadina *f*, lanterna *f*
ma	but	ciò nonostante, comunque, eppure, invece, però, se non che, tuttavia
maglia *f*	sweater, pullover	golf *m*, maglietta *f*, maglione *m*, pullover *m*
magro	thin	asciutto, fino, snello, smilzo *m*, secco (*coll*)
malattia *f*	sickness	disturbo *m*, male *m*, malessere *m*
maleducato	ignorant, impolite	disgraziato (*vulg*), ineducato, scortese, sgarbato, zotico
manico *m*	handle	ansa *f*, leva *f*, maniglia *f*, manubrio *m*
matto	crazy, mad	folle, pazzesco, pazzo, picchiato (*coll*), toccato (*coll*)
medicina *f*	medicine	cura *f*, farmaco *m*, ricetta medica *f*, rimedio *m*

Italiano	English	Sinonimi
membro *m*	member	consociato/a *m/f*, consocio/a *m/f*, iscritto/a *m/f*, socio *m*
misura *f*	size, measurement	dimensione *f*, numero *m*, taglia *f*
modo *m*	method, way, manner	maniera *f*, mezzo *m*, stile *m*, via *f*
molto (adj)	a lot, much, many	parecchio, tanto, un casino di, un mare di, un mucchio di (coll), una folla di (coll)
molto (adv)	very, much	assai, così, proprio, tanto, troppo
morbido	soft	fiacco, molle, soffice, moscio
muro *m*	wall	mura *f*, muraglia *f*, parete *f*
neanche	neither, nor	nemmeno, neppure
negozio *m*	store	bottega *f*, magazzino *m*, supermercato *m*
nome *m*	name	appellativo *m*, cognome *m*, nominativo *m*, soprannome *m*
non	not	affatto, mica, per niente
nonostante	notwithstanding, in spite of	a dispetto di, malgrado
nonostante	although	benché, anche se, malgrado, per quanto, sebbene
nord *m*	north	settentrionale
odore *m*	odor	aroma *m*, fragranza *f*, profumo *m*, puzzo *m* (*vulg*)
omosessuale *m*	homosexual	finocchio *m* (vulg), gay *mf*, lesbica *f*, omosex *mf*
onesto	honest	fedele, leale, retto, sincero
opera *f*	work (a piece of)	lavoro *m*, tesi *f*, testo *m*
operaio/a *m/f*	worker	artigiano/a *m/f*, dipendente *mf*, impiegato/a *m/f*, lavoratore* *mf**, personale* *mf*, stipendiato/a *m/f*
ordine *m*	order	comando *m*, direttiva *f*, istruzione *f*
ospedale *m*	hospital	casa di cura *f*, clinica *f*, infermeria *f*, pronto soccorso *m*
ovest *m*	west	occidente *m*, ponente *m*
padrone/a *m/f*	owner, landlord, employer	possidente *mf*, proprietario/a *m/f*, signore/a *m/f*
paese *m*	country, village	borgo *m*, nazione *f*, patria *f*, stato *m*, terra *f*, villaggio *m*
paga *f*	pay	compenso *m*, guadagno *m*, pagamento *m*, reddito *m*, rendita *f*, ricompensa *f*, remunerazione *f*, retribuzione *f*, salario *m*, stipendio *m*
parola *f*	word	lessico *m*, termine *m*, vocabolario *m*
particolare *m*	detail	dettaglio *m*, sfumatura *f*
passeggiata *f*	walk	camminata *f*, giro *m*
pasto *m*	meal	cena *f*, merenda *f*, pranzo *m*, spuntino *m*
paura *f*	fear	apprensione *f*, panico *m*, spavento *m*, terrore *m*
pausa *f*	pause, break	break *m*, dormitina *f*, intermezzo *m*, intervallo *m*, riposo *m*, siesta *f*
pelle *f*	skin, leather	carnagione *f*, cuoio *m*, pelo *m*
pene *m*	penis	cazzo *m* (vulg), fallo *m*, minchia *f* (vulg), pisello *m*, pistolino *m* (vulg), uccello *m*
per favore *m*	please	per cortesia, per piacere, prego

continues

continued

Italiano	English	Sinonimi
perché	because	ammesso che, dal momento che, visto che
perché	so that, in order	affinché, cosicché, in modo che
perché?	why?	come mai?, per quale ragione?
pericolo *m*	danger	azzardo *m*, rischio *m*
persona *f*	person	anima *f*, creatura *f*, figura *f*, tale *mf*, tipo *m*, tizio *m*
piacere *m*	pleasure	allegrezza *f*, diletto *m*, godimento *m*
pietra *f*	stone	ciottolo *m*, masso *m*, roccia *f*, sasso *m*
pizzo *m*	lace	merletto *m*, trina *f*
poi	then	appresso, dopo, in seguito, quindi
polizia *f*	police	carabiniere *m*, guardia *f*, questura *f*, vigile *mf*
ponte *m*	bridge	cavalcavia *m*, passerella *f*
porta *f*	door	portone *m*, soglia *f*, sportello *m*, uscio *m* (coll)
posto *m*	place, seat	banco *m*, panca *f*, poltrona *f*, sedia *f*, sedile *m*, seggiola *f* (coll)
presente	present	attuale, contemporaneo, corrente, odierno, vigente
presto	soon, early	fra poco, di buon'ora, alla svelta, in anticipo, velocemente
prigione *f*	prison	carcere *m*, galera *f*, penitenziario *m*, prigionia *f*
processione *f*	procession	corteo *m*, parata *f*, sfilata *f*
prossimo	next	appresso, dopo, poi, seguente, successivo
pubblicità *f*	publicity, advertising	avviso *m*, affisso *m* annuncio *m*, manifesto *m*, poster *m*, promozione *f*, réclame *f*
pulito	clean	lindo, mondo, netto
puro	pure	autentico, genuino, schietto
purtroppo	unfortunately	per disgrazia/sfortuna/sciagura
quaderno *m*	notebook	agenda *f*, diario *m*, blocco notes *m*, rubrica *f*, taccuino *m*
qualche volta	sometimes	di quando in quando, di tanto in tanto, ogni tanto, talora, talvolta, una volta tanto
rabbia *f*	rage, anger	collera *f*, furia *f*, furore *m*, ira *f*, stizza *f*
racconto *m*	story, tale	favola *f*, fiaba *f*, narrativa *f*, romanzo *m*, storia *f*
ragazza *f*	girl	adolescente *mf*, fanciulla *f* (coll), giovane *mf*, ragazzina *f*, teenager *mf*
ragazzo *m*	boy	adolescente *mf*, fanciullo *m* (coll), garzone *m*, ragazzino *m*, teenager *mf*
regalo *m*	gift	donazione *f*, dono *m*, elemosina *f*, offerta *f*, omaggio *m*, presente *m*, strenna *f*
regola *f*	rule	canone *m*, legge *f*, normativa *f*
religioso	religious	credente, devoto, pio, sacro, santo
rendimento *m*	performance	performance *f*, produttività *f*
ricevuta *f*	receipt	buono *m*, cedola *f*, coupon *m*, scontrino *m*
richiesta *f*	request	esigenza *f*, domanda *f*, pretesa *f*
ricordo *m*	memory	memoria *f*, souvenir *m*
riduzione *f*	reduction/sale	liquidazione *f*, saldo *m*, sconto *m*, svendita *f*
ristorante *m*	restaurant	*see* locale

Italiano	English	Sinonimi
riva *f*	bank, shore	costa *f*, lido *m*, spiaggia *f*, sponda *f*
roba *f*	stuff, things	beni *mpl*, possessi *mpl*
rotondo	round	circolare, tondo
rottura *f*	break	frammentazione *f*, frattura *f*, spaccatura *f*
rovina *f*	ruin	crollo *m*, rudere *m*
rumore *m*	noise	baccano *m*, casino *m*, chiasso *m*, clamore *m*, fragore *m*, suono *m*
rurale	rural	agrario, agreste, campagnolo, contadino, paesano, rustico
ruvido	rough	aspro, greggio, grezzo, rozzo, scabro
salsa *f*	sauce	condimento *m*, ragù *m*, sugo *m*
salute *f*	health	sanità *f*, igiene *f*
sano	healthy	igienico, in buona salute, salubre, sanitario, salutare
scherzo *m*	joke	barzelletta *f*, beffa *f*, celia *f*, facezia *f*, presa in giro
sciocchezza *f*	foolishness	balordaggine *f*, cazzata *f* (vulg), cretinata *f* (coll), cretineria *f* (coll), fesseria *f* (coll), stupidaggine *f*, stronzata *f* (vulg)
scrittore *mf*	writer	autore/autrice *m/f*, compositore *mf*, giornalista *mf*, novelliere *mf*, romanziere *mf*
scuola *f*	school	asilo *m*, ateneo *m*, collegio *m*, facoltà, istituto *m*, liceo *m*, università *f*
scuro	dark	buio, cupo, fosco, oscuro, tenebroso
se	if	eventualmente, nel caso che, qualora, quando
secco	dry	arido, asciutto
segno *m*	sign	contrassegno *m*, indicazione *f*, indizio *m*, segnale *m*
senso *m*	sense, feeling	effetto *m*, feeling *m*, impressione *f*, sentimento *m*
sentiero *m*	path	corsia *f*, pista *f*, stradicciola *f*, viottolo *m*
sera *f*	evening	crepuscolo *m*, imbrunire *m*, serata *f*, tramonto *m*
sfortuna *f*	back luck	disgrazia *f*, malocchio *m*, sfiga *f* (vulg)
significato *m*	meaning	accezione *f*, senso *m*, valore *m*
silenzioso	silent, quiet	muto, piano, silente, tacito, taciturno, zitto (coll)
simile	similar	analogo, paragonabile, tale
soprattutto	above all	anzitutto, più che altro, specialmente
sorpresa *f*	surprise	meraviglia *f*, sbalordimento *m*, stupore *m*
sostantivo *m*	noun	nome *m*
sotto	below, under	(al) di sotto di, giù, in basso
sporcizia *f*	dirt, refuse	porcheria *f* (vulg), schifezza *f* (vulg)
stanco	tired	affaticato, esausto, sfinito, stufo
stanza *f*	room	aula *f*, camera *f*, locale *m*, sala *f*
strada *f*	road	autostrada *f*, corso *m*, strada principale/secondaria *f*, via *f*, viale *m*, vicolo *m*
studente *mf*	student	allievo/a *m/f*, alunno/a *m/f*, seguace *mf*
stupido	stupid	balordo, cretino (coll), deficiente, fesso (vulg), imbecille, scemo (coll), sciocco (coll)

continues

continued

Italiano	English	Sinonimi
su	on, up	al di sopra di, in alto, sopra
sud *m*	south	meridione *m*, mezzogiorno (coll)
suora *f*	nun, sister	monaca *f*, religiosa *f*, sorella *f*
telefonata *f*	telephone call	chiamata *f*, colpo di telefono *m*
tempo	time, period	era *f*, epoca *f*, età *f*, ora *f*, periodo *m*, tempo *m*, volta *f*
tipo *m*	type, kind	genere *m*, sorta *f*, specie *f*, varietà *f*
tomba *f*	tomb	fossa *f*, sepolcro *m*, tumulo *m*
tra	between, among	entro, in, fra
triste	sad	infelice, lugubre, misero
ubriaco	drunk	ebbro, brillo, ciucco (coll), sbronzo (vulg)
uguale	equal	medesimo, pari, sinonimo, stesso
uomo *m*	man	maschio *m*, gentiluomo *m*, signore *m*, tipo (coll)
vacanza *f*	vacation, holiday	ferie *fpl*, festa *f*, festività *f*
vagina *f*	vagina	sesso *m*, vulva *f*, fica/figa *f* (vulg), fregna *f* (pejor) (vulg)
valore *m*	value	pregio *m*, merito *m*, qualità *f*
vecchio	old	antico, anziano, obsoleto, secolare
veloce	quick	lesto, rapido, sollecito, sbrigativo
vestito *m*	garment, dress	abito *m*, abbigliamento *m*, panni *mpl*, veste *f*
viaggio *m*	trip, voyage	escursione *f*, giro *m*, gita *f*, itinerario *m*, percorso *m*
vicino	near	accanto a, contiguo, presso
vietato	forbidden	bandito, interdetto, precluso, proibito
vista *f*	sight, view	panorama *m*, scena *f*, spettacolo *m*, veduta *f*
zona *f*	area, region	area *f*, circoscrizione *f*, comune *m*, provincia *f*, quartiere *m*, regione *f*

* Many professionals now use the masculine titles to refer to both men and women. Examples include: avvocato/a, dottore/dottoressa, professore/professoressa

Appendix F

Further Resources

By no means comprehensive, the following titles and websites are worthy of a glance.

Grammar Plus

Supplement your Italian grammar library with any of the following titles:

Colaneri, John, and Vincent Luciani. *501 Italian Verbs.* Barron's Educational Series, 1992.

Graziano, Carlos. *Italian Verbs and Essentials of Grammar.* Passport Books, 1986.

Maiden, Martin, and Cecilia Robustelli. *A Reference of Modern Italian.* McGraw-Hill, 2000.

Piluso, Robert V. *Italian Fundamentals.* Barron's Educational Series, 1992.

Ragusa, Olga. *Essential Italian Grammar.* Dover Publications, 1972.

Roberts, Nick. *New Penguin Parallel Text Short Stories in Italian.* Penguin Books, 1999.

La Dolce Vita

Some of the many books written that portray one aspect or another of Italian life include the following:

Barzini, Luigi. *The Italians.* Simon & Schuster Trade, 1996.

Calvino, Italo. *Italian Folktales.* Harcourt Trade Publishers, 1992.

Costantino, Mario, and Lawrence Gambella. *The Italian Way*. NTC Contemporary Publishing Company, 1995.

Grizzuti Harrison, Barbara. *Italian Days*. Grove/Atlantic, 1998.

Hofmann, Paul. *That Fine Italian Hand*. Henry Holt and Company, 1991.

Mayes, Frances. *Under the Tuscan Sun*. Chronicle Books, 1996.

Morante, Elsa. *History: A Novel*. Steerforth Press, 2000.

Spender, Matthew. *Within Tuscany*. Penguin USA, 1992.

The Internet

Use the Internet to supplement your Italian studies. Following are several suggested websites:

About Italian Language Subjects
http://italian.about.com/mlibrary.htm

For one-stop shopping, try the About Italian Language site for thousands of annotated links arranged by topic including grammar, vocabulary, lessons and exercises, idiomatic expressions, online dictionaries, translation, and children's Italian.

The Italian Electronic Classroom
www.locuta.com/

Here's the site we've all been waiting for! You'll have a chance to hear Italian spoken as well as explained in painstaking detail. On this site you'll find games, verbs, vocabulary, idiomatic expressions, and much more, along with a service that connects pen pals interested in nurturing their interests. The Italian Electronic Classroom is a personal favorite.

Acquerello Italiano
www.acquerello-italiano.com/aihome.php3

Sample audio excerpts from the audiocassette magazine for intermediate and advanced speakers. Includes a transcript of the program with a glossary and study supplement.

Audio Anthology of Italian Literature
www.ilnarratore.com/index2.html

Classical and contemporary Italian texts read by narrators, stage actors, and writers available as MP3 audio file downloads.

BBC Italian Language Online for Adults
www.bbc.co.uk/education/languages/italian/index.shtml

Transcripts of the popular BBC television program devoted to Italian and supplementary exercises.

Coniugare i Verbi
www.virgilio.it/servizi/verbi/

High-performance, automatic verb conjugation and resource for studying this crucial aspect of Italian.

The Italian Women Writers project (IWW)
www.lib.uchicago.edu/efts/IWW/about.html

IWW is a long-term research endeavor to preserve and provide access to an extensive corpus of literature written by Italian women authors.

Research Edition of *The Divine Comedy*
www.divinecomedy.org/divine_comedy.html

Three full editions of *The Divine Comedy* online, graphics, maps of the afterlife, and sample manuscript pages from printed versions of Dante. Listen to *The Inferno* as recited by Vittorio Gassman.

Italian Embassy
www.italyemb.org

For the Italian traveler you'll find useful addresses, telephone numbers, directions, travel information, events, and other links to Italian-related information.

Il Cinema

The following is a small selection of the great Italian cinema. These classics have entertained millions of people.

Of course, you can pick up a little Italian from great films such as *The Godfather*, *Serpico*, *Moonstruck*, *Big Night*, not to mention *A Fish Called Wanda*. Once you start listening, you'll hear Italian everywhere!

1900 (Bertolucci)

Accattone (Pasolini)

The Age of the Medici (Rossellini)

Amarcord (Fellini)

Amore (Rossellini)

L'Avventura (Antonioni)

Ciao Professore! (Wertmuller)

Cinema Paradiso (Tornatore)

City of Women (Fellini)

Death in Venice (Visconti)

Divorce Italian Style (Germi)

La Famiglia (Scola)

The Garden of the Finzi-Continis

Italian for Beginners (Scherfig)

Johnny Stecchino (Benigni)

Life is Beautiful (Benigni)

Marcello Mastroianni: I Remember (Anna Maria Tatò)

Marriage Italian-Style (De Sica)

Miracle in Milan (De Sica)

Night of the Shooting Stars (Paolo and Vittorio Taviani)

Nights of Cabiria (Fellini)

Open City (Rossellini)

Paisan (Rossellini)

Padre Padrone (Taviani brothers)

Rocco and his Brothers (Visconti)

La Strada (Fellini)

Swept Away (Wertmuller)

The Spider's Stratagem (Bertolucci) (De Sica)

Two Women (De Sica)

Word List

All feminine nouns (*f.*), irregular masculine nouns (*m.*), and plural (*pl.*) nouns are indicated. Irregular past participles are given in parentheses.

English to Italian

A

a, an   un, uno, un', una
abandon, to   abbandonare
abbey   abbazia *f.*
able   capace
able, to be (can)   potere
aboard   bordo, a
abolish, to   abolire
about   circa
about   di
above, on   sopra
above all   soprattutto
abroad   all'estero
absolutely   assolutamente
academy   accademia *f.*
accent   accento
accept, to   accettare
access   accesso
accident   incidente *m.*
accompany, to
   accompagnare

accomplish, to   compiere,
   superare
accountant   contabile *m./f.*
achieve, to   realizzare
acoustic   acustico
acquire, to   acquistare
across   attraverso
action   azione *f.*
active   attivo
activity   attività *f.*
actor   attore
actress   attrice *f.*
ad   annuncio pubblicitario
add, to   aggiungere
   (aggiunto)
address   indirizzo
adjective   aggettivo
admire, to   ammirare
admission charge   prezzo
   d'entrata
adorable   adorabile
adult   adulto
advance, in   in anticipo
advantage   vantaggio

adventure   avventura *f.*
adverb   avverbio
advise, to   consigliare
aerobics   aerobica *f.*
affection   affetto
affectionate   affettuoso,
   affezionato
affirm, to   affermare
after   dopo
afternoon   pomeriggio
again   ancora
against   contro
age   età *f.*
agency   agenzia *f.*
agent   agente *m./f.*
aggressive   aggressivo
agile   agile
ago   fa
agreement   accordo
agriculture   agricoltura *f.*
air   aria *f.*
air conditioning   aria
   condizionata *f.*
airplane   aereo

airport aeroporto
alarm clock sveglia *f.*
alcohol alcol *m.*
alcoholic alcolico
alive vivo
All Saint's Day (Nov. 1)
 Ognissanti
allergic allergico
allergy allergia *f.*
alley vicolo
almost quasi
alms elemosina *f.*
alone solo
alphabet alfabeto
already già
also anche, inoltre, pure
although benché, sebbene
always sempre
ambition ambizione *f.*
ambulance ambulanza *f.*
American americano
amphitheater anfiteatro
ample ampio
analysis analisi *f.*
ancestor antenato
anchovy acciuga *f.*
ancient antico
and e, ed (before vowels)
angry arrabbiato
animal animale *m.*
animated, lively animato
announce, to annunciare
answer risposta *f.*
antibiotics gli antibiotici
 m. pl.
antiques antiquariato
any qualsiasi
any qualunque
apartment appartamento
aperitif aperitivo
apologize, to scusarsi
appetizer antipasto
applaud, to applaudire
apple mela *f.*
appreciate, to apprezzare
approach, to avvicinarsi
approve of, to approvare
apricot albicocca *f.*
April aprile
aquarium acquario

archeology archeologia *f.*
architect architetto
architecture architettura *f.*
area area *f.*
area code prefisso
argue, to discutere (discusso),
 litigare
aria, air, appearance aria *f.*
aristocratic aristocratico
arm braccio (*pl.* le braccia)
aroma aroma *m.*, odore *m.*
around intorno a
arrival arrivo
arrive, to arrivare
art arte *f.*
arthritis artrite *f.*
artichoke carciofo
article articolo
artist artista *m./f.*
ashtray portacenere *m.*
ask, to chiedere (chiesto)
aspirin aspirina *f.*
assault, to assaltare
assistance assistenza *f.*
association associazione *f.*
Assumption Day (August 15)
 Ferragosto
astrology astrologia *f.*
astronaut astronauta *m./f.*
at a, in
at least almeno
athlete atleta *m./f.*
athletics atletica *f.*
ATM Bancomat
atrium atrio *m.*
attach, to attaccare
attack attacco *m.*
attention!/warning!
 attenzione!
attitude atteggiamento
attract, to attirare
attribute, to attribuire
August agosto
aunt zia *f.*
Australian australiano
Austrian austriaco
authoritarian autoritario
automatic automatico
automobile macchina *f.*,
 automobile *f.*, auto *f.*

autumn autunno *m.*
available disponibile
avalanche valanga *f.*
avoid, to evitare
awaken, to svegliarsi
away via

B

baby bambino
baby bottle biberon *m.*
bachelor scapolo
back, behind indietro
backpack zaino
backward arretrato
bacon pancetta *f.*
bad male
bag (purse) borsa *f.*
baker fornaio
balcony balcone *m.*
ball palla *f.*
bank banca *f.*
bar bar *m.*
barber barbiere *m.*
Baroque barocco
bartender barista *m./f.*
base base *f.*
basement cantina *f.*
basketball pallacanestro,
 basket
bathroom bagno
battery batteria *f.*, pila *f.*
bay baia *f.*
be, to essere (stato), stare
 (stato)
beach spiaggia *f.*
bean fagiolo
bear orso
beard barba *f.*
beast bestia *f.*
beat, to battere
beauty bellezza *f.*
because perché
bed letto
beef manzo
beer birra *f.*
before prima
begin, to iniziare, cominciare
beginning inizio

behave, to   comportarsi
behavior   comportamento
behind   dietro
believe, to   credere
bell   campana *f.*
bell pepper   peperone *m.*
bell tower   campanile *m.*
belong, to   appartenere
belt   cintura *f.*
bench   panchina *f.*
beneath   sotto
berth   cuccetta *f.*
beside, next to   accanto a
best   migliore
best wishes!   auguri!
bet, to   scommettere
   (scommesso)
better   meglio
between   tra
beverage   bibita *f.*
Bible   Bibbia *f.*
big, large   grande
bill   conto
biodegradable
   biodegradabile
biology   biologia *f.*
bird   uccello
birth   nascita *f.*
birthday   compleanno
bishop   vescovo
bitter   amaro
black   nero
blanket   coperta *f.*
blind   cieco
blond   biondo
blood   sangue *m.*
blouse   camicetta *f.*
blue   blu
boarding   imbarco
boat   barca *f.*
body   corpo
boil, to   bollire
bone   osso (*pl.* le ossa)
book   libro
bookstore   libreria *f.*
boot   stivale *m.*
border   frontiera *f.*
boring   noioso
born, to be   nascere (nato)
boss   padrone/padrona *f.*

both   entrambi, tutt'e due
bottle   bottiglia *f.*
bottom   fondo
boulevard   viale *m.*
box   scatola *f.*
box (theater)   palco
boy   ragazzo
bra   reggiseno
bracelet   braccialetto
brain   cervello
brand   marca *f.*
brass   ottone
bread   pane *m.*
break, to   rompere (rotto)
breakdown   guasto
breakfast   prima colazione *f.*
breath   respiro
bridge   ponte *m.*
brief   breve
briefs   gli slip *m. pl.*
bring, to   portare
British   inglese
broadcast, to   trasmettere
   (trasmesso)
broken   rotto
bronchitis   bronchite *f.*
bronze   bronzo
brooch   spilla *f.*
broth   brodo
brother   fratello
brother-in-law   cognato
brown   castano, marrone
bruise   contusione *f.*, livido
brush   spazzola *f.*
buffoon   buffone *m.*
build, to   costruire
building   edificio, palazzo
bulletin   bollettino
burn, to   bruciare
bus   autobus *m.*, corriera *f.*,
   pullman *m.*
busy   impegnato, occupato
but   ma, però
butcher   macellaio
butcher shop   macelleria *f.*
butter   burro
button   bottone *m.*
buy, to   comprare
by   da, in

C

cabin   cabina *f.*
cable   cavo
cable car   funivia *f.*
cafeteria   mensa *f.*
cake   torta *f.*
call, to   chiamare
call oneself, to   chiamarsi
calm   calmo, sereno
calm, to   calmare
camera   macchina fotografica *f.*
camping   campeggio
Canadian   canadese
cancer   cancro
candidate   candidato
candle   candela *f.*
candy   caramella *f.*
canyon   burrone *m.*
cap   berretto
capable   capace
cape   mantello
car   *See* automobile.
car rental   autonoleggio
card   carta *f.*
care   cura *f.*
career   carriera *f.*, lavoro
careful   attento
carnation   garofano
carpenter   falegname *m.*
carrot   carota *f.*
cash   contanti *m. pl.*
cash register   cassa *f.*
castle   castello
cat   gatto
catalogue   catalogo
category   categoria *f.*
cathedral   cattedrale *f.*
Catholic   cattolico
cave   grotta *f.*
CD   cd (pronounced chi-dee)
ceiling   soffitto
celebrate, to   celebrare,
   festeggiare
cemetery   cimitero
center   centro
central   centrale
century   secolo
ceramic   ceramica *f.*, terracotta *f.*
certain   certo

certificate certificato

chain catena *f.*

chair sedia *f.*

challenge, to sfidare

championship campionato

change, to cambiare

channel canale *m.*

chaotic caotico

chapel cappella *f.*

character carattere *m.*, personaggio

characteristic caratteristico

check assegno

check, to controllare

cheek guancia *f.*

cheese formaggio

cherry ciliegia *f.*

chess gli scacchi *m. pl.*

chest petto

chimney camino

chin mento

China Cina

Chinese cinese

chocolate cioccolata *f.*

choose, to scegliere (scelto)

chorus (choir) coro

Christian cristiano

Christmas, Merry Natale, Buon

church chiesa *f.*

cigar sigaro

cigarette sigaretta *f.*

cinema cinema *m.*

circle circolo

circus circo

citizen cittadino

citizenship cittadinanza *f.*

city città

civic civico

civil civile

class classe *f.*

classical classico

classification classificazione *f.*

clause clausola *f.*

clean, to pulire

clear chiaro

clever furbo (slang), intelligente

client cliente *m./f.*

cliff costiera *f.*, rupe *f.*

climate clima *m.*

cloakroom guardaroba

clock orologio

close, to chiudere (chiuso)

closed chiuso

clothing abbigliamento

cloud nuvola *f.*

coast costa *f.*

coat cappotto, giubbotto

coffee caffè *m.*

coin moneta *f.*

cold freddo (adj.), raffreddore *m.*

collaborate, to collaborare

colleague collega *m./f.*

colony colonia *f.*

color colore *m.*

comb, to pettinare

come, to venire

comfort conforto

commandment comandamento

communicate, to comunicare

communism comunismo

community comunità *f.*

company azienda *f.*, ditta *f.*, società *f.*

comparison paragone *m.*

complain, to lamentarsi

compliment complimento

compose, to comporre (composto)

composition composizione *f.*

concentration concentrazione *f.*

concept concetto

conception concezione *f.*

concert concerto

conclude, to concludere (concluso)

condition condizione *f.*

condom profilattico, preservativo

condominium condominio

conference conferenza *f.*, congresso

confess, to confessare

conflict conflitto

congratulations! congratulazioni! auguri!

conjugate, to coniugare

conjugation coniugazione *f.*

connection coincidenza *f.*

conquest, to conquistare

consecutive consecutivo

consequence conseguenza *f.*

consider, to considerare

console, to consolare

consonant consonante *f.*

constitution costituzione *f.*

consumption consumo

contact contatto

contact, to contattare

contain, to contenere

contemporary contemporaneo

contest concorso, gara *f.*

continent continente *m.*

continue, to continuare

contraceptive contraccettivo

contrast contrasto

convenient comodo, pratico

convent convento

conversation conversazione *f.*

convince, to convincere (convinto)

cook, to cucinare, cuocere (cotto)

cooked cotto

cookie biscotto

copper rame *m.*

copy copia *f.*

cork tappo

corkscrew cavatappi *m.*

corn mais *m.*

cornmeal polenta *f.*

correct corretto

correct, to correggere (corretto)

correspond, to corrispondere (corrisposto)

cosmetics cosmetici *m. pl.*

cosmetics shop profumeria *f.*

cost costo, prezzo

cost, to costare

costly costoso

costume costume *m.*

cotton cotone *m.*

cough tosse *f.*

count   conte, conto
count, to   contare
counter   banco, sportello
countess   contessa *f.*
country   campagna *f.*, paese *m.*
couple   coppia *f.*
courage   coraggio
course   corso
court   corte *f.*
courteous   cortese
cousin   cugino/cugina *f.*
cover charge   coperto
cow   mucca *f.*, vacca *f.*
crazy   matto, pazzo
cream   crema *f.*, panna *f.*
create, to   creare
creation   creazione *f.*
credit   credito
credit card   carta di credito *f.*
crib   culla *f.*
crisis   crisi *f.*
cross   croce *f.*
cross, to   attraversare
cross-country skiing
   sci di fondo
crossing   incrocio
crowded   affollato
cruise   crociera *f.*
crunchy   croccante
cry, to   piangere (pianto)
Cuban   cubano
cube   cubo
cultivate, to   coltivare
cultural   culturale
culture   cultura *f.*
cup   coppa *f.*, tazza *f.*
curiosity   curiosità *f.*
curious   curioso
curly   riccio
currency   valuta *f.*, moneta *f.*
current event   attualità *f.*
curtain   tenda *f.*
curve   curva *f.*
customs   dogana *f.*
cut, to   tagliare
cute, pretty   carino
cutlet   cotoletta *f.*, costoletta *f.*
cycling   ciclismo

D

daddy   papà, babbo
dairy store   latteria *f.*
dam   diga *f.*
damaged   danneggiato
damned   dannato
dance   ballo, danza *f.*
danger   pericolo
dangerous   pericoloso
dark   buio, scuro (adj.)
darn!   accidenti!
date   data *f.*
daughter   figlia *f.*
daughter-in-law   nuora *f.*
day   giorno, giornata
dead   morto
deaf   sordo
dear   caro
death   morte *f.*
December   dicembre
decide, to   decidere (deciso)
decision   decisione *f.*
declare, to   dichiarare
decrease, to   diminuire
dedicate, to   dedicare
defect   difetto
defend   difendere (difeso)
define, to   definire
definition   definizione *f.*
degree   grado (temp.),
   laurea *f.* (diploma)
delay   ritardo
delicious   delizioso
democracy   democrazia *f.*
democratic   democratico
demonstrate, to   dimostrare
Denmark   Danimarca *f.*
density   densità *f.*
dentist   dentista *m./f.*
depart, to   partire
department   dipartimento
department store   grande
   magazzino
departure   partenza *f.*
depend, to   dipendere (dipeso)
descend, to (get off)   scendere
   (sceso)
deserve, to   meritare
desk   scrivania *f.*

dessert   dolce *m.*
destination   destinazione *f.*
destiny   destino
destroy, to   distruggere (distrutto)
detergent   detersivo
detour   deviazione *f.*
develop, to   sviluppare
diabetes   diabete *m.*
dialogue   dialogo, discorso
diamond   diamante *m.*
diaper   pannolino
diarrhea   diarrea *f.*
dictatorship   dittatura *f.*
diction   dizione *f.*
dictionary   dizionario
die, to   morire (morto)
diet   dieta *f.*
difference   differenza *f.*
different   differente, diverso
difficult   difficile
digest, to   digerire
digestion   digestione *f.*
dine, to   cenare
dining room   sala da pranzo *f.*
dinner   cena *f.*
direct   diretto
direction   direzione *f.*,
   indicazione *f.*
director   direttore/direttrice *f.*,
   regista *m./f.*
dirt   terra *f.*
dirty   sporco
discothèque   discoteca *f.*
discount   sconto
discover, to   scoprire (scoperto)
discuss, to   discutere
   (discusso)
discussion   discorso, discussione *f.*
distance   distanza *f.*
distinguish, to   distinguere
   (distinto)
distracted   distratto
dive   tuffo
divide, to   dividere (diviso)
division   divisione *f.*
divorced   divorziato
do, to   fare (fatto)
dock   molo
doctor   dottore/dottoressa *f.*
   medico

document documento
dog cane *m.*
dollar dollaro
dolphin delfino
dome cupola *f.*, duomo
door porta *f.*
doorbell campanello
double doppio
down giù
dozen dozzina *f.*
draw, to (design) disegnare
drawing disegno
dream, to sognare
dress vestito
dress oneself, to vestirsi
drink, to bere (bevuto)
drive, to guidare
driver's license patente *f.*
drown, to annegare
drug droga *f.*
druggist droghiere
drugstore drogheria *f.*
drum tamburo
dry asciutto, secco
dry cleaner lavanderia a
    secco, tintoria *f.*
dub, to doppiare
duchess duchessa *f.*
duck anatra *f.*
duke duca *m.*
during durante, mentre
dust polvere *f.*
DVD DVD (pronounced
    dee-vu-dee)

E

each ciascuno, ogni, ognuno
eagle aquila *f.*
ear orecchio
earn, to guadagnare
earrings gli orecchini *m. pl.*
earth terra *f.*
east est, Oriente
Easter, Happy Pasqua, Buona
Easter Monday lunedì
    dell'Angelo, Pasquetta *f.*
easy facile
eat, to mangiare

eat breakfast, to fare la
    prima colazione or fare
    colazione
eat dinner, to cenare
eat lunch, to pranzare
economy economia *f.*
effect effetto
efficient efficiente
effort fatica *f.*, sforzo
egg uovo (*pl.* le uova)
eggplant melanzana *f.*
Egypt Egitto
eighteen diciotto
eighth ottavo
eighty ottanta
elderly anziano
election elezione *f.*
electricity elettricità *f.*
elegant elegante
element elemento
elevator ascensore *m.*
eleven undici
eliminate, to eliminare
embassy ambasciata *f.*
embroider, to ricamare
emergency emergenza *f.*
emigrate, to emigrare
empire impero
empty vuoto
end fine *f.*
enemy nemico
energetic dinamico
engineer ingegnere
England Inghilterra *f.*
English inglese
engraved inciso
enjoy oneself, to divertirsi
enormous enorme
enough abbastanza, basta!
enter, to entrare
entrance entrata *f.*, ingresso
entrepreneur imprenditore
envelope busta *f.*
environment ambiente
Epiphany (Jan. 6) Befana *f.*,
    Epifania *f.*
equipped attrezzato
error errore *m.*
escape, to scappare

essay saggio
essence essenza *f.*
essential essenziale
establish, to stabilire
et cetera eccetera
Europe Europa *f.*
even persino
evening sera *f.*, serata
event avvenimento, evento
ever mai
every ogni
everybody ognuno
everyone tutti
everything, all tutto
everywhere dappertutto
evil cattivo, male
evoke, to evocare
exact esatto
exactly esattamente
exaggerate, to esagerare
exam esame *m.*
examine, to esaminare
excavate, to scavare
excellent eccellente, ottimo
except eccetto
excerpt citazione *f.*
exchange cambio, scambio
exchange, to scambiare
exclude, to escludere (escluso)
excursion escursione *f.*, gita *f.*
excuse, to scusare
excuse me! permesso!
exercise ginnastica *f.*
exist, to esistere (esistito)
exit uscita *f.*
exit, to uscire
exotic esotico
expense spesa *f.*
expensive caro
experience esperienza *f.*
expiration scadenza *f.*
explain, to spiegare
explode, to esplodere (esploso)
export, to esportare
express espresso
express, to esprimere (espresso)
expression espressione *f.*
eye occhio (*pl.* gli occhi)
eyeglasses occhiali *m. pl.*

F

fable favola *f.*, fiaba *f.*
fabric stoffa *f.*, tessuto
face faccia *f.*, viso
fact fatto
factory fabbrica *f.*
fair fiera *f.*
faith fede *f.*
fall, to cadere
fall in love, to innamorarsi
family famiglia *f.*
famous famoso
fantasy fantasia *f.*
far lontano
far-sighted presbite
fare tariffa *f.*
farm fattoria *f.*
farmer contadino/
   contadina *f.*
fascinate, to affascinare
fascism fascismo
fasten, to allacciare
fat grasso
father padre *m.*
father-in-law suocero
faucet rubinetto
fear paura *f.*
Feast of the Assumption
   Assunzione *f.*
feather piuma *f.*
February febbraio
feel, to sentirsi
feeling sentimento,
   sensazione *f.*
felt feltro
ferry traghetto
fever febbre *f.*
fiancé fidanzato
fiancée fidanzata *f.*
field campo, prato
fifteen quindici
fifth quinto
fifty cinquanta
fight, to combattere
filet filetto
fill out, to (a form) riempire
fill up, to (a gas tank)
   fare il pieno

film film *m.*, pellicola *f.*
filter filtro
finally finalmente
finance finanza *f.*
finance, to finanziare
find, to trovare
fine multa *f.*
finger dito (*pl.* le dita)
finish, to finire
fire fuoco
fire, to licenziare
firefighter pompiere *m.*,
   vigile del fuoco
fireplace caminetto
firm fisso
first primo
first aid pronto soccorso
fiscal fiscale
fish pesce *m.*
fish store pescheria *f.*
fist pugno
flea pulce *f.*
flight volo
floor pavimento, piano
Florence Firenze
florist fioraio
flour farina *f.*
flower fiore *m.*
flu influenza *f.*
fly mosca *f.*
fly, to volare
foam schiuma *f.*
fog nebbia *f.*
follow, to seguire
food cibo
foot piede *m.*
for per
foreigner straniero/straniera *f.*
forest foresta *f.*
forgive, to perdonare
fork forchetta *f.*
form forma *f.*, modulo
formal formale
formulate, to formulare
fortress fortezza *f.*, rocca *f.*
fortune fortuna *f.*
forty quaranta
forward avanti
founded fondato

fountain fontana *f.*
fourteen quattordici
fourth quarto
fox volpe *f.*
fragile fragile
France Francia *f.*
free libero
free of charge gratis
French francese
frequent, to frequentare
fresh fresco
friar frate *m.*
Friday venerdì
fried fritto
friend amico/amica *f.*
friendship amicizia *f.*
frighten, to spaventare
frog rana *f.*
from di, da
fruit frutta *f.*
frying pan padella *f.*
fulfillment adempimento
full pieno
function, to funzionare
funeral funerale *m.*
funny buffo
fur pelliccia *f.*
furnishings arredamento
furrier shop pellicceria *f.*
future futuro

G

gain weight, to ingrassare
game gioco, partita *f.*
game room salagiochi *f.*
garage garage *m.*
garden giardino, orto
garlic aglio
gas pump distributore
   di benzina
gas tank serbatoio
gasoline benzina *f.*
gate cancello
generous generoso
genesis genesi *f.*
genre genere *m.*
geography geografia *f.*

German tedesco
Germany Germania
gerund gerundio
get drunk, to ubriacarsi
get on, to (climb) salire
get up, to alzarsi
ghost anima, fantasma *m.*
gift regalo, dono
girl ragazza *f.*, fanciulla *f.*
  (Tuscany)
give, to dare
give, to (a present) regalare,
  donare
glad contento
gladly! volentieri!
glance occhiata *f.*
glass (drinking) bicchiere *m.*
glass (material) vetro
gloves guanti *m. pl.*—
  also singular guanto
go, to andare
goat capra *f.*
god dio
goddess dea *f.*
godfather padrino
gold oro
good bravo
good buono
good day buon giorno
gothic gotico
government governo
grace grazia *f.*
grade voto
gram grammo
grammar grammatica *f.*
granddaughter nipote *f.*
grandfather nonno
grandmother nonna *f.*
grandson nipote *m.*
grapefruit pompelmo
grapes uva *f.*
grappa grappa *f.*
gravity gravità
gray grigio
Greek greco
green verde
greengrocer's fruttivendolo
greet, to salutare
grill griglia *f.*
grilled alla griglia

groceries alimentari *m. pl.*
ground terra
ground floor pianterreno
group gruppo
grow, to crescere (cresciuto)
guarantee, to garantire
guess, to indovinare
guest ospite *m./f.*
guide guida *f.*
guitar chitarra *f.*
gym palestra *f.*
gym suit tuta da ginnastica *f.*
gynecologist ginecologo/
  ginecologa *f.*

H

habit abitudine *f.*
hair pelo
hair (on head) capelli *m. pl.*
hair dryer fon *m.*
half metà, mezzo (adj.)
hall sala *f.*
ham prosciutto cotto
hand mano *f.* (*pl.* le mani)
handle maniglia *f.*
hanger gruccia *f.*, stampella *f.*
happen, to capitare,
  succedere (successo)
happiness allegria *f.*, felicità *f.*
happy allegro, felice
Happy Birthday! Buon
  Compleanno!
Happy Easter! Buona Pasqua!
Happy Holidays! Buone Feste!
Happy New Year! Buon Anno!
harbor porto
hard duro
haste fretta *f.*
hat cappello
hate, to odiare
have, to avere
have to, to (must) dovere
hazel nut nocciola *f.*
he lui, egli
head testa *f.*
headlight faro
health salute *f.*
healthy sano

hear, to sentire, udire
heart cuore *m.*
heart attack infarto
heat riscaldamento
heaven cielo, paradiso
heavy pesante
hectogram ettogrammo
  (*abb.* etto)
height altezza *f.*
helicopter elicottero
hell inferno
hello ciao, buon giorno;
pronto! (telephone)
helmet casco, elmetto
help, to aiutare
help! aiuto!
hen gallina *f.*
here ecco, qua, qui
hernia ernia *f.*
hide, to nascondere
  (nascosto)
highway autostrada *f.*
hill collina *f.*
hire, to assumere (assunto)
history storia *f.*
hitchhiking autostop *m.*
hobby hobby *m.*, passatempo
holiday festa *f.*
Holland Olanda
homeland patria *f.*
homemade della casa,
  fatto in casa
homework compito
honest onesto
honey miele *m.*
honeymoon luna di miele *f.*
honor onore *m.*
hope speranza *f.*
hope, to sperare
horoscope oroscopo
horse cavallo
horse riding equitazione *f.*
hospital ospedale
hostel ostello
hot caldo
hotel albergo, hotel *m.*
hour ora *f.*
house casa *f.*
housewife casalinga *f.*
how come

how much? quanto?
however comunque, tuttavia
hug, to abbracciare
human umano
humble umile
humidity umidità *f.*
humor umore
hunger fame *f.*
husband marito
hymn inno

I

I io
ice ghiaccio
ice-cream gelato
ice-cream parlor gelateria *f.*
idea idea *f.*
ideal ideale *m.*
identification card carta
 d'identità *f.*
identify, to identificare
identity identità *f.*
idiom idioma *f.*
idol idolo
if se
ignorant ignorante
ignore, to ignorare
illness malattia *f.*
illustrate, to illustrare
illustration illustrazione *f.*
image immagine *f.*
imagination immaginazione *f.*
imagine, to immaginare
imitation imitazione
immaculate immacolato
immediately subito
immense immenso
immigration immigrazione *f.*
imperative imperativo
imperfect imperfetto
import, to importare
important importante
impossible impossibile
impression impressione *f.*
improve, to migliorare
in a, in
in a hurry in fretta
in care of (c/o) presso

in fact infatti
in front of davanti a
in season di stagione
include, to includere (incluso)
increase, to aumentare
incredible incredibile
indefinite indefinito
independence indipendenza *f.*
index indice *m.*
India India
Indian indiano
indicate, to indicare
indigestion indigestione *f.*
indirect indiretto
indispensable
 indispensabile
indoor dentro, al coperto
industry industria *f.*
inexpensive economico
infection infezione *f.*
inferior inferiore
infinitive infinito
inflammation infiammazione *f.*
inflation inflazione *f.*
inform, to informare
information informazione *f.*
information office ufficio
 informazioni
ingredient ingrediente *m.*
inhabitant abitante *m./f.*
injection iniezione *f.*, puntura *f.*
injury danno, ferita *f.*
inn pensione *f.*, locanda *f.*
insect insetto
insect bite puntura *f.*
insecure insicuro
insert, to inserire
inside dentro
insist, to insistere
inspiration ispirazione *f.*
instead invece
institute istituto
instruction istruzione *f.*
insulin insulina *f.*
insurance assicurazione *f.*
insure, to assicurare
intelligent intelligente
intend, to intendere (inteso)
intention intenzione *f.*

interesting interessante
intermission intermezzo,
 intervallo
internal interno, dentro
international internazionale
interpret, to interpretare
interpreter interprete *m./f.*
interrupt, to interrompere
 (interrotto)
interval intervallo
interview colloquio
interview intervista *f.*
introduce, to introdurre
 (introdotto)
invitation invito
invite, to invitare
Ireland Irlanda *f.*
Irish irlandese
iron ferro (steel), ferro
 da stiro
irregular irregolare
is è
island isola *f.*
issue questione *f.*
issued rilasciato
Italian italiano
Italy Italia *f.*
itinerary itinerario
ivy edera *f.*

J

jack (car) cric *m.*
jacket giacca *f.*
jail carcere *m.*
January gennaio
Japan Giappone
Japanese giapponese
jeans jeans
Jesus Gesù
jeweler's oreficeria *f.*
jewelry store gioielleria *f.*
Jewish ebreo
joke barzelletta *f.*
joke, to scherzare
journalist giornalista *m./f.*
joy gioia *f.*
judge, to giudicare
juice succo

July   luglio
June   giugno
just   giusto, proprio

K

keep, to   tenere
ketchup   ketchup
key   chiave *f.*
kill, to   uccidere (ucciso)
kilogram   chilogrammo
   (*abb.* chilo)
kilometer   chilometro
kind   gentile
kindergarten   asilo
kindness   gentilezza *f.*
king   re
kiss   bacio
kiss, to   baciare
knife   coltello
knock, to   bussare
know, to (someone)
   conoscere (conosciuto)
know, to (something)   sapere
knowledge   conoscenza *f.*
Kosher   Kosher

L

lace   merletto
lack, to (be missing)   mancare
lake   lago
lamb   agnello
lamp   lampada *f.*
land, to   sbarcare
landing   atterraggio
landlord   padrone di casa
lane   corsia *f.*
language   lingua
large   grande, grosso
last   scorso, ultimo
last, to   durare
late   tardi
Latin   latino
laugh, to   ridere (riso)
laundry   bucato
laundry service   lavanderia *f.*
law   Diritto, giurisprudenza *f.*
   legge *f.*

lawyer   avvocato
lazy   pigro
lead, to   condurre (condotto)
leaf   foglia *f.*
learn, to   imparare
leather   cuoio, pelle *f.*
leave, to   partire
leave, to (behind)   lasciare
left   sinistro
leg   gamba *f.*
lemon   limone *m.*
lemonade   limonata *f.*
lend, to   prestare
length   lunghezza *f.*
leopard   leopardo
less   meno
lesson   lezione *f.*
letter   lettera *f.*
lettuce   lattuga *f.*
level   livello
liberty   libertà *f.*
license   patente *f.*
license plate   targa *f.*
lie down, to   sdraiarsi
life   vita *f.*
light   luce *f.*
light, to   accendere (acceso)
light bulb   lampadina *f.*
lightning flash   lampo,
   fulmine (weather)
line   linea *f.*
linen   lino
linguistics   linguistica *f.*
lip   labbro
liquor   liquore *m.*
list   elenco
listen to, to   ascoltare
liter   litro
literature   letteratura *f.*
little   piccolo, (a little) un po'
live, to   abitare, vivere
   (vissuto)
lively   vivace
liver   fegato
living room   salotto,
   soggiorno
load, to   caricare
loaf   pagnotta *f.*

loan   mutuo
lobster   aragosta *f.*
local   locale
lodge, to   alloggiare
logistics   logistica *f.*
long   lungo
long-distance call   interurbana *f.*
look, to   guardare
lose weight, to   dimagrire
lose, to   perdere (perso)
lost and found   ufficio
   oggetti smarriti
lotion   lozione *f.*
love   amore *m.*
love, to   amare
lunch   pranzo
lung   polmone *m.*
luxury   lusso

M

magazine   rivista *f.*
magic   magia *f.*
magnificent   magnifico
maid   domestica *f.*
maiden name   nome da nubile
mail   posta *f.*
mail, to   inviare, spedire
mailbox   cassetta postale *f.*
maintain, to   mantenere
majority   maggioranza *f.*
man   uomo
manage, to   dirigere (diretto)
management   amministrazione *f.*
manager   dirigente *m./f.*
manner   maniera *f.*, modo
manufacture, to   fabbricare
map   carta *f.*, mappa *f.*
marble   marmo
March   marzo
marina   marina *f.*, lido
mark, to   segnare
market   mercato
marmalade   marmellata *f.*
married   sposato
marry, to   sposare
marvelous   meraviglioso
masculine   maschile
mass   messa *f.*

matches fiammiferi *m. pl.*
mathematics matematica *f.*
matrimony matrimonio
maximum massimo
May maggio
maybe forse
mayor sindaco
me mi, a me
meadow prato
meal pasto
meaning significato, senso
means mezzo
measure misura *f.*
meat carne *f.*
meatball polpetta *f.*
mechanic meccanico
medicine medicina *f.*
meet, to incontrare
meeting congresso, riunione *f.*
melon melone *m.*
mentality mentalità *f.*
menu lista *f.*, menù
merchandise merce *f.*
merchant mercante *m./f.*
message messaggio
messenger corriere
metal metallo
method metodo
Mexico Messico
Middle Ages Medioevo
midnight mezzanotte *f.*
migraine emicrania *f.*
mile miglio (*pl.* le miglia)
milk latte *m.*
mind mente *f.*
minister ministro
minority minoranza *f.*
mint menta *f.*
minute minuto
mirror specchio
misfortune disgrazia *f.*
misfortune, bad luck
   misfortuna *f.*
Miss, young lady signorina *f.*
mix, to mischiare
model modello
modern moderno
modest modesto
mom, mother mamma *f.*

moment attimo
moment momento
monastery monastero
Monday lunedì
money denaro, i soldi *m. pl.*
money exchange office
   ufficio cambio
money order vaglia postale *m.*
month mese *m.*
monthly mensile
monument monumento
moon luna *f.*
more più
more than, in addition to oltre
morning mattina *f.*
morsel, nibble boccone
mosaic mosaico
mosquito zanzara *f.*
mother madre *f.*
mother-in-law suocera *f.*
motive motivo
motor motore *m.*
motorcycle motocicletta *f.*
mountain montagna *f.*
mourn, to lamentare
mouse topo
mouth bocca *f.*
movie director regista *m./f.*
Mr. signore *m.*
Mrs. signora *f.*
much molto
municipality comune *m.*
muscle muscolo
museum museo
mushroom fungo
music musica *f.*
musician musicista *m./f.*
Muslim mussulmano
mustard senape *f.*
mute muto
myth mito

N

name nome *m.*
name of spouse nome
   del coniuge
napkin salvietta *f.*, tovagliolo
narrative narrativa *f.*

nation nazione *f.*
nationality nazionalità *f.*
native language madrelingua *f.*
natural naturale
nature natura *f.*
nature preserve riserva
   naturale *f.*
nausea nausea *f.*
near vicino
near-sighted miope
necessary necessario
necessity necessità *f.*
neck collo
necklace collana *f.*
need bisogno
need, to avere bisogno di
negative negativo
neighbor vicino/vicina *f.*
neighborhood quartiere *m.*
neither neppure
neither … nor né … né
nephew nipote
nervous nervoso
nest nido
never mai
new nuovo
news notizia *f.*
news program telegiornale *m.*
newspaper giornale *m.*,
   quotidiano
newspaper vendor giornalaio
newsstand edicola *f.*
next prossimo
nice simpatico
niece nipote
night notte *f.*
nightmare incubo
nineteen diciannove
ninety novanta
ninth nono
no entrance vietato l'ingresso
no one nessuno
no parking divieto di sosta
nocturne notturno
noisy rumoroso
noon mezzogiorno
normal normale
north nord
Norway Norvegia

nose   naso
not   non
not even   neanche, nemmeno
notebook   quaderno
nothing   niente, nulla
notwithstanding   nonostante
noun   nome *m.*
novel   romanzo
November   novembre
now   adesso, ora
number   numero
nurse   infermiera *f.*

O

object   oggetto
obligation   obbligo
oblige, to   obbligare
obsession   mania *f.*
obtain, to   ottenere
obvious   ovvio
occasion   occasione *f.*
occupy, to   occupare
ocean   oceano
October   ottobre
of   di
offer   offerta *f.*
office   ufficio
often   spesso
oil   olio
old   vecchio
olive   oliva *f.*
on   su
on board   a bordo
on purpose   apposta
one   uno
one hundred   cento
one-way street   senso unico
onion   cipolla *f.*
only   solamente
open   aperto
open, to   aprire (aperto)
operation   operazione *f.*
opinion   opinione *f.*
opposite   contrario
opposite   opposto
optician   ottico
or   o, oppure
orange   arancia *f.*

order   ordine *m.*
order, to   ordinare
ordinal   ordinale
oregano   origano
origin   origine *f.*
original   originale
other   altro
outdoor   all'aperto
outfit   abito
outside   fuori
oven   forno
overcoat   cappotto, soprabito
overdone   scotto,
    troppo cotto
owner   proprietario

P

package   pacco
page   pagina *f.*
pain   dolore *m.*
paint   vernice *f.*
paint, to   dipingere (dipinto)
painter   pittore/pittrice *f.*
painting   pittura *f.*, quadro
pair   paio (*pl.* le paia)
panorama   panorama *m.*
pants   pantaloni *m. pl.*
paper   carta *f.*
paradise   paradiso
parents   genitori *m. pl.*
park   parco
parking lot   parcheggio
parsley   prezzemolo
part   parte *f.*
participate, to   partecipare
pass, to   passare
passing   sorpasso
passion   passione *f.*
passport   passaporto
past   passato
pasta   pasta *f.*
pastry shop   pasticceria *f.*
path   sentiero, via *f.*
paw   zampa *f.*
pay, to   pagare
payment   pagamento
pea   pisello
peace   pace *f.*

peach   pesca *f.*
peak   picco
peanut   nocciolina *f.*
pear   pera *f.*
pedagogy   didattica *f.*
pen   penna *f.*
penalty   multa *f.*, pena *f.*
pencil   matita *f.*
peninsula   penisola *f.*
people   gente *f.*
pepper   pepe *m.*
percentage   percento,
    percentuale *f.*
perception   percezione *f.*
perfume   profumo
period   periodo, punto
permit, to   permettere
    (permesso)
person   persona *f.*
pharmacy   farmacia *f.*
phase   fase *f.*
philosophy   filosofia *f.*
phonetics   fonetica *f.*
photocopy   fotocopia *f.*
photograph   fotografia *f.*
phrase   frase *f.*
physics   fisica *f.*
pie   torta *f.*
piece   pezzo
piece of furniture   mobile *m.*
pig   maiale
pill   pillola *f.*
pillow   cuscino
pink   rosa
pistol   pistola *f.*
place   locale *m.*, luogo, posto
plain   pianura *f.*
plan   programma *m.*
planet   pianeta *m.*
plant   pianta *f.*
plastic   plastica *f.*
plate   piatto
plateau   altopiano
play, to   giocare
play, to (an instrument)
    suonare or giocare
please   per favore, per piacere
please, to (to like)   piacere
    (piaciuto)

please hold!   attendere prego!

pleasing   piacevole

pleasure   piacere *m.*

plural   plurale *m.*

pocket   tasca *f.*

poem, poetry   poesia *f.*

poet   poeta *m.*, poetessa *f.*

poison   veleno

police   polizia *f.*

police headquarters   questura *f.*

police officer   carabiniere *m.*, poliziotto

political party   partito

politics   politica *f.*

polluted   inquinato

pollution   inquinamento

pond   stagno

poor   povero

Pope   Papa *m.*

population   popolazione *f.*

pork   maiale *m.*, porco

portion   porzione *f.*

portrait   ritratto

Portugal   Portogallo

position   posizione *f.*

possibility   possibilità

possible   possibile

post office   ufficio postale

postage stamp   francobollo

postal carrier   postino

postcard   cartolina *f.*

potato   patata *f.*

poultry   pollame *m.*

poverty   miseria *f.*, povertà *f.*

practice   pratica *f.*

praise, to   lodare

pray, to   pregare

prayer   preghiera *f.*

precise   preciso

prefer, to   preferire

preference   preferenza *f.*

pregnant   incinta

prepare, to   preparare

prescription   ricetta *f.*

present   presente

present, to   presentare

preservatives   conservanti *m. pl.*

president   presidente

price   prezzo

priest   prete *m.*

prince   principe *m.*

princess   principessa *f.*

principal   principale

print   stampa *f.*

printing   tipografia *f.*

prison   carcere *m.*, prigione *f.*

private property   proprietà privata *f.*

problem   problema *m.*

produce, to   produrre (prodotto)

product   prodotto

production   produzione *f.*

profession   professione *f.*

professor   professore/professoressa *f.*

progress   progresso

progressive   progressivo

prohibited   vietato, proibito

prohibition   divieto, proibizione *f.*

project   progetto

promise, to   promettere (promesso)

pronoun   pronome *m.*

pronounce, to   pronunciare

pronunciation   pronuncia *f.*

propose, to   proporre (proposto)

protect, to   proteggere (protetto)

Protestant   protestante

proud   orgoglioso

proverb   proverbio

provided that   purché

psychology   psicologia *f.*

public   pubblico

publicity   pubblicità *f.*

pull, to   tirare

punctual   puntuale

pupil   allievo, scolaro

pure   puro

purple   viola

purse   borsa *f.*

push, to   spingere (spinto)

put, to   mettere (messo)

pyramid   piramide *f.*

Q

quality   qualità *f.*

quantity   quantità *f.*

queen   regina *f.*

question, to   domandare

quickly, early   presto

quit, to   smettere (smesso)

quote, to   citare

R

Rabbi   rabbino

rabbit   coniglio

race   corsa *f.*

racket   racchetta *f.*

radiator   radiatore *m.*

radio   radio *f.*

racar   vagone *m.*

railroad   ferrovia *f.*

rain   pioggia *f.*

rain, to   piovere

raincoat   impermeabile *m.*

raise, to   alzare

rare   raro, al sangue

rarely   raramente

raspberry   lampone *m.*

rather   piuttosto

raw   crudo

razor   rasoio

read, to   leggere (letto)

ready   pronto

really   davvero, veramente

receipt   ricevuta *f.*, scontrino

receive, to   ricevere

recent   recente

reception   ricevimento

recipe   ricetta *f.*

recite, to   recitare

record   disco

red   rosso

reflect, to   riflettere (riflesso)

reflexive   riflessivo

refreshment   bevanda *f.*

refrigerator   frigorifero

refuge   rifugio

refund   rimborso

region   regione *f.*

regret, to (to be sorry) dispiacersi (dispiaciuto)
relationship rapporto
relative parente *m./f.*
relaxing rilassante
religion religione *f.*
remain, to rimanere (rimasto)
remainder resto
remember, to ricordare
Renaissance Rinascimento
render, to rendere (reso)
rent affitto
rent, to affittare, noleggiare
repair, to riparare
repeat, to ripetere
report cronaca *f.*, rapporto
represent, to rappresentare
reptile rettile *m.*
republic repubblica *f.*
request richiesta *f.*
reservation prenotazione *f.*
reserve, to prenotare
reserved riservato
reservoir riserva d'acqua *f.*
residence domicilio, residenza *f.*
resident abitante *m./f.*
resign, to licenziarsi
resistance resistenza *f.*
resolve, to risolvere (risolto)
respect, to rispettare
respond, to rispondere (risposto)
responsible responsabile
restaurant ristorante *m.*
result risultato
return, to ritornare, tornare
revision revisione *f.*
rheumatism reumatismo
rhythm ritmo
rib costola *f.*
rice riso
rich ricco
riddle indovinello
right destro
right (legal) diritto
ring anello
ripe maturo
river fiume *m.*
roasted arrosto
robbery rapina *f.*

rock pietra *f.*, roccia *f.*
roll of film rullino
romantic romantico
roof tetto
room camera *f.*, stanza *f.*
root radice *f.*
rope corda *f.*
rose rosa *f.*
round-trip (ticket) biglietto d'andata e ritorno
route percorso, via
row fila *f.*
ruckus baccano
ruins rovine *f. pl.*
run, to correre (corso)
rush hour ora di punta *f.*
Russia Russia *f.*
Russian russo

S

sad triste
safe sicuro
sailboat barca a vela *f.*
saint santo/santa *f.*
salad insalata *f.*
salary salario
sale saldi *m. pl.*, svendita *f.*
sales clerk commesso/commessa *f.*
salmon salmone *m.*
salt sale *m.*
same stesso
sand sabbia *f.*
sandwich panino
Saturday sabato
sauce salsa *f.*
saucepan casseruola *f.*, tegame *m.*
sausage salsiccia *f.*
say, to dire (detto)
scarf sciarpa *f.*
scene scena *f.*
schedule orario, tabella *f.*
school scuola *f.*
science scienza *f.*
science fiction fantascienza *f.*
scissors forbici *f. pl.*
scooter motorino

Scotland Scozia
screwdriver cacciavite *m.*
sculpture scultura *f.*
sea mare *m.*
search, to cercare
seashell conchiglia *f.*
season stagione *f.*
seat posto, sedile
seat belt cintura di sicurezza *f.*
second secondo
secretary segretario/segretaria *f.*
sedative sedativo
see, to vedere (visto)
see you later! arrivederci! ci vediamo!
seem, to sembrare
sell, to vendere
semester semestre *m.*
Senate Senato
send, to inviare, mandare, spedire
sender mittente *m./f.*
sensation sensazione *f.*
sentence frase *f.*
sentiment sentimento
separate, to separare
separated separato
September settembre
serenade serenata *f.*
serious grave, serio
service servizio
set fisso, fissato
set, to apparecchiare
seventeen diciassette
seventh settimo
seventy settanta
severe severo
sex sesso
sexuality sessualità
shadow ombra *f.*
shame vergogna *f.*
share, to condividere (condiviso)
shave, to radersi
she lei, ella
sheet lenzuolo
sheet of paper foglio
shingle tegola *f.*
ship nave *f.*
shirt camicia *f.*

shoe scarpa *f.*
shoe repair calzolaio
shoe store calzoleria *f.*
shop bottega *f.*, negozio
shop window vetrina *f.*
short basso, corto
shorten, to accorciare
shorts calzoncini *m. pl.*
shout, to gridare, urlare
show spettacolo, mostra *f.* (art)
shower doccia *f.*
shrimp gambero
shy timido
Sicilian siciliano
Sicily Sicilia
sick ammalato
side lato, fianco
side dish contorno
sidewalk marciapiede *m.*
sign cartello, segno
signal segnale *m.*
signature firma *f.*
signify, to significare
silence silenzio
silk seta *f.*
silver argento
simple semplice
since poiché, da quando
sincere sincero
sing, to cantare
singer cantante *m./f.*
single singolo
single room monolocale *m.*
singular singolare
sink lavandino
sister sorella *f.*
sister-in-law cognata *f.*
sit, to sedersi
situation situazione *f.*
sixteen sedici
sixty sessanta
size misura *f.*, taglia *f.*
sketch schizzo
ski, to sciare
skiing sci *m.*
skirt gonna *f.*
sky cielo
sled slittino
sleep sonno
sleep, to dormire

sleeping bag sacco a pelo
sleeping pill sonnifero
slender magro, snello
slide diapositiva *f.*
slope pista *f.*, discesa *f.*
slow down rallentare
small piccolo
small bag sacchetto
smell, to odorare, sentire
smile, to sorridere (sorriso)
smoke, to fumare
snack spuntino
snake serpente *m.*
snob snob
snow neve *f.*
so così
so-so così così
soap sapone *m.*
soccer calcio, football
soccer player calciatore *m.*
socks calze *f. pl.*, calzini *m. pl.*
sofa divano
soft soffice
sold out esaurito
soldier soldato
some alcuni/alcune, qualche
some of ne un po' di
someone qualcuno
something qualcosa
sometimes qualche volta, talvolta
son figlio
son-in-law genero
soon subito, presto
soul anima *f.*
soup minestra *f.*, zuppa *f.*
south sud
space spazio
Spain Spagna *f.*
Spanish spagnolo
sparkling wine spumante *m.*
special speciale
spend, to spendere (speso)
spice spezia *f.*
spicy piccante
spider ragno
spirit anima, spirito
spiritual spirituale
splendid splendido
spoiled guasto, rovinato

sponge spugna *f.*
spoon cucchiaio
sport sport *m.*
sports ground campo sportivo
spouse sposo/sposa *f.*
spring sorgente *f.*, primavera *f.* (season)
squid calamari *m. pl.*
stadium stadio
stage palcoscenico
stain macchia *f.*
stairs scala *f.*, le scale *f. pl.*
stall bancarella *f.*
star stella *f.*
state stato
statement affermazione *f.*
station stazione *f.*
stationery store cartoleria *f.*
statue statua *f.*
steak bistecca *f.*
steal, to rubare
steel acciaio
step passo
stepfather patrigno
stepsister sorellastra *f.*
stewardess hostess *f.*
still (again) ancora
stingy avaro, tirchio
stitch punto
stockings calze *f. pl.*, i collant
stomach stomaco, pancia
stone pietra *f.*, sasso
stop fermata *f.*
stop, to fermare
storm tempesta *f.*
story storia *f.*
stove stufa *f.*
straight diritto
strange strano
straw cannuccia *f.*, fieno (hay)
strawberry fragola *f.*
stream rio
stream ruscello
street strada *f.*, via *f.*
stress stress
stress, to stressare
strike sciopero
stroll, to passeggiare
strong forte
struggle lotta *f.*

student studente/studentessa *f.*
study studio
study, to studiare
stuff roba *f.*
stuffed ripieno
stupendous stupendo
stupid stupido
subject materia *f.*, soggetto
subscription abbonamento
substitute, to sostituire
subtitle sottotitolo
suburbs periferia *f.*
subway metropolitana *f.*
succeed, to riuscire
such tale
suffer, to soffrire (sofferto)
suffice, to bastare
sugar zucchero
suit abito, vestito
suitable adatto
summer estate *f.*
sun sole *m.*
Sunday domenica
sunrise alba *f.*
sunset tramonto
supermarket supermercato
sure sicuro
surgery chirurgia *f.*
surgeon chirurgo/chirurga *f.*
surname cognome *m.*,
    nome di famiglia
surprise sorpresa *f.*
surprise, to sorprendere (sorpreso)
surround, to circondare
swallow rondine *f.*
swallow, to inghiottire
swamp palude *f.*
swear, to giurare
sweater maglia *f.*
Sweden Svezia *f.*
sweet dolce
swim, to nuotare
swimming pool piscina *f.*
Switzerland Svizzera
symbol simbolo
symphony sinfonia *f.*
symptom sintomo
synagogue sinagoga *f.*
synthetic sintetico
system sistema *m.*

T

table tavolo (restaurant), tavola
tablecloth tovaglia *f.*
tablet compressa *f.*
tag etichetta *f.*
tailor sarto
take, to prendere (preso)
tall alto
tan, to abbronzarsi
tape adesivo, nastro
task compito, impegno
taste gusto, sapore *m.*
taste, to assaggiare
tax tassa *f.*
taxi tassì
taxi meter tassametro
tea tè *m.*
teach, to insegnare
teacher insegnante *m./f.*
team squadra *f.*
telephone telefono
telephone, to telefonare
telephone call telefonata *f.*
telephone card carta telefonica *f.*
tell, to dire (detto), raccontare
temple tempio
tender tenero
tent tenda *f.*
tenth decimo
terrace terrazzo
thank, to ringraziare
thank you! grazie!
that quello/quella
that which ciò, quel che
theater teatro
theme tema *m.*
then allora, poi
there ci, lì/là
there is c'è
therefore perciò, quindi
thermometer termometro
they loro
thief ladro
thin magro
thing cosa *f.*
think, to pensare
third terzo
thirst sete *f.*
thirteen tredici

thirty trenta
this questo
this evening stasera
this morning stamattina
thought pensiero
thousand mille (*pl.* mila)
three tre
throw, to buttare
thunder tuono
Thursday giovedì
thus dunque
ticket biglietto
ticket counter biglietteria *f.*
tide marea *f.*
tie cravatta *f.*
tie, to legare
tight stretto
tile piastrella *f.*
time ora *f.*, tempo
tip mancia *f.*
tire pneumatico
tired stanco
tissue fazzoletto di carta
to a, in
tobacco shop tabaccheria *f.*
today oggi
toe dito (*pl.* le dita)
together insieme
toilet gabinetto, toilette *f.*
toilet paper carta igienica *f.*
token gettone *m.*
tolerance tolleranza *f.*
toll pedaggio
toll-free number numero
    verde
tomato pomodoro
tomorrow domani
tongue lingua *f.*
tonight stanotte
too troppo
tooth dente *m.*
toothbrush spazzolino
    da denti
toothpaste dentifricio
topic argomento, soggetto
total totale
touch, to toccare
tour giro
tourism turismo
tourist turista *m./f.*

toward   verso
tower   torre *f.*
town square   piazza *f.*
toy   giocattolo
track   binario
tradition   tradizione *f.*
traffic   traffico
traffic light   semaforo
tragic   tragico
train   treno
transfer, to   trasferirsi
transform, to   trasformare
translate, to   tradurre (tradotto)
translation   traduzione *f.*
transport, to   trasportare
trash   rifiuti *m. pl.*
trash can   bidone della
   spazzatura
travel, to   viaggiare
tree   albero
tremendous   tremendo
trip   viaggio
tropical   tropicale
trouble   guaio
truck   camion *m.*
true   vero
trust   fiducia *f.*
trust, to   fidarsi
truth   verità *f.*
try, to   provare
tub   vasca *f.*
Tuesday   martedì
tulip   tulipano
tunnel   galleria *f.*, sotterraneo
turn   turno
turn off, to   spegnere (spento)
twelve   dodici
twenty   venti
two   due
type, kind   specie *f.*, tipo

U

ugly   brutto
umbrella   ombrello
uncle   zio
uncomfortable   scomodo
understanding   comprensione *f.*
understood!   capito!

underwear   biancheria intima *f.*
unemployed   disoccupato
unfortunately   purtroppo
unhealthy   malato
unified   unificato
unique   unico
united   unito
United States   Stati Uniti *m. pl.*
unmarried   celibe *m.*, nubile *f.*
unpleasant   antipatico,
   spiacevole
until   fino a
unusual   insolito
urgent   urgente
usage   uso
use, to   usare
useless   inutile
usual   solito

V

vacation   vacanza *f.*
vaccination   vaccinazione *f.*
vacuum cleaner   aspirapolvere *m.*
validate, to   convalidare
validated   convalidato
validity   validità
valise   valigia *f.*
valley   valle *f.*
value   valore *m.*
variation   variazione *f.*
variety   varietà *f.*
various   vario
vase   vaso
VAT/sales tax   I.V.A. (Imposta
   Valore Aggiunto)
veal   vitello
vegetables   verdura *f.*
vegetarian   vegetariano
vehicle   veicolo
velocity   velocità
vengeance   vendetta *f.*
verb   verbo
very   molto
victim   vittima *f.*
view   vista *f.*
villa   villa *f.*
village   villaggio

vine   vigna *f.*
vinegar   aceto
violence   violenza *f.*
violet   violetta *f.*
visible   visibile
visit   visita *f.*
visit, to   visitare
vitamin   vitamina *f.*
vocabulary   vocabolario
voice   voce *f.*
volleyball   pallavolo *f.*
vote, to   votare
vowel   vocale *f.*

W

wait, to   aspettare
waiter   cameriere
waiting room   sala d'attesa *f.*
waitress   cameriera *f.*
walk, to   camminare,
   passeggiare
wall   muro, parete *f.*
wallet   portafoglio
walnut   noce *f.*
want, to   volere
war   guerra *f.*
warm   caldo
warm, to   riscaldare
warn, to   avvertire
warning   avviso
wash, to   lavare
wasp   vespa *f.*
watch   orologio
water   acqua *f.*
wave   onda *f.*
we   noi
weak   debole
wear, to   indossare, portare
weather   tempo
Wednesday   mercoledì
week   settimana *f.*
weekend   fine settimana *m.*
weigh, to   pesare
weight   peso
welcome! greetings!
   benvenuto!
well   pozzo
well (adv.)   bene

west   ovest, Occidente
wet   bagnato
what   che, che cosa
wheel   ruota *f.*
when   quando
where   dove
wherever   ovunque
which   quale
while   mentre
whistle, to   fischiare
white   bianco
who   chi
wholesale   all'ingrosso
why   perché
wide   largo
widespread   diffuso
widow   vedova *f.*
widower   vedovo
wife   moglie *f.*
wild   selvaggio, selvatico
willing   disposto
win, to   vincere (vinto)
wind   vento
window   finestra *f.*, finestrino
windshield   parabrezza *m.*
wine   vino
wine bar   enoteca *f.*
winery   azienda vinicola *f.*
winter   inverno
wise   saggio
wish   desiderio, voglia *f.*
witch   strega *f.*
with   con
within   fra
without   senza
wolf   lupo
woman   donna *f.*, signora *f.*
wood   legno
woods   bosco, selva *f.*
wool   lana *f.*
work   lavoro
work, to   lavorare
worker   impiegato, operaio
world   mondo
worm   baco
worried   preoccupato
worry, to   preoccuparsi
worse   peggio

wrap, to   incartare
write, to   scrivere (scritto)
writer   scrittore
wrong   torto
wrong, to be   sbagliare

X–Y

x-ray   radiografia *f.*

yawn, to   sbadigliare
year   anno
yell, to   gridare
yellow   giallo
yes   sì
yesterday   ieri
yoga   yoga *m.*
yogurt   yogurt *m.*
you   Lei (polite), tu (familiar), voi *pl.*
you are welcome!   prego!
young   giovane

Z

zero   zero
zipper   cerniera *f.*
zone   zona *f.*
zoo   zoo

Italian to English

A

a, ad (before vowels)   at, in, to, by
a bordo   on board
abbandonare   to abandon
abbastanza   enough
abbazia *f.*   abbey
abbigliamento   clothing
abbonamento   subscription
abbracciare   to hug
abbronzarsi   to get tanned
abitante *m./f.*   resident, inhabitant
abitare   to live
abito   outfit, suit

abitudine *f.*   habit
abolire   to abolish
accademia *f.*   academy
accanto a   beside, next to
accendere (acceso)   to light, to turn on
accento   accent
accesso   access
accettare   to accept
acciaio   steel
accidenti!   darn!
acciuga *f.*   anchovy
accompagnare   to accompany
accorciare   to shorten
accordo   agreement
aceto   vinegar
acqua *f.*   water
acqua non potabile   do not drink water
acquario   aquarium
acquistare   to acquire
acustico   acoustic
adatto   suitable, appropriate
adempimento   fulfillment
adesso   now
adorabile   adorable
adulto   adult
aereo   airplane
affare *m.*   business, deal
aeroporto   airport
affascinare   to fascinate
affermare   to affirm, to assert
affermazione *f.*   statement
affetto   affection
affettuoso   affectionate
affittare   to rent
affittasi   for rent
affitto   rent
affollato   crowded
agente *m./f.*   agent
agenzia *f.*   agency
aggettivo   adjective
aggiungere (aggiunto)   to add
aggressivo   aggressive
agile   agile
aglio   garlic
agnello   lamb
agosto   August
agricoltura *f.*   agriculture

aiutare   to help
aiuto!   help!
al coperto   indoor
al forno   baked or roasted
al sangue   rare
alba *f.*   sunrise
albergo   hotel
albero   tree
albicocca *f.*   apricot
alcol *m.*   alchohol
alcolico   alcoholic
alcuni/alcune   some
alfabeto   alphabet
alimentari *m. pl.*   groceries
all'aperto   outdoor, open air
allacciare   to fasten, to buckle
allegria *f.*   happiness
allegro   happy
allenarsi   to train (sports)
allergia *f.*   allergy
allergico   allergic
allievo   pupil
alloggiare   to lodge
allora   then
almeno   at least
altezza *f.*   height
alto   tall
altopiano   plateau
altro   other
alzare   to raise, lift
alzarsi   to get up
amare   to love
amaro   bitter
ambasciata *f.*   embassy
ambiente *m.*   environment
ambizione   ambition
ambulanza *f.*   ambulance
americano   American
amicizia *f.*   friendship
amico/amica *f.*   friend
ammalato   sick, ill
amministrazione *f.*   management, administration
ammirare   to admire
amore *m.*   love
ampio   ample
anatra *f.*   duck
analisi *f.*   analysis
anche   also

ancora   still, again, yet
andare   to go
andata e ritorno   round-trip
   (ticket)
anello   ring
anfiteatro   amphitheater
anima *f.*   spirit
animale *m.*   animal
animato   animated, lively
annegare   to drown
anno   year
anno bisestile   leap year
annoiarsi   to get bored
annunciare   to announce
antenato   ancestor
antibiotici *m. pl.*   antibiotics
antico   ancient, antique
antipasto   appetizer
antipatico   unpleasant,
   disagreeable
antiquariato   antiques
anzi   and even, but rather
anziano   elderly
aperitivo   aperitif
aperto   open; (all'aperto)
   outside
apparecchiare   to set
appartamento   apartment
appartenere   to belong
applaudire   to applaud
apposta   on purpose,
   deliberately
apprezzare   to appreciate
approvare   to approve of
aprile   April
aprire (aperto)   to open
aquila *f.*   eagle
arancia *f.*   orange
archeologia *f.*   archeology
architettura *f.*   architecture
area *f.*   area
argento   silver
argomento   topic, subject
aria *f.*   aria, air, appearance
aria condizionata *f.*
   air conditioning
aristocratico   aristocratic
aroma *m.*   aroma
arrabbiarsi   to get angry

arrabbiato   angry
arredamento   furnishings
arretrato   backward
arrivare   to arrive
arrivederci!   See you later!
arrivo   arrival
arrosto   roasted
arte *f.*   art
articolo   article
artista *m./f.*   artist
artrite *f.*   arthritis
ascensore *m.*   elevator
asciutto   dry
ascoltare   to listen to
asilo   kindergarten,
   day-care center
aspettare   to wait for
aspirapolvere *m.*   vacuum
   cleaner
aspirina *f.*   aspirin
assaggiare   to taste
assaltare   to assault
assegno   check
assicurare   to ensure, insure
assicurazione *f.*   insurance
assistenza (medica) *f.*   assistance, insurance (health)
associazione *f.*   association
assolutamente   absolutely
assumere (assunto)   to hire,
   to assume
Assunzione *f.*   Feast of the
   Assumption
astrologia *f.*   astrology
astronauta *m./f.*   astronaut
atleta *m./f.*   athlete
atletica   athletics
atrio *m.*   atrium
attaccare   to attach, to attack
attacco *m.*   attack
atteggiamento   attitude
attendere prego!   please hold!
attento   careful, attentive
attenzione!   attention!
   warning!
atterraggio   landing
attimo   moment
attirare   to attract
attività *f.*   activity

attivo   active
atto   document, record
attore *m.*   actor
attraversare   to cross
attraverso   across
attrezzato   equipped
attribuire   to attribute
attrice *f.*   actress
attuale   actual, current
attualità *f.*   current event
auguri!   best wishes!
aumentare   to increase
australiano   Australian
austriaco   Austrian
autobus *m.*   bus
automatico   automatic
automobile *f.* (abb. auto)   car
autonoleggio   car rental
autore   author
autoritario   authoritarian
autostop *m.*   hitchhiking
autostrada *f.*   highway
autunno *m.*   autumn
avanti   forward
avaro   stingy
avere   to have
avvenimento *m.*   event
avvenire   to happen
avventura *f.*   adventure
avverbio *m.*   adverb
avvertire   to warn
avvicinarsi   to approach,
   to get near
avvocato   lawyer
azienda *f.*   firm, company
azione *f.*   action
azzurro   light blue

B

babbo   dad
baccano   ruckus
baciare   to kiss
bacio   kiss
baco   worm
bagnato   wet
bagno   bath
baia *f.*   bay
balcone *m.*   balcony

ballo   dance
bambino   baby, child
banca *f.*   bank
bancarella *f.*   stall, booth
banco   counter
Bancomat *m.*   ATM
bar *m.*   bar, café
barba *f.*   beard
barbiere *m.*   barber
barca *f.*   boat
barca a vela *f.*   sailboat
barista *m./f.*   bartender
barocco   Baroque
barzelletta *f.*   joke
base *f.*   base
basso   short, low
bastare   to be enough, to suffice
battere   to beat
batteria *f.*   battery
bellezza *f.*   beauty
benché   although
bene   well
benvenuto!   welcome! greetings!
benzina *f.*   gasoline
bere (bevuto)   to drink
berretto *m.*   cap
bestia *f.*   beast
bevanda *f.*   refreshment
biancheria intima *f.*   underwear
bianco   white
Bibbia *f.*   Bible
biberon *m.*   baby bottle
bibita *f.*   refreshment, beverage
bicchiere *m.*   glass
biglietteria *f.*   ticket counter
biglietto *m.*   ticket
binario *m.*   track, platform
biodegradabile   biodegradable
biologia *f.*   biology
biondo   blond
birra *f.*   beer
biscotto   cookie
bisogno   need
bistecca *f.*   steak
blu   blue
bocca *f.*   mouth
boccone *m.*   morsel, nibble
bollettino *m.*   bulletin, news
bollire   to boil
bordo, a   aboard

borsa *f.*   bag, purse
borsetta *f.*   purse, bag
bosco *m.*   woods
bottega *f.*   shop
bottiglia *f.*   bottle
bottone *m.*   button
braccialetto *m.*   bracelet
braccio *m.*; braccia *f. pl.*   arm
bravo   good, able
braciola *f.*   chop
breve   brief, short
brioche *f.*   brioche, croissant
britannico   British
brodo *m.*   broth
bronchite *f.*   bronchitis
bronzo   bronze
bruciare   to burn
bruno   brown-haired
brutto   ugly
bucato *m.*   laundry
buffo   funny
buffone *m.*   buffoon, clown,
   fool
buio *m.*   darkness
Buon Anno!   Happy New
Year!
Buon Compleanno!   Happy
   Birthday!
Buon giorno!   Good day,
hello!
Buon Natale!   Merry
Christmas!
Buona Feste!   Happy
Holidays!
Buona Pasqua!   Happy
Easter!
buono   good
burro *m.*   butter
burrone *m.*   canyon
bussare   to knock
busta *f.*   envelope
bustina *f.*   bag
buttare   to throw

C

c'è   there is
cabina *f.*   cabin
cacciavite *m.*   screwdriver
cadere   to fall

caffè *m.* coffee, café

calamari *m. pl.* squid

calciatore *m.* soccer player

calcio *m.* soccer, kick

caldo heat, hot (adj.)

calmare to calm

calze *f. pl.* stockings

calzini *m. pl.* socks

calzolaio *m.* shoe repair

calzoleria *f.* shoe store

calzoncini *m. pl.* shorts

cambiare to change, to exchange

cambio *m.* exchange

camera *f.* room

cameriera *f.* waitress, maid

cameriere *m.*/cameriera *f.* waiter/waitress

camicetta *f.* blouse

camicia *f.* shirt

caminetto *m.* fireplace

camino *m.* chimney

camion *m.* truck

camminare to walk

campagna *f.* country, countryside

campana *f.* bell

campanello doorbell

campanile *m.* bell tower

campeggio *m.* camping

campionato *m.* match, championship

campo *m.* field

campo sportivo *m.* sports ground

canadese Canadian

canale *m.* channel

cancello *m.* gate

cancro *m.* cancer

candela *f.* candle

candidato *m.* candidate

cane *m.* dog

cannuccia *f.* drinking straw

canottaggio *m.* canoeing

cantante *m./f.* singer

cantare to sing

cantina *f.* basement, cellar

caotico chaotic

capace capable

capelli *m. pl.* hair (on head)

capitare to happen

capito! understood!

cappella *f.* chapel

cappello *m.* hat

cappotto *m.* overcoat

capra *f.* goat

carabiniere *m.* police officer

caramella *f.* candy

carattere *m.* character

caratteristico characteristic, typical

carcere *m.* jail, prison

carciofo artichoke

caricare to load

carino cute, pretty

carne *f.* meat

caro dear, expensive

carota *f.* carrot

carriera *f.* career

carta *f.* paper

carta di credito *f.* credit card

carta d'identità identification card

carta igienica *f.* toilet paper

carta stradale *f.* map

carta telefonica *f.* telephone card

cartello *m.* sign

cartoleria *f.* stationery store

cartolina *f.* postcard

casa *f.* house, home

casalinga *f.* housewife

casco *m.* helmet

cassa *f.* cash register

casseruola *f.* saucepan

cassetta postale *f.* mailbox

castano brown

castello *m.* castle

catalogo *m.* catalogue

categoria *f.* category

catena *f.* chain

cattedrale *f.* cathedral

cattivo bad, evil, naughty

cattolico Catholic

cavallo *m.* horse

cavatappi *m.* corkscrew

cavo *m.* cable

celebrare to celebrate

celibe unmarried man, single *m.*

cena *f.* dinner

cenare to dine

cento one hundred

centrale central

centro center, downtown

ceramica *f.* ceramic

cercare to search, look for

cerniera *f.* zipper

certificato certificate

certo certain, sure, of course!

cervello brain

che what, who, which, that

che cosa what

chi who? whom? the one who

chiacchiera *f.* chat

chiacchierare to chat

chiamare to call

chiamarsi to call oneself (to be named)

chiaro clear, light

chiave *f.* key

chiedere (chiesto) to ask

chiesa *f.* church

chilogrammo kilogram

chilometro kilometer

chirurgia *f.* surgery

chirurgo surgeon

chitarra *f.* guitar

chiudere (chiuso) to close

chiuso closed

chiusura festiva *f.* closed for the holidays

ci there

ciao hello, hi, bye

ciascuno each, each one

cibo food

ciclismo cycling

cieco blind

cielo sky, heaven

ciliegia *f.* cherry

cimitero cemetery

Cina China

cinema *m.* cinema

cinese Chinese

cinquanta fifty

cintura *f.* belt

cintura di sicurezza *f.* seat belt

ciò that which

cioccolata *f.* chocolate

cipolla *f.* onion

circa about, approximately

circo circus

circolo circle

circondare to surround

citare to quote

citazione *f.* excerpt, quote

città city

cittadinanza *f.* citizenship

cittadino/cittadina *f.* citizen

civico civic

civile civil

classe *f.* class

classico classical

classificazione *f.* classification

cliente *m./f.* client, customer

clima *m.* climate

cognata *f.* sister-in-law

cognato brother-in-law

cognome *m.* surname

coincidenza *f.* connection, coincidence

colazione *f.* breakfast, lunch

collaborare to collaborate

collana *f.* necklace

collant *m. pl.* stockings

collega *m./f.* colleague

collina *f.* hill

collo neck

colloquio interview

colonia *f.* colony

colore *m.* color

coltello knife

coltivare to cultivate

comandamento commandment

combattere to fight

come how, like, as

cominciare to begin, to start

commesso/commessa *f.* sales clerk

comodo convenient, comfortable

compiere to accomplish

compito homework, task, chore

compleanno birthday

complimento compliment

comporre (composto) to compose

comportamento behavior

comportarsi to behave

composizione *f.* composition

comprare to buy

comprensione *f.* understanding

compressa *f.* tablet, pill

comune *m.* municipality; common (adj.)

comunicare to communicate

comunismo communism

comunità community

comunque however, no matter how

con with

concentrazione *f.* concentration

concerto concert

concetto concept

concezione *f.* conception

conchiglia *f.* seashell

concludere (concluso) to conclude

concorso contest, exam

condizione *f.* condition

condividere (condiviso) to share

condizionale *m.* conditional (verb mood)

condominio condominium

condurre (condotto) to lead, to carry out

conferenza *f.* conference, lecture

confessare to confess

conflitto conflict

conforto comfort, convenience

congratulazioni! congratulations!

congresso meeting, conference

coniglio rabbit

coniugare to conjugate

coniugazione *f.* conjugation

conoscenza *f.* knowledge, acquaintance

conoscere (conosciuto) to know someone

conquistare to conquest

consecutivo consecutive

conseguenza *f.* consequence

conservanti *m. pl.* preservatives

considerare to consider

consigliare to advise, to recommend

consolare to console

consonante *f.* consonant

consumo consumption, waste

contadino/a farmer, peasant

contanti *m. pl.* cash

contare to count

contattare to contact

contatto contact

conte count

contemporaneo contemporary

contenere to contain

contento glad, satisfied

contessa *f.* countess

contestare to challenge, dispute

continente *m.* continent

continuare to continue

conto check, bill, account

contorno side dish

contraccettivo contraceptive

contrario opposite

contrasto contrast

contro against

controllare to check

controllo check, control

contusione *f.* bruise

convalidare to validate

convalidato validated

convento convent

conversazione *f.* conversation

convincere (convinto) to convince

coperta *f.* blanket, cover

coperto cover charge

copia *f.* copy

coppa *f.* cup

coppia *f.* couple

coraggio courage

corda *f.* rope

coro chorus, choir

corpo body

correggere (corretto) to correct

correre (corso) to run

corretto correct

corriera *f.* bus

corriere messenger, courier

corrispondere (corrisposto) to correspond

corsa *f.* race
corsia *f.* lane
corso course
corte *f.* court
cortese courteous
cosa thing, what
cosa c'è? what is it?
così so, thus
così così so-so
cosmetici *m. pl.* cosmetics
costa *f.* coast
costo cost, price
costare to cost
costiera *f.* cliff
costituzione *f.* constitution
costola *f.* rib
costoso costly, expensive
costoletta *f.* rib
costruire to build, construct
costume *m.* costume
cotone *m.* cotton
cotto cooked
cravatta *f.* tie
creare to create
creazione *f.* creation
credere to believe
credito credit
crema *f.* cream
crescere (cresciuto) to grow
cric *m.* jack (car)
crisi *f.* crisis
cristiano Christian
croccante crunchy
croce *f.* cross
crociera *f.* cruise
cronaca *f.* report
crostata *f.* pie
crudo raw, uncooked
cubano Cuban
cubo cube
cuccetta *f.* berth
cucchiaio spoon
cucinare to cook
cugino/cugina *f.* cousin
cui whom, that, which
culla *f.* crib
cultura *f.* culture
culturale cultural
cuocere (cotto) to cook
cuoio leather

cuore *m.* heart
cupola *f.* dome
cura *f.* care
curare to care for, to look after
curiosità *f.* curiosity
curioso curious, strange
curva *f.* curve
cuscino pillow

D

da from, by
Danimarca Denmark
dannato damned
danneggiato damaged
danza *f.* dance
dappertutto everywhere
dare to give
data *f.* date
davanti a in front of
davvero really
dea *f.* goddess
debole weak
decidere (deciso) to decide
decimo tenth
decisione *f.* decision
dedicare to dedicate
definire to define
definizione *f.* definition
delfino dolphin
delizioso delicious
della casa homemade
democratico democratic
democrazia *f.* democracy
denaro money
densità *f.* density
dente *m.* tooth
dentifricio toothpaste
dentista *m./f.* dentist
dentro inside
desiderio wish, desire
destinazione *f.* destination
destino destiny
destro right
detersivo detergent
deviazione *f.* detour
di of, about, from
di solito usually
di stagione in season

diabete *m.* diabetes
dialogo dialogue
diamante *m.* diamond
diapositiva *f.* slide
diarrea *f.* diarrhea
dicembre December
dichiarare to declare
diciannove nineteen
diciassette seventeen
diciotto eighteen
didattica *f.* pedagogy, teaching
dieta *f.* diet
dietro a behind
difendere (difeso) to defend
difetto defect
differenza *f.* difference
difficile difficult
diffuso widespread, diffuse
diga *f.* dam
digerire to digest
dimagrire to lose weight
diminuire to decrease
dimostrare to demonstrate
dimostrazione *f.* demonstration
dinamico energetic
dio god
dipartimento department
dipendere (dipeso) to depend
dipingere (dipinto) to paint
dire (detto) to say, to tell
diretto direct
direttore/direttrice *f.* director
direzione *f.* direction
dirigere (diretto) to manage, to direct
Diritto law
diritto straight (adv.)
disco record
discorso speech, discussion
discoteca *f.* discothèque
discussione *f.* discussion
discutere (discusso) to discuss
disegnare to draw
disegno drawing, design
disgrazia *f.* accident, misfortune
disoccupato unemployed
dispiacere (dispiaciuto) to be sorry

disponibile available

disposto willing

distanza *f.* distance

distinguere (distinto) to distinguish

distratto distracted, absent minded

distributore di benzina gas pump

distruggere (distrutto) to destroy

dito (*pl.* le dita) finger, toe

ditta *f.* firm, business

dittatura *f.* dictatorship

divano sofa

diverso different

divertirsi to enjoy oneself

dividere (diviso) to divide

divieto prohibition

divieto di sosta no parking

divisione *f.* division

divorziare to get divorced

divorziato divorced

dizionario dictionary

dizione *f.* diction

doccia *f.* shower

documento document

dodici twelve

dogana *f.* customs

dolce sweet

dolce dessert

dollaro dollar

dolore *m.* pain

domandare to question

domani tomorrow

domenica Sunday

domestica *f.* maid

domicilio residence

donna *f.* woman

dopo after (prep.), afterward (adv.)

doppiare to dub

doppio double

dormire to sleep

dottore/dottoressa *f.* doctor

dove where

dovere to have to, to must

dozzina *f.* dozen

droga *f.* drug

drogheria *f.* grocery store

duca *m.* duke

duchessa *f.* duchess

due two

duomo cathedral, dome

dunque thus, then

durante during

durare to last

duro hard, tough

E

e, ed (before vowels) and

è is

ebbene well then, so

ebreo Hebrew, Jewish

eccellente excellent

eccetera et cetera

eccetto except

ecco here is, there is

economia *f.* economy

economico inexpensive

edera *f.* ivy

edicola *f.* newsstand

edificio building

effetto effect

efficiente efficient

Egitto Egypt

elegante elegant

elementare elementary

elemosina *f.* alms

elenco list, directory

elettricità *f.* electricity

elezione *f.* election

elicottero helicopter

eliminare to eliminate

emergenza *f.* emergency

emicrania *f.* migraine

emigrare to emigrate

enorme enormous

enoteca *f.* wine bar

entrambi both

entrare to enter

entrata *f.* entrance

Epifania *f.* Epiphany (Jan. 6)

equitazione *f.* horse riding

ernia *f.* hernia

errore *m.* error

esagerare to exaggerate

esame *m.* exam

esaminare to examine

esattamente exactly

esatto exact

esaurito sold out

escludere (escluso) to exclude

escursione *f.* excursion

esistere (esistito) to exist

esotico exotic

esperienza *f.* experience

esplodere (esploso) to explode

esportare to export

espressione *f.* expression

espresso express

esprimere (espresso) to express

essenza *f.* essence

essenziale essential

essere (stato) to be

est east

estate *f.* summer

estero abroad

età *f.* age

etichetta *f.* tag, label

etto hectogram

Europa *f.* Europe

evento event

evitare to avoid

evocare to evoke

F

fa ago

fabbrica *f.* factory

fabbricare to manufacture

faccenda *f.* thing, matter, chore

faccia *f.* face

facile easy

facoltà *f.* school

fagiolo bean

falegname *m.* carpenter

fame *f.* hunger

famiglia *f.* family

famoso famous

fantascienza *f.* science fiction

fantasia *f.* fantasy

fantasma *m.* ghost, phantom

fare (fatto) to do, to make

farina *f.* flour

farmacia *f.* pharmacy

faro   headlight, lighthouse
fascismo   fascism
fase *f.*   phase
fastidio   bother, annoyance
fatica *f.*   effort
fatto   fact
fattoria *f.*   farm
favola *f.*   fable
fazzoletto di carta   tissue
febbraio   February
febbre *f.*   fever
fede *f.*   faith
fegato   liver
felice   happy
feltro   felt
femmina *f.*   female
ferita *f.*   wound
fermare   to stop
fermata *f.*   stop
fermo   still
Ferragosto   Assumption
   Day (Aug. 15)
ferro   iron
ferrovia *f.*   railroad
festa *f.*   holiday
festeggiare   to celebrate
fiaba *f.*   fable, tale
fiammiferi *m. pl.*   matches
fianco   side
fidarsi   to trust
fidanzata *f.*   fiancée
fidanzato   fiancé
fiducia *f.*   trust
fiero   proud
fiera *f.*   fair
figlia *f.*   daughter
figlio   son
fila *f.*   line, row
filetto   filet
filosofia *f.*   philosophy
filtro   filter
finalmente   finally
finanza *f.*   finance
finanziare   to finance
fine *f.*   end
fine settimana   weekend
finestra *f.*   window
finire   to finish
fino a   until, as far as

fioraio   florist
fiore *m.*   flower
Firenze   Florence
firma *f.*   signature
fisso   firm, fixed
fiscale   fiscal
fischiare   to whistle
fisica *f.*   physics
fissare   to set up
fisso   set, fixed
fiume *m.*   river
foglia *f.*   leaf
foglio   sheet of paper
fon *m.*   hair dryer
fondato   founded
fondo   bottom
fonetica *f.*   phonetics
fontana *f.*   fountain
football   soccer, football
forbici *f. pl.*   scissors
forchetta *f.*   fork
foresta *f.*   forest
forma *f.*   form
formaggio   cheese
formale   formal
formulare   to formulate,
   to compose
fornaio   baker
forno   oven
forse   maybe
forte   strong
fortezza *f.*   fortress
fortuna *f.*   fortune
fotocopia *f.*   photocopy
fotografia *f.*   photograph
fra   within, in, between, among
fragile   fragile
fragola *f.*   strawberry
francese   French
Francia *f.*   France
francobollo   postage stamp
frase *f.*   phrase, sentence
frate *m.*   friar
fratello   brother
freddo   cold
frequentare   to frequent
fresco   fresh
fretta *f.*   haste, hurry

frigorifero   refrigerator
fritto   fried
frontiera *f.*   border
frutta *f.*   fruit
fruttivendolo   green-grocer's
fumare   to smoke
fumetto   comic strip
funerale *m.*   funeral
fungo   mushroom
funivia *f.*   cable car, gondola
funzionare   to function,
   to work
fuoco   fire
fuori   outside
furbo   clever, sly (slang)
futuro   future

G

gabinetto   toilet
galleria *f.*   tunnel, gallery
gallina *f.*   hen
gamba *f.*   leg
gambero   shrimp
gara *f.*   contest
garage *m.*   garage
garantire   to guarantee
garofano   carnation
gatto   cat
gattopardo   leopard
gelateria *f.*   ice-cream parlor
gelato   ice-cream
genere *m.*   genre, type
genero   son-in-law
generoso   generous
genesi *f.*   genesis
genitori *m. pl.*   parents
gennaio   January
gente *f.*   people
gentile   kind, polite
gentilezza *f.*   kindness
geografia *f.*   geography
Germania *f.*   Germany
gerundio   gerund
Gesù   Jesus
gettone *m.*   token
ghiaccio   ice
già   already
giacca *f.*   jacket

giallo   yellow

ginnastica *f.*   gymnastics, exercise

Giappone *m.*   Japan

giapponese   Japanese

giardino   garden

ginecologo/ginecologa *f.*   gynecologist

giocare   to play

giocattolo   toy

gioco   game

gioia *f.*   joy

gioielleria *f.*   jewelry store

giornalaio   newspaper vendor

giornale *m.*   newspaper

giornalista *m./f.*   journalist

giornata *f.*   day

giorno   day

giovane   young

giovedì   Thursday

girare   to spin, to shoot (a film)

giro   tour

gita *f.*   excursion

giù   down

giubbotto   coat

giudicare   to judge

giugno   June

giurare   to swear

giurisprudenza *f.*   law

giusto   just, right, correct

gonna *f.*   skirt

gotico   gothic

governo   government

grammatica *f.*   grammar

grammo   gram

grande   big, large

grappa *f.*   grappa

grasso   fat

gratis   free of charge

grave   serious, grave

gravità *f.*   gravity

grazia *f.*   grace

grazie!   thank you!

Grecia   Greece

greco   Greek

greggio   raw, crude

gridare   to yell, to shout

grigio   gray

griglia *f.*   grill

grosso   large

grotta *f.*   cave

gruccia *f.*   hanger

gruppo   group

guanti *m. pl.*   gloves

guadagnare   to earn

guaio   trouble

guancia *f.*   cheek

guardare   to look at, to watch

guardaroba *m.*   cloakroom

guasto   spoiled, rotten

guasto   breakdown

guerra *f.*   war

guida *f.*   guide

guidare   to drive

gustare   to taste

gusto   taste

H

hobby *m.*   hobby

hockey *m.*   hockey

hostess *f.*   stewardess

hotel *m.*   hotel

I

I.V.A. (Imposta Valore Aggiunto)   VAT/sales tax

idea *f.*   idea

ideale *m.*   ideal

identificare   to identify

identità *f.*   identity

idioma *m.*   idiom

idolo   idol

ieri   yesterday

ignorante   ignorant

ignorare   to ignore

illustrare   to illustrate

illustrazione *f.*   illustration

imbarco   boarding

imitazione *f.*   imitation

immacolato   immaculate

immaginare   to imagine

immaginazione *f.*   imagination

immagine *f.*   image

immenso   immense

immigrazione *f.*   immigration

imparare   to learn

impegno   commitment, task

imperativo   imperative

imperfetto   imperfect

impermeabile *m.*   raincoat

impero   empire

impiegato   worker, employee, official

importante   important

importare   to import, to matter

impossibile   impossible

imprenditore   entrepreneur

impressione *f.*   impression

in   in, to, at

in fretta   in a hurry

incartare   to wrap

incidente *m.*   accident

incinta   pregnant

inciso   engraved

includere (incluso)   to include

incominciare   to begin, to start

incontrare   to meet

incredibile   incredible

incrocio   crossing

incubo   nightmare

indefinito   indefinite

indiano   Indian

indicare   to indicate

indicazione *f.*   direction, indication

indice *m.*   index, forefinger

indietro   back, behind

indigestione *f.*   indigestion

indipendenza *f.*   independence

indiretto   indirect

indirizzo   address

indispensabile   indispensable

indossare   to wear

indovinare   to guess

indovinello   riddle

industria *f.*   industry

infarto   heart attack

infatti   in fact

inferiore   inferior, lower

infermiera *f.*   nurse

inferno   hell

infezione *f.*   infection

infiammazione *f.*   inflammation

infinito   infinitive

inflazione *f.*   inflation

influenza *f.* flu
informare to inform
informazione *f.* information
ingegnere engineer
Inghilterra *f.* England
inghiottire to swallow
inglese English
ingrassare to get fat
ingrediente *m.* ingredient
ingresso entrance
ingrosso wholesale
iniezione *f.* injection
iniziare to begin
inizio beginning
innamorarsi to fall in love with
inno hymn
inoltre also
inquinamento pollution
inquinato polluted
insalata *f.* salad
insegnante *m./f.* teacher
insegnare to teach
inserire to insert
insetto insect
insicuro insecure
insieme together
insistere (insisto) to insist
insolito unusual
insulina *f.* insulin
intelligente intelligent
intendere (inteso) to mean
intenzione *f.* intention
interessante interesting
intermezzo intermission
internazionale international
interno internal, inside
interpretare to interpret
interprete interpreter
interrogativo interrogative
interrompere (interrotto)
    to interrupt
interurbana *f.* long-distance
    call
intervallo interval
intervista *f.* interview
intorno a around
introdurre (introdotto)
    to introduce
inutile useless
invece instead

inverno winter
inviare to mail, to send
invitare to invite
invito invitation
io I
Irlanda Ireland
irlandese Irish
irregolare irregular
iscritto student, member
isola *f.* island
ispirazione *f.* inspiration
istituto institute
istruzione *f.* instruction
Italia *f.* Italy
italiano Italian
itinerario itinerary

J-K-L

jeans jeans

Kosher Kosher
ketchup ketchup

là there
Befana *f.* Epiphany (January 6)
labbro lip
ladro thief
lamentare to mourn, to grieve
lamentarsi to complain
lago lake
lampada *f.* light
lampadina *f.* light bulb
lampo lightning flash
lampone *m.* raspberry
lana *f.* wool
largo wide
lasciare to let, to leave behind
latino Latin
lato side
latte *m.* milk
latteria *f.* dairy store
lattuga *f.* lettuce
laurea *f.* degree
lavanderia *f.* laundry service
lavanderia a secco dry cleaner
lavandino sink
lavare to wash
lavorare to work
lavoro work

leccare to lick
legare to tie
legge *f.* law
leggere (letto) to read
leggero light
legno wood
lei she, her
Lei (polite) you
lenzuolo sheet
lettera *f.* letter
letteratura *f.* literature
letto bed
lezione *f.* lesson
lì there
libero free
libertà *f.* liberty
libreria *f.* bookstore
libretto libretto, little book
libro book
licenziare to fire someone
licenziarsi to resign
limonata *f.* lemonade
limone *m.* lemon
linea *f.* line
lingua *f.* language, tongue
linguistica *f.* linguistics
lino linen
liquore *m.* liquor
lista *f.* list, menu
litigare to argue, to fight
litro liter
livello level
locale local
locale *m.* place
lodare to praise
logistica *f.* logistics
lontano far
loro they
lotta *f.* struggle
lozione *f.* lotion
luce *f.* light
luglio July
lui he, him
luna *f.* moon
luna di miele *f.* honeymoon
lunedì Monday
lunedì dell'Angelo Easter
    Monday
lunghezza *f.* length
lungo long

luogo   place
lupo   wolf
lusso   luxury

M

ma   but
macchia *f.*   stain
macchina *f.*   automobile, car, machine
macchina fotografica *f.*   camera
macellaio   butcher
macelleria *f.*   butcher shop
madre *f.*   mother
madrelingua *f.*   native language
magazzino   department store
maggio   May
maggioranza *f.*   majority
magia *f.*   magic
maglia *f.*   sweater, pullover
magnifico   magnificent
magro   thin
mai   never, ever
maiale *m.*   pork, pig
mais *m.*   corn
malato   unhealthy, sick
malattia *f.*   illness
male   evil; fa male   it hurts
mamma *f.*   mom, mother
mancia *f.*   tip
mancare   to lack, to be missing
mandare   to send
mangiare   to eat
mania *f.*   obsession
maniera *f.*   manner, way
maniglia *f.*   handle
mano *f.* (*pl.* le mani)   hand
mantello   cape
mantenere   to maintain
manzo   beef
marca *f.*   brand, type
marciapiede *m.*   sidewalk
mare *m.*   sea
marea *f.*   tide
marina *f.*   marina
marito   husband
marmellata *f.*   jam
marmo   marble
marrone   brown

martedì   Tuesday
marzo   March
maschile   masculine
massimo   maximum
matematica *f.*   mathematics
materia *f.*   subject
matita *f.*   pencil
matrimonio   matrimony
mattina *f.*   morning
matto   crazy
maturo   ripe, mature
meccanico   mechanic
medicina *f.*   medicine
medico   doctor
Medioevo   Middle Ages
meglio   better
mela *f.*   apple
melanzana *f.*   eggplant
melone *m.*   melon, cantaloupe
meno   less
mensa *f.*   cafeteria
mensile   monthly
menta *f.*   mint
mentalità *f.*   mentality
mente *f.*   mind
mento   chin
mentre   while
menù *m.*   menu
meraviglioso   marvelous
mercante *m./f.*   merchant
mercato   market
merce *f.*   merchandise
mercoledì   Wednesday
meritare   to deserve
merletto   lace
mese *m.*   month
messa *f.*   mass
messaggio   message
Messico *m.*   Mexico
metà   half
metallo   metal
metodo   method
metropolitana *f.*   subway
mettere (messo)   to put, to place
mezzanotte *f.*   midnight
mezzo   half
mezzo   means
mezzogiorno   noon
mi   me, to me

miele *m.*   honey
miglio (*pl.* le miglia)   mile
migliorare   to improve
migliore   the best
mille (*pl.* mila)   thousand
minestra *f.*   soup
ministro   minister
minoranza *f.*   minority
minore   smaller, less
minuto   minute
miope   near-sighted
mischiare   to mix
miseria *f.*   poverty
misto   mixed
misura *f.*   measure, size
mito   myth
mittente *m./f.*   sender
mobile *m.*   piece of furniture
modello   model
moderno   modern
modesto   modest
modo   manner, method, way
modulo   form
moglie *f.*   wife
molo   dock
molto   a lot, much, very
momento   moment
monastero   monastery
mondo   world
moneta *f.*   coin
monolocale *m.*   single room, studio
montagna *f.*   mountain
monumento   monument
morbido   soft, smooth
morire (morto)   to die
morte *f.*   death
mosaico   mosaic
mosca *f.*   fly (insect)
mostra *f.*   show (art)
motivo   motive
motocicletta *f.*   motorcycle
motore *m.*   motor
motorino   scooter
mucca *f.*   cow
multa *f.*   fine, ticket
muro   wall
muscolo   muscle
museo   museum
musica *f.*   music

musicista *m./f.* musician
mussulmano Muslim
muto mute
mutuo loan

N

narrativa *f.* narrative, story, fiction
nascere (nato) to be born
nascita *f.* birth
nascondere (nascosto) to hide
naso nose
nastro tape
Natale, Buon Christmas, Merry
natura *f.* nature
naturale natural
nausea *f.* nausea
nave *f.* ship
nazionalità *f.* nationality
nazione *f.* nation
ne some of, about it
né … né neither … nor
neanche not even
nebbia *f.* fog
necessità *f.* need, necessity
necessario necessary
negativo negative
negozio shop
nemico enemy
nemmeno not even
neppure neither, not even
nero black
nervoso nervous
nessuno no one, nobody
neve *f.* snow
nido nest
niente nothing
nipote granddaughter, niece
nipote grandson, nephew
nocciola *f.* hazelnut
nocciolina *f.* peanut
noce *f.* walnut
noi we
noioso boring
noleggiare to rent
nome *m.* noun, name
nome da nubile maiden name

nome del coniuge name of spouse
non not
nonna *f.* grandmother
nonno grandfather
nono ninth
nonostante notwithstanding
nord north
normale normal
Norvegia Norway
notizia *f.* news
notte *f.* night
notturno nocturne
novanta ninety
novembre November
novità *f.* news
nubile unmarried woman, single
nulla nothing
numero number
numero verde toll-free number
nuora *f.* daughter-in-law
nuotare to swim
nuovo new
nuvola *f.* cloud

O

o or
obbligare to oblige
obbligo obligation
occasione *f.* occasion, bargain
occhiali *m. pl.* eyeglasses
occhiata *f.* glance
occhio eye
Occidente West
occupare to occupy
occupato busy, occupied
oceano ocean
odiare to hate
odorare to smell
odore *m.* aroma, odor
offerta *f.* offer
oggetti smarriti *m. pl.* lost property
oggetto object
oggi today
ogni each, every
Ognissanti All Saint's Day (Nov. 1)
ognuno everybody

Olanda *f.* Holland
olio oil
oliva *f.* olive
oltre more than, in addition to
ombra *f.* shadow
ombrello umbrella
onda *f.* wave
onesto honest
onore *m.* honor
opera *f.* opera, work
operaio worker
operazione *f.* operation
opinione *f.* opinion
opposto opposite
oppure or
ora *f.* hour, now
ora di punta *f.* rush hour
orario schedule
ordinale ordinal
ordinare to order
ordine *m.* order
orecchini *m. pl.* earrings
orecchio ear
oreficeria *f.* jeweler's, goldsmith's
orgoglioso proud
Oriente East, Orient
origano oregano
originale original
origine *f.* origin
oro gold
orologio watch, clock
oroscopo horoscope
orso bear
orto garden
oscuro dark, obscure
ospedale *m.* hospital
ospite *m./f.* guest
osso (*pl.* le ossa) bone
ostello hostel
ottanta eighty
ottavo eighth
ottenere to obtain
ottico optician
ottimo excellent, best
ottobre October
ottone brass
ovest west
ovunque wherever
ovvio obvious

P

pacco   package, parcel
pace *f.*   peace
padella *f.*   frying pan
padre *m.*   father
padrino   godfather
padrone/padrona *f.*   boss, landlord, owner
paese *m.*   country, town
pagamento   payment
pagare   to pay
pagina *f.*   page
pagnotta *f.*   loaf
paio (*pl.* le paia)   pair
palazzo   building, palace
palco   box (theater)
palcoscenico   stage
palestra *f.*   gym
palla *f.*   ball
pallacanestro *f.*   basketball
pallavolo *f.*   volleyball
palude *f.*   swamp, marsh
pancetta *f.*   bacon
panchina *f.*   bench
pane *m.*   bread
panetteria *f.*   bakery
panino   sandwich
panna *f.*   cream
pannolino   diaper
panorama *m.*   panorama, view
pantaloni *m. pl.*   pants
Papa *m.*   Pope
papà *m.*   daddy, pop
parabrezza *m.*   windshield
paradiso   paradise
paragone *m.*   comparison
parcheggio   parking lot
parco   park
parente *m./f.*   relative
parere (parso)   to seem, to appear
parete *f.*   inside wall
parte *f.*   part
partecipare   to participate
partenza *f.*   departure
partire   to depart, to leave
partita *f.*   game, match
partito   political party

Pasqua   Easter
passaporto   passport
passare   to pass
passatempo   hobby
passato   past
passeggiare   to stroll
passeggiata *f.*   stroll, walk
passione *f.*   passion
passo   step
pasta *f.*   pasta, pastry
pasticceria *f.*   pastry shop
pasto   meal
patata *f.*   potato
patente *f.*   driver's license
patria *f.*   homeland
patrigno   stepfather
patto   agreement, pact
paura *f.*   fear
pavimento   floor
pazzo   crazy
peccato!   what a shame!
pedaggio   toll
peggio   worse
pelo   hair
pelle *f.*   skin, leather
pelletteria *f.*   leather goods shop
pelliccia *f.*   fur
pellicola *f.*   film
pena *f.*   penalty
penisola *f.*   peninsula
penna *f.*   pen, feather
pensare   to think
pensiero   thought, idea
pensione *f.*   inn
pepe *m.*   pepper
peperone *m.*   bell pepper
per   for, in order to
per favore   please
per piacere   please
pera *f.*   pear
percento   percentage
percezione *f.*   perception
perché   why, because
perciò   therefore
percorso   route
perdere (perso)   to lose
perdonare   to pardon
pericolo   danger

pericoloso   dangerous
periferia *f.*   suburbs
permesso!   excuse me!
periodo   period
permettere (permesso)   to permit
però   but, however
persino   even
persona *f.*   person
personaggio   character, type (of person)
pesante   heavy
pesare   to weigh
pesca *f.*   peach
pesce *m.*   fish
pescheria *f.*   fish store
peso   weight
pettinare   to comb
petto   chest
pezzo   piece
piacere *m.*   pleasure
piacersi (piaciuto)   to be pleasing, to like
piacevole   pleasing
pianeta *m.*   planet
piangere (pianto)   to cry
pianterreno   ground floor
piano   floor, (adv.) softly
pianta *f.*   plant
pianura *f.*   plain
piastrella *f.*   floor tile
piatto   plate
piazza *f.*   town square
piccante   spicy
picco   peak
piccolo   small
piede *m.*   foot
pieno   full
pietra *f.*   stone
pigro   lazy
pila *f.*   battery
pillola *f.*   pill
pioggia *f.*   rain
piovere   to rain
piramide *f.*   pyramid
piscina *f.*   swimming pool
pisello   pea
pista *f.*   track, trail, slope
pistola *f.*   pistol

pittura *f.* painting
più more
piuma *f.* feather
piuttosto rather
plastica *f.* plastic
plurale *m.* plural
pneumatico tire
un po' a little
poco not very much
poesia *f.* poem, poetry
poi then, afterward
poiché since
polenta *f.* corn meal
politica *f.* politics
polizia *f.* police
poliziotto police officer
pollame *m.* poultry
polmone *m.* lung
polpetta *f.* meatball
polvere *f.* dust
pomeriggio afternoon
pomodoro tomato
pompelmo grapefruit
pompiere *m.* firefighter
ponte *m.* bridge
popolazione *f.* population
porco pig, pork
porta *f.* door
portabagagli *m.* porter
portacenere *m.* ashtray
portafoglio wallet
portare to bring, to carry
porto harbor, port
Portogallo Portugal
porzione *f.* portion
posizione *f.* position
possibile possible
possibilità *f.* possibility
posta *f.* mail, post office
postino postal carrier
posto seat, place
potere to be able to, to can
povero poor
pozzo well
pranzare to dine, to eat lunch
pranzo lunch, supper
pratica *f.* practice
pratico convenient, practical
prato field

preciso precise
preferenza *f.* preference
preferire to prefer
prefisso area code
pregare to pray, to beg, to ask
preghiera *f.* prayer
prego! you are welcome!
prendere (preso) to take
prenotare to make a
    reservation
prenotazione *f.* reservation
preoccuparsi to worry
preoccupato worried
preparare to prepare
presbite far-sighted
presentare to present
presente *m.* present
presidente president
presso in care of (c/o)
prestare to lend
presto quickly, early
prete *m.* priest
prezzemolo parsley
prezzo price
prezzo d'entrata admission
    charge
prigione *f.* prison
prima before
primavera *f.* spring
primo first, before
principale principal, main
principe prince
principessa *f.* princess
problema *m.* problem
prodotto product
produrre (prodotto)
    to produce
produzione *f.* production
professione *f.* profession
professore/professoressa *f.*
    professor
profilattico condom
profumeria *f.* cosmetics shop
profumo perfume
progetto project
programma *m.* plan,
    program
progressivo progressive
progresso progress

promettere (promesso)
    to promise
pronome *m.* pronoun
pronto ready, hello
    (telephone)
pronto soccorso first aid
pronuncia *f.* pronunciation
pronunciare to pronounce
proporre (proposto)
    to propose
proposizione *f.* clause
proprietà privata *f.* private
    property
proprietario owner
proprio just, really
prosciutto ham
prossimo next
proteggere (protetto)
    to protect
protestante Protestant
provare to try, to experience
proverbio proverb
psicologia *f.* psychology
pubblicità *f.* publicity
pubblico public
pugno fist
pulce *f.* flea
pulire to clean
pullman *m.* bus
punto period, point, stitch
puntura *f.* injection,
    insect bite
puntuale punctual
purché provided that
pure also
puro pure
purtroppo unfortunately

Q

qua here
quaderno notebook
quadro painting, picture
qualche some
qualche volta sometimes
qualcosa something
qualcuno someone
quale which
qualità *f.* quality
qualsiasi any

qualunque   any
quando   when
quantità *f.*   quantity
quanto?   how much?
quaranta   forty
quartiere *m.*   neighborhood
quarto   fourth, quarter
quasi   almost
quattordici   fourteen
quello/quella   that
questione *f.*   matter
questo   this one
questura *f.*   police headquarters
qui   here
quindi   therefore
quindici   fifteen
quinto   fifth
quotidiano   (adj.) daily
quotidiano   daily paper

R

rabbino   Rabbi
racchetta *f.*   racket
raccontare   to tell (a story)
radersi   to shave
radiatore *m.*   radiator
radice *f.*   root
radio *f.*   radio
radiografia *f.*   x-ray
raffreddore *m.*   cold
ragazza *f.*   girl
ragazzo   boy
ragno   spider
rallentare   slow down
rame *m.*   copper
rana *f.*   frog
rapido   express train
rapina *f.*   robbery
rapporto   relationship
rappresentare   to represent
raramente   rarely, seldom
raro   rare, scarce
rasoio   razor
razza *f.*   breed, race
re   king
realizzare   to achieve
recente   recent
recitare   to recite

regalare   to give a present
regalo   gift, present
reggiseno   bra
regina *f.*   queen
regione *f.*   region
regista *m./f.*   movie director
registratore   tape recorder
religione *f.*   religion
rendere (reso)   to render,
   to give back
repubblica *f.*   republic
residenza *f.*   residence
resistenza *f.*   resistance
respiro   breath
responsabile   responsible
restare   to remain, to stay
resto   rest, change
rettile *m.*   reptile
reumatismo   rheumatism
revisione *f.*   revision
ricamare   to embroider
riccio   curl
ricco   rich
ricetta *f.*   recipe, prescription
ricevere   to receive
ricevimento   reception
ricevuta *f.*   receipt
richiesta *f.*   request
ricordare   to remember
ridere (riso)   to laugh
riempire   to fill out (a form)
rifiuti *m. pl.*   trash
riflessivo   reflexive
riflettere (riflesso)   to reflect
rifugio   refuge
rilasciato   issued
rilassante   relaxing
rimanere (rimasto)   to remain
rimborso   refund
Rinascimento   the Renaissance
ringraziare   to thank
rio   stream
riparare   to repair
ripetere   to repeat
ripieno   stuffed, filled
riscaldamento   heat
riscaldare   to warm, to heat
riserva d'acqua *f.*   reservoir
riserva naturale *f.*   nature
   preserve

riservato   reserved
riso   rice
risolvere (risolto)   to resolve
rispettare   to respect
rispondere (risposto)
   to respond
risposta *f.*   answer, response
ristorante *m.*   restaurant
risultato   result
ritardo   delay
ritmo   rhythm
ritornare   to return
ritratto   portrait
riuscire   to succeed
rivista *f.*   magazine
roba *f.*   stuff, things
rocca *f.*   fortress
roccia *f.*   rock
romantico   romantic
romanzo   novel, fiction,
   romance
rompere (rotto)   to break
rondine *f.*   swallow (bird)
rosa   pink
rosa *f.*   rose
rosso   red
rotto   broken
rovine *f. pl.*   ruins
rubare   to steal
rubinetto   faucet
rullino   roll of film
rumoroso   noisy
ruota *f.*   wheel
rupe *f.*   cliff
ruscello   stream
russo   Russian

S

sabato   Saturday
sabbia *f.*   sand
sacchetto   small bag
sacco a pelo   sleeping bag
saggio   wise
saggio   essay
sala *f.*   room, hall
sala d'attesa *f.*   waiting room
sala da pranzo *f.*   dining room

salagiochi *f.*   game room
salario   salary
saldo   sale, discount
sale *m.*   salt
salire   to climb, to mount
salmone *m.*   salmon
salotto   living room, lounge
salsa *f.*   sauce
salsiccia *f.*   sausage
salumi *m. pl.*   cold cuts, meats
salutare   to greet
salute *f.*   health
salvietta *f.*   napkin
sangue *m.*   blood
santo/santa *f.*   saint
sapere   to know something
sapone *m.*   soap
sapore *m.*   taste
sarto   tailor
sbadigliare   to yawn
sbagliare   to be mistaken
sbarcare   to land, to disembark
scacchi *m. pl.*   chess
scadenza *f.*   expiration
scala *f.*   stairs
scambiare   to exchange
scambio   exchange
scapolo   bachelor
scappare   to escape, to run away
scarpa *f.*   shoe
scatola *f.*   box
scavare   to excavate
scegliere (scelto)   to choose
scemo   silly, idiotic
scena *f.*   scene
scendere   to descend, to get off
scherzare   to joke
schiuma *f.*   foam
schizzo   sketch
sci *m.*   skiing
sci di fondo   cross-country
   skiing
sciare   to ski
sciarpa *f.*   scarf
scienza *f.*   science
sciopero   strike
scocciare   to bother, annoy
scommettere (scommesso)
   to bet
scomodo   uncomfortable

sconto   discount
scontrino   receipt
scoprire (scoperto)   to discover
scorso   last, past
scotto   overdone
Scozia *f.*   Scotland
scrittore   writer
scrivania *f.*   desk
scrivere (scritto)   to write
scultura *f.*   sculpture
scuola *f.*   school
scuro   dark
scusare   to excuse
scusarsi   to apologize
sdraiarsi   to lie down
se   if
sé   oneself (himself, herself ...)
sebbene   although
secco   dry
secolo   century
secondo   second
sedativo   sedative
sedersi   to sit down
sedia *f.*   chair
sedici   sixteen
segnale *m.*   signal, sign
segnare   to mark, to note
segno   sign
segretaria *f.*   secretary
seguente   following
seguire   to follow
selva *f.*   woods, forest
selvaggio   wild, savage
selvatico   wild, untamed
semaforo   traffic light
sembrare   to seem
semestre *m.*   semester
semplice   simple
sempre   always
senape *f.*   mustard
Senato   Senate
sensazione *f.*   sensation,
   feeling
senso unico   one-way street
sentiero   path, track
sentimento   feeling,
   sentiment
sentire   to hear, to smell,
   to taste
sentirsi   to feel

senza   without
separare   to separate
separato   separated
sera *f.*   evening
serbatoio   gas tank
serenata *f.*   serenade
sereno   calm, good weather
serio   serious
serpente *m.*   snake
servizio   service
sessanta   sixty
sesso   sex, gender
sessualità *f.*   sexuality
seta *f.*   silk
sete *f.*   thirst
settanta   seventy
settembre   September
settimana *f.*   week
settimo   seventh
severo   severe, strict
sfidare   to challenge
sfortuna *f.*   misfortune,
   bad luck
sforzo   effort
si   oneself, each other, one,
   they
sì   yes
Sicilia *f.*   Sicily
siciliano   Sicilian
sicuro   safe, sure
sigaretta *f.*   cigarette
sigaro   cigar
significare   to signify
significato   meaning
signora *f.*   Mrs., Ms., woman
signore *m.*   Mr., Sir, man
signorina *f.*   Miss, young lady
silenzio   silence
simbolo   symbol
simpatico   nice, kind
sinagoga *f.*   synagogue
sincero   sincere
sindaco   mayor
sinfonia *f.*   symphony
singolare   singular
singolo   single
sinistro   left
sintetico   synthetic
sintomo   symptom

sipario curtain (theater)
sistema *m.* system
situazione *f.* situation
slip *m. pl.* briefs
slittino sled
smettere (smesso) to quit
snello slender
snob snob
società *f.* company
soffice soft
soffitto ceiling
soffrire (sofferto) to suffer
soggetto subject
sognare to dream
solamente only
soldato soldier
soldi *m. pl.* money
sole *m.* sun
solito usual
solo alone
sonnifero sleeping pill
sonno sleep
sono I am, they are
sopra above, on
soprabito overcoat
soprattutto above all
sordo deaf
sorella *f.* sister
sorellastra *f.* stepsister, half-sister
sorgente *f.* spring
sorpasso passing
sorprendere (sorpreso) to surprise
sorpresa *f.* surprise
sorridere (sorriso) to smile
sosta *f.* stop, pause
sostituire to substitute
sotterraneo tunnel
sotto beneath
sottotitolo subtitle
Spagna *f.* Spain
spaventare to scare, to frighten
spazio space
spazzatura *f.* trash can
spazzola *f.* brush
spazzolino da denti toothbrush
specchio mirror

speciale special
specie *f.* type, kind
spedire to send
spegnere (spento) to turn off
spendere (speso) to spend
speranza *f.* hope
sperare to hope
spesa *f.* expense, shopping
spesso often
spettacolo show
spezia *f.* spice
spiaggia *f.* beach
spiegare to explain
spilla *f.* brooch, pin
spingere (spinto) to push
spirito spirit
spirituale spiritual
splendido splendid
sporco dirty
sport *m.* sport
sportello counter, window
sposare to marry
sposato married
sposo/sposa *f.* spouse
spugna *f.* sponge
spumante *m.* sparkling wine
spuntino snack
squadra *f.* team
stabilire to establish
stadio stadium
stagione *f.* season
stagno swamp
stamattina this morning
stampa *f.* print, press
stanco tired
stanotte tonight
stanza *f.* room
stare (stato) to be, to remain, to stay
stasera this evening
stato state, government, condition
Stati Uniti *m. pl.* United States
statua *f.* statue
stazione *f.* station
stella *f.* star
stesso same
stivale *m.* boot
stoffa *f.* fabric, cloth
stomaco stomach

storia *f.* history, story
strada *f.* street
straniero foreigner, (adj.) foreign
strano strange
strega *f.* witch
stressare to stress
stretto tight
studente/studentessa *f.* student
studiare to study
studio study
stufa *f.* stove
stupendo stupendous
su, sul, sulla on top of, on, up
subito soon, immediately
succedere (successo) to happen
succo juice
sud south
suocera *f.* mother-in-law
suocero father-in-law
suonare to sound, to play
superare to overcome, to accomplish
supermercato supermarket
sveglia *f.* alarm clock
svegliarsi to wake up
svendita *f.* sale
Svezia *f.* Sweden
sviluppare to develop
Svizzera *f.* Switzerland

T

tabaccheria *f.* tobacco shop
tabella *f.* schedule, timetable
taglia *f.* size
tagliare to cut
tale such, like, similar
talvolta sometimes
tamburo drum
tanto so much, so many, a lot
tappo cork
tardi late
targa *f.* license plate
tariffa *f.* fare, charge
tasca *f.* pocket
tassa *f.* tax
tassametro taxi meter
tassì *m.* taxi
tavola *f.* dinner table

tavolo   table (restaurant)
tazza *f.*   cup
te   you
tè *m.*   tea
teatro   theater
tedesco   German
tegame *m.*   saucepan
tegola *f.*   shingle
telefonare   to telephone
telefonata *f.*   telephone call
telefono   telephone
telegiornale *m.*   news program
tema *m.*   theme
tempesta *f.*   storm
tempio   temple
tempo   weather, time
tenda *f.*   tent
tenere   to hold, to keep
tenero   tender, affectionate
termometro   thermometer
terra *f.*   earth, dirt
terracotta *f.*   ceramic
terrazzo   terrace
terzo   third
tessera *f.*   card, ticket
testa *f.*   head
tetto   roof
timido   shy
tipo   type, kind
tipografia *f.*   printing
tirare   to pull
tirchio   stingy
toccare   to touch
toilette *f.*   toilet
tolleranza *f.*   tolerance
topo   mouse
tornare   to return
torre *f.*   tower
torta *f.*   cake
torto   wrong, fault
tosse *f.*   cough
totale   total
tovaglia *f.*   tablecloth
tovagliolo   napkin
tra   between
tradizione *f.*   tradition
tradurre (tradotto)
   to translate
traduzione *f.*   translation

traffico   traffic
traghetto   ferry
tragico   tragic
tramonto   sunset
trasferirsi   to transfer,
   to move
trasformare   to transform
trasmettere (trasmesso)
   to broadcast
trasportare   to transport
trattare   to treat
tre   three
tredici   thirteen
tremendo   tremendous
treno   train
trenta   thirty
triste   sad
tropicale   tropical
troppo   too
trovare   to find
tu   you (familiar)
tuffo   dive
tulipano   tulip
tuono   thunder
turismo   tourism
turista *m./f.*   tourist
turno   turn
tutt'e due   both
tuttavia   however, yet
tutti   everyone
tutto   everything, all

U

ubriacarsi   to get drunk
uccello   bird
uccidere (ucciso)   to kill
udire   to hear
ufficio   office
ufficio cambio   money
   exchange office
ufficio informazioni
   information office
ufficio oggetti smarriti
   lost and found
ufficio postale   post office
ultimo   last
umano   human
umidità *f.*   humidity

umile   humble
umore   humor, mood
un   a, an, one
una   a, an, one
undici   eleven
unico   unique, only
unificato   unified
unito   united
uno   one, a, an
uomo   man
uovo (*pl.* le uova)   egg
urbano   city, local
urgente   urgent
urlare   to shout
usare   to use
uscire   to exit
uscita *f.*   exit
uso   usage
uva *f.*   grapes

V

vacanza *f.*   vacation
vaccinazione *f.*   vaccination
vaglia postale *m.*   money order
vagone *m.*   racar
valanga *f.*   avalanche
validità *f.*   validity
valigia *f.*   bag, valise, suitcase
valle *f.*   valley
valore *m.*   value
valuta *f.*   currency, money
vantaggio   advantage
variazione *f.*   variation
varietà *f.*   variety
vario   various
vasca *f.*   tub
vaso   vase
vecchio   old
vedere (visto)   to see
vedova *f.*   widow
vedovo   widower
veicolo   vehicle
vegetariano   vegetarian
veleno   poison
velocità *f.*   velocity
vendere   to sell
vendetta *f.*   vengeance

vendita *f.* sale
venerdì Friday
venire to come
venti twenty
vento wind
veramente really
verbo verb
verde green
verdura *f.* vegetables
vergogna *f.* shame
verità *f.* truth
vernice *f.* paint
vero true, genuine
verso toward, near, about
vescovo bishop
vespa *f.* wasp
vestire to dress
vestito dress, suit
vetrina *f.* shop window
vetro glass
vettura *f.* carriage,
   railroad car
vi (adv.) there, to you
via *f.* street, way
via away
viaggiare to travel
viaggio trip
viale *m.* boulevard, avenue
vicino neighbor, near (adj.)
vicolo alley, lane
vietato prohibited
vietato l'ingresso no
   entrance
vigile traffic police officer
vigile del fuoco firefighter
vigna *f.* vine
villa *f.* villa
villaggio village
vincere (vinto) to win
vino wine
viola purple
violetta *f.* violet (flower)
violenza *f.* violence
visibile visible
visita *f.* visit
visitare to visit
viso face
vista *f.* view
vita *f.* life

vitamina *f.* vitamin
vitello veal
vittima *f.* victim
vivace lively
vivere (vissuto) to live
vivo alive
vocabolario vocabulary
vocale *f.* vowel
voce *f.* voice
voglia *f.* wish, desire
voi you (plural)
volare to fly
volentieri! gladly!
volere to want
volo flight
volpe *f.* fox
volta *f.* time, occurrence
votare to vote
voto grade
vuoto empty

Y

yoga *m.* yoga
yogurt *m.* yogurt

Z

zaino backpack
zampa *f.* paw, leg
zanzara *f.* mosquito
zero zero
zia *f.* aunt
zio uncle
zona *f.* zone, section
zoo zoo
zucchero sugar
zuppa *f.* soup

Index

W-X-Y-Z